(Re)Negotiating East and Southeast Asia

Studies in Asian Security

A SERIES SPONSORED BY THE EAST-WEST CENTER

Muthiah Alagappa, Chief Editor
Distinguished Senior Fellow, East-West Center

The **Studies in Asian Security** book series promotes analysis, understanding, and explanation of the dynamics of domestic, transnational, and international security challenges in Asia. The peer-reviewed publications in the Series analyze contemporary security issues and problems to clarify debates in the scholarly community, provide new insights and perspectives, and identify new research and policy directions. Security is defined broadly to include the traditional political and military dimensions as well as nontraditional dimensions that affect the survival and well being of political communities. Asia, too, is defined broadly to include Northeast, Southeast, South, and Central Asia.

Designed to encourage original and rigorous scholarship, books in the *Studies in Asian Security* series seek to engage scholars, educators, and practitioners. Wide-ranging in scope and method, the Series is receptive to all paradigms, programs, and traditions and to an extensive array of methodologies now employed in the social sciences.

★   ★   ★

The East-West Center is an education and research organization established by the U.S. Congress in 1960 to strengthen relations and understanding among the peoples and nations of Asia, the Pacific, and the United States. Funding for the Center comes from the U.S. government, with additional support provided by private agencies, individuals, foundations, corporations, and the governments of the region.

(Re)Negotiating East and Southeast Asia

REGION, REGIONALISM, AND THE ASSOCIATION
OF SOUTHEAST ASIAN NATIONS

Alice D. Ba

Stanford University Press • Stanford, California

Stanford University Press
Stanford, California

Printed in the United States of America on acid-free, archival-quality paper

Library of Congress Cataloging-in-Publication Data

Ba, Alice D.
  (Re)negotiating East and Southeast Asia : region, regionalism, and the
Association of Southeast Asian Nations / Alice D. Ba.
      p. cm. — (Studies in Asian security)
  Includes bibliographical references and index.
    ISBN 978-0-8047-6069-0 (cloth : alk. paper)—ISBN 978-0-8047-6070-6
(pbk. : alk. paper)
  1. Southeast Asia—Foreign relations. 2. Southeast Asia—Politics and govern-
ment—1945- 3. ASEAN. 4. Regionalism—Southeast Asia. 5. Regionalism—
East Asia. 6. Southeast Asia—Foreign relations—East Asia. 7. East Asia—
Foreign relations—Southeast Asia. I. Title. II. Title: Renegotiating East and
Southeast Asia. III. Series: Studies in Asian security.
  DS525.8.B33 2009
  341.24'73—dc22

                          2008047523

Typeset by Thompson Type in 10.5/13.5 Bembo

Just as none of us is outside or beyond geography, none of us is completely free from the struggle over geography. That struggle is complex and interesting because it is not only about soldiers and cannons but also about ideas, about forms, about images and imaginings.

Edward Said
Culture and Imperialism (1993)

Contents

Acknowledgments

Like ASEAN, this book is the product of an extended process that has involved multiple renegotiations, much rethinking, and more than one crossroad. Perhaps, it is no surprise given the nature of the process that I have also accumulated a great many debts. My greatest debts are to those who provided guidance and careful comments since the project's earliest iterations. Brantly Womack and John Echeverri-Gent at the University of Virginia not only took considerable time and care in reading early drafts but were also unfailing in their encouragement from beginning to end. In addition, I owe a particular debt to Matthew Hoffmann who read multiple drafts at later stages. I have been fortunate to have him as both colleague and friend.

This manuscript has also benefited from the conscientiousness of its anonymous reviewers. Their pointed comments and constructive critiques served to sharpen the overall argument. Thanks are additionally due to Daniel Green and Stuart Kaufman for their input on certain chapters. I am also indebted to Amitav Acharya and Richard Stubbs, both of whom offered much-appreciated encouragement and comments early in the process; David Elliott at Pomona College, who (unbeknownst to him) put me on this path early on; Yuen Foong Khong for his support; both Muthiah Alagappa at the East-West Center and the Studies in Asian Security Series' editorial committee for their commitment to the project; and Geoffrey Burn for his editorial guidance.

I would be most remiss if I did not also thank some of my fellow ASEAN travelers—especially Mely Caballero-Anthony, Shaun Narine, and Helen Nesadurai, whose intellectual contributions sharpened my thinking. They provided occasional voices over my shoulder, and their friendship made the process enjoyable. Thanks also to my various comrades along the way, especially Patrick Pillai and Dan Slater, both of whom will always be associated with Malaysia for me, as well as Amy Nagle, Peter Ronayne, Christine Spillane, and Kevin Tarmann.

My appreciation also goes to the ASEAN-ISIS network—with particular thanks to the Centre for Strategic and International Studies in Jakarta, ISIS-Malaysia in Kuala Lumpur, and Carolina Hernandez at the University of the Philippines for their help in facilitating interviews, access to materials, and for introducing me to the world of ASEAN "Track 2." Thanks also to those at the Rajaratnam School of International Studies in Singapore, who have provided an intellectual community and have helped to keep me current; the various academics and officials in Bangkok, Jakarta, Kuala Lumpur, Manila, and Singapore who took time from their busy schedules to talk with me; and the ASEAN Secretariat for allowing me to include the ASEAN emblem as part of this book. The library and experts at the Institute of Southeast Asian Studies in Singapore were also invaluable resources.

This project would not have been possible without the funding provided by several institutes at various stages, including the Institute for the Study of World Politics, the Eisenhower Institute, the East Asia Center at the University of Virginia, and the University of Delaware. Thanks also to the Munke Centre at the University of Toronto, especially Joe Wong, for facilitating my ability to work on this project in its last stage. Matthew Davis offered his capable research assistance.

Of course, nothing would be possible or meaningful without the love and support of family. To Mom, Dad, and the best siblings in the world, thanks for always being there for me.

In-Text Abbreviations

AEMM	ASEAN Economic Ministers Meeting
AFTA	ASEAN Free Trade Area
AMF	Asian Monetary Fund
AMM	ASEAN Ministerial Meeting
APEC	Asia-Pacific Economic Cooperation
APT	ASEAN Plus Three
ARF	ASEAN Regional Forum
ASA	Association of Southeast Asia
ASEAN	The Association of Southeast Asian Nations
ASEM	Asia Europe Meetings
CMI	Chiang Mai Initiative
CLMV	Cambodia, Laos, Myanmar, Vietnam
CSCAP	Council for Security Cooperation in the Asia-Pacific
EAEG	East Asia Economic Group
EAS	East Asia Summit
EEZ	Exclusive Economic Zone
EU	European Union
FPDA	Five Powers Defence Arrangements
FTA	Free Trade Agreement
GATT	General Agreement on Tariffs and Trade
IMF	International Monetary Fund
ISIS	Institute of Strategic and International Studies

NAFTA	North American Free Trade Agreement
PMC	Post-Ministerial Conference
PTA	Preferential Trading Agreement
SEANWFZ	Southeast Asian Nuclear Weapons Free Zone
SEATO	Southeast Asia Treaty Organization
SLORC	State Law and Order Restoration Council
SOM	Senior Officials Meeting
TAC	Treaty of Amity and Cooperation
ZOPFAN	Zone of Peace, Freedom, and Neutrality

(Re)Negotiating East and Southeast Asia

Introduction

The ASEAN states have only three things in common: karaoke, durian,[1] and golf.

Popular ASEAN saying

The Association of Southeast Asian Nations (ASEAN) has long posed a puzzle for the study of international relations. On the one hand, states are often divided among themselves; economic interests are more competitive than complementary; unilateralism, as often as not, seems to trump multilateralism. In fact, the open-endedness of past initiatives and the often frustratingly slow pace of ASEAN cooperation have given rise to a common characterization of ASEAN as a "talk shop"—all talk, no action. ASEAN's difficulties and challenges in responding to recent crises—most notably, the 1997 Asian financial crisis, the 2003 SARS crisis, Myanmar, and the recurring environmental haze caused by yearly fires in Indonesia—not to mention recent difficulties in approving a new ASEAN charter seem to further confirm the particular problems of intra-ASEAN coordination.

On the other hand, ASEAN is associated with the transformation of the once volatile and fragmented region that was Southeast Asia. If ASEAN is viewed by many as a "weak" case of regional cooperation, ASEAN's creation in 1967 may be just as widely viewed by others as marking an important turning point in the international relations of Southeast Asia. By this view, with ASEAN's creation, an era marked by highly confrontational politics gave way to a new one characterized by more stable relations and growing cooperation.

In fact, Southeast Asia's economic dynamism, relative stability, and regional initiatives make it easy to forget just how fragile both region and its relations were forty years ago. At the time of ASEAN's founding, conflict and division plagued practically every level of politics. The newness of most states and the legacies of arbitrarily drawn colonial borders practically assured that domestic development in Southeast Asia would be a volatile process. Nor were Southeast Asia's international politics any more stable. At the global level, states found themselves the targets and tools of major power interventions and Cold War designs. At the regional level,

conflict and intervention were no less the norm among ASEAN's founding states (Indonesia, Malaysia, Philippines, Singapore, and Thailand), as
illustrated by the state of relations at ASEAN's founding in 1967: Indonesia
and Malaysia had yet to normalize relations following Indonesia's violent
campaign to "crush Malaysia"; Singapore had just been kicked out of the
Malaysian Federation due to irreconcilable Malay–Chinese tensions; and four
of ASEAN's five members had at least one dispute with another member,
with Malaysia and the Philippines having ended relations already once before over their competing claims to Sabah/North Borneo.

Such territorial disputes, regional rivalries, and major power interventions were considered tremendous, even insurmountable, obstacles to
regional organization. Yet, not only has ASEAN cooperation grown and
deepened, but ASEAN has proven unexpectedly resilient in the face of geopolitical and domestic change. Most important, its regional processes and
so-called weak cooperation appear to have stabilized intra-ASEAN relations
in important ways. Even in "hard" cases of territorial sovereignty, ASEAN
has seen territorial disputes go to international adjudication without incident. Intra-ASEAN relations (among founding members) are so changed
that some even characterize ASEAN states as having achieved the depth
of relations characteristic of a security community defined by dependable
expectations of peaceful change.[2] To be sure, intra-ASEAN regional coordination is still often fraught with difficulty and tension, but the region is
also a more cooperative and stable one than the one that existed forty years
ago. What has never been quite clear, however, is why and how?

While traditional approaches to international relations offer various explanations for why ASEAN cooperation has been challenged and why it should
not work "better," much less is said about how exactly ASEAN has stabilized regional politics or indeed why ASEAN should work at all. In fact, the
usual preconditions and mechanisms identified by approaches as necessary
for cooperation have mostly been weak or missing, making ASEAN an especially challenging, even "least likely" case for regional organization for most
approaches: Realists find few common material interests; liberal approaches
find few democracies (and problematic ones at best); comparativists find in
Southeast Asia's human diversity a weak cultural foundation for unity; institutionalists find in ASEAN few of the consequentialist rules and arrangements that, to them, are key to facilitating cooperation between competitive
and divergent states. Again, all of the above are reasons that ASEAN cooperation is challenged, but they do not explain what ASEAN does, how rela-

tions have stabilized and cooperation expanded and deepened, or what states get out of the ASEAN process.

No less puzzling, especially for approaches that privilege material power, is how this Southeast Asian organization of lesser states came to play a defining role in the creation and development of regional arrangements that now include much larger powers than they. Among the more notable of these arrangements are the ASEAN Regional Forum (ARF), the ASEAN Plus Three meetings (APT), and most recently, the East Asia Summit (EAS). In fact, ASEAN's influence is such that some refer to the "ASEAN-ization"[3] of East Asian and Asian Pacific arrangements. ASEAN-style processes also appear to have facilitated the improvement of states' security and relations vis-à-vis larger Northeast Asian powers, especially and most notably China, a focal point of earlier regional conflict scenarios. Particularly remarkable is the fact that an ASEAN treaty—the Treaty of Amity and Cooperation (TAC)— has today become the most widely accepted and acceded-to regional, indigenous political-security treaty in East Asia and the Asia Pacific.

These are remarkable and dramatic developments for an organization of lesser states for which conflict, not cooperation, had once dominated so many levels of their politics. How did these divergent and competitive states manage to stabilize relations, to expand and deepen areas of cooperation, and become "One Southeast Asia"? How did this organization, self-defined as "Southeast Asian" and as one of lesser powers, come to form the gravitational center of a growing web of post–Cold War East Asian and Asia-Pacific regionalisms? What do these new expanded regionalisms mean for ASEAN as a Southeast Asian organization? And how do we reconcile these transformative changes with the ongoing challenges of intra-ASEAN coordination and collective action?

Regionalism as Ideas and Cumulative Process

These questions drive this study of ASEAN and its evolution. Unlike more traditional approaches, however, my explanation begins not with the material incentives and disincentives of cooperation but instead with ideas—specifically, ideas about Southeast Asia as a distinct but also divided region and for which division at various levels is understood to be a primary source of insecurity and vulnerability. Compared to approaches that stress more material considerations, a consideration of ideas can offer a more complete explanation, one that explains not just the challenges of intra-ASEAN coordination and its continued resistance to more formal, legal mechanisms of cooperation but also its unexpected unity and resilience. Ideas can help us answer the questions left unanswered by more traditional approaches: What ties these diverse states together if not common interests, common threats, or common people? What are the specific ways that the ASEAN process has contributed to the stabilization of relations within ASEAN? What moves regionalism in Southeast Asia and now ASEAN's role in expanded East Asian regionalisms?

Until relatively recently, the study of international relations tended to minimize the role of ideas. But, as various studies now show, ideas can play powerful roles in shaping expectations, behavior, and the world as we know it. In the case of ASEAN, founding ideas about Southeast Asian division as a source of insecurity and opportunity for intervention provide justification for Southeast Asian organization in the absence of other material incentives. At the same time, the same ideas that provided justification for organization also would create normative obstacles in the way of more formal cooperation and centralized coordination.

In addition, I argue for a different conception of cooperation than is usually highlighted by traditional, especially more material, approaches. This is because their view of cooperation as an expression of material gains and constraints tends to be overly narrow, obscuring our ability to see the full range of exchanges taking place between actors. Drawing on constructivist approaches and especially the respective works of Kaye and Barnett, I argue instead that cooperation must be seen more broadly as a social process involving interactive and cumulative social negotiations.[4] While such a conception is inclusive of the bargaining processes and material exchanges emphasized by traditional approaches, its emphasis is nevertheless different, with a primary focus on the exchange of ideas and on how such exchanges reflect, inform, and transform the social content of relationships. By stressing social process, this conception of cooperation also emphasizes that cooperation is not just a discrete bargaining moment or collective action problem but instead a series of cumulative and successive social exchanges. Taken together, these exchanges can transform social contexts and relationships that then make possible (or not) certain kinds of collective and cooperative outcomes. In the ASEAN case, this conception of cooperation as a cumulative and interactive social exchange is further underscored by regional elites who have explicitly conceived regional cooperation as a relationship-building process. In short, the process of cooperation involves not just the negotiation of specific material interests but also social relations, social practices, and indeed social identities.

Talking about Diversity, Divergence, and Unity

How do ideas come to shape politics? And how are social contexts, expectations, and relations shaped and altered? One way is through talking—dialoguing, arguing, framing, affirming, negating. It is through talking that ASEAN's diverse and divergent states have identified, maintained, and pursued points of consensus and agreement on relations and various issues of common concern. It is through talking that ASEAN states have developed new thinking about relations and practices based on a culture of restraint, respect, and responsibility[5] that is dramatically different from 1960s conflict-torn Southeast Asia. It is through talking that states have come to view Southeast Asian regionalism as an appropriate and indeed necessary response to particular problems that might otherwise be better addressed via other means given their different economic and security interests and preferences.

In this sense, traditional and conventional approaches to ASEAN are quite correct. As a dialogue-driven process, ASEAN regionalism is in fact a lot of talk; however, it is not talk without substantive, material effects. ASEAN's talk shop has produced new social norms, a new culture of regional dialogue, as well as new social and institutional practices that stress respect (manifested most notably in a consensus-based regionalism) and nonconfrontational, inclusive engagement. The practical effect of such changes is a regional system based on the nonviolent resolution of problems and the normative belief that states *should* work toward regional solutions. One can criticize ASEAN's norms and practices on a variety of grounds—they are too state centric, undemocratic, and time inefficient—but they are also why interstate conflicts have not escalated to breaking points the way that they did before ASEAN. At very least, if one considers regional stability a precondition of economic growth, then these norms and ideas provide an important foundation on which ASEAN's new economies have been allowed to grow.

Talking, however, has to have a starting point. And my explanation of ASEAN and its dialogue-driven process begins where many explanations do; that is, it begins with the idea of Southeast Asian diversity and division. In fact, if there is one point that most observers of Southeast Asia—Southeast Asianists, international relations scholars of various stripes, comparativists of specific Southeast Asian countries, practitioners—would seem to agree on, it is Southeast Asia's diversity. While the degree of human diversity may vary across different parts of Southeast Asia, there is no denying that this is a place of diverse peoples and influences. That diversity can be seen in Southeast Asia's peoples, geography, and colonial experiences, as well as in national perspectives and geographic orientations. For the Southeast Asianist, for example, the tremendous ethnic complexity of the area means that it is practically impossible to classify or talk about Southeast Asia as one coherent place. These observers are further united by their common conclusion that diversity must mean divergence, if not conflict.

Such themes are especially prominent in discussions of Southeast Asia's international relations, where realist themes of competition and conflict tend to predominate.[6] Here, the realist concept of "national interest" provides the stand-in for "diversity" and "divergence." As the realist argument goes, diversity (different national interests) is the source of political tensions between states, regional rivalries, the problems of regional cooperation, as well as the intergroup conflicts that have been important features of so much of Southeast Asia's post–World War II politics.

Diversity and divergence—these ideas have formed the dominant leitmotif in our understandings and explanations of Southeast Asia's domestic and international politics. And as the dominant leitmotif, these ideas affect both politics and scholarship alike. Indeed, even with ASEAN's expanded membership and the changes that have taken place in Southeast Asia, the very idea of "One Southeast Asia" remains a radical concept. As one longtime scholar of Southeast Asia continued to protest, "I see ten Southeast Asias, not one."

In this sense, diversity's association with division and disunity is more than a theme. It is a strong belief—and it is in treating diversity and its association with division as a belief and a set of ideas about Southeast Asia as a region that I depart from other approaches. In other words, while my argument begins, as others do, with diversity, I argue that diversity's association with disunity and division is at very least as much ideological as it is empirical. Objectively speaking, Southeast Asia *is* an extremely diverse place, but the political significance of that diversity is also the product of social interpretations reinforced by social practice. Some societies interpret diversity as a source of strength and dynamism; others see it as a problem. In the ASEAN case, historical experiences and especially patterned interactions with major powers have contributed mostly to a view of diversity as a source of vulnerability. And that view of diversity affects how ASEAN elites conceive, approach, and practice regional cooperation.

The understood problems of diversity/division provided an important starting point for the intra-ASEAN dialogue on regionalism. Here, states' recent colonial and Cold War experiences provided critical points of reference. Division facilitated various interventions—interventions that, in turn, created additional division.[7] In particular, colonial powers not only drew borders irrespective of geography and peoples, thus creating an important internal diversity, but policies also often exploited and fomented intergroup competition and prevented interactions between Southeast Asian units. Those policies subsequently helped facilitate later Cold War instabilities and interventions. From these experiences emerged not only a commonly held belief and interpretation about the dangers of division but also a correlating conclusion about the need for greater unity. Put another way, if the "problem" of diversity in ASEAN is understood as weak national integration and regional division, then the solution lies in national integration and regional unity.

In this way, I thus depart from past approaches to ASEAN not just in my argument that diversity (and its implications) is also a belief system but also in a second way. Specifically, I argue that alongside beliefs about the dangers of Southeast Asia's diversity and fragility, ASEAN politics are also guided by an important concern for regional unity. As discussed above, ASEAN has been at the center of some remarkable developments—developments that challenge the dominant realist narrative and developments that tell us that diversity and division, while important, are only parts of the ASEAN story.

In short, regionalism is the pursuit of regional unity as a response to the understood problems of division. At the same time, precisely because regionalism begins with the premise of Southeast Asia's diversity, fragility, and predilection toward division, a concern for unity has contrary effects on ASEAN regionalism. Specifically, the understood importance of regional unity, combined with shared understandings about the tenuousness of regional relations, means that even while states are compelled to look to regionalism (unity) as an answer to important security challenges, they are also bound—even morally bound—not to push regionalism too hard or too far, lest the whole project fall apart. In this way, concern for regional unity—even regional unity norm—becomes both driver and constraint on ASEAN regionalism and specific ASEAN initiatives. Given these dynamics, it is perhaps also no surprise that some ASEAN initiatives have been decades-long projects.

A Big-Picture View of ASEAN and
Asia's Post–Cold War Regionalisms

In addition to explaining ASEAN itself, this study also seeks to explain the evolving shape of other, later-developing regionalisms in post–Cold War Asia—APEC, ARF, APT, most notably—and ASEAN's role in their development. Most studies tend to treat each of these regionalisms and regional configurations as relatively distinct phenomena or distinct problems of cooperation; however, I highlight here how they are related, interactive, and even parts of the same process and dialogue.

Specifically, the organizing thesis of this book is that regions and regionalisms in Asia—ASEAN-Southeast Asia, APEC, ARF, APT, "East Asia"— are best understood as parts of a cumulative dialogue or series of social negotiations on the material and normative foundations of regional order—the nature of intraregional ties and obligations, the relationship between major and minor powers, the appropriateness of great power guarantees and intervention.[8] Again, they are cumulative because recent regional expressions and arrangements, as in the case of intra-ASEAN cooperation over time, are all in some way informed by past debates and previous areas of agreement about regional relations and organization. They are also interactive: Regionalisms "talk" to one another in the sense that regionalisms represent not only different geographies but also different and competing ideological conceptions. Thus, unlike some accounts that see these regional arrangements as products of similar functional imperatives, this book treats regionalisms as different and varied in the ideas they represent and consequently what they are supposed to do. And in that these regional processes are both interactive and cumulative, it is difficult to explain something like APT without relating it to other regional ideas and configurations—APEC or ASEAN, for example.

Taking a big picture view also reveals important patterns and rhythms of regionalism in Southeast Asia—in particular, the sensitivity of regionalism to extra-ASEAN changes, especially as regards larger and major powers. My argument draws special attention to the sensitivity of ASEAN and its subsequent regionalism to perceived changes in U.S.–Asia policy, on which so many Southeast Asian interests depend. The sensitivity of ASEAN-Southeast Asia to shifts in U.S. policy have as much to do with U.S. ability to intervene (military and otherwise) as it does states' particular dependence on the United States for economic and political-security goods. Consequently, while ASEAN states are sensitive to shifts in the policies of other larger powers, the United States nevertheless has been the actor with the greatest potential to destabilize the economic and political well-being of Southeast Asian states. No surprise, then, that U.S. policy changes (real and perceived) have proven to provide the most regular catalyst for intra-ASEAN reflection and reevaluation about both intra- and extraregional relations—in short, the ideational opening for change and new directions.

Indeed, as the following chapters detail, how the region should relate to larger, especially major, powers and how ASEAN states can maintain a distinct Southeast Asian space and voice in regions and worlds of larger powers are two facets of an ongoing, even driving dialogue underlying ASEAN regionalism. More to the point, the evolution of ASEAN regionalism must be seen in terms of not one, but two interdependent and intertwined stories—the first, a story about the renegotiation of ASEAN's intraregional relations; the second, a story about collective ASEAN's renegotiations of Southeast Asia's relations with larger powers, especially Northeast Asian powers and the United States. Together, the two stories of ASEAN states' relations with one another and of their relations with major powers thus tell the story of power and ideas and of the ways that the material and ideational interact to produce (and reproduce) the politics and regionalisms we see.

The Plan of This Book

This study proceeds in two parts: Theory and Origins of ASEAN and ASEAN's Post–Cold War Regionalisms. Empirical chapters are organized mostly chronologically so as to highlight the ongoing, interactive, and cumulative dialogues about Southeast Asia's intra- and extraregional relations. Tracing debates over time helps do a number of things. It helps us identify persistent themes and preoccupations; it reveals the rhythms of ASEAN regionalism; it shows us how ideas about region and regionalism have changed over time. Taken together, chapters detail a series of decision-making junctures that have directed the development and course of ASEAN regionalism over time.

Individual chapters are then organized around key debates about intra- and extra-ASEAN relations and the effects of these debates on the shape and content of regionalisms. Taking a process-tracing approach, chapters trace the ways that ideas and arguments connect stimuli and initial conditions into collective regional outcomes. In particular, each chapter highlights the interactions among different ideas and how material changes or perceived changes in states' major power relations serve to destabilize ASEAN's world and catalyze reevaluation about old ideas and practices. That ideational instability opens the door to possible change—modifications and/or new regional expressions—though it may also result in the reaffirmation of old ideas and existing practices.

It should be underscored that the aim of each chapter is not to be comprehensive—for example, there are more comprehensive discussions of the ARF[9] and APEC[10] than what is provided here—but instead to situate and explain their emergence and development in relation to evolving ideas and debates in ASEAN about regions and regionalisms and how they, in turn, feed back into

ongoing dialogues. While each chapter can be read more or less indepen-
dently, each chapter must also be considered as part of a larger narrative about
the evolution of first Southeast Asian regionalism and then Asian Pacific and
East Asian regionalisms. Treating ASEAN and Asia's new regionalisms as
related processes and as parts of a cumulative dialogue over time allows us to
better identify patterns, rhythms, and persistent themes, as well as important
change and evolution that is often overlooked in studies that focus on each
arrangement or development as distinct and discrete phenomena. It is this
combination of continuity and dynamism that recent treatments (theoretical
and practical) of Asia's various regionalisms have not always captured well.

Theory and Origins: Argument in Brief

Chapter 1 fills in different and additional pieces of my theoretical framework. These include the roles played by interacting material–ideational
interactions, a nationalist-bounded regional idea, and the contrary effects
of a regional unity norm premised on the assumed fragility of relations. In
addition, it gives attention to key social processes that have moved, reinforced, changed, and reproduced ASEAN and its regionalisms—argumentation that makes critical causal linkages, consensus seeking in pursuit and in
support of unity, and talking and practice as means of social reinforcement.
Again, ideas are not in and of themselves meaningful or powerful, but these
various processes can help make them so.

Picking up dialogues in the late 1950s, Chapter 2 shows how the politics and
beliefs of the period contribute to a particular physical and normative conception of Southeast Asia. In addition, it gives attention to the politics and forces
behind ASEAN's creation in 1967. While the details of ASEAN's founding
will be familiar to many, the chapter serves a number of important purposes.
First, to explain change and evolution, we have to know where ASEAN has
been. Founding ideas, debates, and circumstances provide an important baseline for comparison and contrast to contemporary developments in the region.
Second, it is not enough to focus on whether ideas "matter" and ignore "where
ideas come from" as some scholars[11] have argued. Rather, the sociohistorical
origins of ideas are critical to explaining not only whether and why certain
ideas have effect but also, I argue, what effect they have.[12]

In particular, I argue that the particular politics and social context of 1960s
Southeast Asia made nationalism an important, initial ideological boundary
for regional ideas and arguments. Indeed, in 1960s Southeast Asia, where
nationalism was the dominant ideology and politics of the day, a nationalist-
regarding regionalism would ultimately be the only kind of regionalism to

have any persuasive power. Forty years later, that original nationalist content continues to inform and bound ASEAN's regionalism(s).

While some may view the use of the term *nationalism* problematic for Southeast Asia given the ways that state borders have often been drawn irrespective of local geographies and populations, *nationalism* is also a most appropriate term because it may best capture the most pressing preoccupations of leaders, as well as the activities going on within state borders. This is especially the case if we understand nationalism not in the sense of the nation-state but instead as an ideological and material process of self-determination and collective construction.

Finally, the chapter fills a need for a systematic and theoretical discussion of the conditions and processes that made this particular idea of region and this particular organization—ASEAN—possible at this particular time, something that is often missing from even very good discussions. In fact, as will be very clear, the idea of Southeast Asia as an organizing principle was a particularly contested concept among Southeast Asian states in the 1960s. Not only did it compete with other geographic conceptions of region, but there was also little clarity about the very contours of Southeast Asia itself. Thus, in Southeast Asia, where organization along these particular Southeast Asian lines has not been supported by history,[13] geography, or efficiency, we need to ask, as Dirlik argues, not only "what" is this region but also "why" this particular region.[14] Why *should* these states attach significance or devote scarce resources to this particular idea of Southeast Asia defined as these ten states, many of which are themselves contested, postcolonial entities? Why not a different idea of region, given "Southeast Asia's" clear material limitations and political obstacles?

Chapter 2 thus highlights how arguments for regional organization give rise to a founding narrative that gives purpose and meaning to the regional idea and project. That founding narrative draws on and brings together a number of key ideas: regional unity as a response to the dangers of national and regional fragmentation, the relationship between fragmentation and intervention, self-determination, and the primacy of the national project, but also the interdependence of national and regional projects. At the heart of this founding narrative is a narrative about Southeast Asia's historical divisions, comprehensive insecurities associated with fragmentation, and the importance of unity as a guiding and normative principle.

This founding narrative about the fragility of nation and region, their relationship to intervention, and the need for unity furthermore has contrary effects on ASEAN's regionalism: On the one hand, it points states toward regional, *Southeast Asian* solutions in response to insecurity; on the other, it calls on member states to be cautious given the fragility of national and regional units. In the shadow of states' recent history of interstate conflict and the omnipresent challenges of state and nation building, actors would draw on that founding fragmentation-intervention narrative to argue that nation-building processes were too fragile and intraregional relations too tenuous to withstand a more demanding regionalism.

In short, ASEAN's founding narrative is most important to explaining not only "why ASEAN?" in the absence of conventional drivers of regionalism but also some of the peculiarities of ASEAN's organizational culture and brand of regionalism—its informal institutionalism, its process-driven regionalism, its eschewal of collective regional balancing strategies, the rituals of ASEAN solidarity. Again, this founding narrative of division and unity will constrain, as much as it will enable and legitimate, later regional efforts.

Chapter 3 then details elites' continued and active search for consensus on questions of regional security and economic cooperation. It showcases the continued weakness of regional ideas and arguments but also material–ideational interactions and their role in reviving a floundering regional dialogue and project. It draws special attention to processes of activist promotion, argument, and reinforcement over time. To illustrate ASEAN's ongoing consensus-seeking process, the chapter picks up on three debates: the Zone of Peace, Freedom and Neutrality (ZOPFAN) as a function of intra-ASEAN debates about great power guarantees and self-determination; ASEAN's response to a reunified Vietnam as a function of regional resilience debates; and ASEAN's 1977 Preferential Trading Arrangements (PTAs) as a function of intra-ASEAN debates about the critical nation–region relationship. The three debates illustrate well, on the one hand, the divergent interests and preferences of ASEAN states and, on the other, the unifying role played by founding ideas. In particular, they show how regional resilience provided an important common interpretation of problems that then made regional unity an important coordinating principle in states' response to new developments and challenges. The three also provide illustrations of the rhetorical struggle between old ideas (nationalism) and new ones (regionalism), with ASEAN's particular brand of informal regionalism the product of that struggle. All three also draw attention to the rhetoric and rituals of ASEAN in the representation of Southeast Asia as "one."

ASEAN's Post–Cold War Regionalisms

Part Two addresses the post–Cold War period of ASEAN regionalism and the expansion of ASEAN processes beyond Southeast Asia. The 1990s were a dynamic period of new ideas, new material challenges, and institutional adaptation. Focusing again on the intra-ASEAN debate, Chapters 4, 5, and 6 turn our attention to how post–Cold War developments destabilize old ideas and open a window of opportunity for new regional initiatives. Chapter 4 details ASEAN's decision to extend membership first to Vietnam (1995) and especially the decisions to extend membership to Cambodia, Laos, and Myanmar (Burma) (1997–1999) despite unclear benefits and other concerns. It highlights intra- and extraregional developments and their challenges to both ASEAN and its regional ideal. By tracing intra-ASEAN debates about expansion, I show how the process of argumentation makes even more explicit the story of "one Southeast Asia" as a struggle for regional ownership vis-à-vis larger, extraregional powers, as well as how that narrative boxes states into a corner, compelling them to go through with membership expansion in 1997 despite strong and publicly expressed reservations by many ASEAN elites.

Chapters 5 and 6 give particular attention to ASEAN's ongoing struggles to manage and define itself in relation to major powers, as well as the ways that more established ASEAN ideas continue to frame regionalist discussions in a post–Cold War context. In particular, chapters highlight how new U.S. economic and political-security priorities introduce both new concerns and new incentives, especially as regards Southeast Asia's relationship with Northeast Asian states, as well as new ideological challenges to both ASEAN and Southeast Asia as a region. These concerns and incentives open the door to new regional thinking and arguments, as states find themselves having to rethink and reconsider how they as Southeast Asian states should relate to other "regional" economies—China and Japan, but also Korea, Australia, and the United States.

Chapter 5 first highlights how questions about U.S. trade policies (regionally and globally) trigger both new initiative in intra-ASEAN trade cooperation (the ASEAN Free Trade Area) and also a search for different regional solutions—notably, in the form of Asia Pacific Economic Cooperation (APEC) and the East Asia Economic Group (EAEG).

Chapter 6 then turns our attention to security. The chapter highlights how uncertain Chinese and U.S. policies compel a reassessment of Southeast Asia as an organizing principle and how ideas once again direct states to particular regional solutions—only in this case, it will be an expanded regional arrangement based on the ASEAN model, namely, the ARF. Also in Chapter 6, I discuss how the ideology of ASEAN regionalism—especially ideas about the importance of reassurance through inclusive, nonconfrontational engagement—are extended from the narrower ASEAN context to the larger East

Asia, but at the same time how it comes into conflict with major powers who conceive regionalism in more legalistic and utilitarian terms. As a political-security arrangement, the ARF draws attention to ASEAN's ongoing structural predicament vis-à-vis larger powers (in this case, China and the United States especially), its evolving dialogue on the value of regional autonomy, and how interactions with a wider region actually solidify members' ideas and identification with a particular diplomatic and institutional culture.

Chapter 7 then draws attention to the effects of the 1997–1998 Asian financial crisis on ASEAN's ongoing debate about how best to negotiate Southeast Asia's relationship with global powers and the global system. The Asian financial crisis proves to be an especially critical turning point in what appears to be an emergent East Asian regionalism in the form of the APT process.

The concluding chapter then reviews the central arguments made in the book and offers some reflections about ASEAN and the prospects for, and significance of, "East Asia" for ASEAN "Southeast Asia." It also considers regional developments in relation to current and ongoing global discussions about the United States and U.S. leadership. While discussions on the changing role of the United States have become de rigueur, these chapters show that in ASEAN, at least, such reevaluations and critical reflections of the United States are not completely new, nor did they emerge suddenly. In fact, current reevaluations have in fact been thirty to forty years in the making.

Most of all, perhaps, the growth and expansion of East Asian economic, political, and institutional activities raise important questions about ASEAN and Southeast Asia as a meaningful entity. While ASEAN ideas about region and regionalism today are also institutionalized in newer East Asian arrangements like APT and the East Asia Summit and consequently will continue to inform the shape and content of East Asia, there is also little doubt that the challenges are great for this coalition of lesser Southeast Asian powers. East Asian developments raise questions not only about ASEAN's thus far privileged place in Asia's post–Cold War regionalisms but also about ASEAN's ability to define and assert Southeast Asian interests and voice within the large arrangements made up of both large and small powers. ASEAN's future role and influence will also depend on how the organization itself is able to adapt and adjust to the challenges emanating from expanded membership and domestic changes within members themselves, as much as shifting great power relations and intensified global challenges. Of course, as these chapters detail, this was also not the first existential crossroads ASEAN has faced. How ASEAN has navigated past survival challenges can provide insight into the organization's future.

ONE

Theory and Origins

Declare the knowledge and the regional identity will take shape. Declare the region's existence as a patch of the earth's surface, and the knowledge will follow.

Craig Reynolds, 1995

1

The ASEAN Paradox and IR Theory

ASEAN is an irrelevant imitation community.

David Martin Jones and Michael L. R. Smith, 2001

Southeast Asia minus ASEAN equals greater political instability, more widespread economic deterioration and almost surely, the ascendancy of expansionist forces that thrive on the weakness, isolation and disunity of others.

Narciso Reyes,[1]
ASEAN Secretary General, 1980–1982

This chapter situates ASEAN and Asia's post–Cold War regionalisms within larger theoretical debates about international relations (IR). It first describes the puzzle that ASEAN presents for dominant IR theories whose utilitarian understandings of cooperation offer limited explanations for ASEAN, its informal consensus-seeking regionalism, and its resilience in the face of change. It then offers an alternative explanation based on constructivist arguments about the role of ideas and social processes (here, argumentation, dialogue, social reinforcement) in the production and reproduction of regions and regionalisms. I build especially on the work of Barnett, Kaye, and Acharya, each of whom have similarly looked to constructivist approaches to explain particular regional politics (respectively, pan-Arabism, Arab–Israeli politics, and Southeast Asia as a security community). My framework, which highlights competing ideas as well as ideational-material interactions in the production of regions and regionalisms in first Southeast Asia and now East Asia, is detailed below.

The ASEAN Paradox

The existence of ASEAN defies most expectations. At the time of its founding in 1967, few expected ASEAN to last one year, let alone nearly four decades, given the volatile state of Southeast Asia's intra- and extraregional relations. Yet, not only has ASEAN seen cooperation deepen, grow, and expand into areas like politics and security that were once too sensitive even to mention, but ASEAN also finds itself today at the center of new arrangements that extend beyond Southeast Asia. If today we see in Southeast Asia a coherent regional entity—as opposed to what one 1954 observer characterized as "a place on the globe where certain groups of peoples, holding little in common, live contiguous to one another"[2]—it is largely due to the existence of ASEAN, whose activities and ideas about Southeast Asia have done much to give both form and substance to this once ambiguous region.

International relations theory has not known what to do with ASEAN. Regional elites associate their organization with milieu-transforming changes in Southeast Asia. Other developing regions identify ASEAN as a model of regional cooperation for their own problematic relations.[3] For such observers, ASEAN provides processes by which members have been able to stabilize their once volatile and fragmented region; to improve their security between one another and vis-à-vis larger, non-Southeast Asian powers; and ultimately to prosper. Yet predominant IR theories view ASEAN's cooperation as weak, inconsequential, even "unworthy of theoretical reflection."[4] Indeed, until recently, ASEAN was barely a mention in IR's mainstream journals and mostly outside its defining debates about world order, multilateral cooperation, international organizations, and regionalism.[5]

Mostly, such conclusions reflect a tendency of approaches to measure cooperation in utilitarian terms—that is, direct material gains and outcomes. Not surprisingly, realists, for whom military power and balance of power are key to security, are most dubious about ASEAN's strategic value. While ASEAN's participants may view regionalism as a way to defend their interests against those more powerful, members have also historically avoided any collective pooling of military capabilities that is central to realist definitions of balancing behavior and world order.[6] Political-security initiatives like ZOPFAN are seen as more or less useless as they offer states little in the way of military or material deterrent against possible territorial encroachment.

But even approaches that are more optimistic about cooperation and the resilience of institutions find it difficult to see the value in ASEAN. In fact, for contractual and neoliberal theorists, as well as realists, it is difficult to see why states would try to cooperate at all because, on the face of it, competing economic and security interests should point states *away* from regional cooperation. For both, the absence of formal mechanisms of cooperation in ASEAN is particularly problematic. Drawing mostly on European and North American examples, approaches argue that the value to be found in institutional arrangements is in their ability to provide "forms of hierarchy in which sanctions are employed to make self-interested choices consistent with the social good."[7] Thus, while they may see information and transparency as important products and facilitators of institutional cooperation, cooperation is nevertheless viewed mostly in terms of formal constraints and binding obligations.

However, if contractual obligations and forms of hierarchy are measures of cooperation, what is one to make of ASEAN's minimalist institutionalism or of the fact that ASEAN's Senior Officials Meeting (SOM), the center of ASEAN agenda setting and top of the ASEAN committee hierarchy,[8] was accorded no formal role in ASEAN for twenty years? What is one to make of ASEAN's founding declaration—a document "so general as to approach the nondescript,"[9] that identified no specific agenda for economic or political cooperation, provided no mechanism for dispute resolution, and established no central coordinating body or authority? In fact, it took ASEAN nine years just to get a minimalist secretariat and fifteen more years after that to upgrade it. By such criteria of cooperation, ASEAN, as well as expanded regional arrangements like the ASEAN Regional Forum and ASEAN Plus Three—arrangements that similarly offer no firm conflict resolution mechanisms or routes of sanction—are all examples of "soft" or "weak institutionalism" that compare unfavorably against the "strong institutionalism" of the European Union, the North American Free Trade Agreement, or the World Trade Organization (WTO).[10] If such formal mechanisms are the criteria for strong cooperation, then, as Katzenstein puts it, "the history of formal regional institutions in Asia is a history of failures so conspicuous, in comparison to Europe, as to beg for an explanation."[11]

However, the preoccupation of traditional approaches also make quite clear why ASEAN has not received more theoretical attention from international relations' main theories: As an example of neither military balancing nor legal contract, ASEAN quite simply offers these theories little to discuss. ASEAN is "weak" because institutional strength is measured in terms of legalization and militarization—neither of which describes ASEAN well. To look at ASEAN's minimalist economic and security initiatives is to conclude that ASEAN is an empty or weak exercise in cooperation—a mere "talk shop." But while ASEAN has certainly had its share of problems, the stabilization of regional relations and growth in cooperation over time counters such an extreme conclusion. Whether or not ASEAN is a security community, Southeast Asia is today more stable, cooperative, and coherent than it was four decades ago. Unlike the situation in the mid-1960s when conflict and intervention were the norm in intra–Southeast Asian relations, today exchanges, dialogue, and collaboration take place regularly at multiple levels and in a variety of areas. Even some contentious territorial disputes—the ultimate realist test—have been referred to the International Court of Justice, shelved, and in some cases, resolved.[12]

My point here is that while utilitarian explanations provide plausible reasons for the limitations of ASEAN cooperation and for why ASEAN has not done more, they have difficulty explaining why ASEAN has not done less. Utilitarian explanations are right to a point: Divergent interests do often make cooperation difficult, more open ended, less binding; and states do often opt for unilateral and bilateral solutions whose gains are more certain or at least less complicated.[13] Nevertheless, absent all the things that theorists say make institutions worthwhile, it is difficult to explain what justifies or sustains the organization, what states hope to gain from ASEAN cooperation, or the whys and hows behind the significant changes since ASEAN's founding. In short, the real puzzle for traditional approaches is not why ASEAN cooperation has not been more materially fruitful but rather why members have pursued ASEAN regionalism for so long if there were nothing going on.

The now-forty-year-old ASEAN thus presents an important puzzle for what have been the dominant approaches of international relations. Left unanswered are the very basic and fundamental questions: Why ASEAN? And what does it do? If ASEAN has mitigated the uncertainty of Southeast Asia's strategic environment—and I will argue that it has—it simply has not done so in many of the ways identified by dominant theoretical accounts. In other words, as Katzenstein argues, the contrast between European and Asian institutions should not lead to the automatic and common conclusion of "Asian failure" versus "European success" but instead openness to different kinds of regional processes and a search for alternative explanations.[14]

This thus provides the starting point for my alternative argument and framework. Drawing on constructivist approaches, my explanation begins with a discussion about the need to think about regionalism as a cumulative, social process. I then turn to the specific pieces of my framework—relational power (ASEAN's small power identity, extraregional uncertainties), regional ideas (especially, a nationalist bounded regional unity norm), and regionalism as a dialogue-driven, consensus-seeking process of social change. I argue that social constructivism's language of ideas, norms, and social process can speak to and capture the dynamics of ASEAN's regionalism in ways that the dominant theories of international relations and their language of material gains cannot.[15]

Thinking Differently about ASEAN Regionalism:
Regionalism as Social Process

I argue that we need to think differently about ASEAN regionalism and about cooperation in general. One of the limitations of more traditional approaches is that cooperation is understood mostly in terms of discrete collective action problems involving the provision and division of direct gains. Similarly, order—the contributions of regional institutions included—is also understood in mostly material and mechanical terms: balance of power, hegemonic leadership, forms of hierarchy, the structure of economic and security incentives. However, order and international institutions can also be understood in social, cultural, and organic terms—that is, the social ideas that regulate interactions and give meaning to relationships.

Thus, rather than thinking about cooperation solely in terms of functionally driven end products or instances of collective action, cooperation is, as Kaye argues, better understood as a dynamic, social "process of interactions" by which actors negotiate, not just specific interests but also new norms and thinking about relationships.[16] Thus for constructivists like Kaye and others, international institutions are more than places where actors go to bargain and negotiate predefined, fixed interests; they are also more than a set of "material rewards and punishments" that constrain state action. Instead, as Johnston similarly argues, institutions are also social environments where actors negotiate their different identities, where they debate ideas, and where they arrive at "collective interpretations of the external world" and how best to respond to it.[17] These social exchanges and interactions then produce changes in how states conceive their interests and themselves in relation to others. Put another way, actors do not enter and exit international organizations exactly the same as they entered it. Viewed in such terms, institutions may be better viewed as "norms builders" as much "norms enforcers;"[18] they are social and socializing arenas, where new ideas, new definitions of self and other, and thus new politics—for better or worse—may emerge, take hold, and reproduce.

By this view, cooperation can be viewed as a dialogue-driven process that aims to identify, seek out, and build on areas of agreement. I argue that ASEAN regionalism is best understood as an ongoing search for consensus and a series of dialogues, debates, and exchanges about both the material and social foundations of regional order: the role of great powers in Southeast Asia, the desire for self-determination, the relationship between nation and region, the causal connection between fragmentation and intervention, the normative idea of Southeast Asia as a distinct region with a distinct point of view. It is through these interactive, cumulative dialogues that regions and regionalisms have been shaped. Most important, states have come to new and common agreement about economic and political-security cooperation through this dialogue-driven process. Consequently, in contrast to 1967, when differences and intra-ASEAN relations were such that states could not even list politics or security as areas for ASEAN cooperation, today not only are both those areas explicitly acknowledged but annual "ASEAN Defense Ministers Meetings (ADMM)" and "informal" meetings of ASEAN defense chiefs[19] have now been made regular and "integral" parts of the ASEAN process. Such developments clearly reflect a radical change in intra-ASEAN relations; but, by many utilitarian accounts, these meetings neither register as significant cooperation nor are they easily explainable.[20]

Thus, Kaye and others argue, thinking about cooperation as a process offers new insights into activities that might otherwise be viewed as empty and pointless.[21] To view cooperation as a cumulative social process allows us to see individual ASEAN initiatives not so much as endpoints to negotiation but rather as parts of larger social trends and series of changes. Individual initiatives may be fraught with problems and fall short of what ASEAN policymakers would like to see, but each also represents points and movement in a larger, more extended social negotiation.

Put another way, to understand cooperation as a cumulative social process is to draw attention to the ways that social interactions and exchanges can create common understandings and the ways that those understandings, in turn, can inform, direct, and constrain subsequent interactions, negotiations, and relations. In this specific Southeast Asian case, exchanges over time have produced new agreement about both intra- and extraregional relations and, most important, a culture of dialogue that forms a basis for more stable relations. That, in turn, has at minimum allowed states to devote more attention and resources to domestic and economic development, improving states' material situation and welfare by almost every indicator. Social constructivist approaches can provide important insight into the kinds of changes and exchanges taking place in ASEAN and the ways that ASEAN facilitates them.

At the same time, such processes—their social dynamics, products, how they contribute to change—have not always been well detailed in ASEAN discussions. Indeed, it is not often clear what the intervening processes were that helped us get from *here* to *there*. For example, constructivist discussions can get caught up in testing the strength or weakness of particular ASEAN norms at particular moments, rather than focusing on the dynamic content of norms and practices over time. Consequently, we know less about "incremental processes of socialization" that build ASEAN as "ASEAN."[22]

Another example of how this critical middle part of the story is sometimes overlooked in discussions on ASEAN can be found in discussions that explain ASEAN norms in terms of history or existing international norms. Specifically, ASEAN's contemporary regionalism is said to be the product of the consultative, consensus-building practices of the Malay village, the Westphalian practices and norms of the international system, the principles of coexistence laid out at the 1955 Bandung Conference, and/or similar in form to Southeast Asia's precolonial empires—*mandala* systems that were highly personal and nonterritorial and whose generally relaxed pattern of intra-regional relations are said to provide kinds of preregions for today's regionalism in Southeast Asia.[23]

These parallels are not unimportant. As argued below, "history" provides important context and prisms that inform and constrain which ideas are more likely to be influential. Such discussions, especially as regards Southeast Asia's historic trading systems and precolonial mandalas, also do us a great service in reminding us not only of Southeast Asian agency and subjectivity—that Southeast Asia was not simply waiting to be "discovered" by the West—but also that Southeast Asia was not always as incoherent as recent history and narratives would lead us to believe.[24]

At the same time, while such parallels and connections are not coincidental, neither are they necessarily causal, as illustrated by the fact that neither Malay village practices nor existing international principles did much to moderate the conflict and confrontation that plagued relations in 1960s Southeast Asia. Moreover, it is worth underscoring that European imperialism had reorganized Southeast Asian life in irrevocable ways and for hundreds of years, such that a very different Southeast Asia emerged after World War II.[25] Indeed, if historical relations had previously been peaceful or close, one would not know it from observing Southeast Asia's first conflictual interactions as new states. As Acharya notes, "[W]ith the advent of European colonialism, much of the commonality and shared consciousness created during these periods was disrupted and, in some cases, severely eroded."[26] In the end, independence did not return Southeast Asia to the regional systems and political forms of the past but instead thrust them into a modern world of nation-states and nationalist conflicts, as evidenced by their destabilizing and divisive conflicts of the 1950s and 1960s.

Thus, the mostly neglected question is exactly how the concept of "region"—historical or newly invented—was made meaningful again after hundreds of years of economic and political division under colonialism, not to mention a period of disruptive intraregional conflict. Also, why did regional elites seize on this *particular* idea of region—defined as these ten states, themselves mostly foreign creations[27]—a region that bore only partial resemblance to its historical predecessors?[28] A focus on social processes—for example, argument, debate, and consensus seeking in promoting, building, and reinforcing a particular region and regionalism—as well as historical conditions can provide insight into these questions.

Toward the twin goals of theory development and explaining ASEAN and its evolving regionalisms, my framework below further elaborates on the conditions and processes, as well as the interacting material-ideational forces, that have made possible social change in Southeast Asia and the interesting role that ASEAN is now trying to play in East Asia and the Asia Pacific. Specifically, I highlight the role played by relational power, ideas, and the dialogue process through which ideas and consensus are promoted, maintained, and renegotiated and through which they have directed the course of ASEAN's regionalisms.

Relational Power

I have thus far emphasized the ideational and social foundations of regional organization in large part because of the realist bias that informs many academic and popular discussions of ASEAN, but this is not to say that power does not matter; quite the contrary. In fact, explanations for ASEAN and its regionalism must consider both material and ideational factors and how they come together if we are to understand and explain ASEAN, its structure, and its processes, as well as resultant Southeast Asian (and now also, East Asian) regionalisms and regional order(s).

While constructivists are right that ideas underlie definitions of material interests and are thus "prior" to the material, there is nevertheless no getting around the fact that ASEAN, despite the tremendous economic growth of member-states, remains a group of lesser powers in a world where material power matters quite a lot. At the very least, in the world we have, it seems important to acknowledge that ASEAN members' relative lack of material capabilities (individually, collectively, internally, and externally) may be a significant factor that structures in important ways their interactions with the world. As O'Brien argues, as powerful as some ideas may be, it nevertheless remains a truism that "Not all groups are equally capable of constructing their own reality, and power relations must be confronted and dealt with in any attempt to build different socio-political arrangements."[29]

In this discussion, I draw attention to two particular ways that relational power affects the course and content of regionalism in Southeast Asia. The first is that ASEAN states, as lesser powers and lesser economies, begin with a narrower range of tools with which to pursue and protect their interests and objectives. They are also more sensitive and vulnerable to changes in major power policies and major power relations as a result. As discussed below, this sensitivity is further intensified by the weak sociopolitical cohesion of many states.[30] Consequently, as regards ASEAN, changes in major power policies and major power relations have provided regular extraregional catalysts for new thinking about regionalism. The second way that relational power matters to ASEAN regionalism is that states' self-identification as lesser powers informs their worldviews and conceptions of what they should and should not do, which in turn colors and constrains what regionalism looks like in East and Southeast Asia.

Major Power Policies and Extraregional Uncertainty. The course, pattern, and development of regionalism in Southeast Asia points to an important relationship between, on the one hand, extra-ASEAN instabilities that are most often a function of major power policy changes and, on the other, new (or sometimes renewed) regional initiatives. Of ASEAN's major power relations, the most important has been the United States, which has been, at one and the same time, provider of important security and economic goods and, to quote Leifer, "intervener extraordinaire."[31] On the one hand, the United States, especially during the Cold War, has been a critical stabilizing force, especially as regarded the major power status quo. The United States has also provided economic assistance, investment, and a market for ASEAN products—all deemed critical for state and regime security. On the other hand, the particular dependence of ASEAN states and economies on the United States for such goods has also made them even more vulnerable to U.S. efforts to intervene. Indeed, the United States has had tremendous ability to meddle and intervene in the affairs of states, as illustrated by a range of different actions, from more military interventions like the U.S. war in Vietnam to efforts to condition aid, trade, investment, and U.S.–Asia security commitments.

At minimum, the tremendous ability of the United States to help or harm Southeast Asia has made ASEAN states most sensitive to changes in U.S. policy. ASEAN states are sensitive to other major powers too, but the comprehensive nature of U.S. power and structure of Cold War dependence on the United States has made states sensitive to the United States much more than to others. Consequently, of extra–ASEAN influences, U.S. policy changes have provided the most regular catalyst for regional initiatives in ASEAN. Such changes do so mostly by creating uncertainty, at times crisis, that triggers a reassessment of the old order and its arrangements and, in turn, a search for alternative ideas and arrangements.

Thus, intra-ASEAN and extra-ASEAN relations are linked in important ways. Each of these chapters consequently details defining ASEAN initiatives and shows each to correlate with extra-ASEAN instabilities associated with larger powers, especially the United States: ASEAN's creation in 1967 (the U.S. war in Vietnam, U.K. retrenchment in the mid- to late 1960s); the ZOPFAN (U.S.–China détente in 1971); the TAC and Declaration of ASEAN Concord (ending of U.S. war in Vietnam); PTAs (1973 oil and food crisis, Nixon shock); ARF, AFTA, and ASEAN 10 (the end of the Cold War); and East Asian—*ASEAN plus*—initiatives (the weak U.S. response to the 1997–99 financial crisis). Viewing it from a big picture perspective, external instabilities have been associated with key decision-making moments in ASEAN's evolution as a regional organization and Southeast Asia as a region.

The strong correlation between ASEAN's major political, economic, and security initiatives, on the one hand, and extra-ASEAN uncertainties, on the other, suggests that the latter significantly increases the likelihood (and may even be a necessary condition) of regional change. As critical juncture theorists and historical institutionalists similarly argue, significant events create a sense of urgency and time pressure that increases the probability for action.[32] As further elaborated below, such events do not in and of themselves explain whether there is change or what kind of change ensues. They do not, for example, explain why ASEAN states might choose a *regional* response to global uncertainties (especially as a regional response was often neither obvious nor immediate). All such events do is to destabilize existing ideas and practices, trigger reassessment, and create pressure to change—for example, by creating situations involving unacceptable consequences,[33] disappointment[34] about existing policies and arrangements, and/or by removing or introducing a new force or factor commonly understood to have critical implications for regional order. However, recognition of events as serious enough to warrant action depends on actors, their interpretations, and often their advocacy. Similarly, whether *regionalism* is the chosen response will depend on what causal linkages and arguments actors make.

Small Power Predicaments; Small Power Identities.   The diversity of Southeast Asia has long challenged our ability to identify one single commonality among states; and, indeed, most efforts usually involve exceptions. However, in our search for commonalities, we may also be overlooking the obvious, namely, a common understanding of their weakness and vulnerability in relation to extraregional forces. Though there are states that view themselves as regional powers or leaders in relation to other Southeast Asian states (Indonesia most notably), ASEAN states share a common identity as (internally and externally) weaker powers in a global system dominated by stronger ones, as well as common predicament involving the tension between dependence, on the one hand, and autonomy and self-determination, on the other.

This identity and tension inform ASEAN states about how the world works and how they see major powers relating to minor powers, as well as understandings of what they as lesser states can and cannot/should and should not do. As Hopf argues, actors' self-conceptions are important because they affect their selection, interpretation, and use of information.[35] It also helps define for actors their own role and ability for agency in particular situations. In ASEAN's case, their categorization of the world in terms of major and minor powers provides states one way to think about commonalities and differences but also plans of action.

In ASEAN, this common identity as lesser powers has also come to inform states' very understanding of "Southeast Asia" (who's in, who's out) and Southeast Asian regionalism and diplomacy. Especially interesting is how ASEAN's dialogue-driven, relationship-building regionalism now also provides the basis for new arguments about its strategic engagement with larger powers. Noncoercive, nonconfrontational, and nonostracizing, this approach is now understood to promote security through inclusive dialogue designed for reassurance, not deterrence. By increasing the sense of security of would-be predators, ASEAN diplomacy is said to neutralize the desire or need for such states to pursue more confrontational and threatening strategies. Today, not only is this inclusive, nonconfrontational, relationship-building approach often argued by elites to be normatively superior to, say, competitive balance of power politics in stabilizing the region, but it is further argued that ASEAN members, *by virtue of their uncontroversiality as smaller powers,* may be best able to facilitate new agreement and stability between greater powers and between those powers and ASEAN as to regional order.[36] In other words, though it may have originally been a function of materially constrained choice, ASEAN's particular mode of regional engagement and role in larger regional arrangements today has come to have a strategic logic—as Johnston characterizes it, an explicitly "counter–real politik" logic—all its own.[37]

Considered to be one of the more distinctive features of ASEAN's corporate identity and diplomatic culture, this diplomatic approach does have some mundane, "practical" roots: distrust between states, different security preferences and perceptions, limited state capacities. These material limitations, as Wendt argues, may make coercive or military strategies less obvious choices and states consequently may be more open to alternative, noncoercive, and nonmilitary kinds of problem solving. At very least, additional steps will be required before lesser states can pursue more coercive strategies. In this vein, Wendt argues that lesser powers may come to appreciate sooner the value of common security over competitive balances of power. As Wendt puts it,

> In policy terms, [relying on the institutional fabric of international society] means that states can be less worried about short-term survival and relative power and can thus shift their resources accordingly. Ironically, it is the great powers, the states with the greatest national means, that may have the hardest time learning this lesson; small powers do not have the luxury of relying on national means and may therefore learn faster that collective recognition is a cornerstone of security.[38]

Of course, more coercive strategies are not completely off limits to lesser powers. As evidenced around the world, lesser powers still have (and frequently pursue) the option of building up their arsenals and pooling their military resources—thus "correcting" their weak status. Interventions (of varying kinds) also remain as options, as illustrated by examples from 1960s Southeast Asia, when Indonesia's leadership, for example, readily launched a violent campaign against its neighbor Malaysia or when the Philippines tried to physically take back Sabah from Malaysia. In short, while material limitations may make more confrontational or coercive strategies less likely as a first policy response, examples from Southeast Asia's own history also make clear that relative power and relative capabilities do not determine the kinds of strategies states pursue. Even lesser states have a range of choice: States can choose more coercive and confrontational strategies as some states did in the 1960s, or they can forego them as ASEAN states did vis-à-vis one another in latter decades. The question is, what accounts for the difference?

Thus, it is important to be clear that my argument about extraregional uncertainties and states' status as lesser powers is *not* saying that such factors *caused* ASEAN to pursue regionalism or its particular form of dialogue-driven engagement or regionalism as a response to perceived economic and security challenges. Rather, my point about the importance of ASEAN states' lesser power status and about extraregional policy changes being important catalysts of ASEAN initiatives is to highlight how this structural dependency is not simply a point of vulnerability but also a starting point for other ideas that will inform views of strategy and identity.

In short, material factors tell only part of the story. To explain the pursuit of ASEAN or Southeast Asian regionalism as a response to political and security challenges, it is thus necessary to turn to other factors—specifically, ideas about Southeast Asia as a region. Especially given that a Southeast Asian or ASEAN response was often not obvious, easy, or economically rational, ideas and argument provide the causal linkages that made regional solutions persuasive, even necessary, responses to perceived and understood challenges.

Founding Ideas, Founding Arguments

Ideas are critical to explaining ASEAN regionalism. Ideas define the social contexts that lead actors to perceive threats in one situation but not another. Ideas also define realms of possibility and appropriateness.[39] In the absence of clear material incentives, ideas are especially useful in helping to explain why diverse and divergent states, as ASEAN states have been, would pursue regionalism as a response to their problems.

ASEAN begins with the normative idea that there is a certain defined area called Southeast Asia and that states in Southeast Asia need and ought to get along with one another by virtue of their geographic proximity, history, and common vulnerability to foreign intervention. This idea is premised on a number of related sub-ideas. These include ideas about Southeast Asia's diversity and history of division and foreign intervention, as well as ideas about national and regional self-determination vis-a-vis those external forces. Taken together, these ideas find expression especially in ideas of *resilience* and "One Southeast Asia" as both regional ideal and plan of action.

Ideas, however, are not significant in and of themselves. Instead, their effect and significance derive from the shared meanings that actors attach to them—in other words, their intersubjective content. That intersubjective content is what gives ideas their causal power and is thus critical to explaining an idea's effectiveness as a coordinating principle or the persuasiveness of one regional idea over another.[40] The importance of looking at the content of ideas becomes especially clear when one considers the many different ideas of region that Southeast Asian states have entertained over the years and those that have failed to take hold. Below, I unpack the regional idea, with particular attention to ideas of *resilience* and *nationalism* as ideological focal points and boundaries.

Regional Resilience—"One Southeast Asia."   As noted, diversity forms an important theme in our understanding of Southeast Asia and its international relations. That diversity is as much perceived as it is real: Southeast Asia *is* an extremely diverse place in practically every respect, but that diversity and especially its political significance are also the products of social interpretations, even active mythologizing. Both the empirical and narrated diversity of Southeast Asia—diversity of peoples, perspectives, interests—pose material and ideological constraints on ASEAN regionalism.

This understanding of ASEAN's diversity may lead us to overstate intra-ASEAN differences and to obscure important areas of agreement among ASEAN states. After all, there would be no ASEAN and no ASEAN regionalism if there were not something that tied these states together. As Emmerson argues, there must be some "minimum common understanding of security" if the process is to mean anything and if "members are not always working at cross purposes."[41] For Emmerson, as it is here, that minimum common understanding is best captured by Southeast Asian conceptualizations of resilience.

Defined as "the capacity of a regional regime to maintain itself against external and internal pressures and conditions that could defeat or divide it,"[42] resilience is most often invoked in terms of *national* resilience—an acknowledgment of the twin challenges of state and nation building. However, in these chapters, I give greatest attention not to national resilience but instead to *regional resilience*. This is not to diminish the importance of national resilience. In fact, national resilience is a critical component of regional resilience. Nevertheless, national resilience, by itself, does not explain why ASEAN states would pursue *regionalism* as the answer to their identified security and economic problems given different interests, perspectives, and preferences. *Regional* resilience, however, does.

Specifically, regional resilience is much like national resilience but on a regional scale. Just as domestic divisions create opportunities for outside actors to intervene and manipulate internal actors against one another, regional divisions will create similar kinds of opportunities. Most of all, regional resilience shares with national resilience deeply held beliefs about the fragility of the political unit—both region and nation. In regional resilience, that sense of fragility is further underscored by Southeast Asia's geographical, as much as political, fragmentation. The idea here, as it is in national resilience, is that a critical source of Southeast Asian vulnerability is to be found in states' own national and regional fragmentation. Regional resilience also similarly expresses a kind of vicious cycle where division leads to intervention, which then deepens existing divisions and subsequently widens the door to even more intervention.

Regional resilience is at the heart of ASEAN's founding argument and founding narrative. It is what makes the idea of "One Southeast Asia" meaningful. In that narrative, causal ideas about the relationship between Southeast Asia's political fragmentation and foreign intervention both draw from, and provide, an interpretive lens through which to understand a relatively recent and violent history of domestic division, intraregional conflict, and intervention by outside powers: Western imperial powers, Japan, Cold War protagonists. In 1960s Southeast Asia, the event that came to most symbolize this causal and interpretative connection was the U.S. war in Vietnam. That war, in which divisions in Vietnam and intra-Southeast Asian divisions opened the door to foreign intervention, would especially help impress on ASEAN's founding states the need for unity both nationally and regionally. Such division, its connection to a reinforcing history of intervention, and the need for unity would be captured in the ASEAN narrative, as expressed, for example, by Carlos Romulo, foreign minister of the Philippines:

> [O]ur historic weakness in Asia lay in our having been fragmented, rendering us permeable to invasion and fractioning our efforts at self-development. . . .It might have been a different story in Southeast Asia . . . [if] we had had a system of mutual consultation among us, a *Musjawarah* . . . when first the great powers appeared in the region. It might have been a different story for my country if during our revolution we had this community of nations to turn to . . . Then we would not have been as terribly alone as we were. And we, the diverse peoples making up Southeast Asia, would not have been set against each other as we became.[43]

It is this narrative that gives power to the ideas highlighted above, as well as meaning to ASEAN activities.

As should be increasingly clear, such understandings of resilience are not just about what others "do to" Southeast Asia (that is, foreign intervention); nor is it about Southeast Asia being the passive object of great power designs. Rather, the causal logic contained in conceptions of resilience point to a clear plan of action—that is, security and self-determination would be secured through unity. Put another way, if fragmentation is understood to be the problem, then the logical answer must be unity. While that unity will be both national and regional, it is the dangers associated with *regional fragmentation* that make *regional unity* an important coordinating and normative principle among ASEAN states.

At the same time, such conclusions about Southeast Asian diversity or division and need for unity produce competing normative pressures that have implications for what ASEAN cooperation looks like. On the one hand, such conclusions create normative pressure in favor of regional cooperation. A concern for regional unity helps explain, for example, why there is cooperation in otherwise unexpected areas as intra-ASEAN trade liberalization.

As further detailed in the following chapters, the driving point is less particular gains as it is the perceived need for greater integration—*unity*. In fact, whereas utilitarian accounts see preexisting interests as drivers of cooperation, in ASEAN the logic is in a way reversed. The idea is that cooperation will also create the uniting interests that are viewed as critical to security.

On the other hand, the perceived need for unity also acts as a normative constraint on how hard and how far states are willing to push cooperation. Specifically, the assumed fragility of intrastate and intra–Southeast Asian relations makes states extremely cautious about forcing other states to adopt initiatives with which they are not comfortable for fear that states and regions—a fragile unity and security—will fall apart. The emphasis is on building and maintaining relationships, not straining and dividing them with difficult and "excessive" demands.

The readily and self-consciously acknowledged obstacles in the way of regionalism in Southeast Asia underscore the point that for those participating in the ASEAN process, "One Southeast Asia" has been a normative, less empirical, idea. "One Southeast Asia" is an ideal, a plan of action, even a guiding principle, but it is importantly not assumed to in fact exist. And herein lie the challenge, tension, and arguably the strength at the heart of the ASEAN process: States are compelled at one and the same time to build greater regional unity but also not to jeopardize what fragile unity exists. Consequently, rather than materially compel other states to act against their preferences and thus upset fragile domestic and regional arrangements, ASEAN states instead take small steps based on what consensus there is and then keep talking in pursuit of new or expanded agreement. Given such constraints, it should thus be no surprise that some ASEAN initiatives have been decades-long projects.

A Nationalist Bounded Regional Idea.   Important to why some ideas trump others is how ideas are framed in relation to more established ideologies and ideas. "Persuasive messages," as Payne argues, "are not transmitted in an ideational vacuum."[44] This means that persuasive ideas are more likely to draw on established ideas than they are to be a complete rejection of all that has come before. Persuasive ideas and persuasive arguments for new practices will be those that are ideationally and socially salient, that is, ideas and arguments that "ring true"[45] and "fit" dominant ideas and ideologies about social realities.[46] This is also what Crawford means when she argues that the ideas and beliefs that form culture provide important "background meaning"—meaning that is both prism and resource for new arguments.[47]

In the ASEAN case, regional ideas and arguments are made more salient by their resonance with the familiar. Here, the regional idea draws particular power and legitimacy from nationalism. In the 1960s Southeast Asian context of decolonization and newly independent states, nationalism was not just the dominant preference or principle; it was the unquestioned belief system of the day. It therefore would have been very difficult to convince newly independent states to sign on to regionalism without some deference to nationalism's core concepts about self-determination, independence, and autonomy.

To be sure, the concepts of the "nation" and "nationalism" are highly contentious in Southeast Asia, given the incongruence of peoples and borders, a legacy of the fact that "[m]ost Southeast Asian countries owe their present boundaries to colonial action" and were drawn with little regard for existing political geographies, the "local way of life," or the peoples that lived there.[48] The result is ethnically and geographically fragmented states, as well as authority challenges for postindependence leaders.

However, in another respect, nationalism is in fact a most appropriate term to describe both the processes and the kind of thinking that have been ongoing in post–World War II Southeast Asia. While nationalism can refer to the unity of state and nation, nationalism can also be understood in Anderson's sense of "imagined communities," the developmental sense of nationalist construction, as well as the political sense of self-determination.[49] Indeed, in all these senses, nationalism captures what has been going on in Southeast Asia. Nationalism here is thus best understood not in the conventional sense of ethnicity but instead as an ideological and material process of political construction: the pursuit of a broad-based political consciousness, the promotion of common identification with the state, the creation of a unifying political ideology, the establishment of a relatively autonomous economy and polity through development.

In particular, new political ("national") communities are being imagined from a preexisting diversity already politicized by colonial policies. Here, authority and legitimacy can also be further exacerbated by ruling elites whose vision of the "nation" may not be sufficiently inclusive. In fact, as Alagappa details, what can emerge is a mutually reinforcing cycle whereby weak "national" identity translates into weak legitimacy and authority, which then leads ruling elites to turn to more coercive means to establish and ensure domestic order.[50] Such actions, then, further undermine domestic legitimacy and exacerbate intergroup conflicts within the state, creating what Ayoob describes as the "third world security predicament" and Job describes as the "insecurity dilemma".[51] In short, the primacy of nationalism as a preoccupation for ASEAN states speaks to pressing concerns about domestic order that are in large part legacies of the colonial era and radically compressed processes of ongoing and simultaneous state and nation building. Such dynamics are why Southeast Asia's most pressing security concerns have tended to be internal, coalescing especially around questions of identity and political legitimacy.[52]

In addition, nationalism can also be understood in terms of the ongoing drive for nationalist self-determination vis-à-vis external forces. Such dynamics are captured, for example, in a variety of politics and social movements—from outright revolutions against colonizing powers, to protests against U.S. bases, to declarations of neutrality, to "Asian values" arguments against external efforts to dictate state policies and development. Such dynamics are also captured by the ideology and policies of economic nationalism—that is, the drive to establish control over one's economy and development as a defensive measure against would-be intruding economic and political forces. Similarly, there is developmental nationalism, which finds expression in various infrastructure and government-led industrialization projects designed to "encourage identification with state and regime," as well as to promote a sense of "national consciousness" and pride through development.[53] In these various ways, nationalism in Southeast Asia is not about the "nation-state" as conventionally understood, but rather about an exercise in self-creation toward establishing the socioeconomic and political foundations that will allow countries to survive vis-à-vis both internal and external forces.

By the same token, then, it is precisely because "nation" is such a contested and problematic concept for Southeast Asia's contemporary states that nationalism is as defining as it is and why it forms an important boundary of the intra-ASEAN dialogue on Southeast Asian regionalism. Here, it is useful to contrast "nationalism" to "sovereignty," which ASEAN and international relations scholars often invoke to explain ASEAN's constrained regionalism.[54] While there are parallels and some similar effects, nationalism is more useful in at least two respects. First, the sovereignty explanation typically views survival in terms of relative power (and thus relative gains) and does not capture well what state elites see to be their ongoing, driving, and most pressing internal and resilience preoccupations. Second, as an expression of a mostly static set of interests, sovereignty also does not capture well the ongoing nature of nation-building projects or the possibility of change.

To return to the argument, in this context of 1960s Southeast Asia, where nationalist priorities and sensitivities were high, any successful regionalism would thus have to be defined in ways that supported, or at very least did not contradict, nationalism's most basic presumptions and priorities. Consequently, ideas of region—*if* they were to be persuasive—could not *but* be defined in national-ist terms. The successful argument—the ASEAN argument—perhaps not sur-prisingly co-opted ideas of national resilience and national self-determination. At the same time, in so doing, regionalism also became importantly bound by nationalism. Not only has regionalism consequently been defined in ways that do not contradict nationalist priorities, but in fact nationalist priorities are legitimated and even actively upheld by "regionalism." This nationalist-bound regionalism has significant consequences for ASEAN institutionalism and integration. Instead of supranationalism, ASEAN regionalism has been a regionalism that has tended to reify—rather than supersede—national perspec-tives and identities. While this nationalist-bounded outcome may be similar to that expected by realists who focus on sovereignty, the explanation here is not only critically different in terms of "why" but also has implications for "what" is produced from it. Where realists see ASEAN's loose institutionalism, for example, as a function of fixed, competitive interests, my explanation focuses on an ideological and normative constraint. Critically also, my argument high-lights the processes by which ideas are promoted, challenged, and reified (see below), thus allowing for change and different outcomes.

Regionalism as Social Process: The Rhetoric and Rituals of Regional Unity

In ASEAN diplomacy, one will find few legal treaties but many declarations of regional solidarity, friendship, and good will. Against conventional views of cooperation and institutions as "purposive institutions with explicit rules, specific assignments of roles to individuals and groups, and the capacity for [collective] action,"[55] the tendency is to view ASEAN's declarations as "cheap talk." A view of cooperation as a cumulative process involving social interac-tions, ideational exchanges, and representational politics reveals, however, that ASEAN's declarations are neither pointless, empty, cheap, nor without real effects for politics.

Specifically, the following chapters give attention to three related pro-cesses, each of which aim to give expression to the idea of Southeast Asia as "one." As part of a dynamic dialogue-driven social process aimed at maintaining and building common understandings and interpretations of problems, each also forms a key part of ASEAN "cooperation." The first is a process of arguing by which some ideas come to be more persuasive than others and by which problems come to be framed and interpreted. The second is a consensus-seeking process aimed at establishing and expanding areas of agreement; and the third is a process that might be best character-ized as social reinforcement whereby certain ideas, even nascent identities, come to be solidified through regular reiteration, social ritual, and social affirmation.

Each of these processes, it should be noted, has been primarily an elite process. The elite nature of the process has reflected what has been a mostly elite decision-making process in Southeast Asia. ASEAN, itself, has been mostly a project of the foreign ministries of ASEAN's member states, though that process has now expanded to include regular participation by ASEAN heads of governments,[56] other ministries (including trade, labor, health, and most recently defense), as well as a small nod to civil society groups that have begun to challenge both the elite nature of the ASEAN process and the discourse of ASEAN regionalism. Nevertheless, as these chapters detail and as illustrated by recent developments concerning the adoption of an ASEAN charter, ASEAN remains a predominantly elite-driven and controlled process.

Additionally it should be underscored that the focus of this study is on *shared* ideas, as opposed to individually held opinions. In tracing the intra-ASEAN arguments and consensus-seeking process, these chapters aim to reveal underlying ideational and normative structures of ASEAN regionalism. Put another way, these chapters are interested in ideas as social, not mental, phenomena.[57] This is why, then, the focus of chapters is on the *public* debate and public exchanges between ASEAN elites as opposed to the individual motivations or individual domestic politics.[58] In addition to getting around the methodological problem of "get[ting] into another's head,"[59] such public exchanges—arguments, justifications, rationalizations, debates—more importantly can reveal key areas of agreement (and disagreement) about social objectives and appropriate action. After all, such efforts, manipulations, and representations would be unnecessary and pointless if there were no cultural stock in representing oneself and one's motives in particular ways.[60]

Regionalism as Consensus-Seeking Process.   One of my driving arguments about ASEAN is that cooperation is best understood as a cumulative consensus-seeking process rather than as a discrete instance of collective action. Put another way, the "struggle for mutual understanding"[61]—in this case about critical nation–region and region–world relationships—is an ongoing one that involves identifying and establishing but also contesting and renegotiating points of consensus on various issues. Toward illustrating this process, chapters detail and trace intra-ASEAN debates about great power arrangements, the nation–region relationship, and Southeast Asia's relationship with larger regions.

Because cooperation involves "a continuing relationship and cumulative dialogue,"[62] the very act of arguing and talking (see below) can be seen as a first important step in the search for consensus—but it is only a *first* step.

That initial exchange then establishes new starting points for discussion and additional consensus-seeking efforts, which then produce other points of consensus and yet other new points to be worked out, and so on. Agreed-on points and principles then become part of an evolving discourse on regionalism, which in turn forms cognitive structures that affect how actors conceive their future range of action, other projects, and their realms of possibility.

The chapters that follow, in fact, show that ASEAN states are in a continual process of clarifying points of agreement. This process of clarification has not been easy—nor has that clarification always produced change in the same direction. Areas of agreement have, in fact, been periodically challenged, undermined, or destabilized by state actions and external policies, prompting reevaluation and renegotiation of the points in question. The larger implication of this is that the social structure on which a regional system is based—collective meanings, shared ideas, norms, relationships—is not static but instead constantly in motion or "in process." This is true whether the system is in process of reproducing itself or in transition. As Wendt notes, "*All* systems, natural and social, are always in process."[63]

Regionalism as Talking and Arguing. The way that states pursue consensus is through talking and arguing. It is through talking and arguing that ASEAN states identify, maintain, and pursue points of consensus. It is through talking and arguing that ASEAN states exercise normative pressure on others to modify or change their positions or behavior. It is through talking and arguing that ASEAN states have developed new thinking about nonviolent resolution of problems—specifically, a culture of restraint, respect, and responsibility[64]—that is dramatically different from 1960s conflict-torn Southeast Asia.

For an organization frequently criticized for being "all talk," it seems especially fitting to consider the role played by talking and arguing in ASEAN. However, in contrast to those who see "talk" as mere "rhetorical shells that give form but no substance to domestic and international arrangements," chapters show that talking can have powerful effects.[65] As Finnemore and Sikkink argue, "[S]peech can . . . persuade; it can change people's minds about what goals are valuable and about the roles they play (or should play) in social life. When speech has these effects, it is doing important social construction work, creating new understandings and new social facts that reconfigure politics."[66]

In fact, "talking," as Onuf argues, may be "the most important way that we go about making the world what it is."[67] The acts of communication—oral, written, other—are the ways in which actors express what they are thinking and who they think they are. When speech takes the form of argument, it becomes a way that actors get what they want. As Crawford puts it, arguments "provide reasons [for action or inaction] that actors think and hope others will find persuasive."[68]

Speech and argument are thus processes by which particular ideas come to influence political life. However, rarely are ideas automatically powerful, or as Higgott puts it, "The presence of a big idea is not of itself a sufficient motor for progress."[69] Ideas—especially radical and contentious ones—will require active, even activist, interpretation, argument, and promotion. Advocates in this sense are important, but so are the arguments they put forward. Arguments make critical linkages among cause, effect, and response. As noted above, for example, the regional idea was made more persuasive because it drew on existing ideas about nationalism. However, this connection was not automatic. Rather, it took active acts of social interpretation—*argument*—to make the necessary linkages between nationalism and regionalism. Thus, to quote Laffey and Weldes, "the 'fit' between new and existing ideas is actively *constructed* rather than simply 'there' in the ideas themselves."[70]

In this process, creative actors therefore play an important role in seizing opportunities and in presenting and arguing for alternative ideas and conceptualizations.[71] In ASEAN, a handful of foreign policy-making elites play an early and critical role in actively pushing particular interpretations of both national and regional security and alternative visions of regional order based on regional resilience. Again, regional ideas in ASEAN were not a priori meaningful but were rather *made* meaningful.

These acts of interpretation are also why regionalism must be understood as something more than just a functional response to problems—whether the problem is the threat of external intervention, the challenge of domestic instability and integration, or the destabilizing effects of regional conflict. Functional needs must still be interpreted in particular ways if, for example, regionalism is to be the solution to the problem. Thus, while a majority of states in other regions of the global south may face similar problems of national integration, regional conflict, and foreign intervention as those faced by ASEAN's founding states, not all regions turn to regionalism as a solution to those problems. This is because states may see a connection between national instability and foreign intervention but fail to identify regional conflict as an exacerbating factor. In other cases, they may recognize the destabilizing effects of intra-regional conflict, but nevertheless fail to attach a particular significance to regional unity. Failing to make these causal connections, states, faced with similar problems of national integration, will more likely turn to nonregional solutions—for example, "international cliency" (thus generating goods for domestic constituencies)[72] or war (creating a rally-around-the-flag effect) as the answer to their problems. In short, ideas and argument are what distinguish Southeast Asia from other regions that may be similarly fragmented but remain "zones of conflict."

Regionalism as Social Reinforcement. Social reinforcement is critical if ideas are to become more than arguments. Social reinforcement is about creating stable patterns—patterned thinking and patterned behavior, habits of thinking and acting whereby actors no longer need to be persuaded as to the merits of particular ideas and practices.

Ideas and practices can be reinforced in various ways, but all will involve in some way a process by which ideas and practices are made more familiar and eventually *normal.* In conflict-torn 1960s Southeast Asia where regional cooperation was *not* normal, for example, ASEAN's founding elites sought to create what they described as a "habit of mind" involving a "growing awareness that . . . [Southeast Asian states] have many problems in common."[73] Toward that end, those elites sought to reinforce initial arguments about the need for ASEAN unity through word and deed. Initially, such efforts mostly took the form of reiteration. Especially in ASEAN's first decade, elites were constantly and self-consciously repeating founding arguments for organization to remind themselves and each other of their common cause and why it was important to work together as this particular group of states. In fact, ASEAN's early meetings were characterized by regular references to Southeast Asia's history of fragmentation and division, as well as arguments stressing the importance of region and regional unity as a defense against foreign intervention, and regional organization as an expression of regional self determination and autonomy—almost as if the case for regional organization had to be continually made. However, as the importance of region and regional organization became more familiar, more accepted, and more unquestioned, such explicit reminders became less and less necessary; the regional idea became more established in Southeast Asian relations; and a culture of restraint began to emerge.

Social rituals can also play a role in reinforcing ideas, especially ideas about community. In the ASEAN case, specific ASEAN rituals serve to give physical expression to the idea of regional unity. Some of the more obvious rituals of regional unity are found, for example, at ASEAN's annual meetings—the locking of hands at every meeting, the wearing of special ASEAN shirts, the collective participation in ASEAN skits and song, and the ceremonial and ritualistic expressions of regional solidarity. These activities all play a part in the regional project and, specifically, the projection and construction of the region as "one" and specifically as "ASEAN." There is also now an ASEAN hymn, a "song for ASEAN," and an ASEAN "song of unity" titled "ASEAN We Are One"[74]—each of which make regional unity its recurring chorus.

These rituals do more than give physical expression to the idea of "One Southeast Asia." They are also the means through which actors experience social bonding and community. As "a medium in which ideas are symbolically expressed, transmitted, and reinforced,"[75] political rituals communicate and reinforce common values and norms. They also define and distinguish social groups; build and affirm social relationships; "enliven . . . collective feelings, which lead individuals to seek out one another and come together."[76] In the ASEAN case, it also helps that those participating in such processes have tended to be the same individuals and elites over the years.

Thus, both the rhetoric and rituals of "One Southeast Asia" can also be seen as part of an ongoing process of regional construction and social reinforcement whereby state elites affirm particular regional ideas over others, project an image of Southeast Asia as unified, as well as experience the idea of Southeast Asia as "one." The important constructivist point here is that the mechanism of change and socialization is not material enforcement—that is, raising the costs of not doing something a certain way (as realist and contractual theorists might argue)—but rather social *reinforcement*.[77] Reinforcement means that the more states talk and act in certain ways, the more they reify certain ideas and practices as normal and natural to a particular community. With social reinforcement, we get greater stability in states' expectations of one another, the strengthening of certain norms, ideas, and practices, and the production and reproduction of cognitive structures. "The power of social practices," as Hopf puts it, "lies in their capacity to reproduce the intersubjective meanings that constitute social structures and actors alike."[78]

Conclusion

For ASEAN, which is frequently dismissed by outside observers as more rhetoric than action, a constructivist process-based approach thus provides us a different way to think about ASEAN and its now four-decades-old regionalism and to explain why so many of ASEAN's elites have viewed Southeast Asia as an important organizing principle despite the limited material rewards attached to specific cooperative initiatives. For much of the last few decades, ASEAN's primary function has had less to do with coordinating cooperation or divvying up gains than it has with the facilitation of an ongoing dialogue about the relationship among nation, region, and the world. This dialogue on what "region" means for them as both smaller and specifically Southeast Asian states has significantly helped to "define the terms of political debate and provide participants in the political arena with a discursive repertoire to be used there."[79] Over time, that repertoire has not only helped to define ranges of possible and appropriate behavior but today to define and distinguish ASEAN itself.

The notion of regionalism as cumulative process also better captures the ways that actors can grow into ASEAN ideas, norms, and practices. Again, an elaboration of these intervening social processes—argument, consensus seeking, social reinforcement—is too often missing from our discussions of ASEAN. Indeed, as the following chapters show, every major ASEAN initiative is in fact the product of and/or a contributor to this process by which particular ideas are (re)affirmed, maintained, contested, or renegotiated. Here, it is worth underscoring that what is important is not what the idea is called but what its content is. It is the content that gives ideas meaning and power, but it can also change. Thus, while references to *noninterference* and *regional autonomy,* for example, may suggest no change, beneath the surface may also be less visible interpretive changes that could then have different implications for state behavior.

The following chapters illustrate the above arguments. The next chapter turns our attention to ASEAN's originating context and founding conditions and the arguments that made possible this particular conception of region at this particular time. In addition to providing a baseline against which to compare and contrast today's Southeast Asia, the next chapter's attention to the sociohistorical origins of ASEAN's founding ideas serves to highlight what exactly the regional idea means in Southeast Asia. That meaning and content are critical to explaining not only whether and why certain ideas have effect but also what effect they have.

Why ASEAN? Why 1967?

FIGURE 1
ASEAN Emblem: "The ASEAN Emblem represents a stable, peaceful, united and dynamic ASEAN . . . The stalks of padi represent the dream of ASEAN's Founding Fathers for an ASEAN comprising all the countries in Southeast Asia bound together in friendship and solidarity. The circle represents the unity of ASEAN."[1]
The Association of Southeast Asian Nations Secretariat

A single wooden stick can easily be broken in half, but a bundle of
wooden sticks tied together will not be broken.

Indonesian saying

Why ASEAN? For almost its entire existence, ASEAN has been the object
of skepticism from various quarters: scholars who see only bilateral conflicts and rivalries, country specialists who see ten very different countries
with different identities, policymakers who question the coherence of an
organization made up of weaker and externally oriented states, as well as
international relations theorists who see an inconsequential organization
defined by divergent interests, limited material capacities, and an aversion
to formal rules and sanctions. How do we explain ASEAN's emergence in
the face of so many centrifugal tendencies and expectations to the contrary?
And why did regional organization succeed in 1967 when it did not in 1961
(Association of Southeast Asia) or 1963 (Maphilindo)?

This chapter gives attention to a number of factors that came together
to make possible ASEAN's creation in 1967: domestic change (especially a
change in regime in Indonesia), crisis and uncertainty (the combined effects
of intraregional conflict and uncertain great power policies), but also ideas
and their advocates. In addition, this chapter also pays attention to ASEAN's
founding arguments, as it is through argument that critical causal connections are made such that alternative ideas and proposals become persuasive. It
highlights how arguments draw complex and critical causal linkages between
division and intervention, national and regional resilience, as well as the
nation-region-world relationship that will justify regional unity in the face of
divergent interests, insecurities, and preferences. This narrative will provide
a kind of genetic code—an ideational DNA, so to speak—that informs the
content of ASEAN regionalism. That narrative, which establishes ASEAN's
raison d'être, will do more than make a convincing case for organization in
1967; it will set the parameters for regionalism in Southeast Asia for decades to
come. The discussion below now turns to the founding context, politics, and
arguments surrounding the creation of ASEAN in 1967.

The ASEAN Prehistory

In 1950s and 1960s Southeast Asia, regionalism was a difficult argument to
make. Most difficult was the argument for an explicitly Southeast Asian
organization. Despite worldwide interest in regional organization and a number of regional ideas offered by Southeast Asian elites, interest in organizing
Southeast Asia as such was both limited and late in coming, a clear indication

that most found the idea either not attractive or not obvious. Instead, elites tended to be drawn to grander and bigger ideas of "Asia": U Aung San of Burma offered a broad vision of Asian federation composed of India, China, and Southeast Asia; Premier Soetan Sjahrir of Indonesia similarly sought a pan-Asian unity that extended beyond Southeast Asia; and perhaps the biggest of them all, the 1947 Asian Relations Conference in New Delhi, brought together "the largest assemblage of Eastern leaders since Kublai Khan," including significant Southeast Asian participation.[2]

The Cold War also inspired its share of "regional" arrangements—mostly in the form of pan-Third World solidarity movements like the Asian-African Conference at Bandung in 1955 or explicitly anticommunist arrangements like Philippine President Quirino's Pacific pact (the first of many such proposals from the Philippines). And still others looked closer to home, defining region more narrowly along ethnonationalist or ethnoreligious lines, as illustrated by a Thai proposed union of Buddhist Mekong countries—Laos, Cambodia, and Thailand—and various proposals for pan-Malay union involving varying combinations of Malaya, Indonesia, the Philippines, Borneo, and New Guinea, as well as southern parts of Thailand. Thus, interest in regional organization certainly existed among Southeast Asian elites, but notably missing was interest in organizing Southeast Asia as such.

The above ideas point to the different ways that elites at the time saw region being cut and expressed. They also underscore the point that "Southeast Asia" was an intensely contested idea at the time given its diversity, as well as the prevailing interests, conflicts, and ideologies of the 1950s and 1960s. Indeed, for many, Southeast Asia's geographical ambiguity, cultural and ethnic heterogeneity, historical porousness to outsiders, as well as its lack of autonomy vis-à-vis other powers and regions, all made highly questionable the claim that "Southeast Asia" represented any kind of coherent or meaningful entity.[3] Even among those who accepted Southeast Asia as a cultural or geographical space, there was still debate about its boundaries.[4] Especially hard to reconcile were the differences between mainland and insular Southeast Asia—which were distinguished by not only geography but also (and consequently) religion and ethnicity, as well as intensity of relations. Such differences justified thinking of the place as two regions, but to think of it as one seemed unimaginable to most.[5] As Charles Fisher, describing the prevalent view at the time, put it: "[For many,] Southeast Asia . . . is so culturally diverse and politically subdivided as to raise doubts in some minds as to whether it constitutes a meaningful entity in any positive sense at all."[6] Indeed, in Southeast Asia, which had been divided among no fewer than five imperial powers with different philosophies about colonial administration, not even colonialism could be said to be a truly unifying experience.[7] No wonder, then, that organizing Southeast Asia as such was so often an afterthought, if it was a thought at all.

Most important, what most seized the imaginations of Southeast Asian leaders in the 1950s and 1960s was not regionalism, but nationalism. This was demonstrated not only by the short-lived nature of most regional proposals—few made it beyond the planning stages, and those that did rarely made it beyond their first or second meeting—but also by various conflicts that consumed Southeast Asian states. Thus, while the end of colonialism may have ended the constraints placed on intraregional interaction and communication—as Richard Butwell observed in 1964, "not for centuries has there been the extent of interaction among Southeast Asians themselves that exists at the present time"[8]—the point here is that independence did not free states to cooperate so much as make conflict with each other.

In particular, in Southeast Asia where the emergence of new polities has invited conflict at all levels of its politics, the 1963 creation of the Federation of Malaysia proved most destabilizing.[9] Not only did the federation's creation immediately put an end to Malaysia–Philippines relations, but it also provided the pretext for Indonesia's three-year policy of violent Confrontation against Malaysia. Singapore's turbulent and brief inclusion and then expulsion from the Federation (1963–1965) similarly both reflected and exacerbated existing regional tensions. In short, regional fragmentation, not integration, seemed to be the dominant trend of the day.

ASA and Maphilindo

In the early 1960s, some elites began to argue for a different regional idea focused on Southeast Asia—but national sensitivities, nationalist rivalries, and intensified patterns of conflict continued to make such ideas less than persuasive. Two short-lived efforts illustrate well both the different regional ideas that competed for attention and the ways that nationalism challenged early regionalist efforts in Southeast Asia: the Association of Southeast Asia (ASA, 1961–1967)[10] and Maphilindo (1963). As the most immediate organizational predecessors to ASEAN, they also offer insight into the changes and conditions that would make possible the emergence of ASEAN.

Of the two, ASA represented the more radical idea as it signified a move away from the ethnic and religious, ideological, and pan-Asian ideas that had been dominating discussions in the 1950s and 1960s. Often described as ASEAN's predecessor, ASA offered an idea of region that was at once more exclusive, focusing on Southeast Asia and not beyond, and more inclusive in the sense that membership was not limited to one ethnoreligious or even ideological group. Though ASA was the initiative of Malaysia's (at that time Malaya's) President Tunku Abdul Rahman, Thailand's participation was especially influential in this respect. As a non-Malay and continental state, Thailand moved ASA away from more "obvious" ethnic or religious organizing principles. Its foreign minister would also actively steer ASA away from purely anticommunist models of organization, as most represented by the U.S.–backed Southeast Asian Treaty Organization (SEATO). It was Thanat Khoman, for example, who persuaded Tunku Abdul Rahman and the Philippines' President Garcia—both staunch anticommunists—to forego the idea of a treaty-based organization that the two originally favored in the interest of downplaying Cold War, political-security themes in favor of less contentious economic matters. In this way, it was thought, ASA would also be made more attractive to Southeast Asia's neutral and nonaligned states.[11]

In theory, Kuala Lumpur and Manila agreed with Bangkok's push for a more inclusive organization and the importance of drawing a wider membership, especially from Indonesia, whose well-known independent identity could offset the strong anticommunist identities of the other three. Indeed, given that all three were well plugged into the Western alliance system (Thailand and the Philippines with the United States in SEATO, the Philippines as host of U.S. bases, and Malaya with the United Kingdom through the Five Power Defence Arrangement [FPDA]), the concern, as Malaya's then-permanent minister of foreign affairs Ghazali Shafie put it, "without Indonesia, the ASA concept would be regarded as American inspired."[12]

However, despite efforts to move ASA away from overtly anticommunist themes, ASA proved unable to overcome the anticommunism of individual members. Consequently, neither Indonesia nor other nonaligned states could be persuaded to join. Indonesian President Sukarno could not see in ASA anything but "an Anglo–U.S. plot to subvert the newly independent states of Southeast Asia" and consequently, to quote Ghazali Shafie, would not "touch ASA with a barge pole."[13] Indonesia's stance and the fact that Southeast Asia's communist states had not been invited to join consequently reinforced the perception of ASA as less than independent. The strongly anticommunist actions and positions often taken by two of ASA's three members also did little to mitigate this perception: Tunku Abdul Rahman found it difficult to conceal his vehement anticommunism; President Garcia, despite an agreement to deemphasize security themes, continued to promote the idea of a broader anticommunist pact and even held a conference of Asian noncommunist powers.[14] For Manila, ASA's more inclusive regional conception appears to have been a second, even third, choice behind anticommunist and Malay-nationalist ideas where regional organization was concerned.[15]

In contrast to ASA, Maphilindo drew from more obvious ethnonationalist ideas of region but proved even less able to manage the centrifugal forces and rivalries pulling states apart. Formed by Malaya, the Philippines, and Indonesia in 1963, Maphilindo was supposed to be an expression of Malay or pan-Malay identity but was in fact the product and ultimately victim of two rival (and irreconcilable) Malay conceptions. The focus of controversy was Kuala Lumpur's planned incorporation of North Borneo (and Singapore) into an expanded Malay union—a new Federation of Malaysia.

Characterizing the federation as a British "neocolonial" plot aimed at the "encirclement of Indonesia,"[16] Sukarno saw the creation of Malaysia as a challenge to Indonesia's regional leadership and his own particular vision for pan-Malay confederation.[17] Jakarta also reportedly viewed Kuala Lumpur's failure to consult it on its plans as a sign of disrespect for Indonesian leadership.[18] As for Manila, newly elected President Diosdado Macapagal's opposition to Malaysia focused on North Borneo, which the Philippines also claimed.[19] Anticolonial nationalism factored large in its opposition. A former U.S. colony anxious to demonstrate its "Asian credentials," the Philippines saw Maphilindo and closer relations with nonaligned Indonesia as an opportunity—to quote a report commissioned by Macapagal—"to boost our prestige in the eyes of fellow Asians, who up to now tend to regard us as Asian puppets"[20] and to express a number of unhappinesses with the United States,[21] including U.S. support for Malaysia's incorporation of North Borneo. The report was also explicit about Manila's interest in a rival Malay confederation like Maphilindo as a way to supplant the proposed Malaysian federation.[22]

In short, Maphilindo was premised on irreconcilable objectives as regarded the political future of Malaysia. Kuala Lumpur joined Maphilindo in the hopes of gaining the others' acceptance of the Federation of Malaysia; Jakarta and Manila conceived Maphilindo to preempt the federation all together—or, as Ghazali Shafie characterized their position, "to render Malaysia unnecessary."[23] So it was no surprise that states would lose interest in Maphilindo once the Federation of Malaysia, complete with North Borneo, became a reality two months later. Just one day after Malaysia's creation, in fact, Manila informed Kuala Lumpur that it would not be extending recognition to the new federation, effectively severing formal relations. More seriously, Malaysia's creation became the pretext for Indonesia's three-year campaign to "Crush Malaysia" (September 1963 to August 1966). A mix of naval blockades, submarine-supplied arms and munitions, organized rebellions and subversions, and Indonesian paratrooper landings on Malaysia's mainland, as well as an international campaign to exclude Malaysia from Third World gatherings, Indonesia's confrontational policies and actions (with Philippine support) in effect constituted a low-level war against Malaysia. As detailed by Gordon, "the infiltration of Malaysia by Indonesian armed volunteers [took place] at such a rate that Malaysia presented a formal complaint to the United Nations Security Council."[24]

Nor was Maphilindo the only organizational casualty as efforts to insulate ASA from the North Borneo issue or from the politics of Confrontation proved futile.[25] While ASA did not completely disintegrate as Maphilindo did, ASA was nonetheless rendered nonoperational by the lack of relations between two of its three members. At minimum, developments made clear not just the tensions between competing "nationalist" visions but also the nationalist obstacles that a more inclusive regionalism would have to overcome. As President Macapagal said to his pro-ASA Vice President Emmanuel Palaez, "Manny, you've got to go slow on this ASA thing; our foreign policy effort has to focus on North Borneo, and everything else must take a back seat."[26] Jorgensen-Dahl put it best, regional organization failed because "North Borneo mattered more than ASA."[27]

Given the failures of Maphilindo and ASA, as well as interstate conflicts and tensions, it was therefore no surprise that much of the world greeted ASEAN's creation in 1967 with more than a little skepticism, yet the organization, contrary to expectations, was able to overcome substantial difficulties, manage conflicts, and even survive important regional and global changes. What made ASEAN different from its predecessors? Three factors are critical to explaining the emergence of ASEAN in the face of strong centrifugal forces: (1) a window of opportunity created by domestic and international developments; (2) a group of transnational elites and advocates committed to an alternative vision of regional order; and (3) the ways that new regional ideas were defined in relation to established nationalist ones.

Systemic and Domestic Openings

Between 1965 and 1967 events in Southeast Asia opened a window of opportunity for new thinking about regional relations and regional organization. These were Sukarno's ouster in Indonesia, the election of a new president in the Philippines, a problematic U.S. war in Vietnam, and confirmation that the United Kingdom would be withdrawing from Southeast Asia. Of these developments, most critical was the regime change in Indonesia set in motion by what officials would describe as a communist power play involving the kidnapping and killing of senior generals in September 1965. Though quickly crushed by the Indonesian army's Strategic Reserve, led by Major-General Suharto,[28] the event provided the pretext for the army to take action against Sukarno forces. After implicating the Communist Party of Indonesia (the PKI) in the power play, the army then moved to eliminate that organization from Indonesian politics; it also froze relations with the People's Republic of China[29] before taking steps to remove Sukarno himself, whose flirtations with communism, the PKI, and China had become of growing concern. Seeing a "threatening linkage between close relations with China and developments in domestic politics [namely, the PKI]," the army concluded that Sukarno's revolutionary politics and communist leanings increasingly served not "Indonesia's interests but those of the PRC, the PKI, and the local Chinese."[30] In March 1966 executive power was transferred to Suharto, who became acting president in 1967 and president in 1968.

The election of Ferdinand Marcos in the Philippines added to the historic opportunity for change that existed between 1965 and 1967 in Southeast Asia. As Gordon details, far more ambivalence toward Indonesia existed in the Philippines than what appeared on the surface during Confrontation. Not all agreed, for example, with Macapagal's argument that North Borneo was essential to Philippine national security or with his decision to support communist-learning Indonesia against smaller and firmly anticommunist Malaysia.[31] In fact, many found the latter decision counterintuitive given the main (anticommunist) threads of Philippine foreign policy; indeed Philippine–Indonesian cooperation "across barriers of ideology and alignment" constituted "one of the great puzzles of [1963]," and Philippine professions of Malay fraternity were "a mystique that defie[d] understanding."[32]

Moreover, in the aftermath of Confrontation, Manila found that Macapagal's policies, rather than improving its regional image as intended, instead further reduced the Philippines in the eyes of its neighbors: Malaysian leaders saw Manila's susceptibility to Indonesian pressure as "another manifestation of the relative shallowness of Philippine policy."[33] Jakarta drew similar conclusions about what it saw to be the ease with which Manila shifted allegiances.[34] Meanwhile, at home, domestic criticism mounted against Macapagal's pro-Indonesia policies in 1964, leading to a search by his critics for a face-saving way out of Macapagal's "foolish" policy stance[35] and a way to repair the relationship with Malaysia. Among those critics included Ferdinand Marcos, then president of the Philippine Senate, soon to become the next Philippine president. Marcos's December 1965 election would open the door for the Philippine–Malaysian rapprochement and the restart-ing of ASA.

Finally, in addition to the opportunities created by domestic changes, great power policies also created new reasons and new urgency for a reconsidera-tion of relations. In particular, U.S. policies and interventions in Vietnam brought front and center the fears and predicaments of lesser states when dealing with much greater powers than they. On the one hand, U.S. mili-tary escalation in Vietnam in 1964 and 1965 dramatically illustrated the link between internal division and external intervention. The fact that Southeast Asia's noncommunist states all faced communist insurgencies and divisions at home made the fear of being "another Vietnam" more than an abstract fear.

On the other hand, fears that anticommunist forces might lose raised the specter of a powerfully, reunified Vietnam that not only would consolidate its influence over peninsular Southeast Asia but also might pay retribution to those who had sided with the United States. Here, Thailand was especially vulnerable not only as a U.S. ally and member of SEATO but also as Vietnam's immediate neighbor. In 1965 and 1966 a growing internal security threat from insurgents backed by Hanoi and Beijing in Thailand's Northeastern provinces also helped keep attention on the potential threat from Vietnam.

For those most closely tied to the great powers, there were also other les-sons. For Thailand, for example, its problematic association with the United States in SEATO provided powerful motivators for reconsidering its rela-tions both with the United States and with its neighbors. As noted above, questions about "the firmness of U.S. commitments in the Southeast Asian area"[36] had already begun to emerge by the mid-1960s and had factored large in Thailand's interest in ASA. Thanat, in fact, would explicitly cite Thailand's disappointments with SEATO as reason for seeking out more indigenous regional arrangements. As Thanat would later explain, Bangkok's support for regional cooperation was "inspired and guided by past events" and specifically "its disappointing experience with SEATO [which] taught it the lesson that it was useless and even dangerous to hitch its destiny to distant powers who may cut loose at any moment their ties and obligations with lesser and distant allies." "[T]he lesson drawn from such events," he concluded, was that "weak nations," if their security were to be truly served, must rely "more on neighborly mutual support than on stronger states that serve their own national interests rather than those of smaller partners."[37]

Nor was Thailand the only one to draw such lessons. Malaysia and Singapore, allies of the United Kingdom and former British colonies, were learning similar lessons. As the United Kingdom confirmed rumors that it would be withdrawing its forces from Southeast Asia,[38] Malaysia's Tunku Abdul Rahman accused the United Kingdom of failing Southeast Asia "when the chips were down."[39] Even Singapore, which, along with the Philippines, worked the hardest to maintain its great power commitments, acknowledged the danger and vulnerability involved in depending on great powers, whose interests "do not necessarily coincide with [that of Singapore]."[40]

Singapore may have found the prospect of Western retrenchment the most worrisome. As a Chinese city-state located among Malay Muslim states suspicious of Chinese communism, however, its immediate concerns focused more on its neighbors than the threats posed by Vietnam or China. Indonesia's Confrontation campaign against Malaysia (of which Singapore had been a part at the time) did little to reassure Singapore about its much larger neighbor. Its insecurity was only heightened by its short and difficult marriage with Malaysia, during which bitter disputes between the two leaderships over the Chinese–Malay ethnic political balance gave way to ethnic riots, ultimately ending Singapore's tumultuous twenty-three-month union with Malaysia.[41]

Moreover, Singapore's union with Malaysia came to a violent end just as events opened the door for reconciliation between Malaysia and Indonesia. In fact, Singapore was less than reassured by its neighbors' rapprochement, and it found even the talk of regional organization suspect, indeed, a possible Malay conspiracy against the Chinese city-state. Malaysia's failure to inform and consult Singapore on its talks with Indonesia, as stipulated in their terms of separation, did little to mitigate that perception or stem the parallels that Singapore drew between its own situation and the "Arab-Israel situation."[42] No surprise that Singapore in the mid-1960s prioritized its extraregional relations. As Singapore's long-time prime minister Lee Kuan Yew characterized Singapore's predicament in 1966:

> The strangest thing about countries is: your best friends are never your immediate neighbours! They get too close and your neighbour's hedge grows and infringes on your part of the garden and the branch of his fruit tree covers your grass and your roses do not get enough sunshine and so many things happen! And therefore our best friends, as has happened with so many other countries, are those who are farther afield and with whom we can talk objectively.[43]

Most important for Singapore, as long as Western powers maintained a military presence in Southeast Asia, there was at least some security for the city-state should relations with its neighbors further deteriorate. Consequently, by Lee Kuan Yew's account, he "worked hard to prolong the British presence."[44] Failing to do that, however, Singapore was forced to take another look at its regional relations as the British withdrawal made it "immediately apparent to the political elite that [Singapore] must . . . achieve an acceptable modus vivendi within the Southeast Asian region . . . "[45]

It was in this context of domestic and international change that states renewed their interest in regional organization in 1966—though politics continued to challenge regional efforts. For some, suspicions and tensions had moreover been intensified by recent conflicts, thus strengthening the barriers to regional organization. And even among regional organization's advocates, there was little agreement as to where they should focus their efforts. Should they restart Maphilindo? ASA? Or should they create a new regional organization all together? Indonesia sought to revive Maphilindo but could not convince Malaysia or Thailand, the latter whose participation as a non-Malay state would have been unclear. According to Thanat, "We are not interested in anything racial . . . we like practical cooperation not cooperation on a racial basis."[46]

Even harder to convince were those in Malaysia. Tunku Abdul Rahman remained deeply suspicious of Jakarta despite the leadership transition. Even Tun Razak, Malaysia's deputy prime minister and strong advocate for working with Indonesia, was unable to disassociate Maphilindo's "racial idea" with Confrontation and declared Maphilindo "dead and buried."[47] Instead, Malaysia pushed to rejuvenate ASA and extend membership to Indonesia. However, here too, post-Confrontation suspicions about Indonesia proved strong, as illustrated by Tunku Abdul Rahman's continued warnings (as late as December 1966) about "the dangers to ASA if a country was admitted whose past behaviour suggested that she would leave any organization when it suited her."[48]

Malaysian concerns about Indonesia were not without justification. Even with Sukarno's ouster, there remained considerable uncertainty about the new government in Jakarta. Not only was Suharto a relative unknown at the time, but Indonesian foreign policy during the transition period was hardly reassuring. Jakarta's continued "angry gestures in Malaysia's direction"—its continued maintenance of troops on the Sarawak border and incursions into Malaysia; its persistent references to "Malaya" as opposed to "Malaysia" in December 1965; and efforts to dissuade the Philippines from normalizing relations with Malaysia during the first three months of 1966, including, at one point, a threat to cut off relations—all gave reason to believe that Jakarta continued to question Malaysia's right to exist. In fact, as late as March 1966 Indonesia continued to make the disbandment of the new Malaysian federation a condition of talks.[49] Even after the formal transfer of executive powers to Suharto, Sukarno forces continued to dominate foreign policy.

Meanwhile, those in Jakarta that favored regional cooperation were not keen on ASA. As the *Far Eastern Economic Review* put it, ASA confronted an "Indonesian nationalism [that] demanded that she should be a founder-member of any regional grouping."[50] This is why, for example, Indonesia originally worked to revive Maphilindo. Failing that, Indonesia began to consider more seriously Thanat's idea that states create a completely new organization that lacked the baggage of its predecessors. In March 1967 Indonesia's foreign minister Adam Malik announced Indonesia's intent to host a Southeast Asian conference to discuss regional cooperation; however, Tunku Abdul Rahman remained to be convinced.

In short, 1965–1967 developments opened new possibilities, indeed a historic opportunity, for regional organization. Most critical was the regime change in Indonesia. Given that Sukarno had been so associated with the radicalization of Indonesian policy toward its neighbors, his removal was essential if there were to be redirection or change in the pattern of Southeast Asia's interstate relations. However, as illustrated above, this change—critical as it was—was still not enough to convince all parties that, this time, regional organization would be any different from past efforts. In fact, for many, recent conflicts made the idea of regional organization as a solution to regional problems even less promising in 1967 than it was in 1961 and 1963. Similarly, uncertainties and changes in the Western commitment to Southeast Asia may have triggered rethinking about old security orientations and regional relations, but intraregional problems were such that regional organization remained a highly uncertain endeavor with debatable benefits. In short, the significance of U.S. and U.K. announcements and the domestic changes in Indonesia and the Philippines lie mainly in the historical and structural opportunity they created to pursue different strategies and ideas about regional order; however, a persuasive argument still had to be made for regional organization.

Arguing for Change

During this 1965–1967 juncture in Southeast Asian politics, a small group of elites played a key role in convincing both domestic constituents and their neighbors that regional organization was worth another try. Among those who played particular roles were Malaysia's Tun Razak, Ghazali Shafie, and home minister Tun Ismail; Thailand's Thanat Khoman, to whom Tun Razak, for one, gave particular credit for "the very big part" he played in (1) facilitating the reconciliation between Indonesia and Malaysia and (2) convincing his friend Tunku Abdul Rahman to reconsider the possibility of a new organization;[51] and Indonesia's Adam Malik, whose advocacy efforts faced considerable challenge at home from Sukarno forces[52] and vis-à-vis its suspicious neighbors. The Philippines' Narciso Ramos and Singapore's S. Rajaratnam also played roles in clarifying the regional ideas that would become the basis for a new regional organization.

Nevertheless, even among regionalism's advocates, there remained important points of disagreement and points for clarification. Thus, even if they were able to convince each other as to the desirability of regional organization, they still had to work out its content. These areas of initial debate included: the nation–region relationship, resilience as self-determination, the desirability of an all–Southeast Asia organization, and the appropriateness of great power guarantees.

Nationalism's Constraints: Resilience and Self-Determination

As developments illustrate, regionalism as an argument faced significant normative obstacles in Southeast Asia, where nationalist sensitivities remained sharp. While Confrontation delegitimated Sukarno's kind of militant "old style nationalism,"[53] nationalism in the sense of self-determination and state or nation building nevertheless remained a powerful ideology in 1960s Southeast Asia. In a postcolonial political context where leaders were at once proud (and protective) of their newly won independence and insecure about their ability to keep that independence vis-à-vis both internal and external forces, Southeast Asian regionalists understood that any persuasive regional argument would have to be mindful of nationalist sensitivities and sentiments. This is one reason, for example, that elites desired a wider ideological membership, especially from nonaligned states. Elites understood that a membership comprised only of Western-leaning and allied states (like ASA, for example) would render suspect the group's autonomy, prompt inevitable parallels to the U.S.–initiated SEATO, and risk its being perceived as "made in Washington"—a sure "kiss of death."[54]

In addition, nationalist sentiments and the fact that most states had only recently gained independence meant that any arrangement that called on states to submit national authority to a regional entity or to their neighbors would be met with intense resistance. This is to say nothing of the tensions and suspicions generated by recent conflicts. In this context, states were therefore highly unlikely to "discard [their] new found nationalism in favor of unclear regional loyalties."[55] Also, for many, it was further felt that national priorities—national consolidation, national development—had to come first, as it was the foundation for everything else, including regional security. Malik, for example, compared the nation–region relationship to a neighborhood made up of individual houses. As he put it, "before . . . neighborliness can be achieved satisfactorily the foundation of each house must be firm and solid . . . [O]nly then will it be able to enter into a neighborly intercourse with the rest."[56]

At this historical juncture in Southeast Asian politics, then, arguments increasingly and explicitly connected regionalism to nationalism's ideas of self-determination, national consolidation, and nonintervention. Rajaratnam, coming out of ASEAN's inaugural meeting in August 1967, may have put it best: "If we are to give life to ASEAN, we must marry national thinking to regional thinking."[57] Thus, arguments prioritized the domestic even at the same time that arguments about resilience were broadened to a regional scale. Drawing on familiar ideas of resilience and preoccupations about division, regionalism's advocates framed regionalism as an act of self-determination. By the same token, it was argued that as long as they remained divided within and among themselves, insecurity and intervention would remain facts of life, and self-determination would elude all.

This linkage between internal divisions and foreign intervention was not completely new. ASA's leaders, for example, understood that there was a "symbiotic relationship" between intrastate and interstate conflicts. This was not just because intraregional instability made it difficult to focus on pressing domestic priorities but also because domestic instability made interstate conflict (and various interventions) a more real possibility. Tunku Abdul Rahman was, in fact, quite explicit about this when he explained Indonesia's radicalism in terms of its economic and political instabilities at home, instabilities that (as he saw it) provided incentives and opportunities for international mischief (on the part of Jakarta vis-à-vis its neighbors but also other states like China that took advantage of Indonesia's divisions).[58] Similarly, in Indonesia, especially among its new leaders, this linkage spoke to established ideas about national resilience (*ketahanan*), which Suharto would define as "ideological, socioeconomic, political, and military strength that together constitute a nation's real capacity . . . to resist [subversion or exploitation]."[59]

A more comprehensive understanding of security that included interdependent internal and external elements was thus not a completely new one; moreover, its familiarity likely gave the regional idea and arguments for regional organization in 1967 an important persuasiveness that they might not otherwise have had. At the same time, recent conflicts also made more salient, more real, and more urgent the connections being drawn. Those conflicts dramatically and empirically illustrated, for example, the ways that domestic and regional instabilities could feed off each other. Picking fights with one's neighbors might deflect attention from problems at home and have a temporary unifying effect but, as the new Suharto regime concluded, it did not remove the fundamental challenges and sources of insecurity within. Real security could only be gained by strengthening one's economy and political situation at home—difficult to do when one is fighting with one's neighbors.

At the same time, though national resilience and national consolidation were familiar ideas, what made the argument radical was that it was being applied on a regional scale. As with factional and civil conflicts within states, the argument was that fighting *between* states similarly provided opportunities for external powers—a China or a United States, for example—to interfere into, and project their own agendas onto, the politics of Southeast Asia, or to manipulate one neighbor against the other. Again, the ongoing war in Vietnam, in which a divided Vietnam opened the door to various foreign interventions, offered a daily and most dramatic lesson as to the dangers of division and the imperative to be both nationally and regionally resilient.

Indeed, elites drew explicit links between their recent divisions (national and regional) and what they saw to be a historic pattern of foreign intervention into Southeast Asia. This linkage was persuasive not only because it seemed to describe well Southeast Asia's security predicament vis-à-vis both internal and external forces but also because it offered states a clear strategy of action. All were familiar with the ways that intra- and interstate conflicts could invite great power interventions. States simply had to look around them to see that linkage: the Cold War division of Southeast Asia and the U.S. war in Vietnam, Soviet aid to Vietnam, U.S. bases in the Philippines, U.S. and Chinese efforts to manipulate domestic politics.[60] These developments all pointed to the intersection between, on the one hand, global politics and great power interventions, and on the other hand, regional and domestic divisions. As Tun Ismail, for example, put it, "Twenty years after the end of World War II, Southeast Asia has not yet learned to live at peace with itself. Intra-regional conflict and confrontation has set nation against nation and balkanization has remained an ever-present threat."[61] In drawing on such themes of balkanization[62] and arguments that outside powers had an interest in keeping Southeast Asia divided, fragmented, and weak, Tun Ismail and others thus made important national–regional–global connections that clearly drew attention to the ways that their own conflicts contributed to their complex and comprehensive security problems.

For these lesser states, the identified linkage between division and intervention was again persuasive because it offered them a clear strategy of action in response to the changes and challenges around them. Specifically, if domestic and regional fragmentation were key sources of Southeast Asian insecurity, the logical conclusion could only be unity and solidarity—*beram-kang* or "survival in togetherness."[63] In this way regional organization—or more accurately, regional solidarity and unity—was linked to key concerns about national stability and foreign interference; peace, they argued, must exist among themselves if they were to fend off foreign attempts at interference in whatever form.[64] In short, national resilience was important, but so was *regional* resilience.

Thus, by connecting Southeast Asia's intra- and interstate conflicts to a pattern of intervention, region to nation, and nation to region, regional organization, as an expression of national and regional resilience, became a plausible solution to their security problems in ways that it might not have been otherwise given their recent conflicts and different preferences. Indeed, Suharto would put it in even stronger terms, arguing that regional organization was something that Southeast Asian states *had to* do for themselves. Regional organization was, in other words, a necessary act of self-determination. As Thanat Khoman argued in 1966:

> The problem is to arouse the conscience of as many Southeast Asian nations as possible to the necessity of combining their strength, or working closely together and presenting a solid front to anyone daring to entertain evil designs against them. If they succeed, not only will each and every one of them be spared from destruction, but the region as a whole will emerge as a strong and free community, capable of serving its own interests as well as those of the world at large. [65]

An "All-Embracing" Organization and Small Power Themes

Regional resilience meant more than the cessation of conflicts; regional resilience, as Thanat's comments make clear, also meant seeking a broad coalition of Southeast Asian states. This meant that the regional idea had to be inclusive of Southeast Asia as a whole, not just those against communism (for example). After all, as long as they allowed ideological differences to divide Southeast Asia, the threat of intervention would remain. While ASA had also been founded on a more inclusive ideal, the politics of Confrontation and the arguments made between 1965 and 1967 now made more explicit the need to bridge the ideological divisions some states had previously been willing to tolerate (and had even perpetuated). The participation of Indonesia—which remained fiercely protective of its independent foreign policy identity—also added strength to this view. Consequently, despite the strong anticommunist sentiments that still existed, there was also agreement early on that the new organization should aim for a wide membership that was inclusive and "all embracing" of Southeast Asia.

Nevertheless, putting these ideas in practice remained a challenge, with ideological divisions especially hard to bridge. Despite Indonesia's participation and Malik's personal efforts to persuade Cambodia and Burma, efforts to draw broader membership in 1967 ultimately proved no more successful than ASA's.[66] In addition, while states were theoretically more committed to an organization inclusive of both communist and anticommunist states, there nevertheless remained considerable concern about extending membership to a state like communist (then North) Vietnam. Debates about extending membership to the two Vietnams point to the tension between, on the one hand, states' suspicions about North Vietnam and, on the other, their belief that real security would be gained only when Southeast Asia was fully united. Philippine Foreign Minister Narciso Ramos attempted to navigate this tension in his statement at ASEAN's inaugural meeting:

> The five ASEAN nations have high expectations for this organization and they truly welcome its expanded membership. We, however, realize that numbers are not the decisive factor in the effectiveness of an international organization. What really matters is a member state's willingness and capability for cooperative endeavors. *Thus, we would have ASEAN's membership limited solely to states within South East Asia and only to those who subscribe to the principles, aims and purposes enunciated in the Declaration and possess mutual interests and common problems shared by the present member countries.*[67]

In so speaking, Ramos outlined the justification for postponing membership for North Vietnam. He also provided what may be the first articulation of the only two conditions ever attached to ASEAN membership: (1) a state must be of Southeast Asia and (2) a state must conform to ASEAN's principles and purposes.

Debates about the two Vietnams also revealed concerns about maintaining an autonomous and nonconfrontational image. Having made the decision not to extend membership to North Vietnam in 1967, states then had to decide what to do with South Vietnam. Given their inability to persuade Southeast Asia's neutral states to join, founding elites feared that including South Vietnam without North Vietnam would look provocative and confrontational and confirm suspicions that the organization was indeed a pro–U.S., anticommunist operation as opposed to one that sought to represent Southeast Asia as a whole. In so doing, they would be making themselves a target for more hostile powers, hurting their future ability to convince other states to join, and, ultimately, deepening rather than bridging regional divisions. As Singapore Foreign Minister Rajaratnam explained, "[South Vietnam's membership] would weaken the [ASEAN] body and . . . divide Southeast Asia . . . Their entry may be looked upon by some as a political act and may also give ASEAN a military bloc outlook."[68] The end result was that neither North Vietnam nor South Vietnam attended ASEAN's inaugural meeting in 1967.[69]

Lastly, debates about membership were complicated by Southeast Asia's conceptual ambiguity as a region. It was all well and fine to say, as Ramos did, that membership would be restricted to the states of Southeast Asia; however, what exactly "Southeast Asia" was remained a question, as illustrated by exchanges as to possibly extending membership to Ceylon (Sri Lanka). Unlike debates about the two Vietnams, whose Southeast Asian status and thus potential eligibility for ASEAN membership were unquestioned, debates about Ceylon focused mostly on whether or not it was in fact a part of Southeast Asia.

The fact that Ceylon had also been invited to join ASA a few years earlier[70] seemed to suggest some precedent for thinking of Ceylon as part of Southeast Asia. However, though Indonesia, Malaysia, and the Philippines all expressed interest in Ceylon's membership in 1967, not all agreed that Ceylon was a part of Southeast Asia. Malaysia, for example, did not think that Ceylon was a part of Southeast Asia but was willing to make an exception to the Southeast Asia–only rule given their inability to draw broader membership. Thus, concluded Tunku Abdul Rahman, "If Ceylon desires to join ASEAN, although geographically she is not in Southeast Asia, Malaysia will support her entry."[71]

Both Jakarta and Manila also had reasons to include Ceylon. Indonesia, a country proud of its "free and active" foreign policy tradition vis-à-vis great (imperialist) powers, shared Malaysia's concern about their inability to draw a wider membership and hoped that a more diverse membership would help give the new organization an independent or autonomous identity more consistent with its own. As for the Philippines, it saw tiny Ceylon as sharing many of the interests and perspectives of founding members as weaker states. The distinctions that elites made between Ceylon and other South Asian powers (notably, India) suggests that Malaysia and others similarly identified with Ceylon as a weaker power much like themselves. Thus, while states were willing to consider Ceylon for ASEAN membership, they were definitely not, as Malik emphasized in 1967, willing to do the same for India.[72]

In the end, Ceylon did not join ASEAN;[73] however, these debates about membership—North and South Vietnam, Ceylon, and also India—reveal areas of concern and agreement as to their regional idea and ideal: (1) the still-evolving and uncertain contours of "Southeast Asia" and (2) small power themes and identification. Their debates and conclusions also underscore the point that, for these elites, regional organization was not to be simply about strength in numbers or about Cold War anticommunism. Rather, regional organization was about Southeast Asia, self-determination, and addressing the intra- and interstate divisions that had made them vulnerable, weak, and ultimately susceptible to various extraregional manipulations and interventions. At the same time, their inability to convince other states to join also meant that the creation of ASEAN *in effect* institutionalized the Cold War division in Southeast Asia. Tun Razak, referring to ASA's similar failure, expressed his disappointment at the 1967 inaugural meeting: "ASEAN has a membership of five countries. Although ASEAN represents the majority of the people of this region, we, as members, must once again admit that it is not fully representative of South East Asia."[74]

Great Power Guarantees

In negotiations over ASEAN's 1967 declaration, the most contentious debates were about states' great power relations, especially the status of foreign bases in Southeast Asia and the appropriateness of great power guarantees. Differences were especially sharp between Jakarta and Manila, which wrangled over Indonesia's efforts to insert a "temporary bases" clause into ASEAN's draft declaration. Differences were so sharp, in fact, that were it not for the mediation efforts of (once again) Thanat Khoman, these efforts to create (yet another) regional organization in 1967 might have been just another historical footnote.

Jakarta's position was informed by at least two considerations. First, as with its interest in wider membership, it had a strong preference for an organization that would reflect its own independent tradition (as opposed to being "pro-West" or "pro–U.S."). In fact, Jakarta argued that the clause was necessary for the survival of the Suharto regime, which could not be viewed at home as supporting U.S. bases or as selling out to anticommunist bloc politics.[75] Second, Indonesia was especially sensitive to foreign bases, as Western powers had recently used operations in neighboring countries to foment trouble against the Sukarno regime.[76]

As for Manila's objections, Antolik argues that they probably had more than a little to do with post-Confrontation concerns about Jakarta given that Manila had expressed no objections to the same clause four years earlier in negotiations over Maphilindo.[77] Manila was also likely sensitive to the implied criticism of its hosting of U.S. bases and its foreign policy as less than independent. Ultimately, compromise focused on the freedom of the hosting state to make that decision (freedom from coercion be it from great powers or neighboring states). Specifically, the resulting clause continued to affirm that "all foreign bases are temporary" as desired by Indonesia but also clearly stated that bases remained "only with the expressed concurrence of the countries concerned."[78] In this way, the 1967 Bangkok Declaration was therefore able to affirm the legitimacy and correctness of both Indonesian and Philippine national identities and perspectives and, at the same time, uphold in principle the idea of regional independence and autonomy.

Despite this compromise, this discussion on the appropriateness of great power guarantees nevertheless raised questions about what ASEAN's own contributions to regional security should be. While ASEAN's rejection of collective defense arrangements is often associated today with a particular non-militaristic "ASEAN way" of doing things, it was not so clear in 1967, as illustrated, for example, by one early draft of ASEAN's founding declaration in which Indonesia—in the interest of self-reliance—had inserted a reference to "arrangements of collective defense."[79] That reference was ultimately removed due to continued concerns of other members about Indonesia and their concern that such arrangements would institutionalize Indonesian dominance.

As in debates about Vietnam's membership, elites expressed concerns that political security references—especially to "collective defense"—would contribute to the perception that the group was anticommunist (as opposed to pro–Southeast Asia), thus dissuading other states from joining. Elites also feared attracting unwanted attention from communist Vietnam and great powers. The argument was that ASEAN states, as lesser powers, should avoid getting drawn into great-power politics. Notably, however, all this did not mean that ASEAN or states as lesser powers lacked the capacity to contribute to their own security. As Rajaratnam explained in July 1967, "The defense of the area in terms of big-power conflicts must remain the concern of the big powers."[80] But "where the small countries can help is by maintaining their own internal security . . . If each of these countries can ensure that its economy is sound, its political system is sound, this is the best contribution that the small countries can make to the defence of the [Southeast Asian] area."[81] Lesser powers might not be able to dictate great-power policies, but they could at least close off opportunities for extraregional manipulations via the unity of both nation and region. In short, resilience, not collective defense, remained the most appropriate response to Southeast Asia's security problems.

Thus, a combination of considerations led states to reject collective defense and ASEAN's militarization. All references to security cooperation were dropped from the 1967 declaration, and there was an explicit move away from anticommunist, military-based, or confrontational stances in the interest of regional inclusiveness. As Tun Ismail argued in 1966:

No country should fear joining a regional community based on these principles [of peaceful development, etc.]. Such a community would not be a military alliance. It would not be an anticommunist alliance. Nor, for that matter, would it be an anti-western alliance. It would stand *for* something rather than *against* something . . . I myself envisage an organization which would be, first and last, pro–South-East Asia, pro-development, pro-regional cooperation, and pro-peace.[82]

Conclusion

Consuelo Cruz argues, "At critical points . . . rival political leaders and entrepreneurs seek to persuade themselves and others that things must either remain as they are or be changed in significant ways."[83] Critical junctures are times of change, uncertainty, and often tumult; they are consequently often associated with search, reflection, and new choices. While existing ideas and strategies can be contested at all times, uncertain and unsettled times are more likely to find actors more receptive to new ideas, interpretations, and visions.[84] These are the times most likely to yield new orthodoxy.[85]

This chapter has detailed just such a juncture in the international relations of Southeast Asia and the conditions and processes that made possible regional organization and new thinking about regional relations in 1967. Of the developments highlighted in this chapter, the most critical was the structural opportunity for change created with the ouster of Sukarno. As long as Sukarno and his forces were in power, as Malik discovered for example, new thinking about regionalism faced a hostile environment in Jakarta; and as long as Sukarno's militant nationalism dominated, Indonesia's neighbors would have found it difficult to change course. Malaysia, especially, would have found it difficult to trust Indonesia enough to work with it again. At very least, Sukarno would have made Indonesia's participation in any new organization unlikely, which, in turn, would have affected the content, if not the survival, of any new regionalism.

In addition, developments point to a role played by changing and uncertain Western security commitments. As highlighted above, these uncertainties were not in and of themselves sufficient motivators for regional organization, but they did inject additional uncertainty and urgency into Southeast Asia's security environment. These uncertainties then intersected with domestic and intraregional changes to widen the opportunity for new ideas and arguments about regional order. These uncertainties were additionally important for drawing into the regional process two states, Thailand and Singapore, that might not have otherwise participated. As detailed above, Singapore had little interest in regional reconciliation or regional relations until the United Kingdom confirmed plans to withdraw from Southeast Asia. Similarly, Thailand, which had no involvement in the Indonesian Confrontation, would also have found indigenous regional organization less interesting. Again, disappointments with SEATO and the United States were key reasons for Thailand's interest in such regional organization beginning with ASA. In short, without the external impetus from the United States and United Kingdom, Thailand's and Singapore's participation would have been less likely in 1967. In this sense, Leifer's characterization of the new organization—the Association of Southeast Asian Nations—as being the institutional product of states' desire for regional reconciliation, though true, is also incomplete given how Thailand and Singapore came to be attracted to the regional process.[86]

More important for this discussion is that the absence of Thailand and Singapore would have affected the shape, content, and thus course of regionalism in Southeast Asia. The absence of Thai participation would have been felt especially acutely given Thanat's critical role in mediating tensions between Thailand's neighbors (first between Indonesia and Malaysia in initial post-Confrontation negotiations on regional organization and then between Indonesia and the Philippines over the temporary bases clause). In fact, without Thanat, it is possible that organization would not have been possible in 1967. The participation of Thailand—a continental, non-Malay, non-Muslim state—as well as Thanat's activist role in pushing for a more broadly inclusive organization also critically shaped the content of founding ideas, founding arguments, and thus the normative foundations of regional organization.

Thanat's role is just one example of why neither domestic nor international change provides sufficient conditions for change. It was certainly not a foregone conclusion that the perceived need for change would result in yet another regional organization. The differences that divided states in the 1950s and early 1960s—different perspectives, competing interests, divergent preferences, mutual insecurities—continued to divide them in 1967, and now there was also the additional baggage of recent conflict. Again, the end of conflict did not necessarily or automatically lead one to regional organization as the alternative. Instead, it took the persistent advocacy efforts of a small group of foreign policy elites. In the ASEAN endeavor, Thanat Khoman, who played a critical mediator role more than once, as well as Adam Malik, who faced a particularly tough audience in Jakarta and in neighboring states, deserve particular mention.

Lastly, the above highlights the importance of arguments—how they are framed, what causal linkages they draw. Even the best of ideas will be passed over if their advocates fail to give proper attention to local contexts or if the arguments they make fail to make sense of the challenges being faced. In 1960s Southeast Asia, this meant respecting nationalist sensitivities; it also meant making regionalism relevant to the processes and priorities of nationalist construction, consolidation, of independence and autonomy. Unlike Europe, these were weaker and newer political entities that not only were trying to negotiate uncertain relations after conflict but were also still in the process of centralizing authority and establishing themselves as legitimate entities at home. Defining their main security challenges as one of division (intra- and interstate), regionalism's advocates thus drew critical connections between division and intervention, between nation and region, and between regional organization and self-determination; only then did regionalism—as an expression of regional unity—offer states a plausible response to their problems. Indeed, drawing on nationalist ideas, regionalism was, as argued by its advocates, a necessary act of self-determination by lesser powers faced with division from within and without. As Rajaratnam explained in 1967, the founding of ASEAN was about smaller powers reclaiming their present and their future:

> If there are people who misunderstand the proposed grouping, or manifest hostility towards it, let us explain that it can only be because as in Europe and in many parts of the world, outside powers have vested interests in the balkanisation of this region. We ourselves have learned the lessons and have decided that small nations are not going to be balkanised so that they can be manipulated, set against one another, kept perpetually weak, divided, and ineffective by outside powers.[87]

Thanat would put it even more simply. As he put it, ASEAN's founding was a "historic event" and no less than "the culmination of the decolonization process that had started after World War II."[88]

Thus, there emerged in 1967, as Malik puts it, new convergence not just about states' national developmental objectives but also how to secure them.[89] At the same time, while regional resilience arguments made national and regional projects interdependent, there was also no question as to which took precedence. Regional resilience meant that each member's security was tied to the others' and that each state had a responsibility to strengthen and stabilize its respective domestic situation (and achieve national resilience) because instability in one affected the cohesion and stability of others. In other words, the *national resilience* of each state formed the foundation for the *regional resilience* of all.[90] Defined thusly, however, regional resilience would have consequences for how regionalism would be expressed. For one, as the next chapter especially details, regionalism could be pursued by individual efforts to bolster and strengthen *national* resilience as a foundation for *regional* resilience. For another, resilience defined in terms of unity but based on the assumed fragility of region and its component units demanded that states both pursue greater unity *and* take care to preserve what unity exists. In both cases, regionalism was obligated to support the national project or, like a house of cards, the whole thing could come tumbling down.

As argued, then, ASEAN's regionalism thus came to be premised not on ethnonationalist ideas, but rather an idea of region that was nationalist *and* regionalist at the same time—nationalist in the sense that it drew on ideas of self-determination and gave primacy to the nation-building project, regionalist in the sense that resilience ideas were being projected on a regional scale and in that nationalist futures were being explicitly linked to their existence as a region. Nationalism—its ideas of self-determination, domestic preoccupations with national consolidation and national integration, anti-imperialism—in fact becomes central to the regionalism that emerged. Again, as one of the few (perhaps only) common ideological frameworks that enjoyed broad agreement in 1960s Southeast Asia, nationalism provided the dominant rhetorical frame against which all other ideas about political organization had to compete or be defined in relation to. The more regionalism could speak to nationalism's established "norms, knowledge structures, and traditional identities," the greater chance it would have a meaningful effect on politics.[91] But, as these next chapters illustrate, it also meant that nationalism would constrain regionalism in important ways. In this context and given the arguments made, it is no surprise that ASEAN's founding declaration explicitly made the "preservation of national identities" an important guiding principle of regional organization.[92]

At this critical juncture, then, emerged not just a new regional organization but a founding narrative about Southeast Asia's history of balkanization and intervention, the dangers of fragmentation and division, Southeast Asia's historic quest for regional unity and self-determination vis-à-vis larger powers. It is, to put it simply, a narrative about the past, present, and future of Southeast Asia. The significance of this narrative is not just that it justifies organization in 1967 but that it also provides states a common social purpose and a common language—a language to which they will return to in their future interactions. Indeed, the ideas and arguments that justify organization in 1967 would set the course for Southeast Asian regionalism by providing "a new agreed-upon grammar . . . [by which] . . . to interpret the appropriateness of future acts that they could not possibly foresee."[93]

3

The Ideas That Bind: Negotiating ASEAN's Ways

> The main reason Southeast Asia—the Balkans of Asia—has held together is through such consensus-building.
>
> *Kishore Mahbubani, 1997*

This chapter gives attention to intervening processes and interactions that both reinforce and give greater clarity to ideas and arguments first established in 1967. In particular, it highlights a process of argument and debate that forms a part of a larger consensus-building process. This process will be key to translating perceived challenges into more collective outcomes. Moreover, in that this process of argument and debate invokes and keeps prominent particular ideas over others, they will not only clarify and reinforce identified ideas and connections but, in so doing, those ideas will also increasingly become "regional" and part of a larger shared expression of "ASEAN-Southeast Asia."

Chronologically, this chapter picks up where the last left off, namely, the creation of ASEAN in 1967. It gives particular attention to ASEAN's founding arguments and ideas—resilience arguments that linked nation to region, fragmentation to intervention, and regional organization to self-determination—and how these arguments and ideas continued to provide centralizing forces in the face of still-strong centrifugal tendencies. Again, if the problem is defined as one of division, then the appropriate solution must be unity. However, as in 1967, these ideas and arguments were also far from having automatic effect and instead continued to rely on activist promotion and activist support from key actors in ASEAN's first decade.

To illustrate states' ongoing search for consensus about regional ideas and regional relations, this chapter details three early ASEAN debates between 1967 and 1978. Two are political-security debates—the first focuses on a 1971 proposal for regional neutralization; and the second, about how best to respond to a newly reunified Vietnam in 1976 and then its intervention into neighboring Cambodia in 1978. The other is economic, specifically regional trade liberalization. These debates reveal the centralizing role played by founding ideas; they also clarify the normative obligations that stem from ASEAN's founding arguments. In particular, resilience arguments that stress unity and assume fragility of relations and of units will come to constrain those who would desire a more binding or more securitized regionalism. Taken together, these three debates as expressions of states' ongoing search for consensus and unity will produce additional points of clarification about ASEAN's modus operandi vis-à-vis key relationships: how ASEAN states should seek security vis-à-vis major and extraregional powers, how ASEAN states should engage non-ASEAN Southeast Asian states, and how ASEAN states should relate to one another—in short, how regionalism in Southeast Asia should be pursued.

Breaking Old Habits

Old habits are hard to break. Consequently, there is very often what Ann Swidler describes as a "cultural lag time" between the point when new ideas are first introduced and when they have greater meaning and thus effect.[1] This certainly was true for ASEAN states, which saw the reemergence of old tensions barely a year into the new organization. The year 1968 saw Kuala Lumpur and Manila suspend relations once again over North Borneo with the former's discovery of Philippine plans to infiltrate the island.[2] That same year also saw renewed tensions between ASEAN's smallest and largest members over Singapore's execution of two Indonesian marines captured during Confrontation. That action—taken despite Suharto's personal appeals for leniency—sparked calls for retaliation by the Indonesian military for the personal and national affront perceived to Suharto and Indonesia, as well as anti-Chinese riots in Jakarta and Surabaya that, by one account, sent "the Singapore ambassador [in Jakarta] . . . flee[ing] for his life."[3] Meanwhile, ethnic riots in Malaysia led to reciprocal threats by Singapore and Malaysia to repatriate the other's workers (45,000 Malaysians from Singapore, 60,000 Singaporeans from Malaysia) with the closing of British bases. For Singapore, especially, such incidents did little to address its still tremendous insecurities as a small Chinese city-state in Southeast Asia. Consequently, despite its decision to join ASEAN in 1967, it continued to direct its attention mostly outside Southeast Asia, prompting some observers to characterize Singapore as "the weakest link in the show of ASEAN unity."[4]

States' quick reversion to old habits pointed to the persistence of old ideas, suspicions, and practices, as well as the continued weakness of the regional idea. Had Thailand and Indonesia (especially Suharto) not been committed to ASEAN and regional relations, bilateral tensions likely would have over-whelmed ASEAN as they had its predecessors. Indonesia's restraint on both North Borneo and the Singapore executions was especially notable given its militancy of only a few years earlier. Indeed, Suharto (with Malik's strong urging) resisted significant domestic and military pressure to take strong action against Singapore, thus controlling the escalation of tensions.

Changing U.S. and U.K. policies in Southeast Asia also played a part in that they helped refocus elites on a common predicament. The United Kingdom followed through on a January 1968 announcement to withdraw from Southeast Asia by the end of 1971 and terminate the Anglo-Malayan Defense Agreement (AMDA), which had played a key role in defending Malaysia (including Singapore) during *konfrontasi*. Tunku Abdul Rahman's disappointment with Malaysia's great power protector was clear when he said in 1969, "Britain has lost the power and the will to exercise the leadership expected of her," leaving a "feeling of emptiness and insecurity in the hearts and minds of those who had previously looked to Britain to leadership."[5]

Questions about the dependability of external guarantors were further driven home by developments in Indochina, especially after the 1968 U.S. defeat at Tet. Subsequent events—including the 1969 Nixon Doctrine, U.S. pressure on Japan to assume more regional responsibilities, and later the U.S. Congress's 1970 repeal of the Gulf of Tonkin Resolution—all gave the impression of a United States that was "tired," "exhausted," and increasingly unable and unwilling to maintain its commitments to Southeast Asian secu-rity.[6] Echoing Tunku Abdul Rahman's sentiments above, Philippine Foreign Minister Carlos Romulo observed in 1969, "Events are beginning to show the diminishing value of reliance on one's friends."[7] For all the ASEAN states, but especially for Thailand and the Philippines, which had supported the U.S. war in Vietnam and thus had concerns about Vietnamese retribution, events provided important reason to rethink the value of external guarantees. "Reappraisal," as Terrill wrote in 1969, was "the order of the day."[8]

Reappraisal, however, did not necessarily mean regionalism—as contin-ued interstate differences and conflicts made clear. All that the anticipated drawdown of U.S. and U.K. forces did was to create urgency to do *something*. And in their common and individual search for an appropriate response to events, particular activist elites and arguments once again played critical roles in drawing states to a regional and specifically ASEAN solution. As in 1967, readily understood ideas of nationalist self-determination provided particular focal points as illustrated, for example, by the fact that all partici-pants attending that 1969 ASEAN meeting made reference to their desire for greater self-determination in their statements. Linking their past inability or unwillingness to address the divisions within to the threat of balkanization from without, regional advocates once again framed the choice as one between regional division and foreign intervention, on the one hand, and regional unity and self determination, on the other.[9] Tun Razak's arguments at that 1969 meeting about the need for "regional actors [to] . . . assert more control over their own regional environment"[10] were typical:

> Unless we are conscious of our responsibilities and ready to take decisive and collective actions to prevent the growth of intra-regional conflicts, our nations will continue to be manipulated against one another. The colonial powers have retreated from this region and the vacuum left by them must be filled by the growth of our own collective power and collective will to survive.[11]

Such statements served to underscore and affirm some key founding ideas and justifications for regional organization: (1) that despite diverse perspectives, states did share a number of attributes that made them "Southeast Asian"— namely, a shared history of foreign intervention and a common predicament of being lesser powers in the global system, as well as geographic proximity; (2) that this shared history and predicament was at least partly a function of their own internal and intraregional divisions; and, consequently, (3) unity and resilience should be regionalism's paramount goals; and (4) Southeast Asia and Southeast Asian regionalism should remain inclusive of both mainland and insular states, communist, nonaligned, as well as noncommunist states—in other words, regionalism in Southeast Asia should be a force for unity, rather than division. Lastly, arguments also made clear that nationalism and regionalism were interdependent acts of self-determination but also that nationalism—the process of national consolidation and resilience—remained the most important foundation of regional security and regional resilience.

As they did in 1967, such arguments in 1969 focused states' attention to the possibilities of regional organization in response to events. Nevertheless, aside from agreement about the need to end their "petty squabbles" and "transcend the narrow confines of our zealous nationalisms . . . [and] great power associations of the past,"[12] there remained a lack of clarity about how exactly ASEAN itself should respond. As Rajaratnam made clear, all that had been decided in 1967 was the creation of ASEAN, little else:

> You may recollect at the first meeting in 1967, when we had to draft our communiqué. It was a very difficult problem of trying to say nothing in about 10 pages. Which we did. Because at that time, we ourselves, having launched ASEAN, were not quite sure where it was going or whether it was going—or whether it was going anywhere at all.[13]

Seen in this light, 1967 had only established some starting points for discussion—and even then, states' commitment to them was far from clear.

In fact, early debates—not just in 1969 but throughout the 1970s—revealed just how much remained to be clarified. Debates about specific proposals, for example, tended to reveal other fundamental questions: What constituted regional cooperation? What kinds of activities were appropriate for ASEAN? What could ASEAN states reasonably expect of other members? What should be the proper relationship between nation and region? How should the relationship between ASEAN and its great power partners be defined?

Such were the questions, for example, that confronted country representatives debating a 1969 Indonesian proposal for ASEAN security cooperation. While this proposal was not adopted (partly due to lingering concerns about Indonesia), the intra-ASEAN debate was nevertheless useful in affirming resilience as the most basic foundation of security and clarifying what resilience meant. From this debate emerged stronger agreement, for example, that a more militarized regionalism was inappropriate for states' regional resilience goals. As Rajaratnam, an opponent of Indonesia's proposal, argued, if ASEAN were to "remain an organization for uniting Southeast Asian nations and not dividing them,"[14] it would be prudent to restrict their focus to economics and trade. Thanat was even more explicit in questioning the appropriateness of such cooperation on resilience and self-determination grounds. Reiterating the position he also took in 1967, Thanat argued, "From our experience, military power alone would hardly be sufficient to cope with the problems we have. Without economic, social, and political progress, we might win with the support of our allies some military battles and still lose the struggle for peace, for freedom . . . sovereign[ty] and independence."[15]

Related debates about the pace and scope of regionalism similarly featured resilience arguments and at the same time underscored the fragility of relations. Indonesia and Malaysia, in particular, referenced the dangers of overstraining a tenuous unity within states, as well as between them, to make the case for a gradualist and broadly defined regionalism. As the argument went, ASEAN regionalism should be defined broadly and loosely, as relations were not ready yet to withstand a more demanding regionalism. Appealing for "patience" from those[16] who would push for more coordinated action from ASEAN, Suharto in his message to ASEAN's 1969 meeting compared ASEAN to a new plant that "needed continued care for its growth [and] continued weeding out of hostile elements." As he put it, the unity and consensus that are conditions for a more concerted regionalism did not yet exist; the first task of regionalism, then, must be on creating those conditions: "The members of ASEAN need more contact with each other, we need a continuous dialogue between ourselves, in order to arrive at a common thinking which will make coordinated and effective action possible."[17]

Malaysian representatives similarly argued for the importance of gradualism and dialogue in pursuit of greater unity and consensus. Malaysia's Tun Razak noted the value of an informal setting and personal interactions— "sport shirt diplomacy"—toward attaining that much desired "foundation of real feeling of good will, mutual respect and understanding, and friendship for one another."[18] Meanwhile, Tunku Abdul Rahman pushed for a broad conception of "regional" cooperation. Southeast Asian diversity meant that a diversity of approaches might be pursued. The important point was that states work together in the interest of greater unity. Cooperation need not be centrally coordinated or even multilateral to be "regional." Indeed, "an enmeshing network of bilateral arrangements between and among different countries of Southeast Asia [was] . . . itself a form of regional cooperation."[19]

In these statements to ASEAN's 1969 meeting were important assumptions about the diversity of members and the fragility of regional relations. Consequently, at the same time that elites affirmed the desirability of regional unity and the belief that greater contact and dialogue were important means by which to attain it, exchanges also began to clarify the competing normative pressures that came from founding arguments. On the one hand, resilience demanded unity—or at least a commitment to work toward that unity; on the other hand, resilience based on the assumption of fragile relations also demanded caution. Thus, while elites all worked on the premise that "togetherness"—"getting together, working together, and planning together"—was, as Tunku Abdul Rahman explained, "the only way . . . to tackle our problems," it was also clear that all believed that togetherness in the sense of unity of purpose, perspective, and identity did not yet exist and most of all should not be taken for granted. In that there remained some very serious differences between states, they needed to proceed cautiously and pragmatically. This meant setting their sights more narrowly, as opposed to looking to potentially divisive grand schemes.

Thus, in addition to reaffirming basic founding assumptions and premises of ASEAN—the importance of resilience, the fragility of regional relations, and the need for greater unity as an expression of Southeast Asia's interest in self-determination—these debates also began to produce ideas about how the ASEAN process should work in pursuit of those objectives. Slowly and gradually, through a diversity of efforts—unilateral efforts at national consolidation, bilateral and multilateral cooperation, regional dialogue, and "sport shirt diplomacy," regionalism would contribute to their common resilience. Slowly and gradually, regionalism through informal and personal dialogue could help create important mutual understanding and common thinking that would make other kinds of cooperation possible. These ideas about regional cooperation—that it should be broadly defined, gradualist, informal, and nonmilitary—offered new starting points for future debates.

Seeking Consensus on ZOPFAN (1971–1978)

Most of all, questions about Western policies and commitments renewed debate about the proper role to be played by great powers in Southeast Asia. In fact, as they were in 1967, differences between members on the great power question remained among the most contentious. At the same time, debates also revealed underlying agreement that was reflective of a common material predicament and ideological disposition—what Girling describes as ASEAN's "great power dilemma"[20] and Acharya, "the classic dilemma of Third World coalitions."[21] Specifically, as lesser powers, these ASEAN states generally understood—albeit to varying degrees—that their own material limitations made necessary some role (economic, as well as security) on the part of larger powers. That acknowledgment, however, existed in tension with a practical concern about abandonment and being made subordinate to major power agendas and priorities. Most of all, reliance on great powers warred with nationalist desires to be the architects for their own security futures and nationalist concern at the ways that such arrangements could make them subject to undue influence.

Given these tensions, it was perhaps no surprise, then, that uncertainties about great power policies prompted regional debates about great power roles in Southeast Asia or that those debates would quickly turn into debates about their own (individual and collective) contributions to the security of ASEAN-Southeast Asia. Indonesia's proposal for intra-ASEAN security cooperation discussed above was part of that debate. But while agreement about the requirements and demands of resilience resolved that debate relatively quickly, other proposals proved more divisive and more difficult to resolve.

In fact, a great range of views existed in ASEAN about the kind of role great powers should play and at what point great power roles challenged basic principles of self-determination. These differences and ASEAN's great power dilemma in general would be brought center stage beginning with a 1968 proposal from Tun Ismail—then member of the Malaysian Parliament and soon to be deputy prime minister under Tun Razak, successor to Tunku

Abdul Rahman. Referencing the deteriorating situation in Indochina and the shifting great power constellations around them, Tun Ismail proposed that the time was "ripe for the countries of the region to declare collectively the neutralization of Southeast Asia."[22] Neutralization became official Malaysian policy in 1970 when Tun Razak became prime minister.

The proposal broke from the past in a few key ways. First, it was a departure for Malaysia, which had previously made the AMDA the "cornerstone" of its foreign policy. Under Tun Razak, neutralization became part of a larger effort to shift Malaysian foreign policy away from the very pro-British, pro-Western orientation of his predecessor and towards a more equidistant stance vis-à-vis major powers. Second, the proposal stood out for being one of the first indigenous proposals of its kind. Previous neutralization schemes had been proposed before, but they were typically proposed by actors external to Southeast Asia.[23] And, third, the proposal was distinguished by its call to neutralize Southeast Asia in its entirety in contrast to previous Cold War–driven proposals that had called for only the neutralization of a single state or only parts of Indochina.[24] It was also notable, given the Cold War division of Southeast Asia, that Tun Razak did not limit his neutralization plan only to ASEAN-Southeast Asia.

In calling for the neutralization of Southeast Asia in its entirety, Tun Razak thus affirmed ideas established earlier—that the Southeast Asian region and thus regional security were to be defined inclusively and not along Cold War divisions. He also emphasized again the need for unity as the best way to neutralize and preempt new division and interventions. Tun Razak explained, "I mention the need to extend the area of peace and neutralisation to include all of Southeast Asia because it is obviously easier and wiser to strengthen the fabric of peace before it is ruptured rather than attempt to eliminate disorder and conflict once they have penetrated into the region."[25]

The proposal, however, met with objections from all the principals: The great powers, despite their interest in retrenching their commitments, opposed the proposal because it limited their options toward Southeast Asia. Non-ASEAN Southeast Asian states remained suspicious of ASEAN in general. Most important, the Malaysian proposal met resistance from other ASEAN members.

Diverging Views

Of the ASEAN states, Indonesia expressed some of the strongest objections. According to Emmerson and others, much of Indonesia's initial lack of enthusiasm for ZOPFAN stemmed from Indonesia's shifting economic and domestic priorities, its related concern that such a campaign would deter Western investment, and its sensitivity to the possibility that enthusiastic support on its part would be misinterpreted as a function of its intent to fill the "power vacuum" in Southeast Asia itself.[26] In fact, Jakarta's opposition may have had the opposite effect, at least in Malaysia. As one Malaysian observer said about Indonesia's objections, for example, "The nature of the ruling regime may have changed in Indonesia since the ousting of President Soekarno but her aspirations for regional dominance are as clear as ever."[27]

Indonesia also had more principled objections that spoke directly to the question of self-determination and relative interpretations of regional autonomy. While Malaysia's proposal was a step toward greater self-determination in the context of Malaysian foreign policy, Indonesia—coming from a different foreign policy tradition—tended to view the proposal differently. Coming from the standpoint of a strong "free and active" foreign policy tradition, Indonesia objected to the plan's mechanism of implementation whereby "the neutralization of the [Indochina] area and possibly of the entire region of Southeast Asia [would be] guaranteed by the three major powers, the People's Republic of China, the Soviet Union, and the United States."[28]

According to an account by Mohamed bin Haron, a senior member of Malaysia's diplomatic service and member of an ASEAN "experts group" on ZOPFAN, what Indonesia found objectionable was the mechanism's suggestion about ASEAN's "certain incapacity to cope with the regional environment."[29] Indonesia's position was that ASEAN states should be developing their own inner strength and resilience, not relying on others. As Indonesia's Foreign Minister Malik put it in 1971, "I strongly believe, that it is only through developing among ourselves an area of internal cohesion and stability, based on indigenous socio-political and economic strength, that we can ever hope to assist in the early stabilisation of a new equilibrium in the region that would not be the exclusive diktat of the major powers."[30]

As for ASEAN's other three members, Thailand was mostly noncommittal but continued to soften what had been a very pro–U.S. stance. Manila tended to view the neutralization proposal—like Indonesia's 1967 temporary bases clause—as a continued indictment of its hosting of U.S. military bases. As for Singapore, the problem with Malaysia's neutralization proposal was not too much great power involvement but too little. Objecting to what it saw to be neutralization's "liquidation of great power presence in the region"[31] and overreliance on the principled self-restraint of great powers, Singapore favored instead a balanced "multipower presence" in Southeast

Asia whereby major powers would check each other and effectively limit the intervention abilities of all.

The Ongoing Search for Consensus

Events in the summer of 1971 helped to keep attention on Malaysia's neutralization proposal despite intra-ASEAN differences. In particular, a surprise U.S. announcement that U.S. President Nixon would be visiting China spoke to states' "worst case suspicion . . . that Washington was buying its way out of the Vietnam War by giving Beijing a regional sphere of interest."[32] According to Malik, this announcement provided an important impetus to reconsider the scope and content of ASEAN cooperation, including Malaysia's neutralization proposal.[33]

In October 1971 ASEAN foreign ministers convened a special meeting to review international developments and their implications for Southeast Asia. For all the ASEAN states, it was clear that Sino-American rapprochement would necessitate, at minimum, a reexamination of their relations with both the United States and China. However, divergent preferences and perceptions prevented members from reaching even a common position on the entry of China into the United Nations.[34] Each member came to the meeting with different ideas about how best to respond to developments: Malaysia continued to support neutralization; Thailand countered with a proposal for a simple ASEAN Declaration of Peace and Neutrality; and the Philippines pressed for a summit of Asian leaders. Unable to reach a consensus, members agreed to meet again the following month in Kuala Lumpur.

As discussed by Heiner Hanggi, the special meeting that took place on November 16–17 was marked by "fierce debates" over both neutralization and the meeting's priorities. At the meeting, Malaysia took up the strongest position in favor of neutralization, while the Philippines and Singapore took up the strongest positions against. By more than one account, Singapore came to the meeting armed with an "elaborate" critique of neutralization.[35] Though the Malaysian proposal, given its reliance on great power recognition, was, as Emmerson puts it, "hardly an invitation to [larger powers] to ignore the region," Singapore and the Philippines seemed swayed by the U.S. argument that "an excessively neutralistic declaration would play into the hands of the neo-isolationists in the United States and would make it more difficult for Washington to maintain the American military presence in the region."[36]

Despite these differences, however, ASEAN states in November 1971 declared the "neutralization of Southeast Asia" to be "a desirable objective" and their intent "to exert the necessary efforts to secure the recognition of, and respect for, South East Asia as a Zone of Peace, Freedom and Neutrality . . ."[37] On the other hand, like the Bangkok Declaration three years earlier, the 1971 Kuala Lumpur (or ZOPFAN) Declaration was short and deliberately vague, a clear indication that members had yet to reconcile their different security preferences.[38] In fact, neutralization, itself, was mentioned only once (as "a desirable objective"), and the declaration failed to specify the mechanism by which ZOPFAN would be implemented (the issue of greatest disagreement). With respect to the great powers, the declaration asked only for external "recognition" and "respect" for the political and physical integrity of Southeast Asia and its states. In short, not only was the 1971 declaration vague in its objectives and mechanisms of implementation, but it also offered no resolution to intra–ASEAN debates.

Thus, by one view, ASEAN's 1971 ZOPFAN Declaration could certainly be argued to be of questionable value. But by another view, the declaration served an important purpose. Specifically, it served to reaffirm common principles: regional resilience as regional security, regionalism as self-determination, regional unity as a defense against interference—all of which were featured prominently in both the ZOPFAN Declaration itself and the joint communiqué issued by ASEAN's foreign ministers. Along these lines, the short ZOPFAN Declaration directly cited the entire fourth paragraph of ASEAN's 1967 founding declaration, reiterating members' commitment to a Southeast Asia "free from external interference in any form or manifestation" and where security and stability were to be the "primary responsibility" of Southeast Asian states themselves.

Most of all, the ZOPFAN Declaration reaffirmed a common commitment to one another at a time when regional relations were still most uncertain. It was a commitment to the idea of ASEAN-Southeast Asia *despite* significantly different preferences. It was also a commitment to the *pursuit* of greater unity and agreement. This point is underscored by the fact that the same 1971 meeting that produced the ZOPFAN Declaration also mandated a senior officials committee (SOC) that would study ZOPFAN conceptually and practically and the ways that it might be made into a "workable concept."[39] In this way, the 1971 declaration is better understood as an agreement to a process—a process of consensus seeking—than it was an agreement to the neutralization of Southeast Asia. In other words, it was a starting point, not an endpoint, of discussions. In this way, the creation of the SOC process also affirmed earlier conceptualizations of regionalism as a gradual, incremental path to greater mutual understanding, mutual agreement, and unity.

The ongoing discussions in both the SOC and in ASEAN at large between 1971 and 1975 illustrate states' continued negotiations and search for consensus on basic principles. Over the course of five sessions, the SOC worked toward accommodating different perspectives, defining the elements and operationalization of ZOPFAN, and clarifying the "guidelines for relations among states within and without the zone of peace."[40] During this time, ZOPFAN continued to evolve, moving increasingly away from the original idea of formal neutralization by great powers toward a position more akin to a political stance of neutrality or neutralism and nonalignment and one that explicitly made resilience its centerpiece.

For example, via the SOC process, the specific terms *peace, freedom,* and *neutrality* were given clearer definition and content. As defined by the SOC, *peace* came to be defined as more than the absence of war, but also "its positive meaning of harmonious and orderly relations." *Freedom* meant "freedom of states from control, domination, and interference by other states in the conduct of their [internal] and external affairs." *Neutrality* meant impartiality in both wartime and peacetime and noninterference in both its direct and indirect forms.[41] In each case, terms were moreover defined broadly to capture better the comprehensiveness of states' security challenges—internal and external but also the interdependence of the two. In short, as defined by the SOC, the absence of extraregional intervention did not by itself make a zone of peace; intraregional conflict had to be absent, too. Thus, through the SOC process, there came to be a "fresh articulation of ZOPFAN"[42] that was an "evocative extension of ASEAN's comprehensive criteria for regional peace, security and stability through structured regional interaction in politics, economics and society, perhaps even defence"—that is, regional resilience.[43]

This is not to say that differences had all been resolved. But what the SOC process did was to shift the emphasis away from great power roles and neutralization (on which there was little agreement) to focus more on the agency of ASEAN states to manage their own security (on which there was much more). The shift in emphasis is notable not only because it reflected a new consensus and different expression of ZOPFAN but also because it demonstrated the ideological pull of arguments for both resilience and greater self-determination even in the face of explicitly identified concerns about "outside powers." As long-time Indonesian analyst of ASEAN security affairs Jusuf Wanandi explains, "ASEAN's blueprint [for ZOPFAN] is based on the ability of countries in the region to manage their own affairs and relations among themselves and, by doing so, create a stable environment in which pressures from outside powers can be nullified."[44] In other words, ASEAN states—through national and regional unity and stability—had it within their own power to prevent interventions from the outside.

The new articulation of ZOPFAN would also offer states a framework by which to approach Vietnam. Here, it is worth underscoring that the SOC process did not take place in a political vacuum. Indeed, throughout the SOC process, developments in Vietnam informed in important ways the dialogue, with the agreement to end the U.S. war in Vietnam in 1973 injecting particular urgency to members' political-security debates. In cases like Singapore, Indochina developments—the U.S. scaling back of commitments, the formal end of the war in 1973, the fall of South Vietnam in 1975—had an especially striking effect. Whereas Singapore previously neglected the region out of distrust for its neighbors, developments now forced Singapore to refocus. In 1972 Singapore's Prime Minister Lee Kuan Yew began a round of "first official visits," beginning with Malaysia. That visit was then followed in 1973 by first official visits to Thailand and Indonesia where, in an act of conciliation, he visited the tombs of the Indonesian marines Singapore had executed three years earlier. In 1974, Lee completed his diplomatic rounds with a first official visit to the Philippines.

As for ASEAN as a whole, ASEAN activities increased as the U.S. war in Vietnam wound down. A special ASEAN meeting was convened to discuss the Vietnam peace agreement, after which states issued a press statement affirming regional unity and resilience as acts of self-determination and as a basic foundation of regional security for Southeast Asia as a whole:

> The meeting recognised that the peace and stability of the area and their own well-being are the primary responsibility of all Southeast Asian countries. The sense of identity and regional cohesion engendered through ASEAN cooperation and . . . developing national and regional resilience could be the foundation on which Southeast Asian countries could assume this responsibility.[45]

In addition, their collective press statement also expressed its gratification that the Vietnam settlement "contained elements . . . similar to the principles enunciated in the Kuala Lumpur [ZOPFAN] Declaration" and the hope that developments in Vietnam "might signify the beginning of the realisation of a Southeast Asian Zone of Peace, Freedom, and Neutrality, free from any form or manner of interference from outside powers."[46] Especially given their differences, the reference to ZOPFAN at this time was notable as both an expression of intra-ASEAN unity and of its all–Southeast Asia inclusive understanding of regional security. It also pointed to the ways that ZOPFAN—once highly contentious—had evolved through the SOC process to become an important expression of ASEAN and its vision for a resilient Southeast Asia.

Vietnam's Challenge to Resilience

One of the clearest obstacles to ASEAN's vision of a Southeast Asian ZOPFAN was Vietnam, which continued to view ASEAN as highly suspect. There is no doubt that, between 1973 and 1978, one of the biggest questions confronting the ASEAN states was how to redefine their relations with Vietnam after a war in which some ASEAN members had played supporting roles. As Rajaratnam put it in 1975, the communist victories in Indochina meant that Vietnam and the Indochina states were now "entering Southeast Asian politics for the first time" and unchecked by other powers; and "[F]or the first time, Hanoi, the new regime[s] which may emerge in Laos, and in Cambodia, would take a good look at a Southeast Asia which is non-communist."[47] ASEAN states all recognized that communist victories in Indochina marked the beginning of a new era in Southeast Asia in which a reunified Vietnam, no longer distracted by wars with Western powers, would now be free to direct its attention (for good or ill) toward ASEAN-Southeast Asia.

As with other issues, efforts to fashion a collective response were complicated by different perspectives and varied degrees of concern—from the almost celebratory tone of Malaysia's Tun Razak to the more cautious tone of the Philippines' Carlos Romulo and Singapore's S. Rajaratnam.[48] For Tun Razak, the end of the Vietnam War signaled the end of foreign domination, intervention, and division in Southeast Asia, creating for ASEAN an historic opportunity to unify the region, "to extend the scope of regional cooperation throughout Southeast Asia," and to create "a family of nations in Southeast Asia that would embrace the whole region" as ideally envisaged.[49] And in that the resolution of the Indochinese conflict had also diminished the reasons and opportunities for great power intervention, "the relevance of the Kuala Lumpur [ZOPFAN] Declaration," he argued, "is surely more evident and its practical realization . . . more urgent and nearer to our grasp."[50]

Others, however, were more cautious. While they too drew on the same themes of self-determination and regional unity as security, they emphasized instead the dangers posed to fragile intra-ASEAN relationships by moving too fast or by extending new membership too soon. Indonesia's Adam Malik warned, for example, that the first priority was not the unification of Southeast Asia but ASEAN's own collective cohesion. Yes, ASEAN should engage Vietnam, but embracing Vietnam prematurely—before ASEAN's own cohesion was assured and before Vietnam's intentions were clear— would only put ASEAN states and ASEAN itself at risk. Thus, as Malik put

it in 1975, openness and inclusiveness had to be accompanied by strength—
"not the strength of arms or armed alliances, but that of ASEAN's identity
and common purpose, of its internal cohesion and functional efficacy." As
he put it, "[T]he goal of widening regional harmony and cooperation [to
the rest of Southeast Asia]" had to be accompanied by the process of "internal consolidation" in ASEAN.[51]

Intra-ASEAN debates about Vietnam between 1973 and 1978 were remi-
niscent of the debates on Vietnam's membership that took place in 1967 in
their tensions and dilemmas. On the one hand, there was much distrust as
reflective of both past conflict and Vietnam's relative capabilities. In this
sense, states' concerns about Vietnam were similar to those they had of other
larger powers—that is, how to persuade these powers to respect and uphold
their right to self-determination, free of interference. On the other hand,
Vietnam as a Southeast Asian state was also critically not like other larger
powers. As such, ASEAN states' concerns about Vietnam's recent militarization tended to be mitigated by an understanding of Vietnam's recent conflicts as the product of the same divisive historical and geopolitical forces
that plagued them as Southeast Asian states. Most important, Vietnam as
a Southeast Asian state was considered to be not only a potential member
of ASEAN but also an essential link in the armor of regional unity. This is
why, as early as 1973, at a special ASEAN meeting held not a month after the
agreement to end the U.S. war, ASEAN foreign ministers issued a statement
that explicitly stated their desire to see the expansion of ASEAN membership.[52] Similarly, following Vietnam's reunification in 1976 and ASEAN
summits in 1976 and 1977, members continued to "express . . . their readiness to develop fruitful relations and mutually beneficial cooperation with
other countries in the region."[53] Ideas about regional resilience are critical
to explaining members' understanding of the challenge posed by Vietnam,
as well as what they understood to be the appropriate ASEAN response.

But though reflective of similar tensions, debates about Vietnam in the
mid-1970s were also not like 1967 debates in at least one critical respect.
Specifically, debates in the mid-1970s included the additional concern
of how Vietnam's membership might affect ASEAN itself. By the mid-
1970s, ASEAN had come to be equated with their common interest in
regional resilience and consequently had gained an importance that neither of ASEAN's predecessors, for example, enjoyed. Such concerns were
uppermost on the minds of those urging caution in ASEAN's dealings with
Vietnam. Attending one of Southeast Asia's first conferences on ASEAN
regionalism in 1974, Abdul Rahim Ishak, Singapore's Senior Minister of

State (Foreign Affairs), echoed, for example, Malik's concerns above about the need to make ASEAN's own cohesiveness and unity their priority before unity of Southeast Asia as a whole:

> [I]t is not desirable that an expansion of the membership of ASEAN occurs at the present time. ASEAN needs to build the links between the five member states. The problem of devising a strong institutional framework which will survive the present leaders of our countries must be our foremost task. The expansion of ASEAN will merely mean the dilution of our ability to communicate with one another without enhancing our capacity to influence regional order and events.[54]

Thus, while there was general agreement that ASEAN should remain open to Vietnamese membership, not everyone agreed that *ASEAN* was ready to bring Vietnam in. In short, regional resilience as ASEAN existed in tension with regional resilience as Southeast Asia. This tension was moreover made more intense with the quick and successive communist victories in Vietnam, Cambodia, and Laos in 1975.

The Rituals and Norms of Regional Amity, Cooperation, and Concord

Given continued intra-ASEAN disagreements about security and the uncertainties of great power commitments, ASEAN states responded to the communist victories in 1975 with notable confidence and openness.[55] The very existence of ASEAN provided states important psychological and symbolic support, a ready framework for a regional response, and ultimately the confidence to approach Vietnam and the post–U.S., post–Vietnam War era in 1976 with cautious openness instead of "negative notions of fear."[56] This was perhaps truest of Thailand and the Philippines, which had been Washington's closest allies in Southeast Asia. Indeed, their joint statement issued July 4, 1975, announced that SEATO "had served its purpose" and that it should be phased out. The two governments also reaffirmed their commitment to the temporary status of foreign bases[57]—a significant gesture on the part of Manila given earlier disagreements with Indonesia on the subject.

Both governments—contrary to expectation—also made it more, not less, difficult for the United States to maintain forces in Southeast Asia. Manila pressed for higher rents and recognition of Philippine sovereignty over U.S. bases. Meanwhile, Bangkok under a new civilian government unilaterally set a deadline for U.S. troop withdrawal from Thailand.[58] At states' annual ASEAN ministerial meeting (AMM) in 1975 a few months earlier, Thai foreign minister Chatichai Choonhaven was in fact explicit in his rejection of old arrangements in favor of new regional relations. As he put it, Southeast Asian states faced a critical choice between a "New

Southeast Asia" characterized by friendship, security, tolerance, and collective self-reliance and the "old Southeast Asia" that was divided, weak, and at war. Speaking to Southeast Asia's "Five Regional Needs"[59]—all five of which emphasized the importance of regional ties—Chatichai then reiterated a previously expressed interest in a meeting of all Southeast Asian states, thus making clear his choice of a new Southeast Asia.

Most important, states responded to developments in Indochina with new ASEAN commitment. As in 1973, ideas about regional resilience as security and self-determination, provided both a common prism through which to interpret events and an important coordinating principle on which states could fashion a response. In particular, ASEAN's twin resilience concerns—ASEAN resilience vis-à-vis a reunified Vietnam and Southeast Asian resilience vis-à-vis all larger powers—meant that efforts to engage Vietnam were accompanied by intensified attention to ASEAN unity and self-strengthening. The years 1975 and 1976 saw notable activity and initiatives from ASEAN that all aimed to project and affirm a united front. In 1976 ASEAN held its first ever summit of ASEAN heads of government. For an organization that had been exclusively the purview of members' foreign ministers, the summit was a significant public affirmation of regional organization and regional unity at the highest levels. That 1976 summit, to be followed by a second summit the next year, also produced ASEAN's first significant initiatives since the 1971 ZOPFAN Declaration: the ASEAN Treaty of Amity and Cooperation (TAC) and the Declaration of ASEAN Concord, both considered steps toward the establishment of a Southeast Asian ZOPFAN.

Given the centrality of regional resilience to ASEAN notions of security, it should be no surprise that ASEAN's first efforts at summitry emerged at this time. After all, ASEAN summitry was a "dramatic demonstration" and visual representation of ASEAN solidarity following developments in Indochina.[60] Both TAC and the Declaration of ASEAN Concord—both milestones in ASEAN regionalism in their formalization of ASEAN's processes and principles of the last nine years—can also be viewed similarly as an expression of ASEAN resolve and unity in the face of evolving challenges. As ASEAN's first (and until 1995, only) treaty, TAC was especially notable. In laying out and codifying for the first time the "fundamental principles" of regional order, including noninterference, nonuse of force, and regional cooperation,[61] TAC signified a shift in thinking about ASEAN; that is, members were now thinking about ASEAN for the long term and not just as a tenuous experiment that might be going, as Rajaratnam earlier put it, nowhere.

Though it gets less attention than TAC, the Declaration of ASEAN Concord was at least equally significant in this respect. Under Concord, ASEAN took its first steps toward institutionalizing regional processes since its founding in 1967. Not only did it commit members to the establishment of an ASEAN secretariat (a physical and tangible expression of region, regional unity, and "institutional rejuvenation")[62] but Concord also identified for the first time the political realm as an area of ASEAN cooperation. Members' willingness to acknowledge ASEAN's political purpose contrasted with their stance ten years earlier when fears and insecurities led states to reject and obscure any political objectives or agendas. At minimum, their willingness to acknowledge ASEAN's political identity—Leifer describes the 1976 summit as ASEAN's "political coming out"[63]—pointed to members' increased confidence in the strength and permanence of their own relations since 1967.

Vis-à-vis Vietnam, both TAC and Concord were thus reflective of both ASEAN's own efforts at self-strengthening and their search for a framework with which to engage Vietnam. This was especially true of TAC, which at once formalized their own relations and provided the basic principles that would guide ASEAN's dealings with a newly reunified Vietnam. The newly signed TAC, like ZOPFAN, was notably made "open to accession by other States in Southeast Asia" from the start. The inclusiveness of TAC and ZOPFAN at this critical moment in time illustrates both important self-confidence and a belief, to quote Rajaratnam, that "different, but not necessarily hostile systems" could coexist in Southeast Asia.[64] At minimum, members' relatively quick normalization of relations with Vietnam—Singapore on August 1, 1973; Malaysia on March 30, 1973; Philippines on July 12, 1976; Thailand on August 6, 1976[65]—pointed to their interest in finding a modus vivendi vis-à-vis Vietnam.

The Limits of Inclusion

More ambitiously, states' "constructive engagement" of Vietnam[66] also reflected a strengthened belief in the processes of resilience and the hope that Vietnam's foreign policy, like Indonesia's in 1967, might be moderated by being part of regional processes. Thus, the challenge before ASEAN, as Rajaratnam would put it in 1977, was not how to create a credible military deterrent against possible Vietnamese aggression but instead "how a non-Communist ASEAN [could] enter into friendly and mutually beneficial relations with three communist states born out of the pain, hatreds, and suspicions of a terrible war."[67]

On this point, ASEAN states continued to develop ideas about the kinds of processes most likely to facilitate the improvement of relations. As noted, the ASEAN process itself began with the idea that dialogue could facilitate mutual understanding—an idea that was now strengthened by both the stabilization of intra-ASEAN relations and demonstrated ability to work toward new consensus as in the ZOPFAN process. In addition, there was also the argument that Carlos Romulo put forth in 1969—specifically that a "posture that [was] neither defensive nor counter-aggressive, but open, positive, and friendly"[68] would be more likely to persuade a potentially hostile Vietnam to look upon ASEAN in less confrontational terms.

For a brief time, a number of high-level diplomatic and trade exchanges between Vietnam and individual ASEAN states gave reason to believe that sufficient openness existed on both sides that new relations might be possible. On July 5, 1976, Vietnam's foreign minister expanded Vietnam's three-point framework for relations to include regional cooperation "for the building of prosperity in keeping with each country's specific conditions," which some viewed to be a sign of Vietnam's new willingness to treat ASEAN as an economic entity (as opposed to U.S. proxy).[69] The same day, Vietnam sent its deputy foreign minister on Vietnam's first "friendship tour" of Southeast Asia, visiting Rangoon and Vientiane as well as all ASEAN capitals except for Bangkok.

Still, there remained important reasons to find Vietnam suspect. For one, Vietnam's selective and varied engagement of ASEAN states led to charges of divide and rule tactics—charges that would increase over the following decade. Moreover, "verbal assaults" on individual ASEAN states and specific ASEAN initiatives helped to keep suspicions alive. In its many references to "genuine neutrality" and "true independence," for example, Hanoi continued to suggest that ASEAN was neither truly neutral nor truly independent. In the same vein, around the time of ASEAN's Bali Summit in February 1976, both Vietnamese and Lao leaderships continued to accuse ASEAN of being just another imperialist-backed creation like SEATO; and in August 1976, Vietnam and Laos successfully blocked ZOPFAN's reendorsement by the Non-Aligned Movement, which had endorsed it just three years earlier. In their call on NAM to support "the struggle of the people of Southeast Asia against neo-colonialism," they not only questioned the legitimacy of ASEAN governments but also suggested Vietnam's continued political, if not material, support for insurgent activity in the ASEAN countries.[70] In fact, despite overtures to individual ASEAN members, Hanoi continued to resist dealing with ASEAN as an organization, thus denying ASEAN and its goals recognition and legitimacy.

In trying to discredit ASEAN and its TAC and ZOPFAN initiatives, Vietnam in essence rejected ASEAN's efforts to define regional security in more inclusive and common terms. As Thanat Khoman, speaking as a civilian, described the situation in 1976: "[W]hile ASEAN nations have repeatedly extended the hands of friendship to Vietnam and the other new Indochinese regimes, the leaders of those countries have responded by shaking their fists at them."[71]

Keeping Up Appearances

Relations experienced an uptick in 1977 due to Vietnam's adoption of a more conciliatory approach toward ASEAN states. Reflective largely of Vietnam's growing tensions with China and Cambodia and related concerns about encirclement, Vietnam upped its efforts to improve relations with ASEAN states. As tensions, border attacks, and other provocations escalated over 1977 and 1978, so too did Vietnam's peace offensive aimed at "win[ning] over, or at least neutralis[ing], ASEAN."[72] Included in this effort was Vietnamese foreign minister Nguyen Duy Trinh's 1977–1978 tour of ASEAN capitals.[73] A similar ASEAN tour by Premier Pham Van Dong then followed, during which he offered to sign a nonaggression pact with each ASEAN capital, an offer that was rejected by collective ASEAN.[74] Hanoi even went so far as to express support for ZOPFAN and publicly acknowledge ASEAN as an economic organization and not the covert tool of U.S. imperialism as it had previously said.

However, whatever optimism ASEAN states may have had for an all-encompassing resilient Southeast Asian regional order came to an end when Vietnam invaded Cambodia/Kampuchea on December 25, 1978. Despite acknowledgment of the security concerns behind Vietnam's action, ASEAN states all viewed Vietnam's intervention as highly problematic and not easily dismissed. Unlike Vietnam's wars with France and the United States, which could be interpreted as wars of national self-determination and wars against foreign intervention, Vietnam's action against Cambodia was viewed less ambiguously as an example of aggression against a neighboring state. Moreover, Vietnam's intervention was especially problematic in the context of ASEAN's recently adopted TAC. Vietnam's unprecedented convening of the foreign ministers of the three Indochinese states in 1979 was also widely seen by ASEAN states as a step toward actualizing Vietnam's long-standing idea of an Indochinese federation and rival to an ASEAN-based regional order.

Most of all, Vietnam's intervention severely tested the unity of ASEAN members. As members tried to fashion a response to events, they found themselves faced with fundamental disagreements about the conflict. Indeed, as Antolik details, members even had trouble agreeing on what to call the Vietnamese action, finally settling on "armed intervention."[75] Such differences not only complicated ASEAN's ability to present a united front vis-à-vis Vietnam but also strained their recently improved relations. Negotiating the differences between Indonesia and Thailand posed a particular challenge. Thailand, as the front-line state, viewed Vietnam's invasion into neighboring Cambodia as a direct threat to itself. Moreover, recognizing that ASEAN's support could only be diplomatic, Thailand turned elsewhere, namely China, for military support,[76] thereby legitimating China's involvement in Southeast Asia. This action put Thailand at odds with Indonesia and Malaysia, both of which considered China, not Vietnam, to be the larger threat to ASEAN security. Both also feared that taking too harsh an action against Vietnam—"bleeding Vietnam white"—would eliminate an important buffer state between China and ASEAN.

Adding to the overall challenge to ASEAN unity was the fact that many also saw in Vietnam's actions an attempt to manipulate intra-ASEAN differences and divide the organization. Antolik best captures the comprehensiveness of the challenge posed to the ten-year-old ASEAN:

> Sustaining solidarity has been stressful; members faced confusion or apathy among external supporters for the ASEAN position, the distasteful reputation of the Khmer Rouge, which ASEAN backs, Vietnamese diplomatic initiatives, factions within the Indonesian and Thai foreign policy making establishments, continuing apprehension about the stability of the Thai government, divisions over the role of China, and apprehensions about Sino-Soviet relations.[77]

In the end, Vietnam's intervention into Cambodia had contrary effects on ASEAN and its notions of regional resilience. On the one hand, Vietnam's action clearly challenged the idea of a unified and resilient Southeast Asia. Thailand's relationship with China also represented a real test of the regional autonomy goals contained in ZOPFAN. And, in fact, it would take some rhetorical contortions to make Thai actions consistent with what was agreed should be the ASEAN project of regional resilience. Within ASEAN, Thai and Indonesian positions also proved especially hard to reconcile. In the end, ASEAN designated Indonesia to be ASEAN's interlocutor in dealings with Vietnam and Thailand its representative in relations with China, thus absorbing into the "ASEAN response" both positions and approaches.

On the other hand, it was also notable that ASEAN elites continued to work on finessing and reconciling the two positions. Through what was often a difficult and trying process, individual elites took concerted effort to focus collective attention on the core areas of agreement. In particular, Vietnam's intervention into Cambodia demonstrated the ways that regional unity—though clearly strained—continued to provide a common interpretive lens and coordinating principle for ASEAN's otherwise divergent states. Shared ideas of region and the importance of regional unity might even have been the *only* significant thing that kept them working together toward a common solution, sustaining the organization at a time of great internal division and stress. In fact, Mochtar Kusumaadmatja, Indonesia's foreign minister throughout the period of Vietnam's occupation, was explicit about the modifications Indonesia had made in support of regional organization: "If it were not for Thailand, the Indonesian reaction [to Vietnam] would have been more flexible."[78]

In addition, Vietnam's actions in Cambodia also furthered ASEAN's development in other ways. While resulting intra-ASEAN divisions over how to respond was a most severe test of ASEAN bonds—certainly up until that point—it is also precisely for that reason that ASEAN's efforts would be so defining for it as an organization. The fact that they were able to work through their differences and not fall apart in the face of great challenge provided an important affirmation of their efforts *and* their solidarity as a group. A sense of solidarity was also helped by the additional opportunities and necessities created by Vietnam's intervention to work with one another within the narrow context of ASEAN and also on the international stage. ASEAN's efforts on the issue vis-à-vis major powers like the United States and China and with international organizations like the United Nations thus brought ASEAN important recognition from the larger international community, which in turn helped to further affirm ASEAN in the eyes of its own members.

Debating the PTA's:
Nationalism's Constraints and ASEAN's Loose Institutionalism

In addition to the above initiatives, the other defining area of early ASEAN activity was trade and economic cooperation. However, despite being one of the few areas explicitly identified by their 1967 declaration as an area for cooperation, ASEAN's early trade initiatives often were just as sensitive and often more difficult, as they were more likely to come into conflict with national development strategies and understood nation-building priorities. Such was the case, for example, with ASEAN's 1977 PTAs, an early, decade-long effort at intra-ASEAN trade liberalization.

In particular, strong nationalist economic priorities and nationalist inse-curities (many the legacies of recent conflict) provided particular obstacles to intra-ASEAN trade liberalization efforts. For one, obvious advantages from such efforts seemed few. Coming from similar levels of development, not to mention a similar climactic zone, ASEAN members mostly had simi-lar comparative advantages and produced similar products (for example, petroleum, coconut, kenaf, sugar, timber, rubber, and increasingly, light manufactured products). Consequently, not only was there little reason to trade with one another, but fellow ASEAN members were often each oth-ers' primary competition. While the structure of their economies and levels of development supported collective bargaining strategies vis-à-vis third markets and other areas of economic cooperation,[79] the bottom line was that intra-ASEAN trade liberalization in the 1970s and 1980s tended to be less economically rational.

Moreover, any interest in trade liberalization tended to come into conflict with nationalist priorities and strategies. As part of their nationalist efforts to reclaim their economies after colonialism, states pursued nationalist import substitution strategies (ISI) aimed at building up domestic and strategic indus-tries. In fact, at the time of ASEAN's founding in 1967, only Singapore had made the commitment to export-led growth. At minimum, such ISI strate-gies—even if designed mostly to protect nascent industries from competi-tion from advanced actors—"created an inherently biased economic policy against intra-ASEAN trade."[80] Such ISI strategies, geared as they were to self-strengthening and development, also tended to politicize any effort that might introduce new competition to domestic industries. As one observer concluded, as sensitive as some agricultural products were, industrial prod-ucts eventually may have done more to "bog . . . down" intra-ASEAN trade liberalization efforts.[81]

This is not to say that there did not exist a "reasonable degree of eco-nomic complementarity"[82] between particular members on some products, but these tended to be limited in number and/or limited to specific bilateral relationships—a questionable foundation on which to base regionwide trade liberalization efforts. As Singapore's Rajaratnam argued in 1968, in such cases bilateral agreements, not ASEAN-wide liberalization schemes, were more appropriate and more likely to succeed.[83] More important, national-ist sensitivities and insecurities remained especially sharp during ASEAN's first years—and this was especially true for ASEAN's most complementary trade relationships.

In the case of Singapore and Indonesia—ASEAN's most and least developed economies—such insecurities deterred both from taking advantage of the complementarities between them. For Indonesia, a free and active tradition intensified fears that trade liberalization would allow more advanced ASEAN economies like Singapore—or outside economies through Singapore—to exploit Indonesia's resources, people, and market and undermine the development of Indonesian domestic industries.[84] The persistent trade imbalance between Indonesia and Singapore—not to mention Indonesia's particular sensitivity about Chinese influence—only reinforced this view. So sensitive was this trade imbalance for Indonesian domestic politics that in 1974 the two governments agreed that the public release of bilateral trade information should be the responsibility of the Indonesian government alone—an agreement that was upheld for nearly 30 years (1974–2003).[85]

In the case of Singapore-Malaysia relations—whose complementarities were such that they were often characterized as "symbiotic"—such complementarities similarly proved no match against nationalist forces and sentiments. In this case, economic nationalism, combined with resentments created from their difficult separation, spurred Malaysia's development of rival services and facilities once provided by Singapore. In other words, interdependence seemed to drive a push for greater differentiation, not integration.[86] As for Singapore, those first few years revealed a persistent distrust toward its neighbors' willingness to uphold stated commitments and about their intentions toward itself.[87] Consequently as in security, Singapore's attention was mostly on partners beyond Southeast Asia. As far as Singapore was concerned, in fact, the less dependent it was on its neighbors, the better. These understood economic and political realities resulted in a more cautious approach toward trade liberalization than Singapore's economic interests otherwise might have suggested.

A Reconsideration

Given such material, political, and ideological obstacles, it was no surprise that states should display little initial interest in intra-ASEAN trade liberalization. This began to change in the mid-1970s as states confronted a looming global economic crisis, as well as new questions about U.S. post–Vietnam War commitments. At the 1974 AMM, for example, each of ASEAN's foreign ministers referred in some way to the troubles brewing in the global economy—troubles that included an ongoing oil and energy crisis and global recession.[88] Describing the world of 1974 as many saw it,

Rajaratnam may have put it best: "Monetary instability, trade uncertainty and uncontrolled inflation are the more readily recognizable symptoms of a world out of control."[89] So pressing were these economic concerns that they almost completely overshadowed developments in Indochina at ASEAN's 1974 AMM.

Economic anxieties moreover remained high as states inside and outside Southeast Asia began the process of normalizing relations with Indochinese states and China following the U.S. war in Vietnam. For ASEAN states, this process intensified existing political insecurities about their own resilience to withstand internal and external communist pressures. In addition, previously discussed questions about future U.S. security commitments and Vietnamese intentions underscored the need to focus on self-strengthening efforts—in particular, the importance of resilience (and specifically economic development as the means to resilience) as the best defense against possible aggressions or subversions inspired from outside.[90] Toward this end, states hoped for economic assistance that would help facilitate their efforts to strengthen their economies from within. Instead, states were disturbed by what they saw to be Washington's general disinterest in ASEAN, as well as signs of new economic interest in communist China and Vietnam. In addition, many elites were reportedly "exercised" by the stress Washington was placing on human rights "in allocating aid and in choosing friends."[91]

This combination of developments began to compel a reconsideration of existing arrangements and new interest in developing regional arrangements. As in the political-security realm, Singapore—for whom global economic uncertainties served to intensify an already high sense of vulnerability—experienced one of the more dramatic reevaluations of regional relations and became ASEAN's strongest proponent for intra-ASEAN trade liberalization.[92] As Indochina and global economic developments continued to evolve, collective steps toward economic and trade cooperation moved forward. A 1974 pledge to take economic collaboration more seriously[93] was followed by new commitments in 1975 to intensify trade negotiations and set guidelines for industrial complementation. Six months later, states agreed "in principle" to lower trade barriers among ASEAN countries. Most indicative of ASEAN's new seriousness toward economic cooperation was the addition of economic ministers (the ASEAN Economic Ministerial Meetings [AEMM]) to the ASEAN process, which had been the exclusive realm of ASEAN's foreign ministers.

The new seriousness with which members viewed ASEAN and economic cooperation was further demonstrated in February 1976 when ASEAN heads of government met in Bali for their first summit. There, they agreed to "the establishment of trading arrangements as a long term objective."[94] A notable product of that meeting was the Declaration of ASEAN Concord, the economic significance of which rivaled its previously discussed political significance. Specifically, the concord explicitly laid out the agenda for ASEAN economic cooperation—cooperation in basic commodities (especially food and energy); industrial cooperation; cooperation in trade; a joint approach to international commodity problems and other world economic problems; and machinery for economic cooperation. One month later, economic ministers directed senior officials to "formulate the necessary guidelines which should govern the operation of such a [preferential trading arrangements] scheme,"[95] which in July was tasked to the newly created Trade Preference Negotiating Group. At a special meeting held in February 1977, states signed the Agreement on the ASEAN Preferential Trading Arrangements (PTAs).

As studies over the next decade demonstrated, these measures—significant though they were in the context of ASEAN's first decade—did little, however, to increase intra-ASEAN trade. "A farce" by one account,[96] the PTAs became legendary for their ineffectualness. Not only did members reject across-the-board cuts for an item-by-item, piecemeal approach toward trade liberalization, but the PTAs also became notorious for their inclusion of "snowplows" and "nuclear reactors"—products that members neither produced nor bought much of. According to Gerald Tan, "For some product categories, up to two-thirds of the items granted preferential tariffs by some countries were not actually traded by them."[97]

Along the way, members did improve the PTAs at the margins, including a 1980 decision to increase reductions to 20 percent and more significantly, to implement the reductions "across the board" for imports valued at less than US$50,000 (later raised to US$10 million), thus replacing the product-by-product approach initially adopted.[98] Still, the effect of the PTAs remained limited. States' structure of trade continued to favor extraregional economies. Moreover, as Stubbs explains, an already existing structural bias against intra-ASEAN trade tended to be reinforced by dynamics of the Cold War—especially the emergence of a "complex web of dependence" whereby "Japan and to lesser extent the United States provide[d] investment capital, and Southeast Asia supplie[d] the raw materials for Japan and the cheap labour for the production of manufactured goods destined primarily for the United States."[99] The result was that ASEAN's trade with Japan and the United States grew and intra-ASEAN trade (limited to begin with) declined.[100]

Also mitigating the effect of the PTAs was the persistence of nontariff trade barriers (quotas, import licensing, import prohibitions, and technical norms)[101] and "exclusion lists" that allowed members to exclude certain "sensitive items." In one case, a member put nearly half of its qualifying list on the sensitive list. In another, an exclusion list was actually longer than its inclusion list.[102] Members' pledge to submit additional items for liberalization each quarter was also diluted by states' practice of padding their lists with items already with zero tariffs or variants of the same product (for example, "plastic sprayers," "aluminum sprayers," and "other sprayers" instead of a single line for "domestic sprayers"). Consequently, when all was said and done, the PTAs covered 16,000 items but less than 1 percent of total ASEAN trade,[103] with various estimates putting the PTAs' effect on intra-ASEAN trade within a range of 0.006 to 5.6 percent.[104]

Pursuing and Respecting Resilience

It has become customary to cite the PTAs as an example of states' divergent interests. And indeed, as highlighted above, this was a big part of the problem. At the same time, given their structure of trade, it remains a bit of a mystery as to why intra-ASEAN trade liberalization would be such a focus of ASEAN economic cooperation in the first place. Indeed, for all the reasons above, intra-ASEAN trade liberalization was not an obvious response to perceived extra-ASEAN challenges. Nor were such efforts cost free, as such efforts proved "extremely demanding of scarce, high-level bureaucratic resources in ASEAN."[105] Viewed in this light, intra-ASEAN trade liberalization (especially in the 1970s and 1980s) seems, in a word, irrational. Here, the process by which states arrived at their 1977 agreement is revealing. It is revealing in the sense that it shows not just tensions among states and state preferences but also ongoing efforts to negotiate exactly what regionalism should mean and entail, especially as regarded the nation–region relationship and the demands of unity. Arguments about regional resilience would especially drive and constrain intra-ASEAN trade liberalization efforts. The PTAs—a nationalist and unity-bounded plan for intra-ASEAN trade liberalization—would be the product of that search for agreement.

Regarding the intra-ASEAN debate, it was clear that while states agreed about the need to strengthen resilience, especially national resilience, in response to new challenges, they diverged in how best to create the conditions to support such efforts. While global uncertainties made Singapore a primary proponent of trade liberalization efforts, others, like Indonesia, tended to put greater stress on industrial cooperation. Nevertheless, as states debated the merits of intra-ASEAN trade liberalization in 1975 and 1977, the idea that states *should* pursue trade liberalization as a region emerged as an important point of consensus—this despite significant differences.

Responding to the crisis brewing in the global economy and a Vietnam no longer distracted by its wars with foreign powers, ASEAN's otherwise divergent states found in regional resilience a common interpretive lens through which to understand their collective problem and response. In that it was believed that greater unity would produce greater security, economic integration became a desirable objective. However, as discussed above, material and social conditions generally did not support intra-ASEAN trade liberalization efforts. The challenge for ASEAN elites, then, was how to create the conditions that would make regional integration possible. In this sense, ASEAN's intraregional trade liberalization efforts reversed the process and logic usually described by dominant theories. Where intraregional trade liberalization initiatives are generally understood as responses to pre-existing regional complementarities and trade, ASEAN trade liberalization and economic cooperation in general were supposed to *create* those trading interests and complementarities in the interest of regional integration and resilience.

In short, the driving force behind intra-ASEAN trade liberalization efforts was not economics but instead politics: Intra-ASEAN trade liberalization (and economic cooperation in general) explicitly served political-security objectives. Thus, the stated aim of the 1977 PTAs was not the promotion of trade or increasing domestic exports per se but instead the "strengthening of national and ASEAN economic resilience" through "the adoption of instruments, as may be appropriate, for ASEAN trade expansion."[106]

The political and normative agenda of region building becomes even more clear when the PTAs are put into context and in relation to a larger set of complementary economic and trade initiatives. Per the Declaration of ASEAN Concord, which identified "broaden[ing] the complementarity of [each member's] respective economies"[107] as a specific aim of ASEAN economic cooperation, these initiatives were designed to encourage specialization through various resource pooling and regional investment schemes—the 1976 ASEAN Industrial Projects (AIP), the 1980 ASEAN Industrial Complementation Scheme (AIC), the 1980 ASEAN Industrial Joint Ventures (AIJV), as well as the ASEAN Brand-to-Brand Complementation Scheme (BBC). While some of these projects proved to be more contentious than even the PTAs, they all pointed to a state-led regional integration process with explicit political-security underpinnings.

The explicit objective of resilience helps to explain not only why states pursued intra-ASEAN trade liberalization in the face of such divergent interests and preferences but also the structure and evolution of the PTAs. Because the overriding priority is regional unity and the maintenance of regional relations (not economic gains), the process by which states negotiated trade liberalization was incremental and consensus driven, much as in the political-security examples above. In addition, as noted above, resilience concerns contained competing normative pressures: While economic cooperation could facilitate closer relations through integration, *premature* economic cooperation could also *jeopardize* regional relations. Illustrations of the latter view were especially evident in ASEAN's earliest years as in the cases of Singapore and the Philippines, which, in 1970 and 1971, drew on a common rhetoric of resilience to caution against overly ambitious economic schemes that could weaken their still fragile relations. "The danger," as Ferdinand Marcos put it in 1971, "is that ASEAN will attempt too much too soon. Our eagerness to concentrate on regional economic cooperation . . . is understandable. But it is better to make haste slowly to prevent discouraging and costly setbacks."[108]

The centrality of regional resilience to ASEAN is most illustrated by the fact that the fragility of relations and the dangers of fragmentation became poignant arguments for *both* action *and* caution on the economic front. Singapore offers one interesting case of a state that drew on the same resilience argument to make the case both for and against intra-ASEAN liberalization. Whereas in 1969 (and 1970 and 1971) Rajaratnam argued, "I for one feel reassured that ASEAN has not attempted any Great Leap Forward . . . because I know that such an attempt, at this juncture of ASEAN's history, would also prove to be the Last Leap Forward,"[109] in 1974 he argued not only that ASEAN was ready for the next step but that its future viability depended on its moving into a "new and more difficult phase of regional cooperation."[110]

Hence, regional resilience became a call to action, as well as a call for restraint. For those arguing for action, the danger was not doing enough and not proving to members ASEAN's relevance to critical questions of economic and political security, the result being defection and the end to regional unity. For those arguing restraint, the danger lay in pushing members too fast such that national stability and regional relations would be jeopardized. As above, protecting ASEAN—as an expression of regional resilience—also became a compelling argument in itself.

Debates about institutional development and especially the role of the economic ministers in the ASEAN process similarly illustrated the competing normative pressures exerted by regional resilience ideas. Though the Concord Declaration's creation of the AEMM expressed a new seriousness of purpose toward economic cooperation, debates also served to make clear that economic cooperation was not to overshadow or undermine their larger resilience goals. In one debate, for example, about whether the AEMM should have primary and sole responsibility for ASEAN's economic dialogues with third parties, foreign ministers countered that such an arrangement would be contrary to the organizational principles of the 1967 Bangkok Declaration and ASEAN's political raison d'être. As the argument went, foreign ministers should remain in charge as a necessary check on imprudent economic ministers whose overly ambitious proposals could put at risk ASEAN's unity, resilience, and existence. And indeed, in reaffirming the special role of the foreign ministers, ASEAN leaders explicitly noted the continued sensitivity of relations and reiterated ASEAN's primary political priorities of good neighborliness, resilience, and unity. (At the Bali summit, only Lee Kuan Yew in fact came out in favor of creating a direct link between the AEMM and the ASEAN Secretariat.)

In short, the message was clear: Economic cooperation was important but insofar as it served regional unity. As Luhilima explains, "Such coordination [by foreign ministers] is primarily meant to oversee and nullify the unpermissable [sic] political and diplomatic implications in all ASEAN activities."[111] ASEAN thus remained, first and foremost, a political exercise, even as it expanded its focus to economic cooperation. Institutionally, as a result, the AMM continued to be the final voice on ASEAN activities and architect of ASEAN guidelines, while the AEMM remained only a semi-independent decision-making body, subordinate to the AMM. This hierarchy was then reaffirmed at their next summit in Kuala Lumpur. Similarly, the fact that the 1977 PTA agreement was signed by ASEAN's foreign (not economic) ministers was not a coincidence but rather a pointed gesture aimed at underscoring the point that economics served a larger political purpose.

Last but not least, debates both revealed and clarified the relationship between nation and region and between national and regional resilience. On the one hand, the relationship between national and regional resilience can be described as mutually supporting—national resilience could not be achieved without stable and peaceful regional relations; regional resilience could not be achieved without national development and stability. On the other hand, debates also made clear that that the national, not regional, project had primacy as a "primary precondition" of the latter.[112] As various ASEAN elites argued, "The immediate concern of South-East Asian countries is not regionalism but how long the component parts of South-East Asia can survive . . . as new nation states created less than two decades ago."[113] Nationalism had to come first.[114]

By extension, regionalism thus had a *responsibility* not to jeopardize the national project—not to risk national stability by pushing leaders and their domestic constituencies further than they felt able to go. In the interest of regional resilience, to quote Singapore's foreign minister in 1972:

> The members of ASEAN have therefore a two-fold duty. One, they have the duty to strengthen their national economies, because strong national economies will make for a strong Association from which all can benefit. . . . Conversely, an Association is only as strong as its weakest member. Therefore, the members of the Association have the duty to see to it that its joint efforts do not act to the detriment of individual members.[115]

In short, the normative obligations contained in resilience arguments point to the ways that regional resilience legitimates and is subordinate to national priorities. In practice, what this meant was that the different national resilience concerns of each individual member tended to trump any interest in a more coordinated regionalism. This is why, for example, the PTAs allowed exclusion lists for "sensitive products." In other words, no state should have to liberalize sectors it deems central to its national development or political integrity.

Ultimately, this concern about the nation-building processes as a primary foundation of regional resilience is also at the root of ASEAN's loose and consensus-driven regionalism—a regionalism that will not impose a majority view on a minority member for fear of jeopardizing that state's national foundations. This is why, then, that Indonesia—as the ASEAN state most sensitive about its sociopolitical integrity and insecure about its own national resilience—had a disproportionate influence on intra-ASEAN trade liberalization efforts.[116] Accommodations made to Indonesia were a big reason why a more ambitious proposal, involving across-the-board tariff cuts as advocated by Singapore and the Philippines,[117] gave way to the tedious "product-by-product" approach toward trade liberalization described above.

The fact that nationalism framed and bound understandings of regionalism had important effects, then, on not only the substance of ASEAN economic cooperation but also its form and process. Such understandings of regionalism not only made it difficult to compel members to adopt or comply with more ambitious liberalization agendas, but also meant that efforts to do so might even be considered illegitimate if they were perceived to undermine the nation-building process. Thus, it is no surprise that from the beginning the 1977 PTA was a voluntary system or that it included exclusion lists, as well as an exit clause that allowed members to suspend tariff cuts if members perceived their local industries or foreign reserves to be in jeopardy. The PTA system also allowed for a graduated level of commitment, whereby members could choose to begin with unilateral concessions and bilateral negotiations that would later be "multilateralised."[118] This "matrix approach" that incorporated less-than-regional activities became one characteristic of ASEAN regionalism. As in states' early efforts in the political-security realm, cooperation and regionalism were thus once again defined broadly to include different kinds of activity: unilateral and bilateral, as well as multilateral.

Conclusion

In detailing ASEAN's early debates on ZOPFAN, Vietnam, and ASEAN's early PTAs, this chapter has highlighted key material–ideational interactions in the production of both specific ASEAN initiatives and in the shaping of ASEAN's evolution its first decade. As in its founding, ASEAN states remained sensitive to global shifts, which became sources of uncertainty and impetuses to reassessment of existing relations. In this context of uncertainty, both ideas and actors played critical mediating roles in framing problems and drawing critical connections between material and ideational claims. In the face of competing interests and preferences, various elites and arguments drew on what had become ASEAN's founding narrative about the relationship between division, intervention, and insecurity. It is through such efforts—whereby regionalist arguments are framed in terms of self-determination, nationalist development, and the relationship between national and regional security—that we get ASEAN regionalism and specific ASEAN initiatives (ZOPFAN, TAC, the PTAs) as appropriate and logical responses to the events and challenges faced by ASEAN states between 1967 and 1977.

In addition, this chapter's discussion of key social processes—argument, consensus-seeking dialogue, and social reinforcement—illuminates a larger process of becoming "ASEAN." As detailed above, much remained unclear about what exactly ASEAN states could and should expect of one another and of their new organization. Continued dialogue was thus critical to clarifying key ideas, concepts, and normative obligations. Similarly, the ongoing process of consensus seeking served to affirm and reaffirm a founding argument about regional resilience.

The debates highlighted in this chapter were thus as much about clarifying and expanding consensus on the nature and scope of ASEAN cooperation as they were about the specific initiatives. Debates about ZOPFAN served to clarify ASEAN ideas about self-determination and their relations with greater powers. Debates about Vietnam give shape to ASEAN's inclusive diplomacy but also reveal the limits of inclusion and the tensions between resilience as *ASEAN* versus resilience as *Southeast Asia*. Lastly, debates about intra-ASEAN trade liberalization give further clarification to the nation–region relationship.

Each debate further serves to underscore the importance of looking at the *content* of ideas. Expanding our vision beyond just what ideas are called, looking at the content of ideas permits us to *see* different kinds of changes; for example, smaller negotiations about what an idea or norm *means*. The content of ideas is also critical to understanding the specific effects that ideas have. For example, as this chapter has shown, regional unity became an important norm in ASEAN; but, without understanding its regional resilience premise, one could easily be led astray as to both its effect and strength.

Also highlighted is a complex process of social reinforcement. Ideas and relationships are reinforced through both rhetoric and practice. Elites in this early period of ASEAN were constantly calling on ASEAN's founding narrative and ideas about regional resilience to remind others of their common cause. Through repetitive argument, ideas became more familiar and more ingrained. But reinforcement of ideas was not just through repetitive argument; it was also through repetitive actions. Through their common work on specific initiatives in the 1970s, ASEAN states demonstrated to one another an important commitment to the process and their ability to achieve not just greater consensus but also greater stability and security in relations. And this too would help reinforce particular ideas and their validity within ASEAN.

In this vein, this is again why Vietnam's intervention into Cambodia was at one and the same time a critical test of ASEAN unity and an ASEAN region-building experience. Divergent preferences and perceptions, combined with unilateral actions, all proved highly fragmenting to a still-nascent ASEAN. Yet, it was also clearly important to states that they try to reconcile different and divergent positions and policies. Such efforts to make coherent different positions clearly showed a concern— even if post hoc—that spoke to the normative concerns of regional unity. Here, too, internal negotiations would create opportunities to clarify what ASEAN was about, as well as new processes that would be part of ASEAN.

External recognition of ASEAN's efforts vis-à-vis Vietnam and ASEAN's ability to survive the significant trials involved in reconciling divergent positions would in the end also affirm for members ASEAN as an entity.

Most of all, this chapter has shown how the concern for regional unity contained in regional resilience exerts different, often contrary, normative pressures on ASEAN's member states. On the one hand, regional resilience demands regional unity efforts—ZOPFAN, regional inclusion, economic integration, a "collective" stance on Vietnam—to address the divisions that are at the understood root of Southeast Asian insecurities. It is also and again what drives a continued consensus-seeking process—ZOPFAN's SOC process or the belabored PTAs process, for examples—in the interest of regional integration despite clear divergences and differences on the part of ASEAN's member states. Again, regional resilience imposes on states a normative obligation to work with one another toward greater agreement and mutual understanding even when (and perhaps precisely because) interests are most divergent. On the other hand, because regional resilience is defined in terms of national resilience and also premised on the fragility of intraregional relations, ASEAN elites are also compelled not to push regional integration efforts in such a way that would jeopardize ongoing national projects or an already fragile regional unity. Together, these competing pressures produce a regionalism that is consensus seeking and consensus driven, as opposed to a majority-rules-based process.

This national–regional dynamic thus has direct bearing on what regionalism looks like in ASEAN-Southeast Asia. In addition to consensus seeking, it also provides the basis for a broadly defined regionalism. Again, the overriding political objective is security through unity and resilience. What this means is that regionalism may be multilateral or bilateral, but also unilateral, as long as efforts all contribute in some way to the greater unity of region and its components or foundational parts. Wanandi's oft-cited characterization of regional resilience captures well exactly this point: "If each member nation [of ASEAN] can accomplish overall national development and overcome internal threats, regional resilience can result much in the same way that a chain derives its overall strength from the strength of its constituent parts."[119] In short, regional resilience enjoins ASEAN members in common cause and as parts of a larger whole, but the nature of resilience is that it can also be achieved mostly through the individual efforts of member-states. By this logic, ASEAN's conception of regionalism may be a collaborative effort but not necessarily a centrally coordinated one.[120]

In the final analysis, few were more cognizant of the differences that divided them than members themselves. ASEAN's member states thus attached particular importance to the collective process. Despite their practical limitations, each of the initiatives discussed in this chapter offered states a way to affirm the regional idea and representations of ASEAN as "one" even when differences remain unresolved. Meanwhile, the consensus-seeking process both allowed states to uphold the unity principle in the face of significant differences and to continue the pursuit for greater unity. Yes, as Alagappa explains, consensus seeking could indeed be long and tedious, but it also reflected an important regard for the collective by ensuring that "the national interests of all member states are taken into consideration, thereby ensuring ASEAN cohesion, a fundamental if unstated objective of ASEAN."[121]

What gave that common activity meaning and what ultimately held these states together were the shared ideas about regional resilience and the importance of regional unity to regional security. The hopes and goals attached to this process by ASEAN elites were as modest as they were ambitious. What they hoped for was not formal integration but instead that members' shared participation in the regional process could create "the development of an ASEAN consciousness"[122] or "habit of mind"[123] that would lead to greater unity and thus security, and ultimately, to quote Suharto, provide "for us the [psychological] incentive to overcome our own difficulties, to rise by our own power and to settle our common problems."[124]

TWO

ASEAN's New Regionalisms

> No one can be certain about the new boundaries created by power shifts, only that the old ones have been eroded. This leads to a necessity for probing, leaving retreat paths open, looking for new ideas, and experimenting.
>
> *Donald Crone 1996: 39*

In Southeast Asia, as elsewhere, the ending of the Cold War had a transformative effect on the regional landscape. For ASEAN states, it was perhaps most of all a chance to end the strategic division between communist and noncommunist Southeast Asia and to achieve its long-stated goal of "one Southeast Asia"—unified, stable, and free from intervention. Indeed, the 1990s was a decade marked by heightened diplomatic exchanges, trade linkages, and political dialogue between the ASEAN states (now six strong with Brunei's admission in 1984) and the states of Cambodia, Laos, Vietnam, and Myanmar (the CLMV states). Those exchanges would help lay the groundwork for those states' membership into ASEAN. The decade also saw tremendous economic growth and political stability, as well as unprecedented initiative and regional cooperation into new and expanded areas on the part of ASEAN states. In sum, the 1990s found the regional project nearly complete: National development seemed assured; regional relations were stable; and the process of incorporating Southeast Asia's remaining members into ASEAN seemed well under way.

At the same time, changes associated with the ending of the Cold War also served as potent reminders that as much as the Cold War had divided Southeast Asia, it had also insulated Southeast Asia as a region in key ways. Uncertainties focused especially on a changing United States, China, and Japan in post–Cold War Asia, which renewed questions about Southeast Asia's integrity as a region, major power roles, and their own ability and agency in defining a changing regional order. Consequently, as much as the decade of the 1990s was a period of regional consolidation, it was also a time of reflection and new thinking about regionalism for ASEAN states. That new thinking included not only a reevaluation of ASEAN but also new interest in alternative arrangements, defined along different regional lines and based on different ideas of regionalism. Now-established ASEAN ideas of region faced particular challenges from the reemergence of Southeast Asia's continental-insular divide, as well as "East Asia" and the "Asia Pacific"—two conceptions of region that differed from ASEAN-Southeast Asia in substance as much as geographic scope.

The following chapters continue to trace the intra-ASEAN dialogue on regionalism, with attention to post–Cold War debates about region and regionalism. Taken together, chapters draw attention to an evolving and widening region whose geographic and political boundaries are highly contested, as well as ASEAN's efforts to adapt and to redefine its role for a wider, more complex regional context. Each of these chapters also highlights the ways that ideas about regional resilience and self-determination still provide important ideological prisms, rhetorical frames, and paths to action. Beginning first with a chapter on ASEAN expansion, chapters then direct the focus to the unprecedented growth in regionalist activities beyond Southeast Asia: Asia-Pacific Economic Cooperation (APEC), the ASEAN Regional Forum (ARF), and the ASEAN Plus Three (APT) framework. Together, these chapters draw attention to the continued intersection between regional and global systems and how old and new ideas continue to come together to produce changing political and regional geographies.

4

The Politics and Rhetoric of "One Southeast Asia"

> When [ASEAN becomes 10], the vision of our founding fathers . . .
> will have been realized. Then we will have succeeded in redressing
> five dark centuries during which a fragmented Southeast Asia all
> too often served as the cockpit of internecine strife and proxy wars,
> abetted and manipulated by extra-regional powers.
>
> *Ali Alatas,*
> *Minister of Foreign Affairs, Indonesia[1]*

> Our leaders said that politically it is good for us to be united as
> one family. Never mind if economic levels are different compared
> to the richer countries . . . We are more driven by sentiment, by
> politics, than by logic and economics.
>
> *Tommy Koh,*
> *Ambassador to the United States, Singapore[2]*

On April 30, 1999, Cambodia became ASEAN's tenth member. Following
the admissions of Vietnam (1995), Laos (1997), and Myanmar (1997), ASEAN
elites hailed Cambodia's admission as completing the "dream" of "One
Southeast Asia." Despite the historical inevitability suggested by the ASEAN
rhetoric, however, the expansion process was in fact not free of conflict or
debate. As in the mid-1970s, debates revealed dual concerns about the readiness and willingness of prospective members to join and support the ASEAN
process, on the one hand, and the corporate resilience of existing members, on the other. In addition to lingering divisions and suspicions about
Vietnam, Myanmar—as a challenge to ASEAN's external legitimacy vis-à-
vis external actors, its now-established practices and mindsets, and ultimately
ASEAN's corporate resilience—became a particularly contentious point
of intra-ASEAN debate. Debates about expansion furthermore took place
at a time when ASEAN was facing new existential challenges: Vietnam's
withdrawal from Cambodia, though welcomed, raised new questions about
ASEAN's ability to remain relevant to members "after Cambodia"—a point
underscored by individual members' attraction to other regional ideas. The
ending of the Cold War brought with it a more competitive global economy

and new pressures on ASEAN's founding members to reconsider a more coordinated regionalism. The advent of the Asian financial crisis in 1997 then compounded all existing concerns, in addition to weakening the ability of both domestic and regional arrangements to support new members and new membership. Given these old and emergent divisions, many wondered if ASEAN could withstand the challenges of the added diversity that new membership would bring. In these circumstances, the advantages, indeed prudence, of expanded membership were far from clear.[3]

What explains ASEAN's decisions to incorporate Vietnam and especially Cambodia, Laos, and Myanmar in the face of such concerns? Popular accounts characterized the process as a balance of power response to China—ASEAN's shift "from balancing North Vietnam to balancing China"[4]—and, to be sure, states found much in China about which to be concerned in the 1990s. At minimum, Vietnam's withdrawal from Cambodia, by ending ASEAN's decade-long de facto alignment with China, raised the possibility of renewed hostilities from the past, a possibility given expression by China's heightened activities around the Spratly Islands and South China Sea.[5]

On the other hand, popular accounts are rarely clear about how expansion—a diplomatic and economic, not military, process—responded to China as an emerging security challenge. For one, ASEAN states continued to eschew military cooperation on an ASEAN scale. For another, of prospective members, only Vietnam offered any deterrent value—and even that was questioned by some ASEAN member-states. As late as 1995 (the year Vietnam was admitted), Malaysian defense officials, for example, expressed the view that Vietnam might in fact *detract* from ASEAN security because of China's particular antagonism toward Vietnam. From their perspective, Vietnamese membership seemed more likely to draw ASEAN states into bilateral conflicts they would rather avoid. Even the Spratly Islands, a primary focus of ASEAN concerns in the 1990s, were characterized as being extensions of Sino-Vietnamese conflicts.[6]

Balance-of-power interpretations similarly often correlate Vietnam's admission into ASEAN with the Philippines' discovery of Chinese structures on Mischief Reef, both of which took place in 1995;[7] however, the fact that ASEAN ministers had already arrived at an informal understanding as to Vietnam's date of admission the previous year suggests that the incident was not defining to the question of Vietnamese membership. Moreover, the fact that Vietnam itself was a competing claimant in the Spratlys dispute and had built garrisons or installations on at least twenty-four islands (the most of any claimant), four of which were part of the same group as Mischief Reef, made Vietnam a less than ideal defender of ASEAN interests on this particular issue.

Lastly, the process of ASEAN–Vietnamese rapprochement was set in motion by Thailand—the ASEAN member with the most cooperative relations with China and with no claim to the Spratly Islands. Not only did Thailand, of ASEAN members, enjoy one of the more cooperative relationships with China (at the time, it was even seeking China's assistance in modernizing its military), but it also played a lead role in persuading other members to engage China in their first official dialogue in the mid-1990s.[8] In short, the expansion process—in its initial impetus (Thailand's policy change), its modes of cooperation (nonmilitary), and the questionable contributions and deterrence value of prospective members—suggests something other than a balance-of-power response to China.

Instead, ASEAN debates during the critical period between 1988 and 1997 reveal a complex set of considerations that involved intramural concerns about regional unity and regional resilience, as much as concerns about extraregional policies. This chapter details the related ways that the "One Southeast Asia" idea as an expression of regional resilience informed and drove the expansion process as a response to those interdependent intramural and extramural challenges. Particular attention is paid to the new and reemergent regional faultlines and challenges to ASEAN's Southeast Asian idea and ideal.

As for China, realists are right: Expansion was very much about China. However, the security challenge posed by China was less military than it was political. Concerns focused especially on the attractiveness of China to mainland Southeast Asian states. It was that attraction that expansion aimed to counter or lessen. Framed in terms of regional resilience, expansion aimed to neutralize openings for foreign influence and domination not only by closing ASEAN ranks but also by offering old and prospective member states a regional path to security. In this sense, ASEAN expansion—like the ASEAN project as a whole—became both an expression of, and the product of, ideas about Southeast Asian agency and self-determination. These ideas would be given additional salience with intensified Western[9] pressure on ASEAN not to admit Myanmar.

New Regional Opportunities and Old Regional Fault Lines

Only twice before had ASEAN seriously deliberated the question of Vietnam's membership—first in 1967 prior to ASEAN's founding and second in the mid-1970s at the end of the Vietnam War. Each of those times correlated with important changes taking place on world and regional stages, but intra-ASEAN differences and concerns about its own corporate resilience combined with Vietnam's disinterest and intervention into Cambodia proved to be insurmountable obstacles. In 1988 developments associated with global changes once again raised the possibility of Vietnamese membership. The steady reduction of Soviet aid to Hanoi over the course of the 1980s helped spur Hanoi's reorientation of domestic and foreign policies, including market reforms and a reconsideration of its relations with ASEAN. These developments seemed to make possible as never before ASEAN's vision of regional order based on regional resilience and unity as articulated in 1967.

Still, ASEAN states' support for Vietnamese membership was neither immediate nor easy. As Chapter 3 detailed, not only had Vietnam's Cambodian intervention challenged ASEAN's norm of nonintervention as contained in TAC, but its policies had also proved extremely divisive to ASEAN—to some, deliberately so, pitting hard-line Thailand and Singapore against a more accommodating Indonesia and Malaysia. Wrote Wanandi in 1985, "There is the impression [in ASEAN] that rather than trying to build the kind of confidence which would enhance Vietnam-ASEAN relations, Hanoi has employed the tactics of splitting ASEAN or playing ASEAN against other countries . . . "[10] The "threat" posed by Vietnam was again not just of a traditional security nature (to Thailand) but also a deliberate attack on ASEAN unity and ASEAN as an organization.

Anti-Chinese policies in Vietnam, which drove an exodus of ethnic Chinese toward ASEAN shores, added to the perceived attack on ASEAN states, individually and collectively. For ASEAN states, the exodus seemed a deliberate attempt to undermine both ASEAN's corporate resilience and the tenuous ethnic balances underlying the national resilience of individual states. As Rajaratnam bluntly put it in 1979, "each junkload of men, women and children sent to our shores is a bomb to de-stabilize, disrupt, and cause turmoil and dissension in ASEAN states. This is a preliminary invasion to pave the way for the final invasion."[11] By 1986 even those more sympathetic to Vietnam began to tire in the face of Vietnam's policies, its attacks on refugee camps across the Thai border, its intensified campaign in Cambodia between 1984 and 1985, and the steady stream of refugees hitting ASEAN shores.[12] Hanoi's continued refusals to work with ASEAN, including its outright rejection of international and Indonesian efforts to bring resolution to the conflict, tested the patience of every member and prompted ASEAN in 1984 to issue what one senior official described as ASEAN's "strongest, harshest, and most strident" communiqué since 1967.[13]

Perhaps not surprisingly, then, ASEAN states responded cautiously to Vietnam's new plan of economic reform and national reconstruction (doi moi), announced in December 1986. ASEAN's 1987 joint communiqué, for example, continued to note Vietnam's continued presence in Cambodia and ASEAN's particular concerns about Vietnam's continued incursions into Thai territory. At the meeting, Thai Foreign Minister Siddhi Savetsila acknowledged Vietnam's stated reorientation of priorities; however, as he put it, Vietnam's intentions would remain "dubious" as long as Vietnamese policy continued to be "one that sows discord and antagonism in relations with Vietnam's neighbors."[14]

Not until two years later did ASEAN–Vietnamese relations experience a real turning point, but impetus came from an unexpected source: Thailand. In 1988 Thailand's new Prime Minister Chatichai Choonhaven unexpectedly reversed Thailand's position of ten years. After a decade of steering ASEAN toward its more hawkish stance against Vietnam, Chatichai unilaterally announced that Thailand would make "rapprochement with Vietnam" one of its "top priorities" in a larger effort to prioritize "economics" over "politics" in foreign policy.[15] Said Chatichai in his now oft-quoted speech to Bangkok's Foreign Correspondents Club in December 1988, "Indochina must be transformed from a war zone to a peace zone, linked with Southeast Asia through trade ties, investment and modern communications."[16] That same month, Chatichai also announced a trade visit to Vietnamese-supported Laos and a tentative trip to Hanoi for the following year[17]—an announcement that was followed by a controversial visit to Bangkok by Cambodia's Vietnam-backed leader, Hun Sen, a visit made more significant by the fact that it was Thailand's first recognition of the regime since Vietnam's 1978 intervention.

Bangkok's radical foreign policy change partly came from a desire to take early advantage of the economic opportunities associated with Vietnam's doi moi policies; but, even more, it reflected the different priorities of Thailand's first civilian government after a long period of military rule. Also factoring large was the personal style of Chatichai, who failed to consult fellow ASEAN members and even his own foreign ministry[18] and who acted against the interests and wishes of the Thai military (which would overthrow Chatichai in 1991).

Chatichai's action was viewed by others at minimum as opportunistic and premature and more seriously as an internal challenge to ASEAN's united front. Thailand's sudden about-face especially upset Indonesia and Malaysia that had supported Thailand's hard-line position in the Cambodian conflict despite reservations and their own preferences. Moreover, in acting ahead of ASEAN, Thailand was also viewed to have usurped Indonesia's designated role as ASEAN's interlocutor with Vietnam, part of the original ASEAN compromise that reconciled Indonesian and Thai positions. Though Chatichai went to Indonesia in January 1989 reportedly to consult Suharto about the changes in Thai policy, the "snap" visit took place only a day before the scheduled Hun Sen visit, only after much publicity, and was quickly ended so that Chatichai could be back in Bangkok in time to receive Hun Sen.[19]

Indeed, Indonesia was most disturbed by Thai actions. As noted in the last chapter, Indonesia had modified its own position to accommodate Thai security interests and understood its own modification as having been a sacrifice made for ASEAN. Thai actions were thus understood to be an affront not just to Indonesia but to ASEAN as a whole and its collective enterprise. Mochtar summed up Indonesian sentiments in a 1990 article: "ASEAN cohesion and political solidarity, slowly built up over a decade since the end of 1978, was dealt a rude blow by Thailand's turn around on the Cambodian question in 1988. Prime Minister Chatichai's gyrations since then have seriously undermined ASEAN credibility."[20]

Indeed, Chatichai's actions had potentially serious implications for ASEAN and its founding ideas. Drawing on "old" nationalist ideas about Thailand's role in mainland Southeast Asia, Chatichai's new foreign policy orientation drew attention to the latent fault line between continental and island Southeast Asia, a fault line that had mostly been obscured by Cold War ideological divisions. As global and regional Cold War conflicts came to an end, the barriers that had prevented Thailand from more extensive (and historical) interactions with its immediate neighbors also began to break down. And for those like Chatichai, such developments created a historic opportunity to reassert a leadership role in mainland Southeast Asia.

Ideas about Thailand as being uniquely positioned to lead and assist in Indochina's transformation were given particular expression through various references to *Suwannaphume*—in essence, a Greater Thailand or Greater Thai Union made up of Tai-speaking peoples from Myanmar, southern China, and Indochina. On Armed Forces Day, January 25, 1989, General Chavalit, head of the Thai army, outlined the role envisioned for the Thai military: "The Thai forces will strive to create a durable peace in order to make it possible for the development of economic cooperation, solidarity, and prosperity in this *Suwannaphume*, with Thailand at its centre."[21]

Such nationalist conceptions were thus a reminder that Thailand's historic ties and orientation had been with continental, not insular, Southeast Asia. As noted in Chapter 2, Thailand was different from ASEAN's other founding members. As the only member not directly involved in the politics of confrontation and as the only continental state in ASEAN, its reasons for joining had been much more tied to its changing U.S. relations than any need for regional reconciliation. Thailand was also not like Singapore, whose commitment had also been periodically questioned. Where geography and history tied Singapore to Malaysia and Indonesia such that Singapore could not ignore its ASEAN relations for long,[22] Thailand's connections to the rest of ASEAN tended to be less apparent. Without the overlapping security vulnerabilities (external and internal) that tied Indonesia, Malaysia, and Singapore for good and for ill,[23] Thai politicians—as one Thai track 2 participant explained— tended to be more "forgetful" when it came to ASEAN. Nor were efforts to remind politicians about ASEAN always welcome—as one acrimonious exchange about expanded membership in the mid-1990s illustrated—even if Thai representatives ultimately recognized the need to reframe policies to account for ASEAN.[24]

Thailand's disregard for the accommodations made for it during the Cambodian conflict, as well as the larger implications of Thai policy for the carefully constructed compromise made in the interest of ASEAN unity, thus "caused apprehension among ASEAN governments" about Thailand's commitment to ASEAN, whose focus and preoccupations tended to revolve more around its island states.[25] In comments made in 1990, Mochtar expressed exactly these concerns: "[Chatichai's] pronouncements on *Suwannaphume* as a Thai sphere of influence encompassing Burma in the west and Vietnam in the east reveal Thailand's possible ambitions or perceptions of its role in Southeast Asia, casting doubt on Thailand's commitment to ASEAN. . . ."[26]

Criticisms appeared to have some effect. Though Chatichai continued to emphasize Thailand's leading role in rebuilding Indochina, there were by 1990 also more references to ASEAN as a framework. Said Chatichai in 1990, for example, "For underlying ASEAN cooperation are principles of order which, if extended to the rest of Southeast Asia, would make the region truly peaceful and its nations one."[27] Greater consideration of ASEAN continued under Anand Panyarachun, who served as Thailand's interim prime minister following Chatichai's ouster by the Thai military in February 1991. Under Anand, references to *Suwannaphume* gave way to characterizations of Thailand being the "gateway to Indochina" and bridge between mainland and maritime Southeast Asia toward the realization of ASEAN's envisioned "united community of Southeast Asian states."[28]

Nevertheless, as ASEAN moved into the 1990s, developments continued to draw attention to the mainland–insular divide. Eased restrictions on the export of Thai currency to neighboring countries led to talk of a "baht economic zone" made up of Thailand and Indochinese states. Similarly, the 1992 creation of the Greater Mekong Subregion (GMS) with support from the Asian Development Bank gave formal expression to the functional and economic division between mainland and insular Southeast Asia. Mekong developments were such that Deputy Prime Minister Suphachai Phanitchaphak felt compelled in 1994 to assure his fellow ASEAN members that his country's enthusiasm for the GMS would not dilute its role in ASEAN. Like Anand and Chatichai earlier, Suphachai assured his neighbors by referencing ASEAN's larger goal of regional unity and integration and by emphasizing how Mekong projects would ease the integration of CLMV states into ASEAN.[29]

In short, while regional and global developments created new possibilities for new membership, they also raised questions about relations among existing members, especially Thailand's commitment to ASEAN. As late as 1995 (the year Vietnam became an ASEAN member), Thailand's then-deputy foreign minister Sukhumbhand Paribatra acknowledged, "There is an underlying tension, and it revolves around the role of Thailand. Many of our maritime friends are not sure where they stand with us."[30]

Chasing the Vietnamese Tiger

Thailand's abandonment of its hard-line position also introduced other challenges. By freeing other members to reassess their own positions on Vietnam, Thailand's policy change opened the door for Vietnamese membership, but it also had the effect of sparking intra-ASEAN economic competition vis-à-vis Vietnam—a competition that only fed concerns about ASEAN's post-Cambodia coherence. Not wanting to be left out, Malaysia, the Philippines, and even Indonesia each began to actively pursue trade and investment opportunities in Vietnam.[31]

Not all looked upon this economic activity with approval. Singapore, in particular, criticized others for (1) jeopardizing ASEAN's objectives as regarded the Cambodian conflict and (2) playing into Vietnam's hands and desire to see ASEAN fragmented and undermined. As Lee Kuan Yew put it in 1989, "You can't have a marketplace while battles are on."[32] While Singapore's own trade with Vietnam led to charges that it was operating under a double standard, Lee distinguished trade from investment that "bring[s] in capital and machinery . . . [and gives] them the implements to earn money to prolong the war."[33] Singapore further noted that because ASEAN's key bargaining strengths lay in Vietnam's need for developmental assistance and access to markets, members' rush to invest in Indochina would only make Vietnam less willing to compromise on areas of ASEAN concern. As Rajaratnam succinctly put it in one 1989 essay, "One of the puzzling aspects of current ASEAN diplomacy is why [ASEAN] should want to throw away the winning card it now holds?"[34]

In fact, Rajaratnam, newly retired from public life, was most blunt in his expressions of distrust toward Vietnam. Characterizing Vietnam's promises to withdraw from Cambodia as "elastic declaration[s] . . . of intent,"[35] he similarly described Vietnam's participation in the Jakarta Informal Meetings (JIM) as Vietnam's "attempt to get from ASEAN what [it] could not get from the United Nations, [namely,] an endorsement of Vietnamese hegemony over Indochina."[36] As for the so-called economic opportunities to be had in Vietnam, Rajaratnam accused Vietnam of once again resorting to divide and rule tactics—in this case, weakening ASEAN unity by mesmerizing its members with visions of an Indochinese "El Dorado" and "Aladdin's cave." Reminding his fellow members of what was really at stake, Rajaratnam got straight to the point: "It would be a pity . . . were ASEAN solidarity to be bartered away for the sake of a few beads and trinkets dangled before it by a smiling tiger . . . "[37] In fact, as late as December 1990, one year after Vietnam had fulfilled its promise to withdraw from Cambodia, Rajaratnam continued to express doubt about the sincerity of Vietnamese motives. Rajaratnam argued, "A nation which has astutely milked the Chinese and the Soviets for 30 years will more likely view eager ASEAN businessmen as fat cows to be milked by them."[38]

Meanwhile, ASEAN members were not the only ones drawn to Vietnam's new economy. As early as 1988, Japan and Australia had already begun to make economic inroads into Vietnam. Between 1988 and 1990 Japan poured 70 million dollars of investment into Vietnam, while Australia, one of the few countries to maintain diplomatic and trade relations with Vietnam during the Cambodian conflict, had become one of Vietnam's most important economic partners.[39] Neither were Japan and Australia the only ones to express interest. According to Hanoi, the period between December 1987 and January 1989 saw over 1,000 trade visits to Vietnam and thirty-five joint projects signed in response to a new investment code.[40] Interest only heightened with Vietnam's promised withdrawal from Cambodia in September 1989, the World Bank's 1990 characterization of Vietnam as Asia's next economic tiger and "another Korea in the making,"[41] and the occasional rumors of U.S.–Vietnamese normalization.

While richer powers were expected to play a role in Indochina, such outside interest nevertheless invoked a sense of entitlement on the part of some ASEAN members. Like Thailand, which viewed itself playing a leading role by virtue of history and proximity, ASEAN states similarly viewed themselves playing a prerogative role in the reconstruction of Indochina by virtue of their Southeast Asian status and particular leadership and interest in the Cambodian conflict. Faced with such external competition, many consequently began to intensify their own economic engagement of Indochina.[42] As one Singapore-based diplomat explained in 1988, "It would be wise for businessmen in the region to get their foot in before the big boys from corporate America start coming."[43]

As for how such activities might affect ASEAN's political rapprochement with Vietnam, statements from officials and top leaders like Malaysian Prime Minister Mahathir made clear that politics should not stand in the way of trade and economic relations with Indochina. In an April 1991 speech, for example, Mahathir acknowledged the still ongoing efforts to "hammer out the acceptable modalities and most appropriate mechanisms" in Cambodia and vis-à-vis Vietnam only to conclude the primacy of economics. Adopting Chatichai's "battlefields to marketplaces" rhetoric, in fact, Mahathir instructed the business community to go forth and prosper: "[T]he Government of Malaysia encourages the fullest private sector participation in the economies of the non-ASEAN states of Southeast Asia. Southeast Asia is no longer a battleground. Let us proceed as fast as we possibly can to turn it into one prosperous marketplace."[44]

Debating ASEAN Expansion: More Divisions Than Solutions?

While Thai policy precipitated much of ASEAN states' initial reevaluation of Vietnam, the signing of the 1991 Cambodian peace agreement officially opened the door for an explicit discussion on new ASEAN membership. The activities of individual members, however, gave additional urgency to the question. Adding to the above concerns were also signs that the activities of individual states were harming ASEAN's collective image in countries like Laos.[45]

ASEAN senior officials took up these concerns in 1991 and 1992 in preparation of a major summit in Singapore. In the face of intramural and extramural challenges, the process of extending membership—while consistent with ASEAN's stated interest in "One Southeast Asia"—also emerged as a process that could serve a number of purposes: It could provide an umbrella framework for various activities of ASEAN's individual members, it could put a less self-interested face on individual activities, and it could help ensure, even privilege, ASEAN's role in Indochina in the face of extra-regional competition. In this sense, expansion became as much about bringing ASEAN into Indochina as bringing Indochina into ASEAN.

In discussions preceding the 1992 summit, however, senior officials decided that neither CLMV states nor ASEAN was ready for new membership and that expansion was thus best postponed. Instead, they advised that ASEAN consider extending the TAC to Cambodia, Laos, and Vietnam as an intermediate measure.[46] Though short of formal membership, extending TAC would at least signal ASEAN's intent to include these states at a later date[47] and at the same time moderate some of the tensions caused by the opportunism of existing ASEAN members. By putting a collective overlay on activities, members' activities might be made a little less zero sum and mitigate some of the potentially harmful effects of intra-ASEAN competition on both old and new relationships.

Nevertheless, the decision to delay membership to Vietnam and Laos in 1991 and 1992 was indicative of important concerns. As in previous debates in the 1970s, questions about prospective members were rivaled only by questions about ASEAN's existing corporate unity and ability to withstand the additional diversity and pressures of new membership.[48] The larger aim of "One Southeast Asia" thus had to be weighed against concerns about how new membership would affect the unity and efficacy of existing ASEAN, including its ability to respond to intensified post–Cold War economic and security challenges. Consensus had already been difficult to achieve among five and six members; increasing the group to eight or ten would only make it more so. Especially given already heightened concerns about post-Cambodia unity among existing ASEAN members, the addition of new members—states whose developmental and ideological perspectives were markedly different from the existing ASEAN six—seemed almost certain to limit ASEAN's ability to project unity and achieve agreement. Malaysian Foreign Minister Abdullah Badawi voiced the views of many at the time, when he said that expansion is a concern for "a grouping that operates on consensus and [therefore] can only progress as fast as its slowest member."[49] Such concerns factored large in the decision to postpone Vietnam's membership in 1992.

A related concern in 1992 was how expansion would affect efforts to create an ASEAN Free Trade Area (AFTA). As will be discussed in more detail in the next chapters, the decision to undertake AFTA in 1992 was a major milestone in terms of ASEAN economic cooperation, with members placing great emphasis on AFTA as the primary mechanism by which to ensure ASEAN's post–Cold War and post-Cambodia organizational relevance and economic competitiveness. Having taken their great leap forward into intra-ASEAN trade liberalization, members had concerns that the introduction of less-developed members would complicate an already difficult process.[50] Arriving at the original common effective preferential tariff (CEPT) mechanism had been difficult for the ASEAN-6, which had already been forced to delay AFTA's launch date from 1993 to 1994 due to administrative and technological problems. If founding members found AFTA's requirements difficult, prospective new members would only find them more so due to their lower levels of development and the fact that they had only just begun the difficult process of reorienting their economies. Said a Vietnamese official in 1994, for example, "This [AFTA] is a tough question for Vietnam where most industries are government owned."[51]

The challenge was even greater with respect to Cambodia, Laos, and Myanmar (the CLM states), for whom the developmental gap was both greater and harder to bridge. Lacking the dynamism and economic potential of Vietnam, these countries would require greater aid and developmental assistance. Customs and tariff moneys furthermore formed a significant portion of their limited state revenues. There were also significant questions about their bureaucratic and technical capability to implement AFTA's requirements. In short, for the CLM states, meeting AFTA's targets would involve more than a question of political will.

Finally, debates revealed growing concerns about how the significant developmental gap between the ASEAN-6 and the CLMV states would affect ASEAN itself. The concern was that the admission of the CLMV states—significantly less open and less developed—might produce in ASEAN two tiers of states: one richer, one poorer; one faster, one slower. There were concerns that such discrepancies in wealth and development would affect even how fully these states would be able to participate in ASEAN life. With close to 300 ASEAN meetings a year at the time,[52] ASEAN membership was no small burden for states with limited material and human resources. For Vietnam, Cambodia, and Laos, the lack of

English-speaking officials would only further hinder their full participation in ASEAN, where English is the working language.

A related but different concern regarded the effect of new membership on ASEAN's principles and norms. While founding members understood that CLMV states were motivated mostly by economic imperatives, the question was whether the CLMV states would respect ASEAN enough not to jeopardize or unnecessarily strain ASEAN's carefully constructed unity. Existing members themselves might not always remember to respect ASEAN but, as illustrated above, there was also enough shared agreement about regional resilience and thus the importance of ASEAN that members could be counted on (even if belatedly and reluctantly) to exercise self-restraint. The question, however, was whether the same could be said about the CLMV states, states that had not taken part in the original founding dialogue and that had not shared the defining and socializing difficulties of ASEAN's early years. Would these states appreciate the role, value, and significance of regional organization in the same ways that founding members did? Would they understand ASEAN's security imperative of regional unity and resilience?

On this point, specific debates also pointed to an awareness that ASEAN's leverage over prospective new members might be limited, especially once new members were admitted. Compared to the European Union and the EU expansion process, for example, the ASEAN 6 (though more economically advanced than the CLMV states) were not so advantaged (in their control over material resources or global legitimacy) in comparison to prospective members to assure conformance to ASEAN norms in the way that the EU did. Thus, for ASEAN states, the admission of new members was far from being a low-risk or "low-cost" approach the way it has been argued in the case of the EU.[53] Especially at a time when ASEAN's future relevance seemed increasingly uncertain, existing intra-ASEAN relations themselves questioned, and future directions debated, the wisdom of admitting new states was far from clear.

Out with the Old, In with the New?

As one way to structure ASEAN's interactions with the CLMV states, elites briefly considered creating a completely new organization. This debate mirrored some of the debates in 1967, when states debated the merits of ASA versus the creation of a new organization. In other words, just as regional organization had to be created anew to accommodate Indonesia in 1967, some believed that the same would have to be done for Vietnam if they were to create a regional order that was accepted by all as truly representative of "Southeast Asian states."[54]

This option appears not to have been debated very long or seriously, however. Practically, ASEAN elites acknowledged that the difficulties involved in creating a new organization were likely to be tremendous. It had been hard enough for the five original members in 1967 to arrive at the minimalist declaration that established ASEAN; there was no guarantee that Southeast Asia's ten states would be able to agree on a new framework. Rajaratnam, a veteran of that original process, made this point in 1989, "The fortuitous combination of circumstances and compulsions that in 1967 persuaded five nations that their survival in a post-Vietnam Southeast Asia required collective endeavors, can never be repeated should ASEAN wither away for one reason or another."[55]

Militating against new organization was also awareness that ASEAN had gained a special significance among members and in Southeast Asian politics that would be difficult to reproduce. Consequently, debates about replacing ASEAN in the early 1990s produced a different outcome than the ones in 1966 and 1967. More to the point, states' two-decades-plus interaction had solidified and reinforced founding agreements and principles, giving ASEAN a strength and legitimacy that neither ASA nor Maphilindo could claim inside or outside the organization. As a result, ASEAN itself became the referent point against which any new idea—be it a *Suwannaphume* or an organizational replacement for ASEAN—had to be measured against and/or justified.

It was no coincidence, then, that the dangers posed to ASEAN and ASEAN unity provided the gravitational center of expansion debates. The fact that questions about new members and concerns about Thai policy were all framed in terms of their common, collective interest in regional resilience and unity (as opposed to individualized interests and offenses) and the fact that Thailand's response was, in turn, to reframe its Indochina activities in more ASEAN-inclusive terms all spoke to an important acknowledgment of the cultural and legitimating capital associated with ASEAN ideas. Notably, also, in expansion debates—compared to previous debates on trade liberalization and ZOPFAN—elites felt less need to invoke the lessons of past conflicts or reexplain why ASEAN and regional unity was necessary and important; it just *was*. In this sense, what these exchanges illustrate was that in the context of Southeast Asian politics in the 1990s, ASEAN had come to have symbolic value in itself—and this became a powerful reason for keeping ASEAN around. Arguing against the creation of a completely new organization in 1992, Mochtar, for example, wrote, "The lesson we have to learn . . . is that when you modernize, you don't necessarily discard the old; you keep it because it has symbolic and emotional value."[56] In 1995 ASEAN welcomed to its ranks Vietnam as its seventh member.

Debating Myanmar: More Divisions

Until 1994, debates about expansion tended to focus on the Indochinese states, an illustration of how the process was dominated by questions about Vietnam. By contrast, Myanmar, though long considered part of Southeast Asia and thus a potential ASEAN member, received little attention. This began to change beginning in 1989, as concerns about Yangon's relations with Beijing grew and as Western countries intensified their pressure on ASEAN to take a harder line toward Myanmar because of its human rights record. While Myanmar, compared to Laos and Cambodia, was a stronger candidate for ASEAN admission due to the legacies of British colonialism (for example, English-speaking elites and administrative frameworks) and stronger economy (unlike Laos and Cambodia, Myanmar was already a member of the WTO at the time of its admission to ASEAN), debates about Myanmar in fact became among the more contentious in ASEAN.

Initially, debates focused on Yangon's treatment of Muslims in Myanmar. Consequently, between 1989 and 1994 intra-ASEAN differences fell mostly along Muslim and non-Muslim lines, whereby Indonesia, Brunei, and especially Malaysia expressed reservations about Myanmar's membership, while Thailand (Myanmar's primary proponent) and the Philippines were the most in favor. In July 1992 Manila proposed that Myanmar be given observer status in ASEAN, but Kuala Lumpur objected because of the 170,000 Muslims who had fled the Myanmar state of Arakan into Bangladesh earlier that year. Argued Malaysia's then–Foreign Minister Abdullah Badawi, "We believe the time has come for a firm stand to be taken as there seems to be no slackening of attacks on the Muslims by . . . [Myanmar's] military."[57]

In 1993 Thailand followed the Philippines with a proposal to invite Myanmar to the AMM that year, a proposal that Malaysia once again blocked only to have Thailand reintroduce it in 1994. That year, however, extra-regional policies and pressures had begun to affect the debate. Of particular concern were China and its activities in the Andaman Sea (basically access to the Indian Ocean via Myanmar), building of naval bases in Myanmar, and assistance in building Myanmar's infrastructure. Adding another extra-regional dimension to the debate were the intensified pressures on ASEAN by its Western dialogue partners to adopt a harder line toward Myanmar because of its human rights record and especially its policies toward 1991

Nobel Peace Prize recipient Aung San Suu Kyi, whose party won an unrecognized landslide election in 1990. Western partners initially directed their criticism at Thailand for its engagement of Yangon, thus allowing collective ASEAN to avoid addressing the problem on the grounds that it was a "Thai" problem. However, especially after ASEAN's 1992 Post-Ministerial Conference (PMC), where both the United States and European partners pressed ASEAN to take a harder line and where U.S. Undersecretary Robert Zoellick "bitterly criticized" ASEAN's "quiet diplomacy" toward Yangon,[58] it was clear that Yangon had become an "ASEAN" problem.[59]

U.S. and European criticisms and their associated political and economic consequences initially had the most effect on ASEAN's more liberal members, Thailand and the Philippines, both of whom did reconsider their initial positions. However, Western pressure also rankled as all members were themselves coming under new scrutiny for their own human rights practices. Malaysia and Indonesia, whose activities in East Timor were also coming under fire, especially viewed Western criticisms as a disturbing trend. By this view, giving in on Myanmar would only legitimate Western efforts to similarly intervene in their own domestic affairs.[60] The result was a reversal of Indonesian and Malaysian positions. Malaysia was persuaded to conclude that Myanmar had made "encouraging progress" in its treatment of its Muslim population;[61] Indonesia began to press for Myanmar's membership; and Thailand was able to invite Myanmar as its "special guest" at the 1994 AMM held in Bangkok.

In fact, U.S. and European criticisms of ASEAN's approach to Myanmar had the effect of destabilizing, eventually reversing, all initial positions; that is, Myanmar's original supporters became the most cautious, while former opponents became its primary advocates. All agreed that Myanmar was eligible for membership; there was also a strong emotional appeal to completing "ASEAN 10" at ASEAN's upcoming thirtieth anniversary in 1997. However, as Western criticisms heightened, differences among ASEAN states about the timing of new membership also intensified.

The debate over Myanmar also revealed both simmering and newer intra-ASEAN tensions. With more liberal Philippines and recently democratic Thailand on one side of the debate and Malaysia and Indonesia on the other,[62] some saw the emergence of a new liberal–illiberal divide in ASEAN, not to mention further confirmation of ASEAN's post-Cambodia fragmentation.

Divisions made their appearance not just at the official "track one" level but also at unofficial or semiofficial (and generally, more liberal) "track two" discussions, which experienced some sharp exchanges, especially between, on the one hand, Thai and the Philippine representatives and, on the other, Malaysia's as to the appropriateness of "moralizing" about human rights.[63] Still, track-two participants generally believed that Myanmar needed to be included in regional processes. In fact, it was at the annual Southeast Asia Forums, first sponsored by Malaysia's Institute of Strategic and International Studies (ISIS) and later under the broader ASEAN ISIS network, that Myanmar in 1989 first reentered the mainstream of Southeast Asian regional processes and dialogues. Nevertheless, by 1996 the very public criticisms made by ASEAN's dialogue partners also increased concerns that Myanmar would be a liability to ASEAN.

Those expressing reservations included Dewi Fortuna Anwar, an Indonesian analyst and later adviser to Suharto's successor B. J. Habibie. In her October 1996 opinion piece in Singapore's *Straits Times*, she listed "at least four compelling reasons for delaying Yangon's full entry into the grouping for a few years," while allowing Cambodia and Laos in as scheduled. Those reasons were: (1) the more immediate need to facilitate entry of Cambodia and Laos; (2) the lack of unanimity within and among member countries regarding Myanmar's membership; (3) Myanmar's questionable motivations in joining ASEAN; and (4) the possible implications of such membership on ASEAN's extraregional relations.[64] Such arguments expressing concern about the potential danger Myanmar posed to intra- and extra-ASEAN relations militated against the arguments of those who saw expansion as a way to expand ASEAN's clout. The fact that Aung San Suu Kyi had "vehemently opposed" ASEAN's extension of membership to Myanmar made it only more likely that ASEAN's reputation would suffer for associating with Yangon.[65]

At the official levels, as in the track-two level, Bangkok and Manila tended to express the most reservations about admitting Myanmar along with Cambodia and Laos in 1997. As ASEAN's more democratic and Western-leaning governments, both the Philippines and Thailand faced greater pressure from both domestic and foreign groups to adopt a harder line. Intra-ASEAN divisions were most evident in October and November 1996, following Yangon's[66] crackdown of prodemocracy activists. Philippine President Fidel Ramos went on record expressing his desire to see Myanmar's membership postponed.[67] Bangkok, meanwhile, felt growing pressure from both foreign and domestic sources, the latter of which had become increasingly outspoken in its opposition as illustrated by various editorial and opinion pieces appearing on the pages of both the *Nation* and the *Bangkok Post* in 1997. Singapore Prime Minister Goh Chok Tong, who had called for the "early realization of our vision of an ASEAN community of 10 nations"[68] just the year before, also publicly expressed reservations. However, Goh pointedly focused on economic rather than political questions about the Yangon regime and its practices.[69]

Meanwhile, Indonesia and especially Malaysia remained firm. As host of their 1997 thirtieth anniversary AMM and chair of that year's standing committee, Malaysia, in fact, had become determined to see ASEAN 10 completed in Kuala Lumpur. At minimum, intra-ASEAN divisions as to how much weight to give Myanmar's human rights practices appear to have been the primary reason for ASEAN's delay in finalizing its decision on expansion. At least twice during that period of October–November 1996, ASEAN reviewed the question of CLM membership and twice decided to postpone the decision.[70] In a move partly aimed at distancing the specific issue of Myanmar from the process of ASEAN expansion, senior officials agreed that, whatever the timing, all three states should be admitted at the same time and as a group.

In the end, Malaysia's wish to see ASEAN 10 take place in Kuala Lumpur was helped by the Philippines, which as host of ASEAN's next meeting in 1998 found itself in a particular bind. Delaying Myanmar's membership in 1997, according to Philippine officials, was not just delaying the inevitable; it also would have more tightly and problematically linked the Myanmar controversy to Manila. As one Philippine official explained, being a democracy made the Philippines most hesitant about admitting Myanmar "under its watch."[71] He further elaborated:

> During the policy-making process in deciding this question, that was part of the main consideration. You have to have a policy and communication plan [as to] how you are going to defend this position to the public . . . That was an important issue . . . [I]f we admitted Myanmar in Malaysia, then the focus of the media would be on Kuala Lumpur . . . [but] it would be a disaster, at least for the Philippines, as the 'champion of human rights' to . . . admit Myanmar.[72]

Accentuating the tension between ASEAN's more and less liberal states were also other differences and simmering tensions. In particular, the debate appears additionally colored by Thai and Philippine irritation with the ways that Indonesia and Malaysia seemed to dominate the ASEAN process. Malaysia's aggressive pursuit of ASEAN 10—one Thai foreign ministry official described it as "bullying"—moreover did little to moderate that irritation. Another Thai foreign ministry official also expressed resentment at what he saw to be Malaysian and Indonesian cliquishness at ASEAN meetings—for example, when they "spoke Bahasa," which "sidelined" non–Bahasa-speaking Thailand and the Philippines. For this reason, he said that Thailand is very happy to admit Laos because it would be "one more close friend of Thailand" in ASEAN.[73]

In fact, this particular tension appears to have provided the opening necessary to break the ASEAN impasse on Myanmar's membership. Specifically, consultations between Bangkok and Manila on the question of Myanmar produced a plan to give them a greater profile through ASEAN's office of the secretary general. That plan was to press for the appointment of Rudolfo Severino, then the Philippines undersecretary of foreign affairs, to the position of ASEAN secretary-general, replacing ASEAN's incumbent Secretary-General Dato Ajit Singh of Malaysia. Consequently, Severino was made Secretary General in exchange for Bangkok's and Manila's supporting Myanmar's membership in 1997. Segundo Romero of the University of the Philippines bluntly characterizes the Philippines decision to support Myanmar's admission as "a quid pro quo for the Indonesian tie-breaking vote that made . . . Severino the new secretary general of ASEAN over Ajit Singh of Malaysia who sought reelection."[74]

A Debate Transformed:
External Interference and Regional Self-Determination

Other forces also contributed to ASEAN's May 31 decision to admit the CLM states in July 1997. As many involved in the process acknowledged, the expansion process acquired a strong momentum of its own that drove the process forward. ASEAN Secretary General Dato Ajit Singh in 1997 may have put it best: "While ASEAN has seen the goal of ASEAN 10 as inevitable and worth striving for, perhaps, it would be fair to say that after 1992, events began to unfurl much faster than anticipated."[75]

Much of that momentum stemmed from preparations associated with ASEAN's upcoming thirtieth anniversary in 1997. As noted, Malaysia, as host of that meeting, was especially keen and determined to see ASEAN 10 take place during ASEAN's anniversary meeting in Kuala Lumpur. Indeed, the fact that it was a milestone anniversary lent to the symbolism of the expansion process. In particular, proponents for expanding ASEAN in 1997 were aided by the galvanizing rhetoric and narrative of "One Southeast Asia"—representations of "One Southeast Asia" as an act of regional self-determination following past and present efforts from outside to balkanize and divide the region—and the strong emotional appeal attached to completing ASEAN's "historic mission of making Southeast Asia one"[76] at

ASEAN's thirtieth anniversary meeting. Consequently, even as concerns about the implications of expanded membership for ASEAN's intra- and extraregional relations intensified, intermediary measures also became increasingly less acceptable as the process progressed.

Western pressures on ASEAN to change course on Myanmar process added to the drama of the "One Southeast Asia" story and thus its momentum. Speaking directly to ASEAN's founding narrative, extraregional efforts to pressure member states and influence ASEAN's decision-making process gave even greater salience to the idea of "One Southeast Asia" as an act of regional self-determination against historical forces. Consequently, while Western objections did initially persuade Bangkok and Manila to reconsider their original positions, their very public efforts to pressure ASEAN states to deny membership to Myanmar ultimately had the opposite effect. Indeed, such pressures had a transformative effect on the intra-ASEAN debate in that they changed what the debate was about. A debate that initially focused on Yangon's treatment of Muslims and then pragmatic questions about its effects on ASEAN as a collective enterprise and then on questions of timing was further transformed again into one about the appropriateness of Western interference and relatedly ASEAN's right to make its own decisions. And, once transformed in this way, it became very difficult for anyone to argue against Myanmar's membership. Not only did self-determination normatively constrain one's ability to argue for a more cautious approach vis-à-vis other ASEAN members, but even those most critical of the Yangon regime strongly believed that external Western actors had no right to dictate to ASEAN what it could or could not do.

Put another way, the very public and at times strong-armed ways some Western powers tried to interfere in ASEAN's decision-making process consequently made even more salient a founding narrative (already emotionally charged on account of ASEAN's thirtieth anniversary) about their collective pursuit of regional resilience vis-à-vis outside forces. The efforts taken by European and U.S. governments during the critical period between fall 1996 and spring 1997 may have played particular roles in pushing the debate to its ultimate conclusion. In October 1996 the EU, following the U.S. lead, suspended all high-level visits to Myanmar and, more important, banned Myanmar's military rulers from visiting the EU. The significance of these decisions was soon made clear. If Myanmar joined ASEAN, the ban meant that Myanmar would be prohibited from participating in any ASEAN–EU meeting in Europe. Similarly, the EU would not attend ASEAN meetings when the ASEAN chair rotated to Myanmar. The EU parliament, in calling for ASEAN to refuse Burma's application "until SLORC [Myanmar's State Law and Order Restoration Council] has stepped from power and democratic rule has been restored," furthermore made explicit that Burma's full membership in ASEAN would harm EU–ASEAN relations. Then, in February 1997, the EU said that any new members (read: Myanmar) would have to individually negotiate their accession into any previously made Europe–ASEAN agreement.[77]

By this point, one could already see that U.S. and European criticisms were having an effect opposite to the one desired. After one particularly acrimonious discussion between ASEAN and Europe over Myanmar in February 1997, for example, Foreign Minister Prachuab Chaiyasarn of Thailand—notably, one of ASEAN's more cautious members on the question of Myanmar—responded that Western countries were putting too much pressure on ASEAN states, which were in a difficult situation. He went on to say, "In Thailand's view, the West should also talk to Aung San Suu Kyi to tone down and lend a hand to the other side to start consultations."[78] A shift in the debate at this point is further suggested by Suharto's February 1997 visits to Cambodia, Laos, and Myanmar, during which he reaffirmed his support for the "speedy admission" of the three countries. As reported by the *Jakarta Post*, "The tour is seen by many observers as a precursor to the three countries' impending admission into ASEAN."[79]

Two months later, in April 1997, the United States announced its decision to impose sanctions on Myanmar. As described by the Thai daily the *Nation*, the timing of the announcement suggested "an astute diplomatic offensive designed to pressure ASEAN" ministers who were meeting the next month to decide the timing of membership.[80] Indeed, State Department spokesman Nicholas Burns made explicit the U.S. position that "We don't believe ASEAN should take this step"—a view also contained in letters written by U.S. Secretary of State Madeline Albright to individual ASEAN leaders.[81] Kent Wiedemann, the U.S. chargé d'affaires in Myanmar, further warned that Myanmar's membership would make it "awkward" for Washington to deal with an ASEAN that included Myanmar.[82] To this, Philippine Domingo Siazon and others explicitly invoked ASEAN's and Myanmar's "right to determine its own affairs."[83] One month later, at a special meeting on May 31, ASEAN ministers unanimously decided to admit all three states in July.

Again, what might have been an intra-ASEAN debate on the merits of the case was turned into an exercise in regional self-determination. This shift in the debate was especially clear in the last few months leading up to ASEAN's thirtieth anniversary celebration in Kuala Lumpur. Thus, even those who questioned the wisdom of admitting Myanmar in 1997 defended ASEAN's unwillingness to bend to Western pressure. Dewi Fortuna Anwar, in the opinion piece cited earlier, for example, concluded her cautionary arguments by defending ASEAN's "prickliness" in its dealings with the West on Myanmar: "[I]t is consistent with ASEAN's objective to establish an autonomous regional order free from external interference that the association refuses to bow to outside pressure about which nations are eligible for membership."[84] ASEAN founder Thanat Khoman was even more blunt in his summation of events. Referring to "a major power [who] enjoined ASEAN not to admit Myanmar," he said,

> This heavy handed, even brutal move had the opposite effect. This galvanized ASEAN members who balked at the unjustified interference. It brought about unanimity where divided opinion existed. Instead of rejecting Myanmar's admission, the latter was admitted unanimously, while the wise decision would have been to delay the admission of the three new candidates, because of their domestic problems, as I had earlier advocated.[85]

China and the Limits of Inclusion

Similar but different questions about undue foreign influence also arose in response to China's activities in Indochina and especially Myanmar. Of ASEAN members, Indonesia's interest in new membership may have been most directly linked to its concerns about China. Viewing China as a potential rival for regional leadership in Southeast Asia, Indonesia saw new membership as adding to ASEAN's political clout.[86] Most important, Indonesia viewed expansion as a means of neutralizing Chinese influence over the CLMV states, which found themselves mostly isolated in the immediate period after the Cold War. In need of both friends and options, these states would find themselves unable to resist China's historic influence and/or material assistance unless given other options.

Such concerns were especially strong in debates about Myanmar and appear to be influential in changing Indonesia's initial objections to Myanmar's membership. Some ASEAN elites, in fact, suggest that Thailand, which favored Myanmar's membership early on, may have deliberately played to Jakarta's fears about China to persuade it to look on Myanmar's membership more favorably.[87] As Indonesia saw it, Myanmar—alienated by much of the international community on account of its military regime, human rights record, and especially its treatment of Aung San Suu Kyi—could not *but* turn to China. For Indonesia, then, bringing Myanmar and the other states into ASEAN became increasingly necessary as a way to offset Chinese influence.

Interestingly, Indonesia's concerns on this point also included existing ASEAN members—specifically Thailand. Thailand's cultivation of relations with China during and after the Cambodian conflict—as with its sudden and unilateral about-face on Vietnam during the last days of that conflict—tended, for example, to reinforce Indonesia's perception of Thailand as a weak link in ASEAN's chain of resilience.[88] As discussed, such concerns about Thailand's orientation had already been an important reason for Jakarta's willingness to accommodate the Thais during the Cambodian conflict.

Thus, vis-à-vis Myanmar and Thailand, as well as Vietnam, Indonesia viewed ASEAN as offering a valuable regional alternative and support community that could mitigate foreign influence in support of regional resilience and security goals. In comments made in 1992, Mochtar spoke directly to the need to keep Southeast Asian states like Thailand and Myanmar within the ASEAN fold:

> The Thais and Burmese are linked to China, because one day China will reassert. Therefore it is very good to have in ASEAN, people with links to communicate through. [But] *it is also very good for the Thais and Burmese to have ASEAN as a group to belong to, when facing this big power. . . . If Vietnam becomes a part of ASEAN, then it won't be alone. So too with the Thais and Burmese.*[89]

As for their approach to China, which was a contrast to their approach to Vietnam, states' individual and collective actions pointed to the region-specific ways with which they viewed ASEAN principles and practices. Relatedly, they illustrated not only the fact that ASEAN was based on very particular ideas of Southeast Asia but also that those ideas had become sharper and stronger over their thirty years of association. For example, China and Vietnam as larger, uncertain powers posed some similar challenges to ASEAN as a group of lesser powers. Such similarities might suggest similar responses—and indeed, there were notable similarities in the ways that states individually and collectively chose to respond to each. As in their approach toward Vietnam, for example, militarization was deemed inappropriate for the identified problems of resilience. In addition, states' approach toward China similarly exhibited a preference for emphasizing coexistence over confrontation. As a result of understood domestic priorities and material limitations, states also took particular effort to mitigate and neutralize any perceptions that ASEAN or its expansion process was "anti-China." Thus, Suharto visited and reestablished relations with China *before* visiting Vietnam, and Thailand sent representatives to Beijing to explain its intentions when it switched its Vietnam policy in 1988 and 1989. Similarly, in 1995, Vietnam's Party Secretary Duo Muoi went to China reportedly to reassure Beijing about Vietnam's impending membership in ASEAN.[90]

These pragmatic considerations notwithstanding, ASEAN's approach toward both powers was also similarly informed by ideas about ASEAN itself; that is, the ASEAN way, so to speak, was that talking and inclusion—not confrontation or coercion—were the better paths to greater agreement. This aspect of ASEAN will be discussed in further detail in Chapter 6, but suffice it to say that by the early 1990s "constructive engagement" and dialogue had become important parts of ASEAN's modus operandi and even regional identity.[91] Drawing on their own experiences and evolution, they believed that no good could come out of isolating China or Vietnam, as that would only encourage mischief at ASEAN's expense.

But while important parallels could be drawn between China and Vietnam, it was also very clear that ASEAN states made important distinctions between the two. For example, as discussed, members viewed Vietnamese membership in ASEAN in much the same way that they viewed Indonesia's in 1967. Regional organization, in other words, offered larger states a legitimate, nondisruptive way to exercise leadership and influence within a regional community. That argument logically should also apply to China; yet ASEAN membership for China was notably never considered a real possibility, even though the ameliorating effects of inclusive engagement and regional organization theoretically applied to China, as much Vietnam.

Instead, as will be discussed in Chapter 6, ASEAN made China a dialogue partner and created the ASEAN Regional Forum, a forum that extended ASEAN dialogue practices and processes but also made clear distinctions between ASEAN and non–ASEAN powers. Put another way, China, as a non–Southeast Asian state, may be an ASEAN dialogue partner, but it may not be a member. By contrast, Vietnam could be made a member because, as Mochtar put it, "[despite] their Marxist system . . . the basic trait of Southeast Asia is there, and I'm sure it can be revived . . . if Vietnam wants to become a member of this greater Southeast Asian entity."[92]

In short, what distinguished China from Vietnam were ideas about Southeast Asia and ideas about regional resilience, and these ideas defined states' realms of possibility and range of response. The parameters set by these ideas also were evident in discussions about other states, many of which shared ASEAN's concerns about China and/or small power or developing power preoccupations. In response to interest expressed by Sri Lanka and Papua New Guinea toward ASEAN membership, for example, Mochtar made clear that size alone did not give one entry into ASEAN:

> We have to be clear about what we mean by Southeast Asia. Sri Lanka and Papua New Guinea were keen on joining ASEAN, but most of my colleagues in the 1980s were not very keen on this. So we started talking about devising a criteria for what we mean by Southeast Asia. The Sri Lankans and the Papua New Guineans are adversarial, they tend to fight about something. Southeast Asians are different.[93]

Clearly Mochtar's memory was selective, ignoring as it did the adversarial histories of Indonesia in the 1960s, Vietnam's recent history in Cambodia, or the fact that, at one point in time, ASEAN seriously considered admitting Sri Lanka based on its size and nonaligned orientation. The significance of his comment lies instead in his invocation of a particular idea of Southeast Asia defined by a particular idea of Southeast Asia and its identification with a less confrontational, dialogue-driven regionalism, as highlighted above.

Singapore PM Goh Chok Tong's 1996 speculative and qualified suggestion that Australia and New Zealand in ASEAN was "a thinkable idea over the horizon"[94] met with a similar response from Malaysia's then-foreign minister Abdullah Badawi:

> Of late . . . some of us in ASEAN appear to be going through some kind of identity crisis. The admission of non-Southeast Asian states has been advocated. The reason presumably, is the growing economic linkages of these states with Southeast Asia, besides their geographical proximity to the region. If we follow this line of reasoning, very soon China, and perhaps even India, should be members of ASEAN . . .[95]

Badawi then put forth one of the more explicit defenses in support of ASEAN as a Southeast Asian organization:

> ASEAN by definition is an association of Southeast Asian nations . . . ASEAN belongs to Southeast Asia. It exists to cooperatively promote the interests of Southeast Asians. . . . [W]e must draw the line somewhere. I suggest we hold the line in Southeast Asia, which is what the Association of Southeast Asian Nations is about anyway. Identity, if we tamper with it, or blur its lines, then we run the risk of losing ourselves, and our commitment to the identity. In this case it is ASEAN that is at risk.[96]

In short, what Mochtar's and Badawi's comments spoke to was an idea of Southeast Asia that was about more than small power status, economic interdependence, or even geographic proximity. And it was that idea—what Barnett describes as the "variable of identity"—that came to "signal" which states were in and which were out, indeed "which states [were] considered more or less valuable partners."[97]

Conclusion and Postscript

In post-Cambodia, post–Cold War Southeast Asia, ASEAN thus found itself confronted with both internal and external challenges. The coincident endings of the Cold War and Cambodian conflicts introduced old and new fault lines—fault lines that called into question in a most fundamental way the empirical reality of "Southeast Asia." Most notable was the reemergence of an old mainland-insular divide, the expression of which came in the form of Thailand's intensified reengagement with its Indochinese neighbors. In particular, the ease with which Thailand put ASEAN aside once circumstances had changed underlined the persistence of old regional fault-lines, as well as new concerns about ASEAN's ability to remain relevant to its members in a changing region and world. The fact that such intramural concerns coincided with growing uncertainties in ASEAN's extraregional relations only ensured that the 1990s would be a time of critical reflection about ASEAN's significance and future directions. In this context, the expansion process as an expression of regional resilience offered members a useful reminder of their common security and relations, as well as an overarching framework and purpose.

On the other hand, that same process also uncovered other tensions and divisions—Muslim versus non-Muslim, liberal versus illiberal—while also introducing to ASEAN a new rich versus poor, core versus noncore dichotomy between old and new members. In this sense, developments since 1997 suggest that many of states' originally expressed concerns were not misplaced. Cambodia and Myanmar have posed particular challenges for ASEAN. In the days leading up to ASEAN's thirtieth anniversary meeting that was to formally accept CLM states as ASEAN members, a power play and coup in Cambodia prevented its admission at the last minute. While Myanmar and Laos were admitted as agreed and ASEAN states continued to work with Phnom Penh, the volatility of that regime dramatically illustrated the potential dangers posed to ASEAN by admitting politically unstable and questionably committed members.

Myanmar's treatment of Aung San Suu Kyi, various troubles and military clashes along the Thai–Myanmar border, and most recently its rejection of international assistance after a devastating cyclone in 2008 have also helped keep alive pre-1997 concerns about Myanmar's readiness for ASEAN membership. Moreover, the unreformed Myanmar regime has become a perennial challenge to the moral and practical authority of collective ASEAN.

No doubt sighs of relief were heard in all ASEAN capitals the day that Myanmar decided to forego its turn as ASEAN chair in 2006. Indeed, problems have been such that some ASEAN elites, including Mahathir, who had so strongly argued for Myanmar membership, have taken the unprecedented step of calling for a reevaluation of Myanmar's membership.

Meanwhile, economic activities, especially in the Mekong region, continue to draw attention to the mainland–insular faultline in ASEAN. In response, ASEAN has tried to inject an ASEAN presence and framework. Just as the expansion process aimed to overarch and unify disparate (and at times competing) activities in Vietnam, the "ASEAN Mekong Development Cooperation" has similarly tried to impose what Simon Hay describes as "a distinctly ASEAN political overlay onto some of the developmental work being undertaken by a number of other [individual and non-ASEAN] agencies."[98]

Other concerns from pre-1997 debates also remain relevant. Of particular note are the continued developmental gap between old and new members and its potential effect on ASEAN's corporate solidarity and efficacy. Moreover, efforts to more fully integrate new members were hindered by the Asian financial crisis, which began the same year that Cambodia and Laos were admitted. Not only did that crisis constrain states' material ability to help new members, but it also refocused members' attention back to their own domestic problems, including renewed ethnic and separatist tensions and economic instabilities, problems they had thought already resolved.

Despite English and technical training from the ASEAN 6, new states nevertheless continue to find full participation difficult. Meanwhile, efforts to accommodate them have only accentuated the divisions between old and new members. Those efforts include, for example, a separate, delayed AFTA timetable for Vietnam and the CLM states to give them more time to meet AFTA's liberalization targets. In 1995 when Vietnam was admitted, ASEAN also amended its consensus-making process on economic matters—a more "flexible" understanding of consensus—to allow certain members to opt out temporarily while others moved ahead. It was also decided that new members would not be required to participate in all ASEAN meetings upon gaining membership.[99]

Such accommodations of new states' economic and bureaucratic limitations thus helped guard against new members slowing down the larger ASEAN process. But while such accommodations responded to key concerns about the effects of expanded membership on ASEAN as a collective and political entity, they also increased the likelihood of a two-tiered ASEAN,

one faster and one slower, "core" and "less core." By allowing states to participate selectively in ASEAN as Laos currently does, ASEAN also increased
the possibility of marginalizing these slower states all together.[100]

The addition of four new members—all from mainland Southeast Asia—
challenges ASEAN in other ways as well. Their membership at once equal-
izes the balance between mainland and insular Southeast Asia and destabilizes
ASEAN's foundational status quo that favored "inner ASEAN." Indonesia's
particular centrality may also be at risk if its own house remains troubled and
Vietnam continues along the positive trajectory that it has been. Moreover,
their numbers—nearly half of ASEAN—also give them the ability to direct
or obstruct the association's directions, something that has been most apparent in recent efforts to adopt an ASEAN Charter (see Conclusion).

The acknowledged difficulties and disagreements associated with meeting these challenges only underline the power of the sentiment attached to
the "One Southeast Asia" idea. This idea, as highlighted above, both framed
states' understanding of challenges—the challenges of Thai unilateralism,
Chinese influence, Western meddling—and in important ways determined
key policy outcomes. Indeed, framed in terms of regional resilience and
regional self-determination, expansion was not just a preferable policy
choice but a historical necessity. As Severino, the former Philippine foreign
minister who replaced Ajit Singh as ASEAN secretary general, put it, "The
only thing worse than a two-tier ASEAN is a two-tier Southeast Asia—a
progressive ASEAN and a lagging portion of Southeast Asia" because the
dangers of *not* bringing the other countries into ASEAN in the end would
be far more troubling.[101]

In the end, especially for those familiar with ASEAN's earliest, most
uncertain days, what may be most notable about ASEAN's expansion process between 1992 and 1997 was the increasing prominence of its founding
narrative. Certainly, few issues brought together ASEAN's founding ideas
and defining practices as did the story of "One Southeast Asia," which as told
was a story about Southeast Asia's historical fragmentation, the difficulties
of regional unity in the face of intraregional differences and extra-regional
"balkanization" forces, and deeply held desire to determine its own future.
Moreover, as ASEAN did battle with the forces from within and without,
the expansion process thus came to be much more than a practical response
to problems but instead a public and assertive expression of an historical
imperative. This narrative—replete with references to ASEAN's "founding
fathers," their "longheld dream" that "all ten Southeast Asian states . . . be
under one roof,"[102] and ASEAN's "historic mission of making Southeast

Asia one"[103]—as well as states' 1997 adoption of an ASEAN flag and song illustrates well Andrew Hurrell's point that with regionalism, "as with nationalism, there is a good deal of historical rediscovery, myth-making and invented tradition."[104] Indeed, the social construction of region and regionalism was never more clear than as in this narrative that saw "One Southeast Asia" as the culmination of a historical struggle for regional self-determination against larger powers. And, as such, Southeast Asia had gained both agency and social purpose.

5

Locating ASEAN in East Asia and the Asia Pacific

> The changing times do indeed call for new approaches, new
> thoughts and attitudes on the part of ASEAN. Otherwise, I'm
> afraid that we run the risk of becoming irrelevant to the emerging
> new world and regional order.[1]
>
> *Anand Panyarachun*
> *Prime Minister, Thailand 1992*

In the area of intra-ASEAN trade cooperation, as in the process of ASEAN expansion, the changing policies and roles of major powers—here, the United States and Japan, as well as China—interacted with rival conceptualizations of region and regionalism to grow a sense of existential threat to ASEAN as a meaningful regional entity. In this case, rival ideas came from without and within—in particular from the Australian-initiated Asia Pacific Economic Cooperation forum (APEC) and Malaysia's proposed East Asian Economic Group (EAEG). Not only did these initiatives threaten to subsume ASEAN-Southeast Asia into larger regional entities, but they also rivaled ASEAN for states' attention, thus intensifying fears that ASEAN was losing its relevance among its own members. Such interdependent global and intraregional concerns challenged ASEAN states to rethink established ideas about region and economic regionalism as something more than an exercise in normative relationship building and in more conventional strategic economic terms.

This chapter begins by outlining a succession of global economic developments over the 1980s that contributed to a building sense of anxiety about the global economy on which ASEAN development and state survival is understood to depend. While none, in and of themselves, proved large enough of a shock to produce a new approach to economic cooperation, they and the intra-ASEAN debates they generated did have a cumulative impact on ASEAN states' decision-making environment. Specifically, they built momentum and a sense of urgency for a new regional approach that would factor large in interpretations of later external catalyzing events—namely, the Maastricht Treaty (signed in 1991, enacted in 1992) and the North American Free Trade Agreement (NAFTA; signed in 1992, ratified in 1993).

The chapter then traces intra-ASEAN debates and states' ongoing search for agreement about how best to respond to new challenges. Even with growing agreement as to the necessity of a regional response to events, the scope and content of that response continued to be debated. The emergence of Asian Pacific and East Asian cooperation schemes moreover widened the range of possible regional responses. They also underscored long-standing questions about the functional and economic utility of Southeast Asia as an organizing principle. Nor had the PTAs discussed in the last chapter done much to change that basic material condition. In fact, intra-ASEAN trade as a percentage of overall trade hardly changed over the course of the 1980s, staying at about 19 percent and never reaching the 21 percent it was in 1970.[2] The regional political economy created by the Cold War also tended to maintain Southeast Asia's extraregional dependencies on the United States and increasingly on Japan.[3] In short, through the 1980s and even into the mid-1990s, the economic incentives for intra-ASEAN trade liberalization remained, to quote Ravenhill, "far from overwhelming."[4]

But while the economics of Asian Pacific and East Asian economic schemes were relatively compelling, both also proved highly contentious. Instead, intra-ASEAN debates revealed greatest normative agreement on ASEAN, not Asian Pacific or East Asian economic cooperation. Rival Asian-Pacific and East Asian schemes in fact made intra-ASEAN cooperation more, not less, persuasive. The result was ASEAN's 1992 agreement to form an ASEAN Free Trade Area (AFTA), a different approach to trade liberalization and improvement from the old PTAs in practically every respect. Meanwhile, Asian-Pacific and East Asian schemes also moved forward but, as detailed below, the fact that intra-ASEAN debates focused on regional resilience, rather than the economic merits of each arrangement, ultimately constrained the creation and ultimately the course of both those arrangements.

"A New World Order"

The decade of the 1980s was a time of growing anxieties about ASEAN's key trading relationships and the global economy. Unstable oil prices, a sluggish global economy, and the troubled Tokyo Round of trade negotiations in 1979 combined to create sufficient concern to warrant their own subject heading ("International Economic Issues") on ASEAN's agenda. "Special" and "deep" concerns expressed about the "concepts of 'selectivity' and graduation' espoused by certain developed countries" in 1979 and 1980 then gave way to "grave concerns" accompanied by "dismay" over the "negative trends in international economic relations" and "the continuing trend towards protectionism" among developed countries in 1981 and 1982. By 1983, members described the international economy as being in a state of "prolonged and serious crisis."[5]

Some relief was expressed toward "the encouraging signs of economic recovery in developed countries" between 1984 and 1987, but sharp downward trends in commodity prices, along with the emergence of new alternatives for traditional primary products, also kept anxieties high, as primary products (though declining as a percentage of total ASEAN trade) continued to dominate ASEAN's total exports.[6] In 1985 Indonesian Foreign Minister Mochtar Kusumaatmadja detailed the long list of challenges that continued to confront ASEAN economies: "escalating protectionism, plummeting commodity prices, high interest rates, declining financial resources for development and exchange rate gyrations."[7] The second oil crisis in 1986 added to a general sense of growing crisis among both elites and the general public.[8] At that year's AMM, Singapore's and Thailand's foreign ministers concluded that certain "global economic and technological trends" had "potentially ominous implications."[9]

Concerns also remained about "protectionist pressures undermining the open market system." Nor did the troubled Uruguay Round of trade negotiations (1986–1994) do much to alleviate those concerns in the latter half of the 1980s. Though ASEAN economies had moved up the production chain, the wider adoption of export-led growth strategies had also made them more sensitive to global economic shifts and uncertainties. Meanwhile, advanced Western economies were experiencing their own economic difficulties, and it soon became clear that ASEAN's relative economic success also made members easier targets—or "scapegoats," to quote Singapore's Ambassador to the United States Tommy Koh—of Western economic anxieties.[10] While Western anxieties focused mostly on the more advanced economies of Taiwan, Korea, and especially Japan, ASEAN economies did not escape the attention of the United States or European community (EC) which made their trade imbalance a regular issue in meetings with ASEAN states.

U.S. policies were a particular concern for ASEAN states. Faced with its own economic slowdown, as well as mounting trade deficits with East and Southeast Asian economies, Washington began to reconsider those economies' "developing economy" status, producing a string of U.S. legislation aimed at creating what Washington saw to be more "equal" and "fairer" terms of trade: The 1985 Multi-Fiber Agreement allowed importing countries to impose two-year (as opposed to one-year) quotas on all varieties of textiles. The 1985 Food and Security Act allowed the United States to create price support schemes for products like rice and sugar—an act that was described by the foreign minister of Thailand, a net exporter of both commodities, as "a very damaging form of trade harassment."[11] For ASEAN economies, the capstone of such legislation was the Omnibus Trade and Competitiveness Act. Dubbed the "Omnibus No-Trade Bill" by the same Thai foreign minister above, that act (which passed in 1988) eventually broadened definitions of what constituted "unfair" trade practices and gave the U.S. trade representative authority to act against identified economies. Subsequently, Indonesia, Malaysia, the Philippines, and Thailand all found themselves on the U.S. "watch list" and under the threat of U.S. trade sanctions. In 1988, the Reagan administration also moved to take duty-free privileges away from Asia's more advanced tigers, including Singapore.[12]

Some directly appealed to the United States to maintain its support for ASEAN economies. As Thailand's then-foreign minister Siddhi Savetsila put it: "[W]e . . . hope that the U.S. will remember that the word liberal connotes both freedom and magnanimity. Hence, even with a level playing field, special consideration without demand for reciprocity should be given to those who are not as strong as the developed, industrialized countries."[13] His comments echoed earlier remarks made by Malaysia's Ghazali Shafie. Characterizing the positions taken by more advanced industrial economies in international trade negotiations as "wealth creating" decisions that had "life and death consequences" for less developed countries, he observed, "While the 'western mind' easily grasps the idea of armies marching across borders, it does not grasp ASEAN's perception of threat to the free market system."[14] Both Siddhi's and Mochtar's comments spoke to a fundamental divergence between, on the one hand, U.S. and European views of ASEAN as strong economic competitors and, on the other, ASEAN states' perception of themselves as "developing" countries that moreover continued to be vulnerable to destabilizing influences from within and without.

But as the Cold War came to a formal close, Western strategic interests for supporting Southeast Asian growth also diminished. Consequently, more pressure, not less, came from North America and Western Europe who were increasingly "intent on treating ASEAN, not as a sturdy little group of noncommunist developing countries to be bolstered economically, but as a full-fledged, economically vibrant bloc which should adapt to western-style respect for human rights and open up its markets."[15] Bringing this new emphasis home was newly elected U.S. President Bill Clinton, who declared a new doctrine of enlarging market democracies in lieu of the old Cold War doctrine of containment. By this new doctrine, ASEAN states, once praised for being bastions of anticommunism, were increasingly censured for their undemocratic, illiberal policies and governments.

Washington's new agenda intensified ASEAN's questions about the role of the United States as a supporter of ASEAN. It also brought to the forefront a strain of ASEAN thinking that had been less prominent in their previous trade relations with the United States—namely, major powers' ability to intervene. Moreover, new U.S. efforts to link trade to other issues (security, labor, and environment, as well as human rights) coincided with the emergence of the United States as the sole remaining superpower, generating various commentary across ASEAN about Washington's unique position to "extract unilateral advantage."[16] In fact, it became increasingly common in ASEAN to characterize Washington's extra-trade agendas as simply another tool of U.S. trade policy, a new form of protectionism, even "a devious attempt to impose conditions for aid and trade."[17]

In short, ASEAN's concerns about the emerging post–Cold War economic order came to focus on two somewhat contradictory perceptions of the United States—the first being of a preponderant power in decline—less competitive, less benevolent, and less able to support the free trade system and its allies—and the second being of a United States economically and politically preponderant, able to extract concessions from the weak at will. Contradictions aside, the two views nevertheless shared a common conclusion: Washington could not be relied on to support ASEAN, and alternatives should be sought.

Arguing for Change:
Old and New Thinking about ASEAN Regionalism

Such changes in the global economy and especially U.S. trade policies through the 1980s set in train a reassessment of old arrangements and strategies, creating both domestic and ideological openings for new strategies. Most important, as Stubbs and others detail, the 1985–1986 regional recession and insecurities caused by unstable commodity prices created opportunity for liberal reformers to have more influence over development and economic policies, facilitating greater adoption of export-led, foreign direct investment (FDI)–driven growth strategies, as well as the creation of new domestic constituencies and coalitions.[18]

These changes opened the door for different arguments for regional trade liberalization. Proponents of intra-ASEAN trade liberalization increasingly portrayed intra-ASEAN liberalization and integration in more conventional economic terms—that is, liberalization as a way to create a larger ASEAN market that could compete against both larger and emerging economies for trade and investment. As early as 1985 the Philippines, Thailand, and Malaysia were making the case for rethinking ASEAN's economic regionalism along those lines and as a response to global uncertainties. Mahathir drew attention to the opportunity of the ASEAN market that existed "before their very eyes" and "at our very door-step." Echoing those views in 1986, 1987, and 1988 were ministers from Thailand and the Philippines who referred to the "immense market opportunity" that a collective ASEAN market offered compared to that of six "disparate" and "fragmented" markets. As Siddhi Savetsila argued in 1988, "the removal of trade barriers to internal trade would transform the appeal of the ASEAN area to foreign investors, who look for economies of scale, leading to production at world market price levels, and consequently to increase exports."[19]

These arguments began to compete with more established thinking about regionalism—thinking that was most apparent in Indonesian arguments. While unstable oil prices had also produced "wide ranging trade, investment and financial sector reforms" in Indonesia[20] as they had in neighboring countries, Indonesia remained the most resistant to regional liberalization schemes. For one, as Mochtar argued, the challenges faced by ASEAN economies were globally sourced and thus required global, not regional, solutions.[21] Most of all, their common interest in regional resilience called for caution. Argued Mochtar in 1986, "ASEAN is a success precisely because it does not try to go too fast . . . The slow pace of integration is the price we have to pay for ASEAN's continued cohesion and success . . . [I]t is better to proceed at a measured pace and succeed, than go fast and fail."[22]

Mochtar was not the only one to draw on resilience to make his arguments. As in prior debates about the PTAs, the normative centrality of resilience to ASEAN was illustrated by the fact that practically all members—whatever their position—made reference to it. Even among those like Malaysia and the Philippines that advocated a more proactive approach based on markets of scale arguments, it was still rare for regional trade liberalization to be justified on purely economic grounds. At their 1985 AMM, for example, their arguments focused on their collective interest in self-determination vis-à-vis uncertain global forces. Expressing concern about ASEAN's dependence on external actors and markets for growth, Philippine Acting Foreign Minister Pacifico Castro argued that it was time for members to cultivate, through economic cooperation, their intraregional ties, which would then provide ASEAN "its own organic dynamism and resilience."[23]

Similarly, Malaysia's Foreign Minister Tengku Ahmad Rithaudeen argued at their 1986 AMM: "The [Tokyo G-7] Summit amply showed that it will be a mistake for ASEAN countries to rely solely on developed countries. ASEAN countries should ingrain in themselves a spirit of self-reliance in executing our development programmes."[24]

As for Thailand, Siddhi Savetsila echoed some of Castro's themes but also tied regional trade liberalization directly to ASEAN's growing existential concerns. As he put it, not only would intra-ASEAN trade liberalization provide ASEAN a "buffer . . . from the more adverse shifts and swings of the world economic situation," but the resulting expansion of intra-ASEAN trade through trade liberalization would build ASEAN itself, thus ensuring its permanence in the face of mounting global and regional changes. Foreshadowing future arguments that would become prominent in the 1990s, he further argued that building ASEAN would help make it the "core building block" in future Pacific economic cooperation.[25]

As before, Singapore drew on regional unity arguments to argue both sides of the debate. As late as 1985, for example, Singapore's Dhanabalan could be heard arguing that the *immaturity* of ASEAN's regionalism would not be able to withstand "the strains of ambitious supranational projects and policies." To those "who feel that ASEAN is making very little progress in economic cooperation within the group and that a new impetus is needed," he warned, "we should always remember that regionalism is a new experience for all of us. It still has to mature . . . "[26]

Just one year, later, however, resilience justified a different conclusion. In response to the "potentially ominous implications in certain global economic and technological trends," Dhanabalan pressed for more than a reconsideration of intratrade liberalization efforts; he also put forth an earlier, controversial proposal to modify ASEAN's definition of consensus to a more flexible "Six minus X principle."[27] To make his case, he significantly fell back on familiar themes. Drawing attention to the "increased competition and price undercutting problems . . . among the ASEAN trio (Malaysia, Indonesia, and Thailand) over markets" and investment, he argued that world developments were encouraging "beggar thy neighbor" policies that now threatened their collective resilience. As he put it, "The slow and deliberate pace of regional cooperation of the past cannot be relevant and adequate for the 1990s . . . The social political pressures of much slower growth may create pressures for some countries to go their own way."[28] In short, more proactive efforts were necessary if they were to neutralize ASEAN's divisive tendencies.

The next year, Dhanabalan's warnings about regional fragmentation were even more explicit in his argument for a new approach:

> ASEAN unity thus far has been built on the basic principles of mutual accommodation, noninterference, tolerance, and understanding. These are the passive requirements of good neighborliness which have served ASEAN well over the past two decades . . . But we need to shift our gears to the more active requirements of cooperation *if we are not to drift apart*.[29]

Meanwhile, global pressures showed little signs of abatement. Finding their members to be continued targets of U.S. domestic interests and legislation, ASEAN in 1989 issued a "stinging" statement on the "growing tendency" of some actors who resorted to bilateral measures to solve their trade problems.[30] Washington's pursuit of various bilateral and regional trading arrangements—for example, with Canada, Mexico, the Caribbean, and Israel—also offered further confirmation of the growing "protectionist mood" in the United States and worldwide. These arrangements provided the focus of a special session of the AEMM in 1989, which expressed concern about the threat to GATT and the "increased danger of trade wars."[31] Talk of new regional trade agreements in North America and Europe and rumors of U.S.–European secret deals added to fears that ASEAN would be shut out of North American and European markets and denied critical foreign investment.[32] By July 1990, ASEAN states in a joint statement concluded, "the possibility that the [Uruguay] round will end as a failure does not now seem unthinkable."[33] And, indeed, the Uruguay Trade Round was suspended in early December 1990.

Normative and Ideological Challenges to "Southeast Asia"

ASEAN's challenges did not end there. As the pressure for change mounted, developments also inspired new interest in extra-ASEAN regional arrangements that challenged not just ASEAN's established modes of cooperation but also the very idea of Southeast Asia as an organizing principle. As previously discussed, Thai activities and peninsular Southeast Asian initiatives had already begun to challenge ASEAN's ideas of a unified Southeast Asia. However, as the 1980s drew to a close, there were also those who began to believe that ASEAN by itself was no longer sufficient for meeting the global economic challenges ahead. For those holding this view, the proper regional response lay in larger, not smaller, arrangements. Two ideas—an Australian vision of APEC and a Malaysian-proposed EAEG—would pose particular challenges. How these debates evolved would have consequences for both ASEAN and the shape and content of subsequent Asian Pacific and East Asian arrangements.

APEC and ASEAN

As far as geographic conceptions go, neither APEC nor the EAEG was especially radical. Certainly, the idea of East Asia had a long history, finding its most significant and recent expression in imperial Japan's envisioned Greater East Asian Co-Prosperity Sphere. As for the Pacific Community idea, it had been debated for at least a decade—mostly at "track 2" business and academic levels, especially the Pacific Basin Economic Council, Pacific Trade Development Conference, and Pacific Economic Cooperation Council (PECC).[34] Within ASEAN, neither idea had much mileage in the 1970s and 1980s. In the case of East Asia, Japanese imperialism remained a significant issue in Japan–ASEAN relations, despite the improvement and expansion of economic relations. Power issues and concerns also plagued the Pacific community idea, as ASEAN states expressed concerns about such a group's institutional challenge to ASEAN and especially about great power domination, intervention, neoimperialism, and conspiracy.[35]

As the Cold War ended, however, both ideas gained new adherents and new attractiveness as a basis for regional organization. As with new arguments for intra-ASEAN trade liberalization, both APEC and EAEG ideas were directly correlated with developments in U.S. trade policy and global trade rounds. Coming on the heels of deadlocked trade talks the previous month, Australia's January 1989 Asia Pacific initiative responded to what Australian Prime Minister Bob Hawke described as "serious cracks . . . in the international trading system"[36] and Australian and Asian fears of being excluded from key markets and trade configurations.[37] Similarly, Malaysia's December 1990 East Asian proposal made a public appearance practically the very day that the Uruguay Round stalled, instead of concluding as it was supposed to do. Despite the circumstances, both ideas nevertheless continued to encounter significant resistance and opposition from and within ASEAN.

As originally proposed, Hawke's APEC did not at first include the United States, whose participation became a key issue in regionalist debates. For ASEAN states, the question of U.S. participation did not have a straightforward answer. On the one hand, as Ravenhill observes, "the dependence of East Asian exports on the U.S. market . . . made the exclusion of the United States from a regional institution a highly risky move."[38] The implementation of the U.S.–Canada free trade agreement in January 1989, especially as it immediately followed the deadlocked world trade negotiations of the month before, only underlined fears about continued access to the U.S.

market. Consequently, of the ASEAN states, only Malaysia supported the original proposal.

On the other hand, including the United States (as the Australian proposal soon did) confronted ASEAN with a different challenge. As discussed, the uncertainties of U.S. policies had intensified ASEAN states' sense of dependence and insecurity. While an arrangement that could assure or facilitate continued access to the U.S. market was desirable, that interest also warred with a growing desire to mitigate and diversify that dependence and vulnerability. As the *Far Eastern Economic Review* put it, "the inclusion of the U.S. [did] not make sense when ASEAN exporters [were] trying to lessen dependence on protectionism-threatened U.S. markets."[39] Moreover, the very fact that Washington was negotiating various trade agreements with others gave additional reason to exclude the United States as a way to leverage bargaining power. This was the argument, for example, of both Mahathir in proposing an exclusive East Asian group and Hawke in making his initial APEC proposal.[40]

Perhaps most of all, the prospect of U.S. involvement intensified ASEAN fears about being dominated in a larger arrangement. As noted above, ASEAN concerns were already evident and well established, especially in track 2 discussions on Pacific community, before Hawke's proposal. For the ASEAN states and for much of the 1980s, whatever benefits could be associated with Asia Pacific cooperation were outweighed by persistent concerns about great power dominance and collusion, the further institutionalization of entrenchment of economic disparities, and the challenges posed to state-led development, as well as the nontrade and noneconomic agendas of Western powers.[41] In this sense, including the United States—a much more powerful actor than either Australia or Japan—was not necessarily reassuring, especially given Washington's new trade and political agendas. Just as troubling, if not more, were the potential implications of Asia Pacific cooperation for ASEAN itself. Taken together, the result was, as Ravenhill puts it, "not just indifference but active hostility from ASEAN" toward formal Asian Pacific cooperation.[42]

Of these concerns, it was notable that the one that provided the dominant frame and argument within ASEAN was the last one about the challenge to ASEAN. While intra-ASEAN debates also produced early agreement against "inward-looking" or "closed" arrangements that might encourage already disturbing trends toward trade blocs, it was the existential threat to ASEAN that came to take center stage in intra-ASEAN debates by midyear. While ASEAN states did vary in their degree of concern—with Indonesia most concerned and Singapore the least—various ASEAN representatives made clear that new arrangements should not "nullify existing forms," "dilute" ASEAN's existing consultations with dialogue partners, undermine ASEAN "identity" or jeopardize ASEAN "cohesion."[43] In debating APEC, arguments thus came to rest less on the economic merits of Asia Pacific cooperation and more on whether such cooperation in fact marginalized ASEAN or detracted from ASEAN cooperation and existing processes.[44]

In fact, as other participants of APEC negotiations observed, ASEAN states displayed a notable unity in their position that ASEAN should not be sidelined, absorbed, or fragmented by any new grouping.[45] That unity moreover gave ASEAN great influence, as acknowledged by Australia's ASEAN-directed lobbying efforts during the first half of 1989. However, despite Canberra's efforts, as one ASEAN representative admitted in July, "Our concerns are not quite allayed."[46] Those concerns moreover remained in evidence up until and even well beyond the first APEC meeting in November 1989. In fact, a September 1989 special informal meeting of ASEAN ministers seeking to clarify ASEAN's position on APEC participation produced a set of conditions and qualifications that made clear ASEAN's still-strong reservations: (1) Asia Pacific cooperation should be based on a "flexible" framework; (2) there should be no new formal body established (in fact, the preference was to call the November meeting an "exploratory meeting");[47] and (3) ASEAN should form the "core" of any new arrangement.[48] On this last point, members considered expanding ASEAN's external PMC dialogues in lieu of Australia's proposal.

Even days before the Australia meeting, many in ASEAN remained conflicted, with Indonesia and Malaysia the most concerned. According to one Indonesian diplomat, "Indonesia would like ASEAN to hijack this [Asia Pacific] initiative but doesn't know how to do it."[49] Even Thailand, which was more amenable to the idea of Asia Pacific cooperation, continued to seek assurances that "the role of ASEAN . . . be maintained" and to make clear it would not support the formation of a new grouping unless ASEAN were at the core.[50] As Thai commerce secretary Subin Pinkhayan put it, "We are not ready to launch another regional body since we already have ASEAN . . . [which] can be extended to cover larger regional cooperation on economic matters."[51] While perhaps not by design, states' collective concern served ASEAN well because it kept the focus of others on ASEAN. In fact, by a number of accounts, ASEAN held "the key" to Australia's Asia Pacific initiative.[52] Not only would any Asia Pacific arrangement lose significant credibility without ASEAN participation, but Japan's full endorsement also appeared to hinge on ASEAN participation.[53]

These concerns for ASEAN made a strong appearance at the November meeting in Australia. There, ASEAN, led by Indonesia and Malaysia, opposed efforts to formalize and make permanent the Asia Pacific grouping with the creation of a secretariat. Instead, ASEAN put forward a previously discussed proposal that Asia Pacific cooperation build on existing ASEAN frameworks, namely, its "ASEAN plus" postministerial consultations with external partners.[54] In making the case for ASEAN, Indonesian Foreign Minister Ali Alatas focused on a few points. First, he reiterated that "ASEAN's identity and cohesion should be preserved and its cooperative relations with its dialogue partners and other third countries should not be diluted." Second, already existing ASEAN mechanisms made unnecessary a completely new arrangement. As Alatas put it, "If we move to a larger intergovernmental body, then isn't it reasonable and logical to start from what we already have?" Third, he argued on the basis of experience and ASEAN's unique status as the region's only long-standing regional organization: "We don't want to squeeze APEC into the ASEAN forum. But ASEAN has experience in developing the only inter-governmental consultative and cooperative process in this region."[55]

Despite their failure to persuade APEC's non-ASEAN members, regard for ASEAN's concerns was nevertheless visible in the final APEC outcome in practically all the most important respects. On the question of future meetings, ASEAN states conceded but got, in return, the privilege of hosting APEC in an ASEAN location every other year, beginning with the next one in Singapore. On the question of membership, ASEAN "strongly resisted" a U.S.-backed proposal to extend membership to the "three Chinas" and successfully pushed that decision to a later date.[56] On the question of ASEAN as an institution, it was agreed that representatives from the ASEAN secretariat would join senior officials in preparing for APEC's next meetings. Most significantly, APEC's informal decision-making structure and institutional design responded to ASEAN's concerns about the prospect of larger members dominating or dictating the agenda against ASEAN states' wishes.[57] Notably, even Singapore, who had pressed for a more formal "European Community-style" organization for ASEAN itself, maintained that "APEC should continue to be a loose, exploratory and informal consultative process."[58]

Consequently, in deference to ASEAN's concerns, APEC adopted a looser institutionalism that was considered more respectful of the region's diversity and different levels of development and, most of all, more consistent with ASEAN's own regionalism. In describing APEC as "a non-formal forum for consultation among high-level representatives of significant economies in the Asia-Pacific region," the meeting's Chairman's Summary thus came to describe the new body in "looser" terms than originally intended by Australia or preferred by APEC's Western participants.[59] ASEAN's concerns were also why there is no reference to "organization," "association," or "community" in APEC's name; instead, it remained, as Australian Foreign Minister Gareth Evans quipped, "four adjectives in search of a noun." While ASEAN states were not alone in their preference for a more informal body (Japan, for example, joined the ASEAN states), the attention others directed at ASEAN in the lead-up process pointed to ASEAN's particular influence.

Other signs of deference to ASEAN were more rhetorical but nevertheless indicative of others' acknowledgment that ASEAN's participation in the process was critical if APEC were to mean anything. For example, up front and in the opening preamble of APEC's first joint ministerial statement is a "recognition of the important contribution of ASEAN and its dialogue relationships" to the development of APEC, as well as "the significant role ASEAN's institutional mechanisms can continue to play in supporting . . . regional economic cooperation."[60] (Aside from thanking the Australians for their hospitality and ability to host a good conference, not even Canberra's initiative received such acknowledgment.) In addition, the 1989 chairman's report explicitly acknowledged ASEAN's concern that Asia Pacific cooperation "should complement and draw upon, rather than detract from, existing organisations in the region."[61]

While ASEAN's concerns were not completely allayed, as illustrated by continued efforts to clarify ASEAN's relationship to APEC throughout the following year, such assurances were sufficient to convince states to take ASEAN's first real step into regional cooperation beyond Southeast Asia. More significantly, it opened the door to (or forced) a rethinking of ASEAN's historical Southeast Asian mandate. The product of that rethinking could be found not just in their collective decision to participate but also in their unexpected counterproposal to base the new Asia Pacific forum on the ASEAN PMC. Efforts also revealed a notable unity about the need to preserve ASEAN. However, ASEAN consensus and unity would then be challenged with a new proposal for an exclusive East Asian grouping from one of their own: Malaysian Prime Minister Mahathir.

Mahathir's Proposal

At just about the same moment in December 1990 that the Uruguay Round "entered its bleakest period,"[62] the press began reporting a Malaysian proposal for a Japan-led East Asian bloc. By Mahathir's account, Malaysia's Ministry of International Trade and Industry originated the idea as a backup to global talks, which Mahathir "immediately" took up and subsequently made his own.[63] Expressing his own frustration with the Uruguay Round's inability to address the issue of agricultural subsidies, a key concern of developing economies, he explained, "I myself was finding intolerable the self-centered negotiating stance of Western nations, which seemed to ignore the voices of developing countries seeking early Uruguay Round agreement."[64] In expressing what Nesadurai describes as Mahathir's "long-held ideas on the dangers of unbridled market forces, his fears of potentially damaging challenges and obstacles for developing countries issuing from the global environment, and his deep resentment against perceived Western manipulations,"[65] the EAEG could also be viewed as a regionalist extension of the populist and nationalist themes that characterized Mahathir's domestic politics.[66]

In responding to growing concerns about the failure of U.S. and European leadership in trade, the above makes clear that Mahathir was not alone in such views; nor was he the first to advocate a new regional response to global challenges. But Mahathir's proposal was also critically different because it was explicitly premised on the argument that ASEAN was no longer enough. Abdul Jabar, a spokesman for the Malaysian Embassy in Washington, D.C., articulated Malaysia's position well: "Malaysia is a small country, and our voice may not be heard. ASEAN is not big enough to carry clout. But if China, Korea, and Japan are with us, perhaps people would pay attention."[67]

In Mahathir's envisioned East Asian group, Japan—as the most advanced East Asian economy—played a particular role. In one sense, Japan was an odd choice, not just because of its past imperial ambitions in Southeast Asia but also because its position on the key issue of agricultural subsidies and protections ran counter to ASEAN interests. (Japan, in fact, was the only one of the APEC economies to support the EC's harder line position on farm subsidies in the just-stalled Uruguay trade negotiations.) However, in another sense, Japan's economic rise in a world dominated by Western power and ideas also made Japan very attractive, especially for a nationalist like Mahathir. For Mahathir, a Japan-led East Asian group importantly addressed what Dirlik has described as the "historical problem" of Western dominance over Asians.[68]

Mahathir was not the only one to look to Japan or East Asia as a response to global and U.S. challenges. As early as 1984, for example, Indonesia had referred to the possibility of an East Asian group. In 1987 both Singapore and Thailand identified Japan as an actor that could fill the role being vacated by the United States.[69] Responding to U.S. Secretary of State Shultz's 1987 "warning" to ASEAN "to look elsewhere instead of America as the engine of [ASEAN] growth," Thailand's Siddhi Savetsila was in fact most explicit in tying Thailand's growing interest in Japan to changes in U.S. policy. As he put it, "[It] is a timely reminder that the world economy that we have known since the end of the Second World War is being fundamentally transformed. Other economic centers are replacing the United States as the engine of growth. The principal one is Japan, which also is becoming more and more important to the Thai economy."[70]

Indeed, Japan's economic presence in Southeast Asia had become considerable. Through aid, investment, and industrial policies, Japan was playing an important leadership role in supporting Southeast Asian growth and development. While Western economies still provided the key markets for ASEAN products, the 1980s—spurred by the 1985 Plaza Accord—saw a dramatic intensification of investment and trade between Northeast Asia and Southeast Asia such that by the end of the decade, "Japan [had] surpassed the U.S. as the region's largest trading partner and aid donor."[71] While debates about wider regional cooperation revealed ASEAN states' persistent reservations about Japanese leadership, economic trends and developments also supported a larger role for Japan and East Asia as a response to changing US policies.

At very least, in the view of Mahathir, Japan could offer additional leadership in the face of U.S. post-Cold War economic retrenchment and the limitations of individual ASEAN economies to play that role. For example, the size of its economy gave Japan an ability to coordinate and provide public goods in ways that Singapore, though the most advanced of the ASEAN economies, could not. In addition, as Malaysia's Trade Minister Rafidah Aziz explained, Japan, as a member of the elite Group of Seven, could "express the region's concerns to the Group of Seven industrialized nations and ensure that investment continued to flow to the region."[72]

Meanwhile, other developments provided additional reasons to think beyond Southeast Asia and specifically to East Asia as an organizing principle. For one, "investment flows from Korea, Taiwan, Hong Kong, and Singapore [were] collectively and in some cases individually dwarf[ing] those of Japan and Western nations, especially the U.S."[73] For another, a growing Chinese economy was also gaining attractiveness as another possible motor of ASEAN growth. With China's economic reforms and the ending of the Cold War, Japan and Korea, as well as ASEAN states, had all initiated and expanded economic and trading relations with China. Even Indonesia, which had been most wary of China, saw economic opportunity by 1990, as illustrated by a historic visit to China that November by a Suharto-led delegation that also included Indonesia's Coordinating Minister for the Economy, Finance, Industry and Development Supervision.

In short, there was much to recommend Mahathir's proposal. Not only did it acknowledge Japan's already considerable economic presence in ASEAN-Southeast Asia, but it also seemed a logical expression of growing economic interdependencies between Southeast Asia and Northeast Asia. Such interdependencies also underscored a point made by regional economists who had long characterized intra-ASEAN economic cooperation as economically irrational. Noting the lack of complementarities between ASEAN economies, Chia Siow Yue and others argued, "The ASEAN regional market is too small for inward-looking regionalism."[74]

In short, trade flows and market forces continued to link ASEAN economies not with one another but with larger trading partners outside the region and increasingly with those in Northeast Asia. In fact, trade within Asia at this point had begun to grow at rates faster than trade between Asia and the rest of the world. Thus, Linda Lim and other economists concluded, "proposals for East Asian cooperation simply "reflected the new realities of ASEAN's international economic relations since the late 1980s . . . "[75] Other academics, noting the artificiality of the Cold War regional economy, saw in these intensified intra–East Asian economic exchanges a return to historical trade and economic relations, relations that had been severed by the Cold War.[76] The idea of a culturally defined East Asian group led by an Asian state also had some appeal in the context of growing cultural and developmental debates about "Asian values," human rights, and the developmental state. Nevertheless, East Asia faced an uphill battle during the early 1990s.

ASEAN and the APEC-EAEG Debate: In Pursuit of Consensus

Given APEC debates and politics of the previous year, it was perhaps unavoidable that Malaysia's East Asian group proposal would be viewed mostly in opposition to APEC. As others have detailed, APEC "won" its first bout with the EAEG for a number of reasons—not the least of which was strong opposition from Washington. For the United States, economic and political-security developments of 1989 and 1990, including Canberra's initial Asia Pacific proposal that excluded it, had begun to sharpen U.S. concerns about its own role and importance in the region. As U.S. Secretary of State James Baker later put it in his memoirs, the "Pacific century" was "rapidly becoming fact . . . My job was to make sure the United States would be a major part of it."[77]

As for the EAEG, the United States—as it did with APEC—brought its significant resources and influence to bear on key allies, in this case leaning especially hard on Japan and South Korea, both of whom were persuaded to oppose Mahathir's proposal.[78] As Baker bragged, "I did my best to kill [the EAEG] . . . My message was simple. All countries are not equal."[79] In this context, U.S. support for a U.S.–inclusive APEC became a way not only to satisfy growing calls for new regional cooperation but also very much to "preempt" the formation of any arrangement that excluded the United States.

This structural situation weighed heavily within ASEAN. For some, the problem with the EAEG, as articulated by Mahathir, was that it seemed to push away the United States at a time when the U.S. economic and political commitment to Asia was the most uncertain. Most, recognizing the truth in Baker's statement, were also ultimately unwilling to risk their ties with Washington, which had come out so strongly against East Asian cooperation.[80] In addition, there were concerns that a Japan-led group that excluded the United States might exacerbate U.S.–Japan trade tensions. Trade tensions, in turn, could affect U.S.–Japan security commitments, which ASEAN states considered an important constraint on Japanese power.

At the same time, the EAEG also found itself stymied and constrained by previous and ongoing debates about APEC and relatedly, ASEAN's now-established institutional-cultural expectations and practices. Both affected the content of the EAEG debate, as well as its directions. As discussed above, the intra-ASEAN debate on APEC settled on two important conditions of ASEAN participation: (1) opposition to "the establishment of an economic trading bloc, as that would be contrary to ASEAN's support for the establishment of a more fair and freer multilateral trading system"; and (2) the preservation of ASEAN's identity and cohesion, as well as its cooperative processes with dialogue partners.

These conditions of ASEAN's participation in the APEC process were formally reaffirmed at ASEAN's February 1990 joint ministerial meeting in Kuching (the "Kuching consensus"), affirmed again at ASEAN's AMM in July later that year, and then again in APEC's 1990 Joint Ministerial Statement. In particular, states continued to emphasize "a loose, exploratory and informal consultative process"; that there be a "pragmatic and gradual" approach to APEC's institutional development; and that cooperation proceed on the basis of equality, equity, and mutual benefit so as to respect different stages of development. As one Indonesian senior official explained, "We don't want institutionalization. We want to be ASEAN-centered, not the other way around."[81] The fact that states still deemed necessary such affirmations and reaffirmations of the above points despite their already having been laid out in APEC's 1989 Chairman's Summary Statement and inaugural Joint Ministerial Statement, point to ASEAN's persistent and particular concerns about APEC's significance for ASEAN despite the decision to go forward.

The perceived challenge to ASEAN represented by APEC moreover combined with intensified concerns about the Uruguay Round to convince states–including, critically, Indonesia—of the need to move beyond ASEAN's old economic regionalism and to intensify its own trade cooperation. In fact, it was Indonesia—which had consistently played the role of "Mr. No" in previous intra-ASEAN trade liberalization debates—that in October 1990 proposed the common tariff scheme (an approach that the Philippine trade secretary described as "radical")[82] that would allow states to finally move beyond the PTAs.[83]

Mahathir's EAEG announcement just two months later, in December 1990, thus entered the fray at a time when the question of ASEAN's participation in larger regional groupings was already particularly politicized and sensitive. While discussions seemed to move states toward greater acceptance of APEC by the end of 1990, that acceptance was the product of a protracted process. Nor had that process alleviated growing concerns about ASEAN's political and institutional relevance. This difficult decision was now challenged by Mahathir's proposal. Moreover, the way that Mahathir first introduced his proposal seemed to challenge the two nonnegotiable conditions of their tentative APEC agreement. The suddenness of the proposal (ASEAN capitals were reportedly taken by surprise by it) and its association with Japan and China (the press characterized the proposal as "an East Asian trading bloc" led by Japan; the proposal also debuted just as Chinese Premier Li Peng arrived in Kuala Lumpur for talks)—all seemed to suggest that ASEAN was being bypassed.

Faced with what Malaysian Trade Minister Rafidah Aziz described as a "cool" response from others in ASEAN, Malaysia immediately began to reframe the concept in ways that were more acceptable to its fellow ASEAN members, which meant in both GATT-consistent and ASEAN-supportive terms. Such clarifications were sufficient to persuade Singapore, which had originally opposed the proposal.[84] Speaking to their two points of agreement, Singapore's Goh Chok Tong on his inaugural visit to Malaysia as prime minister noted that the EAEG would "boost the multilateral free trade system" and "supplement ASEAN." He further emphasized that the EAEG should give "greater meaning to the APEC process without jeopardising [ASEAN's] traditionally important trading ties."[85] At the same time, Goh also agreed with Malaysia that (1) the United States should be excluded "because it has a free trade agreement with Canada"; and (2) the EAEG could strengthen ASEAN's own bargaining power because "ASEAN may not have the same weight in international fora as the East Asia group." Describing a "crescent of prosperity" stretching from Japan through China to Indochina and Myanmar and onto ASEAN, Goh added that his own vision for the region was a "natural extrapolation of Mahathir's idea."[86] Of other ASEAN states, Singapore would be the most supportive of Malaysia's EAEG proposal.

Following on the heels of Goh's visit was that of Thailand's new foreign minister Arthit Urairat on his own inaugural tour of ASEAN capitals in January. During his visit to Malaysia, Arthit, however, would not commit, saying only that ASEAN should be the core for wider regional economic expansion and that too many regional organizations might be "complicating."[87] His position seemed to soften a little following a discussion with Goh Chok Tong in Singapore ten days later—though with the important caveat that they first develop more fully ASEAN's economic role, which he said had yet to be realized despite its twenty-four-year existence.[88] (He expressed similar views toward APEC.)[89] Meanwhile, Malaysian Trade Minister Rafidah Aziz, sent on a tour of ASEAN capitals to explain the East Asia proposal, found the Philippines and especially Indonesia also noncommittal, though both expressed a willingness to study the proposal further.

In response to expressed concerns, Malaysia reiterated its commitment to ASEAN and its intent "not to take any action that will adversely affect it."[90] In addition, while Malaysia continued to maintain a leadership role for Japan in its proposed group, it also made a number of adjustments and clarifications in response to concerns. As early as January 8, during Goh Chok Tong's visit, for example, Malaysian officials had already begun to drop the word *bloc* in favor of *grouping*. By mid-February, the proposal described the EAEG as "complementary" and "supplementary" to as well as "revolv[ing] around ASEAN." As advocated by Thailand, the proposal also emphasized the priority of intra-ASEAN economic cooperation toward strengthening ASEAN and its ability to play that central role. Reframed, the EAEG would also be supportive of both successful global trade negotiations and APEC, as argued by Singapore, and, at the same time, create "a third major force in world economic and trade relations" that would help ASEAN better counter Western trading blocs.[91]

By late February, the EAEG further came to be described as a "step-by-step," evolutionary process, involving first, the creation of consensus—that is, the formation of a "like-minded group of countries" in the interest of consultation and identification of common interests in trade; and second, the "formalization of trade and economic links."[92] Taken together, Malaysia's efforts were able to persuade most to support the initiative "in principle" as long as it did not undermine existing regional processes. However, Suharto—despite consultative meetings with Mahathir and then with Goh Chok Tong the first week of March—remained opposed to the idea.[93] Warning against the danger posed to existing forums, he maintained that intra-ASEAN cooperation should be their priority as it was historically.[94]

Indonesia's resistance to the EAEG and apparent unwillingness to work with Malaysia even in principle seemed particularly hard line, especially given Malaysia's accommodations. Competing personalities, as much as competing ideas, may have factored into Suharto's opposition to the EAEG. Certainly, the two men often seemed at opposite ends of the spectrum. On one end was Mahathir, who could be brash, sharp, and direct, especially about the very global relationships that ASEAN states viewed as essential components to their own prosperity and thus stability. This fact—Mahathir's reputation was well established by the time of the EAEG announcement— made the EAEG an easy target for Washington's growing anxieties about its own role in East Asia and ultimately made the EAEG more politicized than it might have been. Thus, while many in ASEAN were sympathetic to some of Mahathir's arguments[95] and some were "clearly irritated at the U.S. for making such a big issue of the whole thing,"[96] his confrontational approach (not the ASEAN way!) nevertheless made it more difficult for others in ASEAN to accept, especially given Washington's strong reaction. As Singapore's Tommy Koh put it, "Prime Minister Mahathir's mistake was the way he put [the EAEG] and the language was wrong."[97]

On the other end of the spectrum was Suharto, known for his low-key and nonconfrontational leadership. Indonesian–Malaysian differences on the EAEG also were likely exacerbated by the perception that Mahathir-led Malaysia was upstaging Indonesia, which considered itself first among ASEAN equals and the foreign policy of which had recently taken a more activist direction. Mahathir was also viewed as upstaging Suharto, who had recently become ASEAN's last sitting "founding father" following Lee Kuan Yew's stepping down. All these factors likely contributed to what Michael Vatikiotis described as Indonesia's "excessive" and "aggressive" opposition to the EAEG proposal.[98]

Nevertheless, as long as Indonesia (and specifically Suharto) remained opposed, there could be no ASEAN consensus. Twice in March, at two separate senior officials meetings, ASEAN officials punted, agreeing only to give the EAEG further study.[99] This resulted in Malaysia's characterizing the EAEG in even looser terms. As described by Rafidah Aziz on April 6 in her first face-to-face with Tokyo on the subject, the EAEG was now a loose, consultative forum whose goal was "not to form a bloc, but to talk."[100] This characterization of the EAEG as a consultative forum was then repeated at a PECC meeting, as well as by Goh Chok Tong in his effort to "sell" the EAEG to Japan.[101] However, despite the joint efforts of Malaysia and Singapore and greater support from Thailand, ministers meeting at ASEAN's July 1991 AMM still came to no conclusion.

Not until ASEAN's October 1991 AEM, in fact, would there be a formal resolution. Picking up on a recommendation put forward by ASEAN's Institute of Strategic and International Studies (ASEAN-ISIS), a network of ASEAN think tanks, the AEM agreed to adopt Malaysia's East Asian initiative in the form of a "caucus."[102] As outlined in their joint statement, the ministers agreed "to [the] convening of East Asian economies and to meet as and when the need arises."[103]

Feed Back: The ASEAN Free Trade Agreement

The exchanges above illustrate important bounds of the debate created by concerns about ASEAN but also by ASEAN ideas that provided states their regional language and legitimating frames. At the same time, ASEAN itself was not unaffected by APEC and EAEG debates. In drawing on ASEAN to argue for or against new regional initiatives and projects, states nevertheless drew attention to ASEAN's institutional and political limitations. The emergence of alternative regional proposals also played to ASEAN's historic and current sense of fragility—a sense of fragility that was now intensified by the ending of the Cold War and especially Cambodian conflicts discussed in the last chapter. Again, while both events were certainly welcomed, the ending of those conflicts that had been such a focus of attention in ASEAN nevertheless put front and center the question: What next for ASEAN? What would ASEAN do now? Would ASEAN be able to hold the attention of its member states? As noted, this last question was made all the more real by "beggar thy neighbor" policies, "bidding wars" for trade and investment, and the new "scramble" for business opportunities in Indochina.[104] As Indonesia's Coordinating Minister for Economic, Financial, and Industrial Affairs Radius Prawiro put it in January 1992, days before a historic summit in Singapore, "fierce competition rather than mutual cooperation" was taking over ASEAN, contributing to a zero-sum kind of thinking over the region-regarding, collective mindset ASEAN should be promoting, thus threatening regional cohesion.[105]

APEC and the EAEG—as expressions of states' interest in alternative regional configurations—thus intensified, as much as they were constrained by, ASEAN's sense of existential fragility. Moreover, such questions about ASEAN's future and future roles gained even greater prominence over the course of 1991 as states prepared for their upcoming leaders' summit. As with most international summits, ASEAN's scheduled summit exerted pressure to produce something important and meaningful; but, in this case, the pressure was made even greater by questions about ASEAN's post-Cambodia relevance and the fact that the summit was only ASEAN's fourth in twenty-five years.

As noted above, the combined and interactive challenges from global trade rounds, U.S. policies, and APEC and EAEG proposals had already begun to expand states' openness to new intra-ASEAN trade cooperation. But developments over the course of 1991 no doubt intensified all the trends and concerns above. In particular, moves toward regional single markets in Western Europe and North America provided very real manifestations of what had previously been abstract fears about Western protectionism and the collapse of global talks. Indeed, of the four press releases put out by ASEAN's economic ministers in 1991, three of them specifically addressed the protracted Uruguay Round negotiations and their feared breakdown.[106]

In April 1991 Thai Prime Minister Anand followed Indonesia's October 1990 common tariff scheme with a proposed ASEAN free trade area. By midyear, all five members advocated intensified intra-ASEAN cooperation in the interest of maintaining their own economic and political viability and toward better positioning ASEAN to lead (and not to be subsumed by) larger regional arrangements.[107] In July ASEAN foreign ministers—citing North American and European efforts to link the environment and human rights to trade, the threat posed by North American and European trade agreements, and the likely diversion of investment to Eastern Europe and Mexico—agreed to forward a proposed ASEAN free trade area to leaders to consider at their summit scheduled for January 1992.[108] In October 1991—the same month that the Paris Peace Accord officially ending the Cambodian conflict was signed—ASEAN's economic ministers approved Indonesia's common tariff scheme, which was then merged with the Thai proposal to create an ASEAN free trade area.

At the 1992 summit in Singapore, leaders formally endorsed a new common effective preferential tariff scheme (CEPT). Their declaration made

clear the concerns that had led them to that historic decision: the "formation of large and powerful economic groupings among developed countries"
and its implication for an open global trading regime, the need to reconcile
ASEAN with newer regional arrangements, and ASEAN's post-Cambodia
relevance and unity.[109] On this last point, Indonesia's Minister of Trade
Arifin Siregar was blunt: "If ASEAN does not rapidly form the AFTA, it
is feared that ASEAN countries might join other planned free trade zones
outside ASEAN which would only weaken ASEAN unity."[110]

Thus, ASEAN took its "great leap" forward into intra-ASEAN trade liberalization. In fact, in practically every respect, the 1992 CEPT was a significant improvement over the PTAs. Most notably, the CEPT from the out-
set dropped the PTA's product-by-product approach for a sector-by-sector
approach to intra-ASEAN trade liberalization. In so doing, the CEPT thus
addressed ASEAN's past practice of padding lists with inconsequential products. In addition, where the PTAs operated by having members list product
by product the items that were to *receive* preferential treatment, the CEPT
asked members to list product by product items that were to be *excluded* from
the scheme. In other words, where the PTAs allowed states the semblance
of doing something by adding individual items (however inconsequential)
to inclusion lists, the CEPT required states to take the active step of adding
(and thus having to justify) products on exclusion lists. Thus, the structure
of the framework created a political and social deterrent from members creating overly long exclusion lists. In addition, unlike the PTAs, which had
called only for a minimum tariff reduction (10 to 15 percent), CEPT directed
all members to reduce tariffs on intra-ASEAN trade toward a common tariff
rate of 5 percent or lower by the year 2008 (which later would be moved up
to 2003).[111]

As further indication of members' new thinking about intra-ASEAN economic cooperation, states adopted a Framework Agreement on Enhancing
ASEAN Economic Cooperation based on a new "flexible" understanding
of consensus (a proposal that Singapore had advocated first in 1980 and then
again in 1987). Via the "6-minus-X" formula,[112] the CEPT allowed all those
members desiring of action to proceed forward and opponents of action to
delay their participation in intra-ASEAN trade arrangements.[113] In this way,
the new formula increased the likelihood that trade liberalization would
move forward. Not only would it guard against one member holding everyone else back, but flexible consensus also would exert material and social
pressure on members to participate for fear of being left behind and/or
being branded uncommitted to ASEAN.

Toward improving ASEAN's institutional ability to administer new economic agreements, members also established an experienced intragovernmental body, the Senior Economic Officials Meeting (SEOM), to oversee the implementation of the CEPT agreement and AFTA scheme. The SEOM replaced ASEAN's five national economic committees that had once overseen economic cooperation, thus offering a more centralized process. Both the ASEAN Secretariat and the Secretary-General were also upgraded: The Secretariat was given an "expanded mandate" to "initiate, advise, coordinate, and implement" ASEAN policies and action plans; the Secretary-General now became the Secretary-General of *ASEAN* and not simply of the ASEAN *Secretariat*. In addition, the Secretary General was given an extended term (five years from the previous three) and furthermore was to be "appointed on merit and accorded ministerial status."[114] Finally, ASEAN heads of state at the Singapore summit also agreed to hold regularized summits every three years, instead of calling them as necessary as they had done over the last twenty-five years. As the Singapore Declaration highlighted, each of these measures was necessary "to strengthen ASEAN."[115]

The 1992 CEPT scheme was by no means a perfect agreement. Critics noted, for example, the long time frame, its lack of a dispute resolution mechanism (which has since been adopted), its permitting of individual exclusion lists, and its lack of specificity on a variety of issues (how to determine ASEAN content, rules of fair competition, and the harmonization of standards). To be sure, at a mere eight pages (compare to NAFTA's nearly 2,000), it was clear that the CEPT—like the 1967 Bangkok Declaration twenty-five years earlier—had left many details to be worked out in the future.[116] Consensus would continue to be sought.

Conclusion

In sum, intra-ASEAN debates about economic regionalisms in the 1980s and 1990s continued to illustrate the ways that global uncertainties and changes interacted with longstanding concerns about both national and regional resilience to set the stage for new economic regionalisms. In this case, questions about U.S. trade policies interacted with troubled global trade negotiations to exert pressure for change at both domestic and regional levels. Initial questions proved insufficient to convince states to take that great leap on economic regionalism, but they did build on one another over the course of a decade to destabilize existing ideas about key relationships, approaches, and arrangements. Questions built up over a decade created domestic, structural, and normative opportunity for new ideas about liberalization to take hold; they also generated a slow-building sense of crisis that, in turn, sustained ongoing debates about change. The various concerns interacting and building on one another over the 1980s mitigated against the hope that things would improve and intensified pressure on all that something must be done.

Here, it may be useful to think about the particular roles of Maastricht and NAFTA—both of which were explicitly identified as reasons for AFTA. As concrete manifestations of states' decade of concerns about the global economy, both made it more difficult for states like Indonesia to hold out for a global solution. At the same time, Maastricht and NAFTA did not transform the debate, nor did they move the debate in new directions. After ten years of intra-ASEAN debate and insecurity, Maastricht and NAFTA were not transformative developments so much as they were the straw that broke the camel's back.

At the same time, the above chronicle of debates also makes clear that uncertainty in and of itself is insufficient to push states to a new level of intra-ASEAN trade liberalization. Moreover, the same domestic, normative, and structural changes above created opportunities for new arguments not just about intra-ASEAN cooperation but also for new non–Southeast Asian regional arrangements. These ideas, which took the form of APEC and the EAEG, challenged both ASEAN solidarity and even the very idea of Southeast Asia as an organizing principle. In debating APEC and the EAEG, ASEAN itself became the focal point of debates. Just as resilience provided the legitimating frames for intra-ASEAN cooperation, ASEAN itself—in other words, preserving ASEAN as an institution, process, practice, even identity,[117] as much ASEAN unity—increasingly became over the course of the 1990s a key argumentative frame that ultimately bound and shaped the content and development of APEC and EAEG frameworks. Precisely because there was normative agreement about ASEAN's value to Southeast Asia, ASEAN came to offer itself an important rallying and unifying point in the search for consensus on new arrangements.

The role played by ASEAN as the main rhetorical focal point of debates about Asia Pacific and East Asian cooperation can be traced back to founding agreements and arguments about ASEAN's importance to intraregional relations and overall resilience. Underlying ASEAN remain states' founding assumptions about the fragility of intra-ASEAN bonds, the very premise of regional resilience arguments. In the late 1980s, this particular rhetorical frame was given additional centrality by coinciding and growing fears about ASEAN's post-Cambodia fragmentation and the existential threats to

ASEAN represented by the EAEG and especially APEC. Here, ASEAN provided an important point of agreement and certainty in the face of uncertain developments (be it about the specifics of Asia Pacific and EAEG proposals or about world developments in general). It also provided the language, as well as prism through which to understand and thus respond to uncertain developments. This is not to say that there were not also other lenses in the viewfinder, but importantly it was the ASEAN lens that they all shared.

Lastly, this chapter has also illustrated some ways that debates about APEC and EAEG fed back into discussions about intra-ASEAN trade liberalization. In other words, shared understandings about ASEAN may have bound the development of both APEC and the EAEG, but ASEAN itself was not unaffected by them. For example, in drawing on ASEAN to delegitimate or legitimate new regional initiatives and projects, states also highlighted ASEAN's institutional limitations and the understood fragility of relations. Especially in the context of post-Cambodia insecurity and the presence of actual regional alternatives to ASEAN, this highlighting of ASEAN's weaknesses created additional momentum for new action. Noordin Sopiee, who himself was an influential advocate of the EAEG idea in Malaysia, summarized well the argument:

> We must act with determination and efficiency to strengthen ASEAN. We must concentrate on ASEAN cohesion and strengthen ASEAN capabilities. If we are not careful and if we fail to respond to the present multi-directional challenges to ASEAN solidarity, it is possible that ASEAN will be peripheralised not only in the Pacific but also in the world and even within South East Asia.[118]

In this way, ASEAN itself became an important rallying point, which in turn produced AFTA, new economic decision-making processes, and an upgraded secretariat and secretary general.

The debate between APEC and the EAEG fed back into the ASEAN process in other ways, as well. For one, the tensions between Suharto and Mahathir had lasting effects at very least in terms of ASEAN's clout in APEC. If unity once gave ASEAN unusual influence over the founding of APEC, ASEAN disunity diminished their ability to better direct that forum's directions and development. For another, the particular emphasis placed on ASEAN and Southeast Asia as an organizing principle in debates about APEC and the EAEG meant that states' participation in these other larger frameworks had to be reconciled. Thus, ASEAN elites offered various conceptualizations toward that purpose: "concentric circles,"[119] "expanding and intersecting circles,"[120] a "nucleus for . . . [Asian Pacific] initiatives,"[121] and "fulcrum for wider cooperation in the Asia Pacific, particularly in the

EAEC and APEC."[122] Most significantly, according to these new conceptualizations, smaller groups like ASEAN could exist within larger groups
without losing their identity or purpose.[123] But while these conceptualizations may have given greater legitimacy to ASEAN's new regional activities,
they also altered and expanded what had been ASEAN's historic Southeast
Asian purview, which subsequently introduced new tensions even at the
same time that it gave ASEAN new relevance.

6

ASEAN of and Beyond Southeast Asia:
The ASEAN Regional Forum

It is better to talk than not to talk, and it is better to talk to people
you know.

Bangkok Post (25 July 1994)

We reject the possibility of ASEAN evolving into a regional, collective security arrangement or military alliance. We are able to
do this because of our belief that to win friends, one should not
create enemies.

Mahathir bin Mohamad,
Prime Minister of Malaysia, 1987[1]

As regional and global systems transitioned into a new era, economics and
trade were not the only areas where new challenges were compelling new
thinking about regionalism. In the political-security realm, as well, ASEAN
states found themselves confronted with parallel concerns about major
power roles, intra-ASEAN unity, and indeed the future of Southeast Asia as
a meaningful region and organizing principle. This chapter traces the process by which ASEAN's founding consensus about security and understandings about its identity as a Southeast Asian organization are destabilized and
the subsequent process of debate and consensus searching that follows. This
chapter shows how old ideas—resilience as unity, self-determination, inclusive engagement, and perhaps most important, the idea of Southeast Asia as
a distinct region—continue to constrain collective endeavors but are also
adapted for new conditions.

In detailing these processes, this chapter picks up on four intertwined,
interactive debates. The first two are continuations of older debates, namely,
the appropriateness of external security guarantees and a Southeast Asian
ZOPFAN. The latter two—whether to extend ASEAN's Treaty of Amity
and Cooperation and ASEAN processes beyond Southeast Asia—focus on the
appropriateness of ASEAN principles, processes, and modes of engagement
beyond Southeast Asia. The products of these debates will be a refined U.S.–
ASEAN security relationship, a new Southeast Asian Nuclear Weapons Free

Zone Treaty (SEANWFZ)—only ASEAN's second treaty—an expanded regional purview, and, most significant, the creation of the ASEAN Regional Forum (ARF), the Asia-Pacific's first official security dialogue and states' first ASEAN-led institutional foray into ASEAN-plus regionalism. These efforts and adaptations are significant for expanding ASEAN beyond its originating conditions. They will also help give ASEAN's coalition of lesser powers a much more influential role in shaping the emergent post–Cold War regional system and order than they or anyone else ever expected they would play.

Renegotiating ASEAN's Great Power Predicament

As before, uncertainties about the U.S. security commitment to Southeast Asia played a particular role in catalyzing new thinking about existing arrangements. The prospect of U.S. retrenchment drew attention to long-standing concerns about the dependability of U.S. security commitments, states' vulnerabilities as smaller powers, and the wisdom of U.S.–centric arrangements. Though Moscow became less of a concern in the early 1990s, ASEAN states, as during previous times of U.S. uncertainty, tended to see a reduced U.S. security commitment to Southeast Asia as opening the door for China and Japan to play larger, less predictable roles in Southeast Asia.

This time, the ending of the Cold War and Cambodian conflicts added new intensity to their concerns. On Japan, concerns focused on the critical U.S.–Japan security relationship, long considered by ASEAN states to be a positive constraint on Japanese power. The ending of the Cold War weakened Washington's strategic interest in supporting a country that had become a major economic power and even formidable economic rival. The result was heightened U.S. pressure on Japan not just to open its markets but also to assume larger responsibility for both its own security and the security of the larger region.

The particular concern of ASEAN states was Japan's possible remilitarization. For example, if Japan saw the United States as insufficiently protecting it from North Korea or China or if it felt that its considerable economic and trade interests in Southeast Asia were at risk, Japan might feel compelled to remilitarize and even to renew its imperial ambitions in Southeast Asia.[2] Such were, for example, some of the arguments offered by a 1994 Tokyo-commissioned report that recommended that Japan develop autonomous capability as a hedge against further deterioration of U.S.–Japan relations.[3]

Meanwhile, the ending of the Cambodian conflict, combined with post–Cold War uncertainties about U.S. commitments, added to the questions about China. ASEAN concerns would grow with reports of China's military modernization and heightened Chinese activity around the Spratly Islands, to which ASEAN members (Malaysia, Philippines, Brunei, and after 1995, Vietnam) were also claimants.[4] Technical acquisitions and the building of an airstrip in the Paracel Islands further pointed to a growing ability to project its presence southward and an interest in "extend[ing] its sovereign jurisdiction deep into the heart of Southeast Asia."[5] The South China Sea would in fact become the defining issue of ASEAN–China relations in the 1990s and even a litmus test for Chinese intentions.[6]

At the same time, as highlighted by the discussion below, collective ASEAN was in fact slow to change. The defining ASEAN initiatives of the 1990s—the ARF, an expanded TAC, the SEANWFZ treaty—all took years to come into fruition as appropriate responses to regional changes. Partly, this was because states perceived greater strategic ambiguity in the changing security landscape than is often emphasized.[7] But partly, also, it was because the processes of argument and consensus seeking were also cumulative, involving first the desensitization of critical security issues, then growing familiarity with potential options, before collective ASEAN would be convinced to pursue new (and in the case of the ARF, radically new) directions. The discussion below traces these processes and shows how ASEAN's defining post–Cold War political-security initiatives were the products of these cumulative and interactive processes.

The Manglapus Initiative

Questions about U.S. security commitments in Southeast Asia emerged as early as 1986. That year Philippines' People Power revolution ousted Ferdinand Marcos, brought into power a new democratic government, and opened the door for more nationalist voices, especially those more critical of the U.S. presence in the Philippines, to gain influence. As most notably symbolized by President Aquino's decision to visit ASEAN neighbors before Washington, the regime change represented an opportunity for Manila, which had been very pro–United States under Marcos, to pursue a more independent foreign policy.[8] That window of opportunity widened further with Aquino's June 1986 convening of a Constitutional Commission. Charged with the drafting of a new Philippine constitution, that commission considered new constitutional provisions for U.S. bases in the Philippines. The new government would also come under pressure from communist forces, which made elimination of U.S. bases a key demand in their negotiations with Manila in 1987. In newly democratic, post-Marcos

Philippines, Manila's relationship with Washington and especially U.S. bases had become hot and sensitive subjects of debate, as well as tests of one's nationalist credentials.

Pro–U.S. forces were able to defeat more extreme proposals that categorically banned foreign military bases, troops, and facilities from Philippine national territory, but two clauses in the new constitution kept the door open for further challenge. The first allowed U.S. bases to remain only until 1991 (the expiration date of the extant agreement), at which time all foreign bases would be banned from the Philippines "except in accordance with a new treaty duly concurred by the Senate" or if deemed necessary by Congress, popular referendum, or plebiscite. The other provision restricted nuclear weapons from the Philippines. In the new constitution's Declaration of Principles, the former U.S. colony asserted that "the Philippines, consistent with the national interest, adopts and pursues a policy of freedom from nuclear weapons in its territory."[9] In short, while both permitted continuation of U.S.–Philippine security arrangements, both also made clear that their continuation was temporary and conditional.

The latter provision in fact provided the basis for subsequent legislation outlawing the possession, storage, and transport of nuclear weapons in Philippine territory.[10] Introduced in August 1987 and ratified by a wide margin in the Senate in June 1988, the legislation put back some of the bite that had been lost in the earlier redrafting of the new Philippine constitution. It also aligned the Philippines, which had long battled its pro-American image abroad, with more independent forces and recent nuclear weapon–free zone initiatives in Latin America, the South Pacific, and closer to home, ASEAN's own calls for a Southeast Asian ZOPFAN and nuclear-free zone, the latter of which U.S. bases in the Philippines had posed a key contradiction.[11] It was immediately apparent to most that the legislation had potentially serious implications for U.S security commitments in Southeast Asia. Similar (and, in fact, less strict) legislation passed in New Zealand in 1985 had already led to the suspension of U.S.–New Zealand security commitments and, in effect, the end of the ANZUS security alliance.

This, then, was the domestic, regional, and global context from which newly confirmed Foreign Secretary Raul Manglapus was speaking when he launched his challenge to ASEAN's carefully constructed, founding consensus on U.S. basing arrangements. Specifically, in August 1987, as Manila prepared to renegotiate U.S. bases in the Philippines, he began calling on ASEAN states to have an open discussion and reach a collective decision on U.S. bases and their contributions to ASEAN security. Even more radical, he suggested that the burden of the U.S. security presence be dispersed and shared throughout the region.[12] At minimum, he hoped that confronting others with the prospect of a U.S. departure would result in some collective affirmation of the bases' contribution to overall ASEAN security. Such affirmation and support from ASEAN, he believed, could help blunt some of the nationalist pressure at home against the bases.

The appeal to his fellow ASEAN members also reflected a widely held view in the Philippines that others in ASEAN had been allowed to free ride on its efforts, enjoying all of the security benefits of U.S. bases without paying any of the political costs in terms of both domestic and international constituencies. By this view, U.S. bases in the Philippines had allowed others in ASEAN to champion national and regional self-determination but at the same time be relatively assured of the comforting presence of the United States nearby. When he characterized the Philippines' hosting of U.S. bases as "a national and regime sacrifice for the good of ASEAN," Manglapus was in fact explicit on this point. As he put it, "The Philippines has borne the burden of the bases for the last 40 years for the defense of Southeast Asia."[13]

Both the impetus behind the Manglapus initiative and the challenges it faced illustrate both material and normative dimensions of states' lesser power predicament,[14] as well as the ways that the predicament played out within, as much between, states. Domestically, it played out in the streets of Manila and between executive and legislative branches of the Philippine government. Though members of Aquino's own party sponsored the nuclear-free legislation aimed at limiting and even eliminating U.S. bases, the Aquino administration ultimately chose to preserve the U.S.–Philippine security relationship at least until 1991, when the current agreement expired. Ruling that the regulation of nuclear weapons was a presidential, not congressional, authority, the Philippines' Department of Justice also exempted the United States from the new legislation's restrictions on nuclear weapons.[15]

Such actions aligned the Aquino government with more pro–U.S. forces. As noted above, strong pressure existed at home from forces that viewed U.S. bases as vestiges of American colonial rule.[16] As Aquino discovered her first year, even reports of U.S. political support could bring on charges of "vassalage" to the "Great White Father."[17] Meanwhile, abroad and within ASEAN, Manila faced criticism from those who identified the Philippines with the United States. The (London) *Times* characterized Aquino's predicament thus: "[S]he feels vulnerable at home—where the left uses the bases as a popular rallying cause for the faithful. Abroad she feels exposed and isolated."[18]

However, if Manila could convince others in ASEAN to offer their collective support, it could give its position greater legitimacy. After all, it would confirm, then, the argument that the Philippines was acting for ASEAN and for the larger good of the region as opposed to acting as the client state of the United States. Thus, Manglapus's call was repeated by Aquino herself at ASEAN's 1987 summit in Manila. Referring to the "Philippine factor" and its role in "securing [the] airspace and sea lanes that are vital to the economic stability and growth of our neighbours in South-East Asia," Aquino called on ASEAN to acknowledge publicly the importance of U.S. bases: "ASEAN is first about friendship and responsible statesmanship . . . and the wisdom to see that . . . devotion to national security requires an equal commitment to the security of the region, the hemisphere and the world."[19] As Manglapus later explained, "[Aquino's remarks were] a diplomatically disguised invitation for all to join in the political responsibility for U.S. bases and rescue the Philippines from the divisive and polarizing domestic issue of being the lone bases host in Southeast Asia."[20]

The problem, however, was that the same predicament that faced the Philippines also faced its neighbors, who found the Manglapus initiative too direct, too public, and thus too overt a challenge to their own efforts to establish independent foreign policy identities. This was particularly true of Indonesia, which was seeking to become the next chairman of the Non-Aligned Movement (a position that, to its embarrassment as a founding member of NAM, it failed to win that year). The Philippine proposal also directly challenged Indonesian-led efforts to establish a SEANWFZ. Proposed in 1984, SEANWFZ was conceived as supporting ASEAN's larger ZOPFAN objectives and had moreover recently gained momentum following the successful conclusion of the South Pacific's Rarotonga Treaty. Manglapus's request for common support for U.S. bases in the Philippines thus conflicted with Indonesia's SEANWFZ efforts, not to mention ZOPFAN. As Manglapus acknowledged, "If the option of retaining [the bases] is chosen, we will have to find a modus vivendi by which the facilities can continue alongside with our policy of neutrality and a nuclear weapons-free area."[21]

It was perhaps no surprise, then, that ASEAN was unable to give Manila what it asked for. Both Jakarta and Kuala Lumpur certainly understood the stabilizing role played by U.S. bases in the Philippines, but the desired public affirmation was simply too direct an approach given the identities they had established for themselves at home and abroad. Indonesia, especially, took issue with the implied suggestion that Indonesia could not take care of its own security, as well as Aquino's disregard for an informal agreement not to raise the subject at the summit.[22] As for others, Singapore and Thailand expressed some support but the question was otherwise officially dropped due to the perceived irreconcilability of Jakarta's and Manila's public positions. Amplifying the perceived danger this question posed to ASEAN unity, and indeed ASEAN itself, was knowledge that differences between Jakarta and Manila on the bases nearly prevented ASEAN from being established at all in 1967.[23] Consequently, members refused to address Manila's request, and there was no mention of the matter in leaders' 1987 summit declaration—though there were Philippine accounts that ASEAN leaders had conveyed their support in a confidential report.

Singapore Answers Manila's Call

After a year of relatively little activity on the subject, the debate was reignited on August 4, 1989, with Singapore's announcement that it would provide U.S. forces in the Pacific expanded access and support. Negotiations over the course of 1989 and 1990 produced a memorandum of understanding (MOU) allowing for a "modest increase" in U.S. maintenance and repair facilities in Singapore. A second MOU followed in 1992. As an extension of the first, that agreement moved a naval logistics unit supporting the U.S. Seventh Fleet from the Philippines.

From Singapore's perspective, the decision was a necessary response to developments over the course of 1988 and early 1989. U.S.–Philippine negotiations over just an interim agreement to cover the last two years of their extant basing agreement had nearly broken down in 1988 over questions of compensation. Also in 1988, the Philippine Senate passed its antinuclear legislation, raising new questions about the legality of U.S. bases. Adding to the questions were intensified efforts to push ASEAN's own SEANWFZ—efforts that Washington characterized as "unhelpful" and problematic to its current basing arrangements and ability to maneuver in Southeast Asia tactically and politically.[24] In fact, from 1988 and into 1989, no less than six high-ranking officials (including President Reagan himself in March 1988) publicly stated their objections to ASEAN's proposed SEANWFZ.[25] Meanwhile, President Aquino continued to stall on setting a date for renegotiating the bases. Uncertainty about the future of U.S. bases in the Philippines was such that Washington in early 1989 decided to suspend the $42 million previously allocated for military-related construction projects in the Philippines.

For tiny Singapore, whose sense of insecurity tended to be more acute due to its size and history with its neighbors, such developments convinced it that something had to be done to facilitate a continued U.S. security presence in Southeast Asia; otherwise, as Singapore's Minister of State for Foreign Affairs George Yeo explained, a "whole chain of events . . . would follow": U.S. withdrawal would lead to a rearmed Japan, which would cause China and Korea to accumulate arms, which would then heighten Indonesian and Malaysian insecurity, which would then have implications for Singapore. The negative chain of events described by Yeo thus revealed not only Singapore's concern about larger Northeast Asian powers but also its continuing insecurity about its closest neighbors. As Yeo put it, the thought of Asia without the United States was "frightening." [26]

While Singapore's action likely hurt Manila's bargaining position vis-à-vis Washington, Manila was quick to offer support. As Manglapus put it, "Singapore is saying that we're no longer alone."[27] Thailand, though mostly supportive, stayed out of the debate by characterizing the action as a "bilateral issue" between Singapore and Washington. The response from Jakarta and Kuala Lumpur, on the other hand, was "pungent and public."[28] Both saw the action as contrary to their nationalist and regionalist interest in self-determination. Both also found the agreement problematic on account of Singapore's proximity to them—a point illustrated by Jakarta's and Kuala Lumpur's new willingness to support U.S. arrangements in the Philippines over new ones in Singapore. In Indonesia, a 1950s incident when the United States used Clark Air Base to supply rebelling forces outside Java provided the key historical referent for its concerns. As a *Jakarta Post* editorial explained, if there are those who wonder, "What . . . could be the cause of the apprehensions that apparently continue to exist among Indonesians about this relatively small American presence in Singapore," it is because Indonesians see the U.S. presence as existing to counter Indonesia.[29] Not helping these concerns was Singapore's failure to consult with either Jakarta or Kuala Lumpur.[30]

However, in their criticisms of Singapore, Jakarta and Kuala Lumpur notably drew on collectivist themes and established regional frames. Specifically, they criticized their neighbor for undermining their common and collective security, for being insufficiently region regarding, and for its insensitivity to the sentiments of its ASEAN neighbors. In contrast to Singapore's view that it was *preserving* the regional status quo, Indonesia and Malaysia charged Singapore with "*destabilizing*" the status quo and security of the region which had been "fairly free from the influence of superpowers." By contributing to the "proliferation of bases" and "arms" into the region, Singapore's action, they argued, was "without logic," had set back their collective interest in a Southeast Asian ZOPFAN and SEANWFZ, and had "undermin[ed] peace processes" in Southeast Asia.[31] Even the youth wing of UMNO, Malaysia's ruling party, got into the act with its characterization of Singapore's decision as a betrayal of ASEAN principles and efforts to bring peace and neutrality to Southeast Asia.[32]

Most of all, both Indonesia and Malaysia made clear that they would not tolerate the creation of any new foreign bases. Referencing ASEAN's 1967 Bangkok Declaration, one high-ranking Indonesian official suggested that Singapore's action challenged the founding principles and founding consensus on which ASEAN had been built.[33] Another official put it in even stronger terms: "Indonesia's stand is clear. A new foreign base will create instability within the region . . . [I]t would mean a setback for ASEAN . . . I assure you, Indonesia will not remain calm if the Singapore Government offer of a military base to an outside power becomes fact."[34]

ASEAN themes, especially about regional resilience and balkanization from without, were also played up in the Indonesian and Malaysian press, which criticized Washington for trying to destroy ASEAN unity and Singapore for allowing Washington to do so. In Malaysia, *Berita Harian Malaysia* compared the situation to the Middle East: "If Israel, a small country with U.S. military support, can succeed in destroying unity in the Middle East, it is not impossible that one day, with the U.S. military presence in Singapore, ASEAN may face the same fate."[35] Singapore's second MOU with the United States the following year would prompt a similar response from retired Indonesian Lt. General and former ambassador to Japan Sayidiman Suryohadiprojo, writing into the *Jakarta Post*. Charging both with fomenting division within ASEAN, he found Washington guilty of imagining threats and pitting regional states against one another. As for Singapore, the former ambassador took the city-state to task for its insufficient ASEAN spirit. As he put it, if the United States was in Singapore "to safeguard the security of Southeast Asia against one or more of its member states," and "if that is the consideration of the [Singapore] people in favor of a U.S. military base in Singapore, then those people have discarded the ASEAN spirit of mutual trust and cooperation."[36]

Such exchanges, including criticisms of Singapore's lack of consultation and the explicit linkages made between regional division and foreign manipulations, illustrate the ways that the shared language of regional unity continued to frame intra-ASEAN debates. However, these exchanges ultimately did more than just affirm core principles. In making states reassess and clarify their positions, these exchanges would also narrow areas of a disagreement and facilitate a new, explicit consensus as regards the great power question.

Specifically, there emerged new agreement that particular kinds of foreign arrangements—temporary and commercial—were within ASEAN bounds of acceptability. For example, both critics and defenders of Singapore tended to focus on questions of permanence and whether new arrangements were in fact "bases" as measures of their appropriateness. Citing the Bangkok Declaration's temporary bases clause, Manglapus, for one, defended U.S. arrangements in Singapore (and the Philippines) on the grounds that they were "temporary realities" and thus consistent with ASEAN's "long-term" ZOPFAN objectives.[37] Both Malaysian and Indonesian officials also focused on this distinction in their objections to "foreign bases" but not "maintenance facilities." As Mahathir put it, "Malaysia has never objected if American forces use facilities in Singapore for supplies, maintenance and servicing of its warships and planes. The establishment of permanent bases, however, will change the character of ASEAN" and was thus unacceptable.[38] Lee Kuan Yew, after a meeting with Suharto, was also explicit in emphasizing that there would be no U.S. base in Singapore "whatever happens."[39] This point would be reaffirmed in 1992 following the second Singapore–U.S. MOU.

From this process of criticizing, defending, and reconciling emerged explicit agreement that commercial agreements—because they were temporary and forged between two sovereign parties—were acceptable and not contrary to ASEAN goals and principles. As a result of this new clarification, Singapore's second MOU two years later was much less controversial than the first. While Indonesia and Malaysia still complained about Singapore's failure to consult or provide sufficient advance notice of the details, both were also quick (this time, within days not weeks of the original announcement)[40] to state that it was a nonissue. As both made clear, "As long as the U.S. does not set up a permanent base in Singapore, we have no objections."[41]

Beyond the New Consensus

On the surface, such accommodations may seem relatively minor. After all, ASEAN's 1967 Bangkok Declaration did note the "temporary" character of foreign bases, and Indonesia and Malaysia did understand the role played by the United States as a "stabilizing agent" even if they did not wish to say so publicly.[42] In addition, new agreements increased the U.S. presence in Singapore only modestly. Not only did the two countries already enjoy close security cooperation, but U.S. warships already had permission to dock in Singapore for maintenance, supplies, and rest. Even with the 1992

MOU, the number of U.S. personnel to be stationed in Singapore remained relatively small (under 200).[43]

Normatively, however, the Philippine and Singapore initiatives had begun to do something quite significant. They had forced a taboo issue that had been constrained by both identity claims and the demands of regional unity out into the public. Manglapus himself spoke to this point in his reflections on ASEAN's reluctance to discuss the issue in 1989: "Perhaps, [ASEAN] does not feel that such an item [question of foreign bases] on the agenda would be constructive in strengthening the unity of ASEAN. Since it is evident that we hold different views, therefore [we would] rather not talk about it."[44] By forcing discussion, however, both Philippine and Singapore initiatives began a critical process of desensitizing the issue of extraregional security arrangements. Where previously states found the issue so divisive that they did not wish to talk about it, the issue was now discussed more openly. Signs of change could be found in Mahathir's public affirmations of existing U.S. arrangements. Indonesia was less public in its support, but still there were signs that Jakarta might be moderating its position. Such signs included an Indonesian study that viewed U.S. arrangements in the Philippines as a necessary, albeit still short-term, fact of Southeast Asian security.[45]

Most illustrative of the normative change were new efforts to pursue arrangements along the Singapore model. In fact, all six ASEAN members, including Malaysia and Indonesia, subsequently took steps to negotiate their own commercial arrangements with the United States.[46] As early as late 1990, around the time of the first U.S.–Singapore MOU, Brunei had already offered the United States additional access and Malaysia had begun to make known that the U.S. military was welcome to do business in Malaysia too.[47] The September 1991 Philippine Senate decision not to renew U.S. bases and then the actual closing of the bases in 1992 created additional opportunities for both Washington and various ASEAN capitals to forge additional "access" arrangements. All, however, continued to draw a distinction between "bases" and "facilities." As Singapore analyst Chandran Jeshurun put it, intra-ASEAN exchanges made it clear that while facilities were now fine, even appropriate, "bases" was now officially "a bad word."[48]

This refined consensus provided the starting point and basis for states' subsequent calls in 1992 for a continued U.S. political-security role in Southeast Asia in response to heightened questions about ASEAN's Northeast Asian neighbors. U.S.–Japan trade tensions and growing U.S. pressure on Japan to assume a larger regional security role focused particular concerns on Japan. Over the course of 1989 and 1990, representatives of Singapore, Malaysia, Indonesia, and the Philippines, in fact, all noted their concerns about the U.S.–Japan relationship and the dangers of a remilitarized Japan—the latter of which was also the subject of an awkward exchange between Malaysia and Japan at their postministerial conference (PMC) in 1990.[49]

The general trend continued into 1992, which saw U.S.–Japan frictions over trade, burden sharing, and U.S. basing arrangements worsen such that U.S.–Japan relations were characterized as suffering "the worst downturn in decades."[50] The year 1992 also saw Japan successfully amend Article 9 of its constitution, which subsequently allowed the sending of peacekeepers abroad and prompted enough ASEAN concern that Japanese representatives felt compelled to address the issue at ASEAN's postministerial conference that same year.

As for China, 1992 was also a year of sharpened security concerns. In fact, up until 1992, ASEAN's external Northeast Asian concerns had mostly focused on Japan. ASEAN's July 1992 AMM/PMC, especially, marked a shift in ASEAN states' attention toward China. Of note was the passage of a new Chinese law authorizing the use of force in defense of China's South China Sea claims and China's contract with an American oil exploration company, again with the promise to use force to protect its claims.[51] As a result of these activities, the subject of China dominated the July 1992 AMM in ways that it had not previously.[52] Not only was the South China Sea explicitly mentioned as a concern in ASEAN states' 1992 joint communiqué, but ministers also took the additional step of issuing a collective Declaration on the South China Sea, calling on claimants to exercise restraint and commit to a peaceful resolution to the problem.

Such concerns about their relationships with Japan and China would strengthen ASEAN's consensus on the need to keep the United States positively engaged in Southeast Asia. The consensus was expressed most strongly at ASEAN's July 1992 ministerial meeting, when every one of the ASEAN foreign ministers openly voiced his desire to see Washington playing a continued political-security role in Southeast Asia. Nevertheless, the conditions of the earlier consensus also still held as members made clear that permanent bases remained unacceptable.[53] As Malaysia's defense minister affirmed and qualified, the United States will continue playing an important role in Southeast Asia, but "that role has to be defined and redefined in the context of current developments . . . there is a common stand that you cannot go back to the conventional style of having military bases."[54] In this sense, the real challenge faced by ASEAN states increasingly was not just how to keep the United States engaged in Southeast Asia but rather how to redefine that commitment and the U.S.–ASEAN relationship in ways appropriate for both ASEAN's material and normative realities.

Time to Talk Security

At the same time, the same uncertainties that provided a basis for states' new willingness to explicitly support a qualified U.S. presence also amplified questions about the wisdom of relying on Washington for security. As even those most supportive of a continued U.S. presence argued, developments made clear that regional stability should not solely or even mainly "depend on military might" and on "powerful states."[55] To do so was to make themselves vulnerable to changing foreign agendas that may or may not be consistent with those of ASEAN-Southeast Asia. As Manglapus argued, the United States could only meet the "short term immediate requirements of security."[56]

The result was a parallel and interdependent debate about regional agency, the possibilities of regional organization, and ASEAN's own contributions to regional security. As the Philippines' Defense Secretary Fidel Ramos argued, "The foundation of regional stability and security in our region would be truly solid if the ASEAN countries could forge close collaborations among themselves and reduce their dependency on outside actors for their defense and nation-building requirements."[57] Here, the Philippines, as the member state most directly affected by U.S. developments, once again took the lead in pushing for ASEAN action beyond the existing consensus.

In addition to continued efforts aimed at convincing ASEAN to take "collective responsibility" for U.S. bases in the Philippines,[58] various representatives—including Manglapus, Aquino, and Ramos—also began pushing for a more proactive ASEAN regional security role and even greater intra-ASEAN defense cooperation. While Manila's hoped-for ASEAN conversation explicitly on U.S. commitments never materialized, Manila did persuade others at their 1990 AMM to hold a more general dialogue on "the security situation in Southeast Asia."[59] That decision was not completely without precedent. Just that January, South China Sea concerns provided the justification for an intra-ASEAN track-2 "workshop." Now known as the South China Sea Workshops, the intra-ASEAN dialogue was expanded to include non-ASEAN claimants in 1991.[60] Nevertheless, this workshop in 1990 and after 1991 remained a relatively constrained process, limited in scope to the South China Sea and in membership to ASEAN states and other claimants. The decision to approve Manila's request for a regional dialogue was thus significant in that it tentatively opened the door to a dialogue with a more expansive agenda and participation.

Other developments provided additional pressure on ASEAN states to expand beyond their comfort zone. Of particular note was the fact that others outside ASEAN were also increasingly interested in holding a broader regional forum on security. Both Australia and Canada, for example, had been circulating different proposals for new regional security dialogues, versions of which were presented at ASEAN's 1990 PMC. As in trade debates, Australia proved to be an especially persistent proponent for an Asian Pacific dialogue with proposals in 1987, 1988, and 1990 (and one more in 1991). Canada also argued for a new regional dialogue, especially a North Pacific dialogue of Canada, Russia, Japan, South Korea, North Korea, China, and the United States—a proposal that notably did not originally include ASEAN. Both Australian and Canadian proposals envisioned a kind of Asian-Pacific version of the Conference on Security and Cooperation in Europe (CSCE).

These proposals added to ASEAN's existential concerns already in evidence in other debates over APEC and new ASEAN membership. As in APEC debates, the perceived challenge posed to ASEAN lay not only in the fact that proposals came from outside the region but also in their push for Asia-Pacific arrangements that potentially could subsume ASEAN. Here, it may be no coincidence that the same 1990 communiqué that endorsed Manila's proposed security dialogue also continued to warn against the dangers that APEC posed to ASEAN. In other words, following their experience in APEC, ASEAN states may have been more inclined to seize the initiative from others. Also in that same communiqué were instructions to plan for another summit so that ASEAN could properly "strengthen itself," "chart new directions to enhance intra-ASEAN cooperation," and thus "prepare itself for the challenges of the 1990s" and in response to the "dramatic" strategic and economic changes associated with the ending of the Cold War.[61]

Other political-security developments added to a growing sense of ASEAN's diminished importance both within and outside the group. For example, Thailand's relations with Japan and China added to the questions about Bangkok's commitment to ASEAN, especially given its new mainland orientation (discussed in Chapter 4). During a 1990 tour of ASEAN capitals, Thai Army Commander General Suchinda Khraprayun in fact felt compelled to reassure his ASEAN neighbors that there was no new

Tokyo–Bangkok alignment in the works.[62] Meanwhile, Washington's unilateral decision to withdraw its support for the ASEAN-initiated coalition in
Cambodia—a decision announced just days before ASEAN's 1990 meeting
that gave the green light to Manila's proposed security dialogue—seemed
proof of ASEAN's diminished importance vis-à-vis external actors.[63]

Over the latter half of 1990 and early half of 1991, proposals from
Canberra and Ottawa, as well as Moscow, continued to generate debate.
ASEAN's concerns focused on the form and source of extraregional proposals as much their content. As in APEC debates, many in ASEAN found the
legalism of Western approaches—as associated with the CSCE, for example—as an avenue for Western powers to commit ASEAN states to undesir-
able agendas.[64] References to the CSCE were made especially problematic
by that body's recently activist efforts to link human rights to political and
security cooperation. Various ASEAN representatives further argued that
the institutions of the West did not account for Asia's diversity or the particular needs of developing states. As Alatas put it, "We have to be careful
not to think that certain things that work in one region ought to be translated to another."[65] In fact, "CSCE"—as a product of a different region,
different conditions, and different agendas—became a kind of bad word
in ASEAN such that any reference to it practically guaranteed a proposal's
defeat (especially if initiated by Western powers). Not surprisingly, Canada
and Australia dropped references to the CSCE in later proposals.[66]

Such extraregional pressures over the course of 1990 and 1991 thus added
to the pressure and momentum behind Manila's dialogue on regional security. And so it was that eighty government officials and academics in "their
individual capacities" and from twenty countries convened in Manila for
the first session of a two-part seminar to discuss "regional security, [coun-
try] perceptions . . . , alternatives to the U.S. security umbrella and prospects for regional security cooperation."[67] Characterized by some in the
press as "ASEAN's first regional security cooperation talks," the June 1991
Manila seminar thus began to clarify both regional challenges and parameters of cooperation, especially ASEAN's role and response.

Manila in particular continued to press ASEAN to "arrive at an open
consensus on security in the region"—a consensus that "must not evade"
the question of extraregional roles but at the same time not forgo ASEAN's
strong interest in self determination and resilience.[68] Referring to the
problems of SEATO, as well as recent Australian and Canadian proposals,
Manglapus argued that it was time to correct the mistakes of the past when
regional security proposals were born outside Southeast Asia. As he put it,

"The post-cold war world has come to acknowledge that regional security must be conceived in the region and not in the capital of some outside power."[69]

In his efforts to impress on others the need for ASEAN to articulate a clear position, Manglapus also spoke to growing anxieties about ASEAN's future coherence, relevance, and ultimately regional resilience. Framing the choice as one of acting versus fragmenting, he argued, "Consensus is now an imperative not only because the solidarity of ASEAN demands it but because in the post–Cold War period the global standoff that once deterred regional conflict is gone, permitting the intensification of intra-regional tensions." He concluded, "ASEAN must produce its own response; ASEAN must discover a single lesson from its varied past, colonial and historical, and articulate a single answer."[70]

While the Manila Seminar failed to produce the single answer Manila desired, it did help solidify a growing conclusion "that the time [had] come to discuss security issues on a more structured basis."[71] This, too, would be one of the key conclusions of ASEAN's Institute of Strategic and International Studies (ASEAN-ISIS). Meeting June 2 through 4, 1991, immediately before the Manila Seminar, that group proposed "that an ASEAN-PMC initiated conference be held . . . for the constructive discussion of Asia-Pacific stability and peace . . ." That recommendation was then included in a memorandum sent to ASEAN governments that same month.[72] The convening of a second South China Sea Workshop—the first full meeting of all South China Sea claimants plus ASEAN states—five weeks later was also indicative of a larger trend and growing consensus as to the need for more regular and expanded security dialogue.

Thus, by ASEAN's July 1991 AMM, various developments and activities had contributed to "a growing mood" in favor of an expanded security role for ASEAN.[73] Taking "note of the increasing interest in issues relating to peace and security in the region" evidenced in various proposals and the Manila Seminar, ministers at that AMM agreed to expand the PMC agenda to include security; they also agreed that "ASEAN and other countries in East Asia and the broader Asia Pacific should engage in regular constructive consultations." At the same time, ministers remained notably reluctant to go beyond existing ASEAN frameworks as illustrated by their conclusion that ZOPFAN, TAC, and the PMC process remained "appropriate bases for addressing the regional peace and security issues in the nineties."[74]

These conclusions were immediately put to the test at the PMC that followed. There, ASEAN ministers confronted persistent and growing pressure from dialogue partners who wished for a new regional security framework. As noted above, Australia and Canada had by this time both been peddling proposals for a new security dialogue. At the 1991 PMC Japan threw yet one more into the ring. (According to one ASEAN source, ASEAN at this point had no less than five different proposals to consider.) However, as with the Australian and Canadian proposals, ASEAN had specific objections. Though ASEAN ministers were now more receptive to the idea of a security dialogue and now willing to talk security in the PMC, they nevertheless objected to the Japanese proposal's attempt to "operationalize" and "institutionalize" the dialogue with the creation of a regular senior officials meeting and committees. Ministers also expressed objections to the suggestion of some dialogue partners that the PMC be transformed into "an exclusive forum on security."[75]

In short, there were specific aspects of Japan's proposal that were still deemed out of conformance with ASEAN ideas and ASEAN's preferred approaches. In the end, the primary problem with the Tokyo proposal may have been the same one that plagued Australia's and Canada's, namely, that it came from outside ASEAN. This point is underscored by ASEAN's continued rejection of other proposals despite their efforts to accommodate ASEAN concerns. Canberra's and Ottawa's proposals were both reframed to emphasize informality, inclusiveness, and without reference to the CSCE. Yet, not only did these accommodations fail to convince, but, as Caballero-Anthony observes, "the more the non-Asian states tried to push their ideas, the more reservations the member states of this region had [about them]."[76] Similarly, ASEAN's many concerns with Tokyo's proposal—despite its explicit rejection of European models as inappropriate for Asia—illustrate that ASEAN's concerns were not just limited to non-Asian states.

Still, the Japan proposal was symptomatic of the new thinking emerging in and around ASEAN. Most of all, the number and persistence of proposals for a regional security dialogue sent a very clear message to ASEAN: Not only was there strong consensus and momentum for an expanded regional security dialogue among non-ASEAN regional states, but ASEAN was now facing growing competition from rival frameworks, as well. In a sense, previous concerns that ASEAN would lose itself within a larger grouping now warred with the growing fear that ASEAN might be bypassed altogether if it did not take greater initiative.[77] As one Singapore diplomat described ASEAN's new security agenda in 1991, "We are nudging ourselves, or [are] being nudged [by developments] into this way of thinking."[78] This "way of thinking" was then given official expression and sanction by ASEAN leaders meeting in Singapore in January 1992, when they endorsed the recommendations of

ASEAN's senior officials (and 1991 AMM) and agreed that "ASEAN should intensify its external dialogues in political and security matters by using the ASEAN Post Ministerial Conferences" toward enhancing regional security.

Extending ASEAN Beyond Southeast Asia

The 1992 Singapore Declaration thus opened the door even wider for a regularized regional security dialogue that extended beyond ASEAN. Reservations and differences remained as elites continued to search for the right format. As one official admitted about ASEAN's first discussions on security in January 1992, "This is very much an evolving process. How it will turn out, I do not know."[79]

But while much uncertainty remained about specific outcomes, it was also pretty clear by the 1992 Singapore Summit that the general parameters of ASEAN's response had also more or less been established. In fact, various meetings and consultations leading up to the January 1992 summit—from the Manglapus Initiative to the Manila Seminar to the 1991 AMM/PMC to the 1992 Singapore Summit, as well as a growing number of track 2 gatherings—had begun to produce important points of consensus as to the basic requirements of security and what an ASEAN response might look like. These ideas would continue to refine and strengthen in 1993 and 1994, as states prepared to hold their first meeting of the ASEAN Regional Forum.

A few points are worth highlighting. For one, it was pretty clear by January 1992 that ASEAN's response to the challenges above would take the form of an extended regional security dialogue and that it would moreover be based on existing ASEAN frameworks. Here, it is worth recalling that ASEAN had earlier proposed to base APEC on the ASEAN PMC only to have the idea turned down. Meanwhile, efforts to "harden" the APEC process despite agreement not to (see next chapter) may have strengthened elites' commitment to an ASEAN-based framework. Suggestions that APEC might expand beyond its trade agenda would also further push and reinforce ASEAN's decision to commit to the creation of an expanded security dialogue.

For another, the process of consensus seeking itself had come to give legitimacy, momentum, and form to the idea of a regional security dialogue. This was not just because actors seeking consensus on the question were already in fact talking regional security but also because various meetings and consultations had begun to transform Manila's original request into a more regularized process. For example, in just 1991 alone, there had been at least four ASEAN-sanctioned "informal" forums (the Manila and Bangkok Seminars and two South China Sea Workshops)[80]—all of which were notably cited by the 1992 Singapore Declaration as a basis and precedent on which the PMC could develop an extended political-security dialogue.[81]

The search for consensus on whether to hold a regional security dialogue also produced other points of agreement. In particular, discussions made clear that there continued to be little support for collective militarization, an "ASEAN alliance," or arrangements that focused exclusively on "traditional" security questions.[82] The reasons for states' objections are important as they highlight the ways that founding and normative ideas about ASEAN continued to inform security thinking and to moderate even states' new consensus about the need to maintain a U.S. political security role in Southeast Asia.

In particular, objections to more traditional alliances and exclusive security arrangements reflected ideas about resilience, ASEAN unity, as well as the assumptions about the value of informality, inclusion, and dialogue. On the first point, many questioned the appropriateness of such arrangements for ASEAN's primary security challenges, which were still more internal than external.[83] This was one reason cited by Malaysian foreign minister Abdullah Badawi (acting as chair of ASEAN's 1991 standing committee) for why ASEAN opposed Japan's suggestion that there be a forum devoted exclusively to security.[84] Others worried ASEAN states diverged too much in both their threat perceptions and their security preferences to make such collective military cooperation possible or practicable.[85] For Ali Alatas, ASEAN should "remain true to its essence and that is economic, cultural, and even now political cooperation, but not a defense pact."[86]

In addition, underlying ASEAN's objections to collective militarization were also ideas about the processes most likely to facilitate improved relations between uncertain actors. As states grappled with the question of U.S. security guarantees and proposals for new defense cooperation, states began to articulate more clearly the merits of informal, inclusive, dialogue-driven engagement. For example, Badawi and others warned that defense pacts and arrangements that focused exclusively on military security contained a dangerous logic: In assuming both conflict and enemies, they made retaliation and intervention by others more likely. An exclusive security focus suggested a military bloc, and, to quote Badawi, "the creation of a military bloc would invite the establishment of a counter bloc."[87]

Rather than exclusive, traditional security arrangements, elites tended to argue instead for a more informal, comprehensive dialogue-driven process. No doubt, as in APEC, elites' interest in informality also reflected a practical concern about limiting the ability of larger powers to dominate agenda and process. At minimum, a more informal process better accounted for the diversity of actors, views, and preferences. But these debates between 1990 and 1992 expressed even more clearly that informal dialogue also served other important purposes. Specifically, the argument was that informality created an environment in which people, especially possible adversaries, would be more willing to engage, work, and talk with one another. This logic of informality could be found in a variety of ASEAN venues and processes—the Jakarta Informal Meetings on Cambodia[88] and ASEAN itself.

The growing consensus about the value of informal dialogue could also be found in the growth of ASEAN-related track-2 activities and dialogues, especially after 1991. Such examples of track-2 dialogues included the Manila Seminar and the South China Sea Workshops, in which individuals participate in their "private" and "individual capacities." Similar to the justifications for informality above, the logic underlying track-2 dialogues was that individuals without the baggage of their official roles and responsibilities will be more likely to talk freely about sensitive topics and to have "frank informal discussion[s]"[89] that could lead to improved agreement, mutual sensitivity, and trust. As Wanandi explained in 1991—likely with reference to ASEAN-ISIS's own 1991 Memorandum to official ASEAN about creating a multilateral security forum—governments can be more hesitant toward sensitive issues; thus, "unofficial" groups can play a role in developing and desensitizing those issues through public discussion.[90] In this sense, informality may also be viewed as a first step of a multistep, gradual or evolutionary approach to security and cooperation.

Acknowledgment of the role played by informal discussion and specifically track-2 processes in facilitating new consensus could be found in ASEAN ministers' 1993 joint communiqué that recognized the work of the ASEAN-ISIS network for the first time, as well as the establishment of the Council for Security Cooperation in the Asia-Pacific (CSCAP) in 1993.

In addition, especially as states considered how best to manage an uncertain China relationship, arguments for informal, inclusive dialogue began to express a more explicit strategic logic. Specifically, dialogue aimed to engage, as opposed to disengage. At minimum, as one ASEAN official put it, "it is better to . . . engage China now when it wants to be in than to let it go off on some unilateral track."[91] More positively, inclusive engagement also contained a proactive logic. Singapore's Foreign Minister Wong Kan Seng spoke to this logic in 1992 when he described ASEAN's new consultative dialogues with China and Russia as a process that "builds confidence . . . while minimizing conflict. It is this approach, of broadly engaging our neighbours in

Southeast Asia and others in the larger Asia-Pacific that will help promote and strengthen conditions for regional peace and stability."[92]

Put another way, in contrast to the confrontational "bloc" logic associated with "defense pacts," inclusive, informal dialogue operated on the premise that uncertain actors could find common security with one another. As Manglapus put it in his opening remarks to the Manila Seminar, "We are here . . . to listen to each other, hopefully to make new friends but certainly not to abandon old ones. For even our old friends have made new friends of their old antagonists."[93] Thus, as hard-minded and practical as ASEAN elites were, the idea of inclusive dialogue reflected an important belief that relationships could in fact be transformed through dialogue and engagement. (They might still hedge their bets, but there is the belief that engagement and dialogue—given the right conditions—can potentially transform relationships and at very least, produce relationships that are more predictable, stable, and thus mutually secure.[94])

In short, as ASEAN states began to talk about regional security within ASEAN and with those outside ASEAN, the logic of inclusion, engagement, and dialogue became more prominent in elite thinking and arguments about how to respond to ASEAN's changing and expanding regional arena. These ideas were not entirely new. These ideas were drawn from ASEAN's own positive experiences with an informal, inclusive regionalism. Such thinking was also in evidence in the mid-1970s vis-à-vis other states in the Southeast Asian region, especially Vietnam before its intervention into Cambodia. However, until 1990–1991, little attention was given to the possibility of extending these processes outward, beyond Southeast Asia. In fact, there were important reservations about whether ASEAN processes would be as effective or as appropriate for non-Southeast Asian powers.[95]

On this point, the decisions to include the Soviet Union and especially China as potential dialogue partners and then to expand the PMC agenda to include security were significant. While ASEAN had been holding dialogues with third parties since 1972 and postministerial conferences since 1978, it was not until 1991 that ASEAN began to use the dialogue process more directly as a political-security mechanism. Previously, postministerial conferences primarily served as opportunities for ASEAN states to dialogue established economic partners toward gaining important trade or developmental assistance. The invitation to Beijing and Moscow—both of which attended their first AMM as observers in 1991—thus signified a rethinking of the PMC process and a starting point for ASEAN's new expanded security dialogue.

Through the multilayered, multitracked, cumulative consensus-seeking process discussed above, all these ideas thus came to find expression in the ASEAN Regional Forum in 1994, where the logic of informality and the premium placed on dialogue were clearly in evidence. The format of the discussion was loose, focused more on spontaneous and organic discussion rather than a strict agenda or "rigid road map." China and Russia were also both invited despite not yet becoming official ASEAN dialogue partners. ASEAN planners of that first ARF meeting went so far as to remove the "heavy conference table" in order to provide a more informal, comfortable environment for discussion.[96]

All this is not to say that there was no role for more conventional security measures or support for greater intra-ASEAN defense cooperation. But what this debate made clear was that certain kinds of security cooperation were less appropriate than others for both ASEAN and ASEAN's understood challenges. At minimum, more traditional security cooperation should also be supplemented and complemented by more dialogue-driven processes. For example, some discussion focused on ASEAN's "well established network of defense security cooperation between ASEAN members at a bilateral level" and whether it should be "enhanced" with what Aquino described as "the regionalization of ASEAN security."[97] Here, elites rejected more radical Philippine proposals for an ASEAN alliance but expressed greater interest in an ASEAN "consultative mechanism" that would allow greater "consulting, dialoguing, [and] exchanging [of] information," visits and training between ASEAN defense establishments.[98]

Defending "ASEAN"

Creating the ARF did not eliminate the dangers to ASEAN. Though ASEAN's leading role in the ARF was, as Leifer notes, unprecedented for a group of lesser powers, the ARF was also an unwieldly forum of states with different interests and different institutional approaches. Of particular note were tensions between ASEAN and Washington, which had not been initially supportive of the new forum. The Bush administration, especially, viewing various proposals as rivals to its own existing, U.S.–centric network of bilateral alliances and arrangements, expressed strong opposition to Australian, Canadian, Japanese and ASEAN proposals on the grounds that states in Asia should remain with the "tried and true, tested [U.S.] security arrangements."[99] Only at the last minute, in the summer of 1993 as the ARF was to be announced, did Washington (under a new Clinton administration) agree to participate.[100]

Nor did ARF sessions necessarily bring about a coming together of minds. Instead, as Simon observed, the ARF's early history revealed "a division on security issues comparable to APEC's split on economic matters. ASEAN states and China preferred to keep discussions general to avoid disagreements, while the United States, Australia, Canada, and Japan preferred to devise practical CBMs (confidence building measures) capable of early implementation."[101] The first meetings of the ARF also revealed significant differences over membership and substance that taken together translated into growing dissatisfaction with ASEAN's centrality and leadership in the ARF, especially among the ARF's Western participants.

In particular, the same tensions between ASEAN states and Washington witnessed in other issue areas (for example, APEC, trade, and ASEAN expansion) also plagued the development of the ARF. But for ASEAN states, it would seem particularly egregious that Washington, especially given its late support for the ARF, would question ASEAN's role.[102] Washington's efforts to dictate the agenda would also come across as problematically high handed, an attempt to circumvent regional and indigenous preferences and visions. As one Singaporean diplomat said about an early disagreement over ASEAN's invitations to Beijing and Moscow to participate in security dialogue, "The United States is trying to hold onto the old patterns of doing things as long as possible, but the old patterns no longer hold."[103]

Providing additional context to these tensions was also a new sense of confidence among ASEAN states that now competed with old fears and insecurities. Similarly, the sense of concern created by shifting major power relations was increasingly matched by a sense of opportunity. ASEAN-Southeast Asia was no longer the "backwater" it had been at the end of World War II. Individually, collectively, and even institutionally, ASEAN states "felt" successful. Not only did such success free states to look beyond their borders and embolden them to be more ambitious in their national and regional foreign policy agendas, but it also gave states greater confidence to engage larger powers in an uncertain environment. For ASEAN states, ASEAN–U.S. debates in the ARF were thus increasingly not just about how to stabilize the regional security environment but also about ASEAN's right and prerogative to define the emerging regional order. Similarly, ASEAN–U.S. tensions made the ARF increasingly as much about moderating an unchecked United States as an uncertain China.

Indeed from the first debates about whether to rotate ARF leadership among both ASEAN and non-ASEAN states (each meeting is cochaired by one ASEAN and one non-ASEAN member), ASEAN has been "fiercely protective" of its leading role.[104] ASEAN's 1992–1994 decisions that cumulated in its creation of the ARF, thus taking the dialogue initiative away from others, mostly served it well in this sense. Precisely because the ARF is an ASEAN initiative, ASEAN has been able to define the forum's goals, scope, and processes in ways that it might not otherwise have been able to had the forum originated from other actors. The fact that the ARF is founded on the ASEAN PMC also has given ASEAN states great influence over ARF membership. Similarly, the fact that ARF meetings immediately follow ASEAN's annual meetings also gives ASEAN greater profile and influence over the ARF's agenda and priorities. A 1995 concept paper further affirmed "ASEAN's proprietary hallmark" on the ARF by making it "the repository of all ARF documents and information and [actor that would] provide the necessary support to sustain ARF activities."[105] To quote Mahathir, "ASEAN created the Asean Regional Forum. ASEAN must stay the course to ensure that the ARF process is not steered into a direction which ASEAN does not wish to pursue."[106] Indeed, it is worth underscoring that Asia's first official security dialogue is not the *Asian* Regional Forum, but rather the *ASEAN* Regional Forum.

Such efforts have not stemmed the challenges to ASEAN's role. Debates over membership and process have been especially contentious. As noted above, Washington has criticized ASEAN for unilaterally taking steps to allow for Beijing's and Moscow's participation. Similar criticisms would be leveled at ASEAN in 1995 over Indian membership. Most of all, as in debates about ASEAN's expanded membership, U.S. efforts to pressure ASEAN to deny Myanmar's membership met with particular resistance from ASEAN elites who believed that it was well within their right as an indigenous regional organization to decide the scope and membership of regional processes. As Thai Foreign Minister Kasem S. Kasemsri put it, "Who participates in ARF is a matter for ASEAN to decide."[107]

Differences over Myanmar spoke to larger differences about the value of including and engaging uncertain powers without conditions. As highlighted above, ASEAN states saw value in informality, dialogue, and inclusion but these values and logics tended to sit in tension with the primacy that Western states like the United States placed on efficiency and explicit, binding rules. If ASEAN states saw value in the simple rituals of getting together and in their collective affirmation of regional processes, Western participants tended to view the same as obstructionist, if not a waste of time.

Such debates over membership, process, and substance ultimately had the effect of sharpening ASEAN's sense of "difference" and identity as a non-Western organization with different institutional values and practices. Efforts to defend ASEAN practices and priorities similarly sharpened ideas and arguments. For example, while the logic of informality, dialogue, and engagement had been important features of ASEAN regionalism *within* ASEAN, the above debates highlight important reservations about their appropriateness beyond Southeast Asia. In the process of arguing and defending ASEAN and its practices within the ARF and vis-à-vis non-ASEAN actors, however, arguments about the extended relevance of ASEAN's nonconfrontational, inclusive, and dialogue-driven regionalism gained greater prominence and complexity in their causal claims.

Most notably, ASEAN states, drawing on ideas of region, their identity as lesser powers, and the logic of inclusion, came to make a novel argument about the particular role that they, as lesser powers could and should play. In contrast to the conventional view that power should have pride of place, ASEAN elites not only defended ASEAN's right to take the helm of expanded processes as indigenous Southeast Asian states and in the interest of self-determination, but they also increasingly argued that their smaller power status made them *uniquely* and *most appropriately* positioned to lead the ARF. As Jose Almonte and others explained, "Because ASEAN is non-threatening—it is seen as having no hidden agenda—and because their [great power] relationships are still unstable," ASEAN has the unique ability to convince uncertain, larger powers to talk.[108] In this way, exchanges and debates about ASEAN's centrality in the ARF solidified ASEAN's tentative steps to play a role beyond its normal Southeast Asian ambit.

Reconciling ASEAN–Southeast Asia with Asia Pacific Regionalism

The decision to extend ASEAN processes and institutional attention beyond Southeast Asia was not without its problems.[109] The decision to embark on the ARF may have been aimed primarily at neutralizing extraregional political challenges, but fears that new Asia-Pacific arrangements might subsume ASEAN and render Southeast Asia irrelevant as an organizational principle also remained very real. In short, now that the member states had taken this radical step, they faced the significant challenge of maintaining ASEAN's and Southeast Asia's political, institutional, and geographic meaning vis-à-vis both Southeast Asian and non-Southeast Asian states.

In fact, this concern was very much a part of the pre-ARF search for consensus highlighted above. Pre-ARF debates may have helped produce stronger consensus in favor of expanded regional security dialogue, but they revealed even stronger consensus that ASEAN must not be sidelined or marginalized in the effort. Thus, it should be no surprise that ASEAN's expanded regional activities have been accompanied by parallel efforts to intensify, strengthen, and "enhance" intra-ASEAN cooperation. If the Manila Seminar focused on ASEAN and Asia Pacific Cooperation, the Bangkok Seminar focused on intra-ASEAN cooperation. If the Singapore Declaration opened the door for the development of an expanded security dialogue, it also directed ASEAN itself to consolidate, deepen, and expand intra-ASEAN coopera-tion. Similarly, the South China Sea Workshops opened not with a general convention of claimants but instead with ASEAN states meeting on their own the first year, before opening the process to other claimants the next. In the particular case of the South China Sea Workshops, it is also worth not-ing that the only nonclaimants participating in the Workshops are ASEAN states. (Put another way, ASEAN plus other claimants participate.)

Similarly, if there are to be upgraded security consultations with PMC partners, then ASEAN would also have to upgrade its own security con-sultations, for example, with the introduction of new consultations among ASEAN's foreign and defense officials in June 1992. Another meeting fol-lowed in early 1994. Defense officials have met on a regular basis since 1996 as part of a newly endorsed Special Senior Officials Meeting (SSOM). (In line with ASEAN's desire to maintain a nonconfrontational identity, the SSOM notably avoided the word *defense* to describe their meetings.) ASEAN defense officials have also since become regular participants in the ARF and ARF-related meetings.[110] In short, states clearly thought it impor-tant that ASEAN's expanded Asia-Pacific activities be accompanied by par-allel efforts to intensify and strengthen intra-ASEAN cooperation.

Maintaining Boundaries: TAC, ZOPFAN, and SEANWFZ

Part of ASEAN's self strengthening effort would also involve renewed attention to existing ASEAN frameworks—in particular, ZOPFAN, TAC, and SEANWFZ—each of which as affirmations of "ASEAN-Southeast Asia" gained new salience as states expanded ASEAN beyond its his-torical regional mandate. ASEAN's renewed attention to ZOPFAN and SEANWFZ is especially interesting given their Cold War connotations. As highlighted in Chapter 3, despite its intra- and extraregional contra-dictions, ZOPFAN early on came to have a kind symbolic power in the ASEAN discourse as an expression of a particular regional ideal—not of

Cold War neutrality but instead of a distinct Southeast Asian space that was resilient, unified, and self-determining. Indonesia's 1984 SEANWFZ proposal also helped keep the ZOPFAN ideal alive—though it too faced significant extra- and intraregional obstacles because of Cold War geopolitics and Vietnam's intervention into Cambodia. Perhaps not surprisingly given the nature of past obstacles, the ending of Cold War and Cambodian conflicts seemed to open up new possibilities for both initiatives. Adding to that sense of possibility were also new nonproliferation and test ban treaties in other regions. Indeed, developments seemed to make both region and world finally "ripe for the implementation of SEANWFZ" and a Southeast Asian ZOPFAN.[111] As noted, Jakarta's desire to take advantage of this opening was an important obstacle in the way of Manglapus's original initiative.

Most of all, SEANWFZ and ZOPFAN initiatives, as well as TAC, assumed new relevance and significance as developments continued to blur the lines between Southeast Asia and Northeast Asia. In particular, the late 1980s and early 1990s saw new proposals to extend principles that had been explicitly and exclusively Southeast Asian beyond Southeast Asia. These proposals renewed old debates about the proper role of larger powers but also introduced newer debates and tensions as to how to situate and defend a Southeast Asian political and geographic space within a larger East Asia and Asia Pacific.

A 1987 Thai proposal to extend TAC's principles of peaceful coexistence and mutual noninterference to non–Southeast Asian states illustrated especially well the tensions. Specifically, Bangkok proposed to "expand . . . the number of signatories to TAC beyond the region" to include the U.N.'s "permanent five." At the center of the ASEAN debate were two questions: (1) should TAC be extended to non–Southeast Asian powers; and (2) if so, should there be separate protocols for Southeast Asian and non–Southeast Asian states?

Bangkok's argument was that extending ASEAN's norms and practices was a good way to raise ASEAN's regional and international profile.[112] The Thai proposal, however, immediately met with Indonesian opposition. From Indonesia's perspective, wider accession opened the door for external powers to intervene in ASEAN affairs. In addition, Indonesia appeared to view the Thai proposal as a particular danger to a Southeast Asian ZOPFAN.[113] Indonesia was especially concerned that it would allow non–Southeast Asian powers on ASEAN's High Council for dispute settlement as outlined by TAC's Article 14. On December 15, 1987, a compromise solution came in the form of an amended TAC. The new protocol read, "[TAC] shall be open for accession by other States in Southeast Asia. States outside Southeast Asia may also accede to this Treaty by the consent of all the States in Southeast Asia which are signatories to this Treaty and Brunei Darussalam."[114] Thus, the protocol opened the door for non–Southeast Asian accession but significantly made such accession conditional on the agreement of all ASEAN members. Addressing Indonesian concerns about TAC's High Council, the amendment also stipulated that Article 14 could "apply to any of the States outside Southeast Asia which have acceded to the Treaty" but *only in cases where that state is directly involved in the dispute to be settled by regional processes.*[115] Thus, ASEAN allowed for conditional and qualified non–Southeast Asian accession to a treaty that had originally been limited to Southeast Asia alone.[116]

The debate, however, continued into the early 1990s, especially as states began to consider broader Asian Pacific cooperation more seriously. As noted above, an important point of agreement that emerged by early 1992 was that if Asian Pacific cooperation was to be the new reality, then it should be premised on existing ASEAN frameworks and processes so as to guard against ASEAN's marginalization. In the context of this newly articulated consensus, Bangkok viewed TAC as offering one such ASEAN framework on which to build new expanded cooperation and at the same time assure ASEAN's place and prominence in new arrangements. Put another way, TAC offered one way to "ASEAN-ize" emergent Asia Pacific security processes. At ASEAN's 1992 summit, Thai Prime Minister Anand Panyarachun appealed directly to ASEAN's shared interest in self-determination. As he put, it "A new world order is something that cannot be imposed on us . . . We need to speak up, to tell outsiders how we view a new world order, what kind of role we want to play." [117]

Jakarta's view, however, was quite different. Rather than an opportunity to expand and preserve ASEAN's influence, it tended to view the extension of TAC beyond Southeast Asia as a threat not just to the ASEAN content of Southeast Asian order but indeed to the very concept of Southeast Asia itself. This latter view was perhaps most apparent in Alatas's characterizations of an extended TAC as a threat and rival to a Southeast Asian ZOPFAN.[118] In Alatas's defense of ZOPFAN and a distinct Southeast Asian zone, Indonesia continued to express concern that expanding TAC would legitimate non–Southeast Asian intervention into Southeast Asian affairs through the TAC's High Council. Big power contributions to regional security, he argued, should be made through ZOPFAN, not via intervention.[119] Conceding that "it would be good for the principals contained in the treaty to be observed by outside countries," Alatas nevertheless maintained that formal accession by outside powers was not necessary. As he would put it on more than one occasion, "In our opinion, the Treaty of Amity and Cooperation is meant as a treaty for Southeast Asian countries."[120]

In response to such concerns, ASEAN foreign ministers in July 1993 adopted a new ZOPFAN Programme of Action. That Programme of Action was significant in a number of respects. For one, it was the first time that ASEAN laid out and endorsed an operational strategy in pursuit of a Southeast Asian ZOPFAN. There were four main elements to the "new ZOPFAN": (1) a code of conduct governing relations between states in Southeast Asia and those in the Asia-Pacific region; (2) Cooperation within ASEAN and with other Southeast Asian countries; (3) A blueprint to engage friendly powers in dialogue on political and security matters; and (4) A framework to promote the observance of the U.N. Charter.[121]

In addition, the programme was significant for its effort to provide a basic framework for ASEAN's relations with a widening region. It also made clear that though ASEAN was now looking beyond Southeast Asia, its basic principles and treaties still remained very much Southeast Asian in their content. In this sense, the timing of the programme is significant. Adopted at the same meeting that foreign ministers announced the creation of the ARF, the new ZOPFAN Programme of Action can be seen as another example of how ASEAN's new Asia Pacific efforts were accompanied by parallel efforts to intensify and deepen intra-ASEAN cooperation. These clarifications then cleared the way for a more activist promotion of TAC in the ARF,[122] the result being the ARF's endorsement of an *ASEAN* treaty as its code of conflict, another affirmation of the ARF's ASEAN content.

Lastly, the programme was also the first time that ASEAN articulated TAC, ZOPFAN, and the SEANWFZ as parts of a single plan. And just as TAC gained new life, so too did ASEAN's proposed SEANWFZ. In December 1995 the ten states of Southeast Asia declared their part of the world a nuclear weapons free zone. In the context of changes and challenges described above, the SEANWFZ treaty had great symbolic significance as both an expression of what states saw to be their regional authority over matters affecting Southeast Asia and as a formal affirmation of Southeast Asia as a geographic space. Put another way, the SEANWFZ's significance lies in its attempt to validate both the content and contours of Southeast Asia.

On the first, the question of regional authority, the debate had particular resonance as a result of continued opposition from nuclear powers. The treaty most immediately responded to recent nuclear tests conducted by China and especially France, whose tests took place in the South Pacific. Initial efforts to persuade nuclear powers to support the ASEAN initiative were encouraged by a relatively positive response from the United States. However, at the last minute, Washington withdrew its support, citing a standing policy of neither confirming nor denying the presence of nuclear weapons on U.S. ships. The United States, along with Britain, France, and Russia, also objected to what was characterized as a "no first use" clause banning the use or threat of nuclear weapons. China also particularly objected to the treaty's inclusion of states' exclusive economic zones (EEZ).[123] Opposition from the nuclear states (despite ASEAN efforts to accommodate concerns), in turn, destablized the intra-ASEAN consensus in favor of the treaty.

Yet all ten Southeast Asian states signed the treaty in December 1995 on the premise that the treaty would send an important message to the world and especially to major powers—namely that this was Southeast Asian space and that it was within the purview of ASEAN as a Southeast Asian organization to establish guidelines for behavior within that space. Thus, even Singapore, which felt that additional accommodations should be made if the treaty were to be practicable, still supported the treaty in principle.[124]

It was also notable that though ASEAN dropped the "first use" clause, it maintained the reference to the EEZs. No doubt, the reference to the EEZs reflected concerns about Spratly claims, but states' decision to maintain that reference can also be seen as part of a larger effort to clarify, define, and maintain the geographic space of "Southeast Asia." Indeed, the 1995 SEANWF treaty held particular symbolism as regarded ASEAN and its historic mandate. In addition to being only ASEAN's second treaty (the first being TAC), the SEANWFZ treaty was also the first ASEAN treaty to be signed by all ten Southeast Asian states; as such, it also represented the first formal expression of "One Southeast Asia."

Taken together, then, the SEANWFZ can be seen as a notable show of solidarity and independence in the face of great power objections, as well as a notable affirmation of "Southeast Asia" at a time when developments were questioning "the very category of Southeast Asia."[125] Malaysia's *New Straits Times* explained why the SEANWFZ should still be relevant four years after the ending of the Cold War:

> Without [the Cold War's] geopolitiking in the background, Southeast Asia can take its own side in asserting its claims to peace and sovereignty in its own corner of the planet. ASEAN's push for a genuinely nuclear-free zone is not just a case of striking while the iron is hot. After a long gestation, the opportunity for the

region to assert its own identity is more than just a relief—it is the chance of a lifetime to throw off the shackles of the past and to build on the lasting ties of the near future.[126]

On March 27, 1997, Indonesia became the seventh member to ratify the treaty, thus bringing the treaty into force.[127] It was registered with the United Nations June 26, 1997.

Conclusion

In sum, the 1990s proved to be a dynamic period of change and adaptation as ASEAN moved beyond its established geographic and normative comfort zone. Global and regional changes, combined with political challenge from within and without, pressed states to rethink their own roles and capacities as lesser powers to shape the regional order in Southeast Asia and beyond. That rethinking moreover would gain even sharper clarity as ASEAN began to defend the role it had carved out for itself in Asia Pacific security vis-à-vis larger actors unaccustomed to playing more subordinate roles.

The political-security initiatives pursued by ASEAN during the 1990s are notable in more ways than one. They are notable as examples of new and clarified consensus, as well as states' new willingness to expand into a new political-security realm of cooperation and most significantly beyond Southeast Asia. The ARF is a particular example. As Leifer notes, the ARF stands out not only for its being the Asia Pacific's first official level security framework but also for the unusual leadership role played by smaller powers:

> Within the Asia-Pacific, there is no other historical example of a group of lesser states assuming such a diplomatic centrality in fostering a multilateral security arrangement that involved all major regional powers. That centrality would also seem to be at odds with the experience of the nineteenth-century Concert of Europe . . . based on the role of major powers as defining members.[128]

These initiatives are commonly explained as a function of ASEAN's great power concerns: China, Japan, and also the United States. But this chapter also makes clear that "new ASEAN thinking"[129] and new ASEAN initiatives were products of more than great power flux. For one, ASEAN states as a whole were pretty resistant to the idea of an expanded regional security dialogue. For another, too many differences existed in ASEAN to conclude that there was any one clear response to perceived material challenges. Rather, this chapter makes clear that there was a lot of searching and feeling around going on about the nature of challenges facing ASEAN and its member states, about whether a response is necessary, and what kind of response was most materially and normatively appropriate for understood needs.

In that process, concern for ASEAN took center stage. Actors, as they did in past debates, continually drew on established themes of regional self-determination, fragmentation, intervention—in short, regional resilience—as well as the idea of a distinct Southeast Asian region to make important causal and normative claims in justification of new initiatives and in defense of old ones. Talking, debating, and arguing are the processes that intervene to bring certain ideas to the forefront, make acceptable new ideas and proposals, and (in this case) create a general momentum for a particular policy and strategic response to new challenges.

As highlighted above, these processes were not just interactive but also cumulative. Philippine and Singaporean initiatives forced dialogue and began to desensitize the great power question. Subsequent exchanges then contributed to a narrowing of differences on the question of great power security arrangements, which then gave way to a more explicit consensus in favor of, to quote Ali Alatas, a "quadrangular structure of relations"[130]—as opposed to single U.S. power or no major powers—in Asia (a position closer to Singapore's original 1970s position than that of the Philippines or Indonesia). As one key premise of the ARF, this new agreement about the desirability of engaging different actors was critical to that forum's creation.

In other words, ASEAN states' consensus on an expanded regional forum emerged only after multiple sessions, reinforced challenges, and reinforced exchanges. Arguments cumulated such that by January 1992 both the regional response—an extended security dialogue between ASEAN and other East Asian and Asian Pacific states—and its particular features (the dialogue should be informal, inclusive, dialogue-driven, nonmilitary, gradual) were quite established. The fact that the ARF would mirror ASEAN's own features no doubt made that entity more persuasive; but, again, the decision to extend ASEAN processes beyond its founding mandate and regional purview was hardly automatic. Today the ARF may seem like a "logical" response to material change and a "natural" extension of ASEAN's processes, but the above makes clear that this was not always the case.

The importance of such ideas and processes is not to deny as, Leifer most notably argues, that the ARF is an expression of ASEAN's collective interest in major power balance.[131] As highlighted above, major powers can and do play important roles in Southeast Asia; lesser powers ignore them at their own peril. Similarly, major power changes can provide important impetuses for action and certainly opportunities for reflection. Rather, the point is that a full explanation of ASEAN's particular political-security initiatives of the period requires attention to the ideas, argument, and consensus-seeking processes that mediated the differences between states and that moved states toward particular adaptations and particular regional solutions.

Lastly, the intra-ASEAN dialogues highlighted above and in the last chapter also point to an ongoing reassessment of ASEAN itself—not just the parameters of ASEAN political-security cooperation but also its historical Southeast Asian ambit. As detailed in this chapter, the challenges faced by ASEAN have a mixed effect. While ASEAN's expansion into Asia-Pacific regionalism challenged its identity and processes in important ways, ASEAN's defense of them also led to a deepening and expanding of intra-ASEAN cooperation, as well as clarifications about the kinds of roles that ASEAN can and should play beyond Southeast Asia.

In particular, this chapter has given attention to how conflicts with out-side (Western) powers over ASEAN's regional processes force a clarification and defense of ASEAN practices and ASEAN-centered arrangements. In that process, arguments that a "policy of friendship is better than a policy of containment"[132] grew more prominent, as did the general (as opposed to Southeast Asia–particular) importance of inclusion, informal and regular dialogue, and engagement in transforming uncertain non–Southeast Asian relationships into cooperative ones. In short, these conflicts produce a more explicit argument about what ASEAN's ways and practices are about, what such practices do, and what ASEAN is, as well as their broader application beyond Southeast Asia. Indeed, ASEAN states have come to argue that they, as lesser powers, are especially well suited to lead regional processes.

Similarly, in a context where China's forays into the South China Sea were challenging the "utility and legitimacy of Southeast Asia as a strategic category,"[133] where Western powers were actively promoting their own regional security agendas and models, and where ASEAN itself had become increasingly concerned about its continued relevance after Cambodia, the importance of bolstering ASEAN and deepening intra-ASEAN coopera-tion took on new significance. Thus, the development of the ARF was accompanied by an equally significant effort to deepen and regionalize intra-ASEAN security cooperation and consultations.

Altogether, then, these political-security measures stand out not only for their attempts to define an extended ASEAN regional order but also for ASEAN's continued efforts to affirm and defend a distinctly Southeast Asian space and content. Even as region and regionalism widened, efforts like the 1993 ZOPFAN Programme of Action, the 1995 SEANWFZ Treaty, and reconsideration of TAC pointed to efforts to maintain an ASEAN core and to affirm the idea of Southeast Asia as a distinct entity even within larger regional arrangements.

Indeed, between 1991 and 1997 ASEAN states appeared to enjoy a strengthened and sharpened consensus about the value of their own institutional processes, regional values, and collective practices. But even so, the question in the post–Cold War, post-Cambodia era nevertheless remained whether non–Southeast Asian powers, with different histories, ideas, and identities, as well as different capabilities, would find the same value in ASEAN ideas, principles, and practices.

Renegotiating East Asia:
"The Idea That Will Not Go Away"

All financial crises are educational, but some are more educational than others.

Financial Times, 1998[1]

Between 1997 and 1999, ASEAN states watched a fast-moving crisis quickly destroy what had taken decades to achieve: economic growth, national stability, regional confidence. Economically, the crisis destabilized economies, undermined investor confidence in the region, and invited the interventions of external powers. Politically, it unseated more than one government, destabilized communal relations, renewed separatist pressures, and contributed to the fragmentation of Southeast Asia's largest state. Individually, the financial crisis took away the livelihoods of people at every level and sector of the economy. Institutionally, the crisis undermined the legitimacy of long-standing national and regional arrangements in Southeast Asia.

For ASEAN, in particular, events did much to shatter its reputation of a successful regional organization. The image of a region falling apart was only intensified and underscored by the limitations of existing governance arrangements to respond not just to economic crisis, but also to the environmental haze created by burning fires in Kalimantan, political crises in founding states, domestic turmoil in Cambodia, and an emerging crisis in East Timor. In short, for ASEAN states, the so-called Asian financial crisis was no less than a comprehensive survival threat that shook the very foundations of national and regional resilience.

Much has now been written (and debated) about the causes for the 1997–1999 Asian financial crisis.[2] Though there remains much disagreement about primary causes, most agree that the crisis involved some combination of domestic and international dynamics. This chapter does not explain the crisis' root causes; instead, it addresses the crisis in relation to ASEAN's ongoing dialogue about Southeast Asia's relationship with greater powers and its effect on both ASEAN and its thinking about ASEAN-plus regionalism.

This chapter gives particular attention to the postcrisis trend toward East Asian regionalism. As discussed previously, changing major powers' and especially U.S. policies in the early 1990s helped catalyze new thinking about ASEAN and other regionalisms. The late 1990s were no different from the early 1990s in this respect—but the regional outcome would be different. Where the first half of the decade saw Asia-Pacific regionalism(s) ascendant, the latter half would see East Asia ascendant. This chapter investigates interactive material, discursive, and social forces that help produce this shift. In its explanation, it gives particular attention to the material and social effects of ASEAN's interactions and exchanges with its Western partners.

This chapter begins by picking up on the EAEG–APEC debate as a way to highlight how this debate contributes to a post–Cold War social context that is increasingly defined in oppositional terms. East–West tensions combine with new regional processes to grow a sense of "East Asian" difference. These new ideational and social dynamics will, in turn, inform how actors (in ASEAN) viewed the 1997–1998 financial crisis, its origins, and what ought to be the appropriate response. The chapter focuses especially on U.S.-ASEAN tensions over East Asian responses to the 1997–1998 financial crisis and how these tensions shift the debate in favor of East Asia. The chapter concludes with some observations about what this East Asian trend means for ASEAN.

The Emergence of "East Asia"

"ASEAN" and the "West"

As discussed in Chapter 5, APEC won the initial round in the APEC–EAEG debate. The early 1990s also saw APEC gain momentum due in part to new attention from the United States, which focused on APEC as a way to neutralize regional interest in more exclusive groupings and in particular the EAEG. Partly, APEC also benefited from Indonesia's new receptiveness towards APEC—which was partly reflective of improving Australian–Indonesian relations, especially Canberra's astute diplomacy and deference toward Suharto.[3] In fact, Indonesia experienced a remarkable—and to many, still inexplicable—reversal on APEC. From being one of APEC's strongest critics, Indonesia became one of its key supporters. However, as discussed by Ravenhill, Suharto's new APEC activism came at a cost, especially to ASEAN. Especially in the lead up to the 1994 APEC summit in Bogor, Suharto's willingness to bypass ASEAN norms of consensus in pursuit of a contested agenda undermined ASEAN solidarity from within, contrib-

uted to the perception of incoherence from without, and likely contributed to ASEAN's diminished influence in APEC.[4] At minimum, Suharto's
conversion was instrumental to efforts by APEC's advanced, industrialized
Western economies to get past the constraints originally imposed on APEC
by ASEAN and its Kuching consensus in pursuit of a more activist trade-
liberalization agenda.

Suharto's conversion thus made possible APEC's controversial trade
liberalization agenda, an agenda that ultimately may have worked against
APEC as a regional institution. It was at Bogor, for example, that APEC
adopted what many now consider an unachievable agenda of trade liberalization with fixed timetables. Andrew Elek is especially critical in his
assessment that Bogor set APEC "up for disappointment."[5] Battles between
APEC's Western and Asian memberships in 1995 and 1996 over Bogor's
implementation were also especially divisive. In light of the challenges to
both the understood process and agenda of APEC, the result was diminished ASEAN interest in APEC.

On the other hand, the problems and tensions associated with Bogor
reflected deeper, more fundamental problems. As discussed in Chapter 5,
APEC was not founded on any fundamental agreement (be it on substance
or process) but instead on ad hoc compromises. Even at the time of APEC's
adoption, political support from ASEAN members for the arrangement
was far from overwhelming. Only Singapore's support could be described
as "enthusiastic." Thailand, Indonesia, Philippines, Malaysia, and Brunei
offered "hedged to reluctant support."[6]

Such founding tensions meant that significant fault lines—material and
normative—existed just beneath APEC's surface. Moreover, early and subsequent interactions between members not only tended to confirm and exacerbate differences but created an institutional climate that was hardly helpful
to the coming together of minds. In particular, APEC would find itself constrained by the early tensions between the United States and Malaysia and,
consequently, the constructed opposition between APEC and the EAEG.
Just as Mahathir's confrontational rhetoric made U.S. acceptance of the
EAEG less likely, the strongly worded U.S. opposition and activist efforts
to undermine the EAEG—efforts that continued into the Clinton years[7]—
similarly did APEC no favors where Mahathir was concerned. Tensions
were also exacerbated by Malaysia's view that it had made significant modifications to its EAEG proposal in response to U.S.–related concerns. Already
a skeptic of APEC, Mahathir consequently became the strongest defender
of the Kuching consensus on which ASEAN's participation had originally

been based. By all accounts, Mahathir "resist[ed] . . . all efforts at APEC institution-building."[8] Moreover, the more that others tried to intervene in EAEG debates, the more critical and firmly obstructionist Mahathir became in APEC. And because APEC continued to operate by consensus, Malaysia was able to constrain the directions and development of that body just by saying "no."[9]

As for the rest of ASEAN, disappointment in the early 1990s focused on APEC's limited efficacy vis-à-vis global trade rounds and, relatedly, their differences with other APEC members whose "intransigence" on agriculture and textiles were viewed as "jeopardizing" the success of global trade negotiations.[10] Founding differences between ASEAN economies and more advanced Western economies about APEC's development versus trade liberalization agenda also remained salient. Those differences were intensified by continued differences with Western participants over a host of attached issues, including human rights and democratization, as well as trade and security. Again, despite dramatic economic growth, ASEAN states strongly identified themselves as internally and externally vulnerable economies. Moreover, there was a strong sense that lesser and advanced economies had different roles and responsibilities. Those views led to very different ideas about what APEC should do and what their respective responsibilities within APEC should be. Where the United States believed that APEC's primary objective should be trade liberalization (fair trade through free trade), ASEAN economies tended to believe that APEC should help facilitate the development and institutional capacities of lesser economies (in short, fair trade through development). At very least, ASEAN states felt that more advanced economies should be more understanding of development challenges and more tolerant of the particular constraints (the comprehensiveness of survival threats from within and without) that justified their state-led and authoritarian development strategies.

Moreover, differences between APEC's Asian and Western participants continued to exist as much on process as substance. As discussed, ASEAN's participation had been gained mostly through promises to keep the new process informal, consultative, and gradual; however, those conditions were slowly eroded with, first, a 1991 decision to "endow APEC with a clear institutional personality" and then a 1992 decision to create an APEC secretariat in Singapore. U.S. President Clinton's 1993 calls for a "Pacific Community" and a leaders' summit in Seattle were also viewed as attempts to further institutionalize the APEC process. Meanwhile, a 1993 suggestion from U.S. Defense Secretary William Perry that Washington would like APEC to become more of a security arrangement not only went against what ASEAN saw as APEC's purposes but also rekindled fears about Washington's hidden agenda vis-à-vis APEC.[11]

Thus, by Bogor there already existed significant tensions and unease about APEC's directions. In fact, as Gallant and Stubbs observe, even when APEC was making its greatest strides, there were significant intra-APEC divisions on both content and process. On one side was the neoliberal view of market-led, "firm-based" development, functional cooperation, and comprehensive, goals-oriented, legalistic regionalism. On the other was the "Asian view" of "network-based" development, as well as gradualist, process-driven, voluntary regionalism. Moreover, according to Gallant and Stubbs, the more APEC advanced, the sharper these differences seemed to become.[12]

Consequently, as in the ARF, the negative interactions between ASEAN states and more advanced, usually Western powers in APEC—including the persistent criticisms of ASEAN on human rights and democratization grounds—had the effect of sharpening ASEAN arguments in defense of existing practices and, in turn, reinforcing them within the ASEAN context. In this vein, for example, Mahathir's original arguments for an East Asian group—which had been originally framed in mostly instrumentalist and populist terms—also picked up additional "cultural" dimensions. Specifically, that argument would refer to a particular "Asian" way of diplomacy and interaction with others. That "culture," as Mahathir would put it, was about not dictating to others what they could or could not do; it was also about respect for others. Moreover, until countries like Australia learned to act properly, they could not be part of "East Asia."[13]

Such tensions in APEC, along with Mahathir's tenacious and continued efforts to promote the EAEG idea every chance he could, ensured that discussion on an East Asian group continued. ASEAN's compromise EAEC decision—however unsatisfactory Mahathir may have found it—also kept the East Asian idea in play as a ready-made prospective response to future challenges, a point underscored by the fact that the EAEC was a regular agenda item at each of ASEAN's annual meetings between 1991 and 1997.[14]

ASEAN and Northeast Asia

In the meantime, ASEAN states were continuing to expand their relations with Northeast Asian states and economies. Moreover, as ASEAN began reaching out beyond Southeast Asia, ASEAN itself created new institutional opportunities for East Asian interaction that made East Asian get-togethers less radical and more familiar. In particular, ASEAN's 1991 decisions to make

South Korea a full dialogue partner and to include China as an observer meant that there were now official forums—first the PMC, and then the ARF—for ASEAN states and their Northeast Asian counterparts to meet. APEC, too, provided a regular setting and opportunity for East Asian states to interact. Even if states did not meet nominally as "East Asia," these institutional forums nevertheless created important opportunities for rethinking their relations with one another and as East Asia.

For example, it was on the sidelines of the first meeting of the ARF in 1994 that ASEAN states first met with China, Japan, and Korea for an "informal lunch" of "6+3" to discuss the principles of the EAEC as "an issue of mutual interest."[15] An initial agreement to meet on an as-needed basis soon gave way to a Singaporean proposal to hold more regular meetings between Southeast Asia and Northeast Asia. That proposal then led to the introduction of annual meetings of "7+3" (ASEAN-6, with new member Vietnam, plus China, Japan, and Korea) held after ASEAN's annual ministerial meetings. ASEAN and Northeast Asian states would also get together in preparation for a new set of meetings with their European counterparts, the first of which met in March 1996 (see discussion below). Then, in July 1996 Malaysia proposed an informal summit of "7+3+3" (the additional three being Cambodia, Laos, Myanmar) for December that year. Plans were then made to convene such a meeting at ASEAN's informal leaders' summit scheduled for December 1997 in Kuala Lumpur. This would be the first informal meeting of what is now known as "ASEAN Plus Three."

These meetings and interactions of ASEAN plus Northeast Asian states, though informal, represented de facto meetings of something that was beginning to look like "East Asia." Taken against the backdrop of continued dissatisfactions with the APEC process and negative interactions with Western powers in APEC (and the ARF), the growth of East Asian activities could thus be seen as a commentary on APEC, more generally Asia-Pacific regionalism, and its perceived limitations and problems. At minimum, as Terada argues, these meetings between ASEAN and Northeast Asian states could be seen as part of a process of "acclimation" by which states became more comfortable with the idea of East Asian organization.[16]

Also catalyzing thinking along East Asian lines was a new sense of confidence born of economic growth (a confidence that sometimes sat in tension with the insecurities described earlier). This sense of confidence combined with the perennial criticism from the West (former imperial powers and interveners that they were) to produce a kind of nationalist or regionalist narrative about the rise of East Asia. As characterized by Kishore

Mahbubani, the new thinking was no less than a "psychological revolution" involving a growing sense that ASEAN and Asia more broadly had important contributions to make to a larger civilizational and political discourse.[17] ASEAN elites increasingly spoke not only of "Asian values"[18] but also of an "Asian renaissance"[19] and an "Asian way" as an assertion of a distinct positive value system, as much as defense against Western criticisms.

From this period also emerged ambitious representations of East Asia as the "third pillar" of the post–Cold War economy, alongside North America and Europe. It was this kind of thinking that was also partly behind Goh Chok Tong's proposal in October 1994 that "Asia" should have a meeting with "Europe." That proposal became the basis of the Asia–Europe Meetings (ASEM)—an "informal" and "multidimensional" process involving biennial summits of European and Asian heads of government, regular meetings between ministers (foreign ministers are the "driving force," but finance ministers have met as many times[20]), as well as regular, supporting consultations between East Asian senior officials.[21] ASEM's inaugural summit would take place in March 1996.

As highlighted above, ASEAN's interest in ASEM was both a product of newfound confidence and a reaction to the perceived problems of Asia Pacific processes, U.S. efforts to dictate the APEC agenda, perceived failures of U.S. economic leadership,[22] and an intensified perception that ASEAN and its concerns were being actively sidelined in APEC. Commenting on ASEM's value and significance as "the first gathering among Asian and Western leaders on an equal basis," Ramon Rosario, chair of the influential Phinma Group of Companies in the Philippines and former Philippine ambassador to Germany and Japan, was explicit: "In APEC, we [ASEAN states] are not equal with the United States. Can you imagine how we feel when leaders of APEC, a five-year institution, tells ASEAN, a 28 year organization, what to do? That's why APEC has not received such an enthusiastic response from Asians."[23]

In addition, on the parts of most Asian (Japan again remained the most reluctant one) and European states, APEC had created a need for Asia and Europe to forge new, independent links as counterpoints to the United States.[24] For the ASEAN states, their APEC experience and especially the sense that ASEAN was losing its influence in that body helped generate new support for arrangements that did not necessarily include the United States. The launching of NAFTA in 1994 also furthered this view. The fact that the United States now had institutional links within North America through NAFTA, with Europe through NATO, and with East Asia through APEC

brought back Mahathir's old question as to "why it is proper for some countries to come together and protect themselves while others may not do so."[25]

Indeed, ASEM was in an important way a turning point in terms of
East Asian regionalism.[26] Not only did ASEM afford individual East Asian
states the opportunity to work with one another (as in ARF and APEC, for
example), but it also marked the first time that "Asia" was meeting as "Asia."
Equally important, ASEM also marked the first time that "Asia" was being
recognized by external—and perhaps importantly, Western[27]—actors as a
legitimate entity with equal standing. In this sense, ASEM was, as Gilson
notes, a notably different kind of arrangement than APEC. Unlike APEC
in which "the point was to combine a range of states within a coherent unified framework," ASEM assumes two distinct entities in an interregional
(as opposed to intraregional, transregional, or global-regional) process. Nor
did it take much prodding for most to see that the members of this process
were also the very same actors that made up Mahathir's EAEG—in essence,
ASEM operationalized the EAEG idea.

ASEM did bear some important similarities with APEC, however. For
one, ASEM, like APEC at its founding, reflected ASEAN's influence and
concerns. ASEM was and remains very much a process of consultation as
opposed to a formal organization. In fact, even more than APEC at its
founding (and perhaps precisely because of the lessons of APEC), ASEM
contained an even greater stress on the principle of "equal partnership."
ASEAN's centrality in ASEM was also more evident by virtue of the fact
that Goh Chok Tong proposed and initiated the process. ASEM could even
be described as ASEAN-led, at least vis-à-vis "East Asia." It was agreed, for
example, that ASEAN should take the lead in organizing the "Asia" side
of ASEM. This meant that just as the EU could decide who constituted
"Europe," ASEAN could determine the critical question of who constituted "Asia." While states chose to leave the definition of "Asia" open, they
did decide that for the sake of "manageability," "Asia" would initially com-
prise the ASEAN states plus the three states of Northeast Asia.[28]

But also like APEC, the ASEM process similarly contributed to a sharpened sense of difference between ASEAN states (and China, Korea, and
Japan), on the one side, and EU on the other.[29] Despite ASEM's rhetoric
of equal partnership, for example, the relationship was still very much one
between advanced, industrialized economies and lesser-developed economies with all its related tensions. On both sides, expectations of the process
and of each other tended to reflect their different histories, levels of development, and institutional values. The EU states tended to view democrati-

zation and human rights as important organizing principles. In contrast, the ASEAN states—as they did in ASEAN and in APEC—placed priority on development, capacity building, and resilience over questions of political or economic liberalization.

In ASEM, these tensions were immediately evident. ASEAN states, especially, found themselves once again the subject of considerable criticism on questions of human rights, democratization, and ASEAN's way of dealing with internal problems of other states. In fact, within two months of their first summit, senior officials preparing for the first meeting of ASEM foreign ministers in February 1997 divided over the subject of East Timor and Myanmar. As in ASEAN's relations with the United States, Myanmar, especially, had also been a perennial thorn in the ASEAN–EC/Europe dialogues for much of the 1990s, but in 1997 the issue was renewed by ASEAN's preparations to extend ASEAN membership to Myanmar later that year. It was also not lost on ASEAN that the European states making the most of these questions were also former imperial powers.

In their objections to Myanmar, the European side of ASEM—much as happens when admitting new members to the EU—tried to impose conditions on ASEM participation. For the ASEAN states, the EU approach was not, as Singapore Foreign Minister Jayakumar explained, the "ASEAN way." Rather than the European approach of "prenuptial agreements," the ASEAN way was to "marry first" and then work with the new family member in a "quiet nonconfrontational manner."[30] Even more important, however, European efforts to dictate participation on the Asian side (and ASEAN membership) violated understandings of noninterference, as well as their prior agreement that ASEAN should determine ASEM's Asian membership. In addition, and just as important, such efforts were viewed as a sign of disrespect for ASEAN (hence the emphasis that a number of ASEAN officials at that meeting placed on "mutual respect" or as Jayakumar put it, there should be "no finger pointing"). Across ASEAN, EU efforts to intervene in ASEAN decision making were considered, in a word, "inappropriate."[31]

In short, by the end of 1997, ASEAN states and their Northeast Asian counterparts were meeting with greater frequency and regularity. Their interactions with one another and with Western trade and dialogue partners were increasingly being expressed in terms of what Stubbs describes as "a functioning—if somewhat embryonic" East Asian regionalism.[32] Just as important, these early interactions and exchanges informed the understood content and direction of relations and of regionalisms. They also would inform how different sides understood the nature of the 1997–1998 crisis.

The Asian Financial Crisis: Competing Interpretations

The devaluation of the Thai baht in July 1997 set off a financial crisis that quickly spread across East and Southeast Asia before moving on to Brazil and Russia. According to Milner, the Asian financial crisis may have been unparalleled in its depth, speed, and scope.[33]

As the financial crisis spread through Southeast Asia and East Asia, it is interesting how little the rhetoric, discourses, and political dynamics described above did not change. In fact, the pre-1997 exchanges between ASEAN and Western dialogue partners very much fed and informed their respective interpretations of the crisis and how to respond. For the United States and the European Union, the problem was one of liberalization. Decision makers in Washington, in Europe, and in the headquarters of institutions like the IMF and World Bank all tended to see the crisis in terms of insufficient liberalization in Asia. Economically, the crisis was a function of lax macroeconomic policies and ASEAN states' failure to sufficiently liberalize their financial markets (which led to distorted valuations, easy money, and bad investments)—that is, poor "economic fundamentals." Politically, the crisis was a function of illiberal regimes, greedy elites, crony capitalism, and bad governance. In short, ASEAN states had done it to themselves.

In contrast, ASEAN states tended to see the crisis differently. While not completely ignoring the fact that there were domestic sources to the crisis, ASEAN elites tended to see the crisis, at very least, as much a function of an unrestrained global economy. Characterized by some as the "first post–Cold War 'crisis of globalization' "[34] and neoliberalism,[35] the Asian financial crisis—as viewed by the ASEAN states—illustrated all too well how the "expansion of global markets, institutions, and certain norms . . . progressively reduce[ed] the purely domestic aspects of politics everywhere."[36]

At very least and especially as the crisis wore on, the general ASEAN consensus was that, whatever their domestic problems, the crisis was extreme and that their policies, in the words of Higgott and Phillips, "were not so distorted as to warrant the scale of financial and economic chaos which dominated 1997 and 1998."[37] The indiscriminate nature of the crisis, hitting various economies "with little regard to the real differences in their economic fundamentals," also tended to reinforce these views.[38]

This tendency to focus on external, global sources of the crisis also reflected both a structural and ideological disposition. Viewed through the prism of past experience, ASEAN states understood that significant asymmetries of power between themselves and Western powers, especially the United States, gave external states great capacity to mete out harm as well as benefit. That understanding moreover interacted with regional ideas and understandings about themselves as weak, fragmented powers vulnerable to foreign intervention. Thus, it is no surprise that *all* the ASEAN states (not just Mahathir, for example) tended to see the crisis largely in terms of foreign security threats—in this case, foreign speculators and global/transnational actors—playing off the weaknesses of Southeast Asian actors.[39] Such a social context also makes it easier for conspiracy theories to take root.

In Search of Regional Solutions:
The ASEAN Swap and Asian Monetary Fund

Not surprisingly, different interpretations of the sources of the crisis led to very different understandings about the response. Western states tended to focus on correcting domestic problems of states. This was at least one reason that such importance was attached to IMF reforms, for example. Such conditions included mandatory cuts in government spending, removal of government subsidies, higher taxes, greater transparency, liberalization of currencies, the end to "prestige projects." As IMF Managing Director Michel Camdessus put it, the priority ought to be on putting one's own house in order.[40] Similarly, the World Bank began touting "good governance" as a condition of aid and development.

As for ASEAN, different understandings of the crisis tended to lead to different solutions. As the Thai crisis quickly became regionalized, ASEAN minister's first collective statement on the crisis came in their 1997 Joint Communiqué under the heading "International Currency Manipulation."[41] In that statement, ASEAN "foreign ministers expressed serious concerns over well coordinated efforts to destabilize ASEAN currencies for self-serving purposes, thus threatening the stability of all ASEAN economies." In line with their interpretation of the crisis, ASEAN states focused on the need for mechanisms that would either better regulate speculation or better respond to it. At the front end, as Malaysian Deputy Prime Minister Anwar Ibrahim argued, mechanisms needed to be in place to guard against crises developing in the first place. Specifically, the liberalization desired for and pushed for by the United States and different global organizations needed to be accompanied by "an effective mechanism" to "regulate, supervise and protect the markets, particularly the emerging markets against speculators and abusers."[42]

At the back end, the crisis similarly revealed the deficiencies of existing mechanisms to manage and respond to emerging and full-blown crises. Despite the IMF's focus on surveillance and early warning mechanisms after the Mexican peso crisis, for example, there was the view—a view that grew over time—that the IMF had failed to adequately protect the ASEAN economies from harm, react quickly to the crisis unfolding in Southeast Asia, or moderate the crisis once it began.

Faced with a growing crisis, states thus began a search for supplementary arrangements that could make up for the perceived deficiencies of existing and nonexisting global regimes. And in the search for better ways to respond to the crisis, ASEAN states, as they did before, turned to regionalism as one solution. Here, ASEAN provided an early unifying focal point of efforts. Specifically, a particular mind-set—informed by notions of regional resilience and normative arguments that regional problems should be (to quote Thai Finance Minister Thanong Bidaya) "solved by regional integrated solidarity"[43]—directed much initial attention to ASEAN. Almost immediately, for example, Malaysian Deputy Prime Minister Anwar invoked resilience arguments in calling for "a collective strategy" to fight an "economic war" waged by Western syndicates.[44] As he explained, it was precisely because Southeast Asia was weak and divided that foreign attackers attacked them and were now picking them off "one by one."[45] The fact that ASEAN's annual meeting serendipitously took place just after Bangkok and Manila floated their currencies also helped draw attention to ASEAN as one response to the crisis. In their first joint ministerial statement of the financial crisis, ministers called on ASEAN to intensify ASEAN cooperation "to safeguard and promote ASEAN's interests in this regard." Regional proposals included Suharto's idea of a "regional safety net" that would help countries deal with similar crises and attacks, as well as a Thai proposal for an ASEAN currency.

Of particular note was the idea of a resuscitated and improved ASEAN "swap arrangement fund." Originally set up in 1977[46] and coincidentally due to expire in 1997, the ASEAN swap arrangement had already been a subject of discussion amongst ASEAN central bankers in mid-February 1997, as well as ASEAN finance ministers working on the early realization of AFTA in early March.[47] In fact, ASEAN finance ministers—already noting ASEAN's heightened vulnerability to speculative attack and acting on a suggestion from the IMF's managing director Michel Camdessus—asked the IMF in March 1997 to assist them in reworking that arrangement toward creating a more extensive regional currency defense mechanism that was also more reflective of the changes and challenges of the new global economy. Despite some concerns about the mechanism given new members whose economies and currency regimes were much weaker, finance ministers agreed to proceed with the idea "in principle" and to continue consultations with the IMF towards its further development.[48] As part of what Malaysia would immediately dub the "ASEAN fund," Malaysia also proposed that funds be set aside to help provide training in insurance, banking, and finance to personnel from ASEAN member-states (current and prospective).[49]

As the crisis became regional and as ASEAN states depleted individual resources defending their currencies in July 1997, attention increasingly focused on the fund as a source of short-term liquidity. That idea found support in ASEAN, especially from Indonesia, Malaysia, and the Philippines, who reportedly harbored doubts about the surveillance capabilities of the IMF.[50] The idea also received particular attention from Thai Foreign Minister Prachuab Chaiyasarn. Despite having just agreed to an IMF bailout package, the IMF's belated response and concerns that the package was still not big enough fueled Thailand's interest in regional arrangements as an additional line of defense against foreign exchange attacks.[51] The fact that neither the United States nor European countries made direct contributions to the package also added to the interest in a regional backup plan.

The problem, however, was that every ASEAN member by August 1997 was either already in trouble or anticipating trouble. Not only did that mean that the current ASEAN account would be insufficient to address the extent and depth of the financial crisis, but it also meant that individual states would be less willing to increase their contributions as they would need funds themselves for their own defense.[52] (Malaysia, Singapore and Indonesia had also each already promised funds to Thailand's IMF package—US$1 billion, 1 billion, and 500 million respectively). By one account, anything less than a US$100 billion account "would not be viable."[53] Thai Finance Minister Thanong Bidaya further noted that ASEAN's inadequacies went beyond not having enough money. As he explained, "We don't have the expertise. We don't have the technical know-how. We don't have anything. We just know that when one of us in trouble, the others should pack together to help."[54]

Meanwhile, the crisis worsened and spread. It was at this point and in the lead-up to a September 1997 meeting of ASEM finance ministers that ASEAN senior officials and finance ministers began to talk more seriously about an "Asian fund" as opposed to just an ASEAN fund. As Philippine Finance Secretary Roberto de Ocampo explained, "The reason it was originally called an ASEAN fund is because the present currency crisis is prevalent, or was felt most strongly in the ASEAN economies, but the original proposal has obviously been overtaken by events."[55]

Most of all, the extent of the crisis made clear that any viable regional response would have to involve Japan as the regional actor with the greatest capacity and resources. Preparations for a September meeting of ASEM economic ministers provided the opportunity for ASEAN senior officials to approach Japan, which was cautious but saw an opportunity to exercise (and be recognized for) regional leadership.[56] It helped that Japan's vice minister of finance for international affairs, Sakakibara Eisuke, had himself been advocating a proposal for an Asian fund and in August 1997 had just floated the idea to countries that had contributed to Thailand's rescue package.[57] ASEAN's interest thus presented a particular opportunity for him to push his idea through. As envisioned, Sakakibara's proposal would model the Asian monetary fund (AMF) or financial rescue fund on the precedent set by the United States in its supplementary package to Mexico during the peso crisis.[58] Most important, the proposed "regional facility . . . would be prepared to disburse pre-committed emergency funds more promptly than the resource-strapped IMF"—thus correcting the perceived problems of both U.S. and IMF responses.[59]

The annual meetings of the IMF and World Bank the same week provided additional opportunity for Japan and ASEAN to develop further ideas for some kind of regional mechanism and to try them out on the United States and IMF, neither of which supported the idea of a fund independent of IMF authority. Both the United States and IMF saw the ASEAN-Japan proposal as a way to avoid IMF conditionalities, which, in turn, would increase "moral hazards."[60] U.S. Treasury Secretary Rubin reportedly also lobbied China at the IMF meeting to oppose the Asian fund proposal. Despite Japan's and ASEAN's efforts to frame the new facility as "supplementary" and "complementary" to the IMF, U.S. and IMF authorities remained extremely "skeptical."[61]

Nevertheless, ASEAN elites continued to push for a regional facility. Not only did recovery still seem elusive for Thailand, despite IMF assistance and conditions, but the crisis had also now spread to Indonesia, raising additional concerns about both regional stability and ASEAN itself. As the chairman of the Indonesian Bankers Association explained, "If only the IMF would really honour its commitments, the formation of an ASEAN fund would not be necessary."[62] The "destructive competition" between ASEAN states themselves added to the sense of comprehensive threat, prompting Philippine President Fidel Ramos' calls for a " 'common front' in the face of speculative attacks on our national currencies."[63]

Pledging his personal commitment to the creation of a financing facility, Ramos as that year's ASEAN chair promised to pursue the matter vigilantly at the upcoming APEC meeting in late November. However, before the APEC meeting could take place, Japan—faced with strong opposition and pressure from the United States and the IMF—withdrew its support for the proposal. Meanwhile the emergence of another proposal had the effect of neutralizing some of the interest in an Asian monetary fund.

Specifically, at a meeting of Asian and Pacific central bankers convened by the Philippines in Manila, the United States and IMF put forward an alternative proposal for a regional surveillance network. This proposal had in fact been foreshadowed by U.S. Treasury Secretary Robert Rubin in his responses to ASEAN-Japan campaigns for an Asian fund at the previously mentioned meetings of the IMF and World Bank.[64] The so-called Manila Framework had a few key features. It focused on surveillance by "peer pressure" and strengthening domestic financial systems and regulatory capacities. On the key point of additional funds, the proposal offered a cooperative financing arrangement that would supplement IMF resources—but only under "exceptional circumstances" and only after a potential recipient had exhausted its IMF loans. In addition, while any Asian country was theoretically able to contribute to the fund, such contributions would be made in consultations with the IMF and on a case-by-case basis.[65] Most important, the new network would not operate independent of the IMF. It also would not be led by Japan. The Manila Framework, despite being so constrained, was subsequently able to satisfy at least temporarily the growing demand for some kind of regional mechanism.

The persuasiveness of the proposal was likely aided by Ramos' personal efforts at APEC and within ASEAN and perhaps most of all by some relief that Washington was finally taking an interest in Southeast Asia's crisis. The personal efforts of U.S. President Bill Clinton—"the good campaigner that he is" (to quote the Singapore *Straits Times*)[66]—in mobilizing support for the framework at APEC also likely helped seal the deal. Even Mahathir expressed some satisfaction with the meeting, the process, and the outcome—though he still pressed for more action at the global level.[67] The Manila Framework was endorsed at both APEC and by ASEAN leaders at their informal summit the next month. While the "ASEAN fund" was mantained, most continued to see such a fund as too "small" to be of much use.[68]

The Search Continues

Despite Washington's successful efforts to preempt a Japan-led AMF at the end of 1997, interest in East Asian regionalism remained and grew. For one, the crisis continued to unfold, hitting Indonesia especially hard in 1998. For another, the alternative Manila Framework, however welcomed it was in December 1997, remained underdeveloped, just as IMF arrangements remained insufficient. Moreover, there was also a relatively strong concern in ASEAN that IMF conditions might in fact do Indonesia more harm than good. Their preference was to help shore up the Indonesian *rupiah* first, but again ASEAN lacked the resources to do so. Consequently, they could only appeal, as Fidel Ramos did, to the IMF for flexibility and to "refrain from pushing already battered economies to the depths of depression."[69]

Faced with nowhere else to turn to, states like Indonesia had to accept IMF aid and consequently all its conditions. But, as noted above, the appropriateness of those conditions had become the subject of some debate both inside and outside ASEAN. Meanwhile, Indonesia's economy got worse, communal riots erupted, and its government fell. Later, critics would cite a list of "questionable judgments" for exacerbating, rather than alleviating, the economic and human costs of the crisis.[70] The opaqueness of IMF decision making only added to the criticisms.

For the rest of ASEAN, Indonesia's collapse was viewed with tremendous and particular concern. Not only were they concerned that Indonesia's economic crisis would make their own economic situations worse, but they also feared that Indonesia's political troubles would spill over into neighboring states. In addition, given Suharto's role in the founding of ASEAN, the possible collapse of that government began to raise questions about ASEAN's own survival.

The worsening crisis consequently kept attention on the insufficiency of existing arrangements. Washington—because of its positions on conditionality, its failure to contribute to the Thai bailout package, and its slow and "reluctant"[71] assistance to a collapsing Indonesia—was a particular target of unhappiness among not just ASEAN elites but also ASEAN publics. States also saw Washington constrain assistance from international institutions like the IMF and World Bank only to then actively prevent states from pursuing their own regional solutions. On this last point, Washington's active opposition to their proposed AMF seemed especially unreasonable given its reluctance to provide assistance to Asian economies itself or through other mechanisms.[72] Moreover, ASEAN states could not help but notice that

Washington's response to their financial crisis stood in significant contrast to its reaction to the Mexican peso crisis a few years earlier. In that crisis, Washington (and Ottawa) provided massive amounts of emergency financing to offset the private capital being drawn out of that country. Not only did it set up a fund to help its neighbor, but it also "strong-armed" allies and international organizations into contributing to it.[73] Yet, it then objected to efforts from Japan to do the same for Asia. U.S. readiness to help Brazil and Russia in 1998 also contrasted with its reluctance in Asia.

All this would contribute to a sense of bitterness, even betrayal in ASEAN, whose members felt they deserved better treatment for having been loyal Cold War allies.[74] Especially given past U.S.–ASEAN differences over trade, human rights, and regional organization, there was also widespread suspicion that Washington was secretly pleased that a rising, more assertive, more confident Asia had received a deserved comeuppance.[75] At minimum, U.S. actions (or, in this case, inaction and opposition) during the 1997–1998 crisis played to ASEAN's long-standing questions about the dependability of U.S. commitments and to the need to take greater regional initiative. Such views made both regional and non–U.S.-based options more attractive and more persuasive.

Rethinking APEC

The above dynamics thus had the effect of affirming and intensifying, rather than diminishing, the perceived need for alternative, more independent frameworks. One such framework might have been found in APEC given that its membership included all the relevant principals.[76] Certainly, U.S. and Japanese membership meant that APEC had a capacity that ASEAN lacked. Jesus Estanislao, for example, explicitly argued for a larger role for APEC on the grounds of ASEAN's smallness, which, as he put it, meant that "ASEAN alone cannot go very far."[77] By 1997 APEC was also a relatively established process compared to more nascent "ASEAN plus Three" or "10 plus 3" arrangements. As noted above and discussed further below, the first informal summit of ASEAN and Northeast Asian states, for example, did not take place until December 1997, lacked an official name, and was an event held in conjunction with the ASEAN summit, rather than being an event in and of itself. Nesadurai describes the Asian financial crisis as having been a prime opportunity (ultimately missed) for APEC to regain momentum among its members.[78]

However, APEC's response was limited primarily because the United States, as it did on the specific question of Japan's AMF proposal, continued to prioritize existing global arrangements. In addition, reflective of U.S. interpretations of the crisis as a crisis of incomplete liberalization, APEC continued as normal, pursuing what was still a highly contested trade liberalization agenda. While the November 1997 APEC meeting did endorse the Manila Framework, APEC itself offered no additional or credible cooperative response to the crisis. In the words of one Indonesian official, "APEC was not there. It responded slowly."[79]

Nor did APEC's 1998 meeting bring any additional relief. Liberalization was once again the focus but now it focused on political liberalization as a problem of ASEAN states. At that meeting in Kuala Lumpur in 1998, a year when Indonesia seemed to be falling apart and when instability was the norm across Southeast Asia, the United States chose instead to press home a solution of "good governance." Most notably, U.S. Vice President Al Gore chose to make what one observer described as an "intemperate" speech that prioritized "tweaking the nose of the host (Mahathir)" instead of focusing on what ASEAN states saw to be some serious survival threats.[80] At minimum, in the context of anti–Suharto demonstrations the year before and recent anti-Mahathir demonstrations, Gore seemed to advocating—or, at least, applauding—such efforts to bring down regimes. In the end, not only did that speech reinforce an already sharpened precrisis sense of difference between ASEAN and APEC's Western membership, but for many it further raised questions about Washington's ability to act or help ASEAN in a fair and neutral way.[81] This sentiment fed a growing sense that APEC was "irrelevant" to solving ASEAN's problems.[82]

A 2003 decision to develop an East Asian regional bond market illustrates well APEC's diminished relevance among its ASEAN and Asian membership. Here, the existence of a previous and parallel APEC effort aimed at the creation of securitization and guarantee mechanisms for regional bond markets made APEC a logical body to take the lead. But instead, Asian (Northeast Asian, as well as ASEAN) states decided to pursue a specifically East Asian initiative.[83] One Japanese source put it simply, "People are not satisfied that APEC is the right body."[84]

Rethinking ASEAN

ASEAN too experienced a rethinking, though of a different sort and with a different outcome. As highlighted above, the crisis began with states being more or less in agreement about the crisis's causes, what they thought were the primary priorities and issues, and what they thought was missing or needed to better manage both current and future crises better. Early on, states also coalesced around ASEAN—in particular its ASEAN fund—as a possible regional response to global challenges. There was also agreement about that fund's limitations and the need to look beyond ASEAN for help.

But as the crisis wore on and worsened, the limitations of ASEAN became more apparent, as did states' competitive tendencies. Efforts of individual members to distance themselves from their neighbors no doubt added to a growing sense of a region in disarray. Such efforts stemmed largely from the perception that investors were making decisions based solely on their common geographic location and with little regard for the specifics of individual situations. In this sense, the indiscriminate nature of the crisis confirmed just how successful ASEAN's efforts to construct "One Southeast Asia" had been. In other words, though their interdependencies were still greater with non–Southeast Asian economies than with each other and though ASEAN elites themselves continued to doubt ASEAN's and Southeast Asia's regional coherence, the financial crisis, especially its contagion effect, made quite clear that foreign investors, at least, did in fact see Southeast Asia as "one."

In fact, both actual and perceived ASEAN solidarity faced a series of tests, one after another: environmental haze, new political turmoil in ASEAN's founding states (Mahathir's sacking of his deputy prime minister, Anwar Ibrahim; Indonesia's falling apart; a change in government in Thailand), an emerging crisis in East Timor, ASEAN's limited effect on new and prospective members. These developments, especially as they followed on the heels of contentious debates over Myanmar, further destabilized ASEAN members' established norm and practice of not interfering in their neighbor's affairs and added another layer to already difficult intra-ASEAN debates.[85] The continued absence of an effective *ASEAN* response—especially given states' earlier rhetoric and what ASEAN Secretary General Severino would describe as the world's overly high expectations of ASEAN[86]—added to the impression that their once-rising institution was now fast on its way to becoming a "sunset organization."[87] In May 1998 domestic unrest and financial crisis forced Suharto to step down, an event that Yang Razali Kassim would later characterize to be as "earth-shaking [to ASEAN] as the financial crisis that swept the region."[88]

Not only that, but others noted that ASEAN's internal troubles were opening the door for divisive tactics from major powers. And indeed,

ASEAN's troubles gave its critics—already not pleased with some ASEAN practices and priorities—new opportunities to press particular agendas and more ammunition to challenge ASEAN's centrality in wider regional arrangements like the ARF. As some observing the crisis in Southeast Asia noted, "it is precisely such internal divisions that have allowed the U.S. to maintain its own hegemonic position by practicing a strategy of divide and rule."[89] At minimum, such internal tensions limited their ability to influence important crisis-related policy decisions and their ability to better deal with major powers. In this sense, member actions seemed to undermine important regional resilience objectives vis-à-vis larger powers that had been an initial premise for regional organization in ASEAN. As Severino lamented in March 1998, states appeared to lose sight of the "ideal of regional solidarity and cooperation" on which ASEAN had been founded. And in fact, reports of a "disintegrating ASEAN," troubled AFTA efforts, and a diminished ASEAN in the ARF had become regular news items by September 1998. As Severino put it, "People started expecting ASEAN to fall apart, they claimed that ASEAN had fallen into disarray, that ASEAN countries have been fatally damaged by the financial crisis and so on . . . "[90]

At the same time, true to understandings of regional resilience, such interacting intra-ASEAN and extra-ASEAN concerns also seemed to mobilize efforts to regroup. The growing realization of ASEAN's postcrisis loss of credibility vis-à-vis non-ASEAN members, as much ASEAN's failure to help individual economies, became a particular argument for new ASEAN initiative.[91] Singapore Foreign Minister S. Jayakumar may have said it best:

> In 1998 I pointed out that ASEAN faced a crisis of confidence. Today we must ask ourselves why the regional economic recovery has not translated into a restoration of international confidence in ASEAN. We may not like the perceptions of ASEAN as ineffective and a sunset organization. We may question whether they are justified. But they are political facts. Perceptions can define political reality. If we continue to be perceived as ineffective, we can be marginalized as our dialogue partners and international investors relegate us to the sidelines.[92]

Faced with this problem as framed, the answer for ASEAN would have to be "deeper integration, closer cohesion and greater openness." "On this response," as one Asian journalist put it, "hangs the future of Southeast Asia."[93]

As states began to reassess ASEAN, it is worth underscoring that despite a general intra-ASEAN conclusion "that ASEAN . . . [did] not have the institutional capability or the stature to react to the crisis in an effective fashion,"[94] states notably still saw ASEAN—unlike APEC—as an important framework for addressing the challenges associated with the crisis. While ASEAN lacked the funds or the know-how to form a regional monetary fund on its own, intra-ASEAN debates and efforts continued to affirm the need for ASEAN as a vehicle for regional and national self defense. Thus, the ASEAN Fund remained an important focus of ASEAN ministers, who in October 1998 agreed to the creation of a surveillance process, which would then be put under the supervision of central bank officials, with support from ASEAN Surveillance Coordinating and Technical Support Units.

In addition, states continued to develop other ASEAN trade and investment initiatives as a way to recenter, self-strengthen, and ultimately (they hoped) regain their former resilience and competitiveness. It is notable, for example, that despite the severity of the financial crisis and earlier suggestions (especially from Malaysia) that AFTA might be delayed, ASEAN states not only maintained their commitment to AFTA but in October 1998 also sped up their tariff reduction time table to 2003. States also adopted short-term measures (loosening national equity requirements, for example) to facilitate new investment.[95]

States also renewed attention to streamlining ASEAN's decision-making processes in the interest of better coordination and efficiency. Building on earlier decisions to introduce "flexible consensus" (1992) and a majority-rules dispute resolution mechanism (1996) to the AFTA process, ASEAN states continued to debate the question of "qualified majority voting" and the specific possibility of expanding their "ASEAN minus X" principle to technical policy matters as a way to streamline ASEAN cooperation.[96]

In short, ASEAN, compared to APEC, saw considerably more activity as a response to the growing crisis—and this was despite ASEAN's already obvious and acknowledged political and material limitations. While AFTA later saw some backtracking and continued to have limitations for various reasons,[97] such actions during the crisis did point to a general view that AFTA remained important to both the overall ASEAN project and the specific challenge of the financial crisis. Thailand especially would push the idea that "AFTA is the way to get out of the region's economic crisis."[98]

Nevertheless, despite efforts to strengthen ASEAN, the shared assessment remained that ASEAN was limited in some critical and fundamental ways. With neither influence nor presence at global negotiating tables or global halls of power, ASEAN states were simply limited in their ability to influence or defend themselves vis-à-vis critical decisions being made at the global level and by Washington. Thus, even at the same time that states saw ASEAN as an important part of their response, they also continued to look for other alternatives beyond ASEAN, as well as APEC, which as discussed above reflected too much the perceived problems at the global level to offer any meaningful assistance. In short, by the end of 1998 the predominant conclusion was just as Mahathir had argued early on, that ASEAN was too small and APEC too big. "To this end," as the *Jakarta Post* would later put it, "ASEAN, while painfully recognizing its own institutional and geopolitical weakness, has acknowledged . . . that the East Asian region could be much stronger and influential in world affairs if the three major Asian powers up north are eventually brought into the picture."[99]

The reassessments of ASEAN and APEC, as well as U.S. and global arrangements, consequently directed more and more attention to the potentials of East Asian frameworks. That interest was moreover offered venue and audience via the previously discussed "informal" meetings that ASEAN continued to hold with its Northeast Asian counterparts throughout the crisis, beginning with preparations for their first official informal gathering on the sidelines of ASEAN's 1997 summit. In addition to offering states forums to discuss, debate, and solidify ideas, these talks also facilitated the growth of new government-led regional efforts that now existed alongside what had been a mostly market-driven regionalism. The very holding of these sessions also helped make "East Asia" more and more "real," tangible, and practical as a framework.

In fact, indicative of East Asia's new persuasiveness among states, East Asian regional activities grew in quantity, quality, and across issues. Among the more notable developments was the development and regularization of the APT process at the top leadership level. Not only have leaders met every year since 1997, but in 1999 they took the significant step of officially recognizing their "informal meetings" as the ASEAN Plus Three (APT) process. Moreover, that high-level summitry is now further supported by separate meetings of APT Finance, Economic, and Foreign Ministers; Senior Officials Meetings, and Senior Economic Officials Meetings. The year 2000 then saw the emergence of "two big ideas": the East Asia Study Group to explore the possibilities of East Asian integration and East Asian free trade.[100] Tasked with identifying areas for future cooperation, that group would conclude both the "necessity and inevitability" of "East Asia."[101]

Just as notably, the APT process, which began as a consultative process, has seen a remarkable growth of activity at the functional level since 1997. In addition to the above, such activity also includes increasingly regular ministerial meetings between the ten states on a growing number of issues—for example, health (two meetings as of 2006), labor (at least five meetings as of 2006), and tourism (six meetings as of January 2007). There have also been growing consultations and emergent cooperation in areas of energy, drug trafficking, and agriculture, including the creation of a rice reserve system and an emergency communication network among energy ministers. In July 2003 ASEAN and the three Northeast Asian states also agreed to create an "APT governing group" to study the possibility of an East Asian oil stockpile toward assuring a stable energy supply.[102] According to Severino, as of late 2007, there were no less than forty-eight different mechanisms in place managing and facilitating cooperation between APT states.[103]

Perhaps not surprisingly, given the primary nature of the crisis, the most activity has taken place in the financial sector. In May 2000 APT finance ministers, meeting in Chiang Mai, "agreed to strengthen our policy dialogues and regional cooperation activities in, among others, the areas of capital flows monitoring, self-help and support mechanism and international financial reforms." The "Chiang Mai Initiative (CMI)" identified the creation of a regional surveillance mechanism and regional financing mechanism as particular areas of interest and cooperation.[104] The first would provide a kind of early warning system on capital flows. The second would involve a regional network of bilateral swap and repurchase agreement facilities—or bilateral "swap" agreements.

Building on the 2000 decision, APT members in 2001 agreed to convene an ASEAN+3 Study Group comprised of senior finance and central bank officials whose mandate was "to discuss frameworks and modalities to enhance the effectiveness of [APT's] economic review and policy dialogue."[105] As a result of their study, APT senior finance and central bank deputies now meet informally, usually twice a year, to discuss economic and policy issues; the first meeting took place on April 4, 2002. The year 2002 also saw seven countries[106] agree to exchange information on short-term capital flows. While information exchanges have been mostly based on self-reporting, the growth of bilateral swaps is expected to demand a more formal, structured process.

In light of previous debates and U.S. objections, the decision to develop a regional financial arrangement was especially significant. Building on an identified need to "enhance . . . self-help and support mechanisms in East Asia" through greater monetary and financial cooperation under "the ASEAN+3 Framework,"[107] the emergent mechanism could be viewed as a reincarnation of their earlier, defeated AMF, especially given the role of Japan. In this case, the mechanism would build on a multibillion-dollar Japanese initiative (the Miyazawa Initiative) set up in late 1998 to assist crisis-affected economies. Then, in May 2000, ASEAN finance ministers, with their Northeast Asian counterparts at Chiang Mai, "agreed in principle to pool hard currency resources" toward protecting Asian countries from speculative attacks.[108] Notably, the CMI had two components—an ASEAN component in the form of an expanded ASEAN swap and an extended network of bilateral arrangements among ASEAN countries, China, Japan, and Korea.[109]

The latter has seen particular growth. In 2001 the thirteen states implemented a series of bilateral arrangements to exchange currency among their central banks. In 2005 at a meeting of the Asian Development Bank, a Japanese initiative doubled the size of the CMI's currency account; it also raised the amount members could draw without IMF conditions (from 10 percent to 20 percent), and took new steps toward multilateralizing the CMI's bilateral swap agreements.[110] As of May 2007, a total of sixteen arrangements (at a total of US$80 billion) between eight countries had been signed.[111]

ASEAN, "East Asia," and "ASEAN Plus Three": What's in a Name?

Thus, the late 1990s saw the emergence of a notable "East Asian" trend in regional activities since 1997, a contrast to the early 1990s when it seemed that the "Asia Pacific" was the trend of the future. The expansion and intensification of the APT process was (and continues to be) especially striking, proceeding at a pace that has surprised even those closely involved in ASEAN. But what does this East Asia trend mean for ASEAN's coalition of smaller, Southeast Asian economies? While few see the APT process as a substitute for ASEAN,[112] the APT certainly raises questions about ASEAN. Some regional elites have already expressed their expectation that at some point ASEAN will in fact be subsumed under the APT or some "East Asia" process. Most, however, continue to see ASEAN as an important representation of Southeast Asian interests and that of smaller powers and consequently argue that ASEAN will continue playing a necessary, even "pivotal" role in the ongoing reorganization of East Asia.

As many in ASEAN argue, however, if ASEAN wants to claim ownership of both smaller and wider regional process, ASEAN must be strengthened institutionally, economically, and politically. Those making this argument include former Secretary General Rodolfo Severino, who has argued that ASEAN must speed up trade liberalization. Carolina Hernandez, a long time track-2 participant from the Philippines, has similarly argued, "ASEAN needs to reinvent itself not just in terms of its norms and codes but even in the way members deal with one another."[113] Some, prioritizing ASEAN and generally concerned that ASEAN may lose its relevance inside and outside Southeast Asia, have even justified East Asia as the "catalyst to get [ASEAN's] act together again."[114] Toward this end, elites at both track 1 and track 2 levels have continued to debate and develop intra-ASEAN integration efforts alongside their East Asian activities. In addition to the initiatives already discussed, there have been proposals to strengthen the ASEAN Secretariat and to create an ASEAN regional debt ratings agency.[115] Recent debates, efforts, and adoption of the ASEAN Charter can also be seen as the culmination of that post-Asian financial crisis process and debate (see Conclusion).

Indeed, over the decade since the Asian financial crisis, persistent concerns about ASEAN's own voice being lost amidst the East Asian activity have remained an important driver and subject of ASEAN activities and debates. Especially illustrative of these concerns have been debates about whether to give institutional expression to the APT process—for example, through the establishment of a secretariat and whether to rename the APT to explicitly reference "East Asia." The main proponent for doing both has been Mahathir, who in 2002 offered $10 million in seed money to set up an APT secretariat in Kuala Lumpur and pushed to have the APT's name formally changed to express its East Asian identity.[116] But this proposal met with consternation all around: New ASEAN members were "bewildered" and concerned that they would be even more marginalized in the larger setting; old members mostly felt that the APT process was still too new to take those steps.

Most of all, members were concerned that ASEAN itself would be lost. As long as ASEAN is in the title, there is no doubt about its existence. "ASEAN plus Three" also explicitly makes ASEAN the center. However, "East Asia" potentially renders ASEAN invisible. The creation of an APT secretariat, a formal and physical expression of the East Asia idea, was viewed as similarly problematic. With the exception of the Philippines, ASEAN's other founding members all expressed particular concern that an APT secretariat would "steal the shine" from the ASEAN Secretariat,[117] if not pose a potential threat to ASEAN itself. As one ASEAN diplomat put it, ASEAN would both "lose its luster as a regional entity" in the face of a new East Asian entity and "be 'neutralised' by the North Asian giants, especially China."[118] Similarly, one long-time reporter for Bangkok's *The Nation* summarized: "Deep down, opponents [of the APT Secretariat] fear the new secretariat will transform ASEAN+3 to 3+ASEAN . . . "[119]

Thus, despite some desire to support the proposal on account of Mahathir's impending retirement—a "gift" to a long-time ASEAN leader—Thailand and others argued and agreed that first priority go to "strengthen[ing] the ASEAN secretariat"[120] in Jakarta so that ASEAN would be better able to manage the APT process. That way, as the director-general of the ASEAN Department of Thailand's foreign ministry put it, when an East Asian secretariat materializes, "at least we will continue to steer it."[121] In short, despite consensus about the value of APT processes, their growth and expansion have also not eliminated concerns about ASEAN itself. The emergence of the East Asia Summit in December 2005 would introduce even more questions.

Conclusion

The 1997–1998 Asian financial crisis marked an important juncture in an ongoing intra-ASEAN debate about ASEAN-plus regionalisms. In particular, the crisis revealed in the most dramatic way the deficiencies and insufficiencies of existing governance arrangements at all major levels—global and regional, as well as domestic. This chapter has detailed especially the process by which ASEAN states came to important reconsiderations of existing global and regional arrangements and how that process contributed to new ASEAN thinking about East Asian regionalism.

As highlighted above, the growth of East Asian regionalism, especially after 1997, reflected more than just a growing interdependence among Southeast Asian and Northeast Asian states. (After all, interdependence also characterized APEC, which declined in importance after 1997.) Rather, it was the product of complex, interactive forces and processes, key pieces of which were already in play before the crisis began. Intra-APEC debates, for example, helped sharpen both ASEAN choices and identity vis-à-vis Western members of APEC. Meanwhile, opportunities provided by ASEAN for Southeast Asian and Northeast Asian states to meet provided a chance for actors to familiarize themselves with one another and with the very idea of "East Asia." Mahathir's particular efforts also kept the East Asia idea alive, despite its earlier defeat and continued contentiousness. All these pre-1997 developments were important to understanding and explaining the expansion of East Asian processes since 1997. They are what made "East Asia" a ready idea, process, and response to the developments of 1997–1998.

In this sense, the crisis did not create "East Asia" so much as it intensified and sped up existing processes already in train. Put another way, the Asian financial crisis played midwife to ideas and processes that had already been gestating for quite a while. At minimum, the crisis seemed to affirm and deepen the sense of difference—difference in interest, perspective, and worldview—that had already been growing throughout the 1990s. Indeed, as illustrated by Gore's 1998 speech to APEC, the specific issues of contention from earlier debates, rather than abating, remained alive and well throughout the 1997–1998 crisis. Myanmar, in particular, came up as an issue between ASEAN and its Western partners at practically every regional meeting. At the height of the crisis, the EU denied Myanmar officials visas, which prevented their participation in EU–ASEAN dialogues, an action that prompted a similar move from the United States. Madeleine Albright and Al Gore also made Myanmar and human rights a focal point of their interactions with ASEAN. In a related but different vein, a suggestion from Mahathir to revisit the Universal Declaration of Human Rights became the subject of a sharp exchange between, on the one hand, Albright and Undersecretary Stuart Eizenstat and, on the other, Mahathir at a 1997 ARF meeting. Rather than backing away from Mahathir, however, that exchange notably rallied others in ASEAN to Mahathir's defense. In particular, the Philippines' Siazon (among others) argued that not only might the Human Rights Declaration benefit from review, but review was also the right thing to do given that so many countries were not represented at the Charter's original drafting.[122]

Such differences reflected a difference in opinion, but even more significantly, an absence of shared belief. In particular, there was a tendency not to believe the sincerity of the other's arguments. If Western partners tended to view ASEAN's cultural and developmental defense as a cover for status quo interests in regime survival, ASEAN elites were often similarly suspicious of Washington's human rights and democratization rhetoric. As many put it, Western actors are motivated by a need "to cater to the international media's agenda,"[123] and a desire "just to score points . . . [so that] they look good to their people."[124] No wonder that APEC often faced such an uphill battle. Its problems reflected not just divergent interests but also the fact that participants were coming from different worlds and increasingly speaking different languages.

Indeed, APEC's diminished importance illustrates the ways that a weak founding agreement—that is, the weakness of shared beliefs about what that arrangement exists for—can have lasting effects, especially on the patterns of interaction that emerge and shape an institution's social context. As discussed, APEC's founding was based on a set of ad hoc compromises rather than on any fundamental agreement about objectives or process. It is this lack of normative agreement about "why APEC"—not APEC's loose regionalism or even its diversity of membership—that makes APEC "weak." Linda Lim once described APEC's 1998 Early Voluntary Sectoral Liberalization (EVSL) initiative as one that seemed "doomed with birth defects."[125] In essence, the same could be said about APEC more generally. It is possible that APEC's birth defects could have been overcome. Leadership might have facilitated more durable agreements; but that did not happen. If members had agreed on the value and indeed validity of the consensus-building process, that too might have helped, but again, there was no agreement on objectives or process.

Instead, interactions between APEC's Western and ASEAN members ultimately produced not habits of cooperation but instead "othering" tendencies, even habits of confrontation (especially between Malaysia and the United States). Interactions did little to persuade APEC's skeptics (in ASEAN or in the United States) to the validity or legitimacy of either APEC's content or process. The APEC process may have been created in the hopes of "Pacific community" (however defined) but in the end may have done more to weaken it. At minimum, these debates and interactions affected how each side interpreted the Asian financial crisis and thus their understandings of the response. In the end, for ASEAN states, APEC offered no true alternative to existing arrangements. In this sense, Kahler's characterization of APEC's troubles is correct. Specifically, he argues that APEC is unnecessary because there are global regimes that already do what APEC functionally does (or is supposed to do). However, the above discussion also suggests that, for ASEAN states, at least, the relevant redundancy is not economic or functional as argued by Kahler but instead very much political.[126] APEC is, in other words, made less important to ASEAN states by the fact that its politics and content mirror arrangements already in existence (and identified as the problem) at the global level.

Lastly, this chapter has highlighted important dynamics in ASEAN itself, as well as its particular role in facilitating recent East Asian regional trends, including an East Asian response to the crisis. For example, ASEAN leaders took the lead in public debates and framing choices. Mahathir and Goh Chok Tong, especially, kept the East Asian idea on the agenda such that it was a ready option when the crisis hit. Other ASEAN leaders also took the lead in arguing with global actors about regional priorities. These public arguments drew on and deepened existing dialogues about Asia's place in the world. In addition, ASEAN provided important institutional opportunities for Northeast Asian and Southeast Asian states to get together. ASEAN venues—including the "ASEAN plus" meetings that informally began in 1994, solidified in 1997, and then were given a name in 1999—provided not just opportunities for communication and transparency, but an important opportunity to identify, agree, and indeed bond over common problems and their common struggles with other actors.

The role played by ASEAN in facilitating East Asian trends speaks to the particular politics of East Asia but also ASEAN's institutional legitimacy in East and Southeast Asia. Similarly, the continued relevance of ASEAN as a regional framework in the context of the 1997–1998 crisis also speaks to its important normative strengths vis-à-vis rival arrangements. Again, not only was it the case that states turned to ASEAN early on, but they continued to do so even after ASEAN's political and material limitations were quite apparent. One may ask why ASEAN did not become more marginalized among Southeast Asian states as APEC did in the aftermath of the 1997–1998 crisis, when both arguably failed to offer effective frameworks to contain or manage it. The answer lies in different expectations and different founding agreements. For one, despite an early interest in an ASEAN response, there was nevertheless a strong understanding of ASEAN's material limitations. Put another way, ASEAN elites in 1997 and 1998 did not really *expect* ASEAN to be able to respond to the crisis on its own—though the crisis did generate an interest in developing greater capacity and better mechanisms to respond better in the future.[127]

In addition, compared to APEC, ASEAN's mandate was both stronger and broader. Unlike APEC, ASEAN states understood ASEAN to be a multi-issue, comprehensive association, whose contributions to regional stability were widely acknowledged by Southeast Asian elites. Most of all, ASEAN was "stronger" for the strength of its founding agreements. Despite political, normative, and material challenges, states still fundamentally agreed about the necessity of unity as a basis for overall national and regional resilience. Elites and officials may worry about ASEAN's future and efficacy, and they may question their own unity, but they do not doubt ASEAN's larger purpose or raison d'être. Similarly, they believe in the ASEAN process—how it works— even if they think it could use improvement or modifications. Neither is true of APEC. To be sure, the crisis triggered a fundamental (and still ongoing) reassessment of what ASEAN does, how it should relate with others (inside and outside ASEAN), as well as how it should work. Nevertheless, the strength of founding agreements and a general belief that ASEAN's processes had served them well meant that both the resulting reassessment and thus consequences for organization were more constrained. Compared to APEC, the reassessment was much less about ASEAN's reason for being and rather more about how it could improve in ways that would better serve those reasons for being—and, importantly, save the organization.

Current East Asian trends may prove to be ASEAN's greatest challenge as far as competing regional frameworks are concerned. And as in APEC, EAEG, and the ARF debates in the early 1990s, the development of APT and now the East Asian Summit (see Conclusion) will similarly compel ASEAN to debate and argue for new directions, in addition to rethink its role and place in East Asia both practically and ideationally.

Thus far, ASEAN has found ways to conceptualize Asia's new regionalisms in ways that do negate ASEAN but instead continue to acknowledge a role for Southeast Asian organization. East Asia's particular political dynamics, where only ASEAN offers any "comfort level" in relations, are also likely to support, at least in the short to medium term, the centrality, influence, and even leadership of this group of small-to-middle powers. Nevertheless, if ASEAN is to maintain that centrality, it will have to demonstrate its own organizational coherence and clarity of leadership. Intensified efforts to deepen and expand ASEAN integration efforts especially speak to concerns about ASEAN. It is again no coincidence that, as East Asian activities have intensified, so too have initiatives like the ASEAN Economic Community[128] and the ASEAN security community that are targeted specifically at building and expanding ASEAN regionalism. Similarly, it seems certain that members themselves will continue to argue that ASEAN plays an indispensable role in bringing together other actors with more problematic relations. As Carolina Hernandez, a long-time track-2 participant from the Philippines, put it, "Why do people look at it as an either-or situation? Without ASEAN, you cannot have the 'plus three.' All three need ASEAN. If you leave the three alone, it will be difficult, because they still need to arrive at some kind of regional reconciliation among themselves which ASEAN has been able to do."[129]

Conclusion

> [A]s with all organizations and entities, ASEAN will have to realize that it will not be nor can it be the ultimate creation.
>
> *Thanat Khoman,*
> *ASEAN founding father*[1]

These chapters have described dramatic and unexpected changes in Southeast Asia's international relations. At the center of these changes has been the Association of Southeast Asian Nations, a group of diverse states that has managed to create a stable and prosperous region that is the envy of many in the developing world. Moreover, ASEAN's group of lesser powers now finds itself the gravitational center of a host of regional arrangements that include much larger powers than themselves. To be sure—and as these chapters highlight—ASEAN is not without its limitations, and many of its strengths are also sources of weakness. Nevertheless, ASEAN has played a role in both Southeast Asia and now beyond Southeast Asia that is unexpected from more material and power-based accounts. In this conclusion, I revisit the arguments made at the beginning of this study as to the roles played by interacting material, ideational, and social forces in the construction of regions and regionalisms in general and in Southeast Asia, Asia Pacific, and East Asia in particular. I conclude with some reflections on what the dynamics described in these chapters mean for the future of ASEAN, East Asia, and U.S.–ASEAN relations, as well as for our theoretical understandings of cooperation and the processes of change.

Complex Interactions:
Power, Agents, Ideas, and Social Processes

Chapters in this study have highlighted the ways that regions and regionalisms are products of complex interactions and intersections. Together, they also offer a contrast to material explanations that fail to account for the variety of exchanges, interactions, and changes that take place in world politics. In the specific case of Southeast Asia, material explanations have been less able to "see" what ASEAN does, ASEAN's underlying driving objectives and dynamics, or how it has helped to stabilize expectations among states. As detailed in these chapters, today's ASEAN regional order is a complex system that reflects interacting material and ideational structures, entrepreneurial action, and critical interactions between extraregional and intraregional forces, as well as cumulative, iterative social exchanges about Southeast Asia's intra- and extraregional relations.

Extraregional Triggers and Social Change

In thinking and practice, actors tend to follow routines until something happens to make them think or behave otherwise. It is thus no surprise that change and especially turning points—be it with respect to the modus operandi of particular actors or the life of an institution or political system—have often been correlated with dramatic events of particular material consequence. So it has also been with ASEAN, for which material changes—both real and perceived—have provided important impetuses and opportunities for new ideas to enter and shape the political discourse, a discourse that, in turn, has redefined Southeast Asia's international relations.

These chapters have highlighted regionalism's particular sensitivity to material and extraregional uncertainties, especially in U.S. policy, which have provided regular catalysts for intra-ASEAN (re)negotiations about states' extra- and intraregional relations and, in turn, new regional initiatives. Each of the initiatives discussed in this volume, for example, has been associated with a rethinking of regional relations that was prompted by uncertainties in ASEAN's extraregional relations. The strong correlation between ASEAN's major political, economic, and security initiatives and extraregional changes suggest that such extraregional triggers significantly increase the likelihood of regional change in ASEAN.

On the other hand, the chapters also make clear that such extraregional and material developments by themselves provide only indeterminate explanations, especially as regards specific ASEAN responses. Underscoring this point is the considerable debate that has accompanied each of ASEAN's initiatives—from ASEAN's founding all the way to current "ASEAN plus" initiatives. The key to explaining particular changes lies in identifying the intervening processes and forces—entrepreneurial action, particular interpretations, the process of argument for example—that direct actors to particular actions as appropriate responses to challenges.

In fact, even the need for change is not always immediately evident. Rather, individual agents and actors have played key roles in pushing for change. Practically all of ASEAN's major initiatives—beginning with its founding—have involved activist or entrepreneurial efforts. In some cases, individuals played direct roles in the creation of new initiatives—for example, ASEAN's founding (Tunku Abdul Rahman, Thanat Khoman, and Adam Malik), ZOPFAN (Tun Razak), SEANWFZ (Alatas and Suharto), the expansion of TAC (Anand), and AFTA (Anand). In other cases, individuals played less direct roles in introducing or facilitating normative changes that made possible different initiatives later in time. These include Chatichai in ASEAN expansion and Manglapus and Aquino in the creation of the ARF, as well as Mahathir and Goh Chok Tong in "ASEAN plus Three" initiatives. To be sure, each of these individuals was responding at least in part to opportunities and challenges created by perceived material changes; but that fact makes the roles played by these individuals no less significant. Indeed, the cases above illustrate not only a critical role played by agency in promoting particular solutions but also the importance of that agency in *recognizing* and exploiting perceived openings.[2]

Founding Arguments, Founding Ideas, and Founding Conditions

These chapters have also highlighted the important mediating roles that ideas play in politics. Ideas provide prisms through which actors interpret the significance of events and that direct actors to particular actions over others. They can also make the critical difference between systems of amity and systems of animosity. In Southeast Asia, ideas have been critical to explaining how diverse and divergent states came to see Southeast Asian regionalism as an important response to their identified problems of domestic, regional, and global order.

Specifically, the ASEAN case highlights how ideas shape regional politics through arguments about the relationship between intraregional and extraregional forces. Arguments make important causal claims and connections that provide the basis for actors' understandings of both their challenges and the appropriate response. Here, ASEAN's founding arguments have helped make meaningful and thus influential two big ideas in the shaping of regional order. The first is the belief that there does exist some space called Southeast Asia and that "Southeast Asia" should provide ASEAN its organizing principle. The second big idea is resilience—states' common understandings of themselves as weak, fragmented powers and the understood vulnerabilities of that division, especially in relation to various foreign forces.

However, neither of these ideas would have had the influence and centrality they have had in regional life were it not for particular arguments—in this case, a founding argument about *regional* resilience. In drawing critical causal connections between *regional* division and foreign intervention and between *regional* unity and self-determination, regional resilience is what made the case for regional organization. Again, if the problem is identified as one of division and fragmentation, then the logical solution must be one of unity and organization. Regional resilience is what makes "Southeast Asia" a meaningful and thus powerful organizing principle. This founding argument about regional resilience is critical to explaining not just "why ASEAN?" but also its particular regional politics. It is also what ultimately distinguishes Southeast Asia's regional politics and regional order, not only from the regional politics of South Asia, the Middle East, or Northeast Asia but also from the liberal regionalism of Western Europe. In short, different arguments and different ideas will give rise to different politics.

At the same time, these chapters have also highlighted how arguments and ideas are themselves conditioned by their material and social environment. As above, material changes can be important sources of instabilities—instabilities that give ideas and arguments a chance that they might not otherwise have had. But, also, material realities and conditions can inform and influence ideas. Here, material considerations—domestic constraints; limited resources; the absence of an immediate, shared military threat—informed initial preferences for a nonmilitarized regionalism. Similarly, troubles in the Thai–U.S. relationship attracted Thailand to regionalism and, in so doing, expanded regional consultations and agendas beyond Southeast Asia's insular states. Without Thailand—as a continental state and in Thanat's particular advocacy efforts—regional organization might have been premised on a very different idea of "region" than the inclusive Southeast Asian idea that emerged. The same is true of Indonesia's participation, which hinged on its changed domestic politics. In short, both "Southeast Asia" and resilience—which are today important sources of regional normative and identity claims through practice and argument—were originally influenced in important ways by particular material conditions at ASEAN's founding.

Similarly, the above chapters make clear that ideas themselves are context bound. Rarely have successful ideas come from nowhere or been created wholly from new cloth. Instead, as Checkel argues, they are both constrained and enabled by "the broader social discourse in which they are embedded."[3] Regionalism in 1960s Southeast Asia was made more persuasive—indeed possible—by the fact that it was framed in ways that resonated with a broader social discourse of nationalism—the challenges, vulnerabilities, and priorities of nation building; the historical dangers of division, fragmentation, and intervention; and the persistent and pressing desire for self-determination after centuries of subjugation. Here, regional resilience arguments were especially key in making regionalism consistent with existing normative priorities and interpretations. Regional resilience is what reconciled nationalism and regionalism—ideas and ideologies that might otherwise have been defined in opposition to each other. Regional resilience is what made the case for regional organization.

Founding ideological constraints and conditions, as with the material, have similarly had lasting effects on what ASEAN became. ASEAN's defining tensions, paradoxes, and institutional identity, as well as its rituals of solidarity and culture of talking, are all products of a regionalism that had originally been framed in *both* nationalist and regionalist terms. These chapters have highlighted especially how the concern for both national and regional unity, which is at the core of regional resilience arguments, produces contrary normative pressures on ASEAN. On the one hand, regional resilience demands unity—or at least a commitment to work toward that unity; on the other hand, regional resilience based on the assumption of both regional and national division also demands caution. Consequently, ASEAN's regionalism is informal, less rule bound, and most of all dialogue and consensus driven. Again, the process of consensus building—the pursuit of unity through talking without jeopardizing the unity that exists—is itself an expression of regional resilience arguments. As detailed in these chapters, such tensions and characteristics have been most obviously evident in ASEAN's trade liberalization efforts but are also evident in the processes that produced key security initiatives like ZOPFAN and the ARF, as well as APT.

In this sense, ASEAN's founding argument does not merely justify regionalism as a response to particular material challenges, nor does it simply make regionalism possible given a particular normative context. Founding arguments provide regionalism its social purpose and raison d'être, and as such affect its objectives and what it looks like. As underscored below, this point has critical implications for our assessments and understandings of not just ASEAN but also ASEAN's "spin-off" regionalisms—APEC, ARF, APT, and other "East Asian" processes.

Making and Reinforcing the Argument

In addition to the interactive influences of material and ideational forces, these chapters have highlighted some processes by which ideas come to shape politics. As recapped above, for example, the process of argument is a key intervening process that connects stimuli to action. How stimuli interact with existing ideas and expectations is thus key to explaining whether there is change, as Legro and others have argued;[4] however, just as important are the arguments that establish causal connections as to whether and how to respond. Southeast Asia's own history—as well as the many parts of the developing world that remain violent and conflict prone despite sharing with Southeast Asia similar material constraints and challenges—is testimony to the fact that needs have to be identified and interpreted in certain ways before regionalism is seen as the answer to the problems of division, conflict, and intervention. In the absence of arguments tying nation to region, fragmentation to intervention, unity to security, there would be no ASEAN—and certainly not the ASEAN we know today.

At the same time, arguments are not just static sets of causal claims and ideas. In fact, these chapters illustrate that arguments evolve and adapt and moreover can be made more persuasive over time. What this means is that the process of argumentation may—and most often does—involve more than a one-shot exchange. Actors, for example, constantly respond and adjust to new information—not just about material experiences, as highlighted in more economic accounts but also ideational and normative changes created by previous arguments. In particular, these chapters have highlighted a process of consensus seeking, involving familiarization and reiteration, as well as debate, clarification, and modification. Put another way, arguments that may not be immediately persuasive may also be incrementally made more persuasive down the line.

In these chapters, the ARF and APT initiatives offer particular examples of how arguments that were first rejected were made possible later by the normative changes they introduced. In the case of the APT—the "EAEG by another name"—entrepreneurial efforts by Mahathir, as well as Goh Chok Tong, helped make a previously radical idea more familiar, ensured its prominence among a range of possible regional responses debated, and ultimately offered an "obvious" regional alternative to the ideas and arrangements that had disappointed when the 1997–1998 crisis hit.[5]

The ARF is another example. When first introduced, the idea of ASEAN participating in, let alone leading, an expanded security dialogue was a radical idea that was almost immediately rejected. Such a proposal went beyond ASEAN's founding mandate, seemed contrary to ASEAN norms as regarded political-security cooperation, and stretched ASEAN's originating regional purview. However, Manila's persistence in challenging ASEAN's security taboo and persistence in talking about the need to talk about security helped make the idea more familiar and acceptable. Not only did Manila put "new thinking" on the agenda at a time when others would have preferred to go on as usual, but ASEAN's consensus-seeking process itself helped build momentum for an expanded dialogue as the appropriate response to uncertainties in ASEAN's great power relations. To be sure, ASEAN's 1993 decision to create the ARF was also influenced by other factors—the political challenges posed by extraregional proposals, as well as major power uncertainties—but Manila's efforts nevertheless helped create the normative conditions that made an expanded security dialogue a "logical" response to those extraregional challenges and "natural" extension of ASEAN processes.

Consensus seeking can also begin with agreement on a basic principle, which is then expanded and consolidated through debate, modifications, and clarifications as to its component parts. ZOPFAN, AFTA, and indeed ASEAN itself are all good examples of initiatives that began by identifying what some call the "lowest common denominator" but were subsequently developed through a process of consensus seeking that clarified, modified, and expanded states' initial agreement. It is also worth underscoring that each of these initiatives has been enabled and (ultimately) made more meaningful by ASEAN's commitment to the consensus-seeking process as an expression of regional unity and regional resilience.

The above cases highlight also how the reiteration of arguments and ideas can remind, affirm, and thus maintain previous points of agreement. The more an argument is made, the more it leverages a particular viewpoint and, as above, at least diminishes some of the normative obstacles against it. This is not to say that all arguments will ultimately become more persuasive—as above, arguments still have to "make sense" of perceived realities—but repeated arguments can increase the prominence of particular interpretations. This kind of reinforcement has been evident throughout ASEAN's existence and across initiatives, but it was perhaps most critical in ASEAN's earliest years when elites felt compelled to ritualistically repeat a founding narrative of intraregional division, conflict, and balkanization by external powers. That ritualistic retelling of ASEAN's founding story—the dangers of division, the need for unity, the problems of intervention, the challenges of self determination—served to remind others and themselves of their common cause and constraints. Repeated enough, this narrative increasingly took on the properties of social discourse and social fact.

To underscore the point, the processes by which ideas come to influence world politics can involve extended social processes, involving normative familiarization, normative adjustments, and normative reinforcement.

This is especially so with arguments that are promoting particularly novel ideas or initiatives, as those ideas and initiatives will be more vulnerable to challenges from old orthodoxies, new information, and charges of inconsistency. Thus, if ideas and arguments are to "take" and have more lasting effect, they must be supported by processes that maintain and affirm their validity. Even established ideas will need to be maintained—for example, through rhetoric and discourse, action and routine—if they are to remain influential. Both established and more radical ideas will, in other words, need reinforcement if they are to have lasting effects.

Lastly, words do not just reinforce ideas; they can also have important context-creating effects. As Khong argues about ASEAN's inclusive engagement rhetoric, for example, rhetoric can create new expectations and new normative pressures that shape both interpretations of reality and ultimately behavior. Drawing on David Campbell, Khong writes,

> Once a particular discourse acquires "greater value," it becomes the conventional wisdom of the day. That is one reason why, in the present fluid security environment, many ASEAN officials prefer the language of engagement and dialogue as opposed to that of containment or constrainment. Speaking the latter language, they fear, might only help make it into a self fulfilling prophesy.[6]

In short, while many may disparage ASEAN's "talk shop," these chapters provide evidence that talking—arguing, debating, consensus seeking, reiterating—can have some significant and complex effects on politics and social systems. Not only can talking help loosen the normative barriers in the way of particular ideas, produce clarifications and modifications that are critical to new agreement, and maintain existing agreement, but it can also create new social realities. Indeed, it is through talking that ASEAN states have promoted, reinforced, and reproduced a particular conception of region and a particular politics.

If rhetoric can shape practice, practice can also reinforce and shape the rhetoric. ASEAN's rhetoric of "One Southeast Asia" offers a notable example. In 1967 the idea of "One Southeast Asia" was fraught with all sorts of normative and empirical contradictions. However, every year that ASEAN states were able to maintain—*practice*—regional unity and every year that ASEAN's relations and overall regional security situation improved, the idea of "One Southeast Asia" gained substance, and arguments for regional resilience gained increased credibility. One can debate the extent to which such ideas were directly responsible for material changes, but the key point is that the stabilization of relations and all its benefits (growth, prosperity, legitimacy, international recognition) followed and are associated with the creation of ASEAN in 1967.[7] Consequently, by 1995 and 1997 "One Southeast Asia" as the basis for regional security was less a matter of argument but a matter of shared belief, with its own dynamics, as illustrated by ASEAN's expansion politics and process.

ASEAN's shared belief and practice of inclusive engagement as a strategic response to uncertainty offers another illustration of how practice can reinforce ideas and beliefs. In 1967 inclusive engagement was a barely formed argument—and to the extent that it was, it was limited to Southeast Asia. In other words, the argument was about an inclusive Southeast Asia (that is, regional resilience) not inclusion as a general principle. It was important to include Vietnam, for example, because regional resilience called for Vietnam's inclusion. It was only later that the inclusion and its associated conflict-mediating effects came to have more universal application, and only later that it became a more general principle of ASEAN's collective diplomacy. Specifically, both the argument and the belief that including and engaging are better than excluding and confronting were reinforced through practice and the successful amelioration of intra-ASEAN conflict associated with that practice. Similarly, the extended arguments about the value of inclusion, dialogue, and consensus that developed from states' defense of ASEAN practices vis-à-vis Western actors were later given additional validity by ASEAN's improved relations with China. In other words, the validity of inclusive engagement—essentially a belief in the possibilities and benefits of common and cooperative security—is reinforced by the stabilization and improvement of relations between ASEAN and China, as well as within ASEAN itself. In short, talking and doing can reinforce ideas and transform arguments into ways of thinking and acting.[8]

All this is not to say that ASEAN states do not appreciate more conventional security measures, but ASEAN rhetoric and experience have also convinced states that such measures are both not enough and potentially problematic for regional security. Indeed, forty years of talking and doing have produced a security culture that increasingly focuses on the mitigation of conflict through dialogue, inclusive engagement, and common security—the logic of security with, not security against.

Similarly, this is not to say that all problems in ASEAN have been resolved or that repeated social interactions always produce improvements in relations. For example, ASEAN's annual confrontations with Western powers in APEC and the ARF have had differently reinforcing effects. In the face of persistent and repeated Western criticism of ASEAN-style institutionalism and conflict management, for example, ASEAN states have had to sharpen and clarify their arguments about what ASEAN does and how ASEAN works. The result is a reinforced sense of difference but also a reinforced argument about the merits of both ASEAN's ways and ASEAN centrality. From these interactions has emerged a particular and novel argument that ASEAN states' lesser power status makes them in fact uniquely qualified to lead regional processes and to reassure uncertain actors—what Johnston characterizes as ASEAN's "counter-real politik ideology" or discourse about political change, security, and socialization.[9] This relatively new argument and belief have helped give ASEAN the wherewithal to go beyond its founding regional ambit and to engage actors like China which, unlike Vietnam in the 1970s, lies outside Southeast Asia and thus beyond regional resilience arguments.

Thus, interactions—as Karl Deutsch argued long ago—can have consolidating and reinforcing effects on relationships. But the 1990s examples of ARF and APEC also underscore the point that processes and interactions may reinforce "negative" as much as "positive" conclusions about processes and others. They also illustrate the insufficiency of looking at interactions without consideration of the context and quality of interactions—and not just in the sense of duration and density, as sometimes emphasized.[10] For example, to quote Checkel, "prolonged contact in sessions marked by intense bargaining is likely to have quite different effects on actors than meetings devoted to puzzling and joint puzzle solving."[11]

In both the ARF and APEC, interactions have tended to be more confrontational and divisive in both substance and style. In both arenas, ASEAN states have found themselves the regular targets of Western criticisms on trade, governance, human rights, ASEAN institutionalism, and Myanmar. Moreover, such exchanges have persisted over the life of both arrangements and even at the height of major economic or political crisis. Not surprisingly, exchanges between ASEAN states and Western partners, especially the United States and the EU, have tended to reinforce, not lessen, perceived differences. Disagreement about how regional cooperation should be pursued (for example, rules-driven versus dialogue-driven and consensus-driven) is not just an additional point of difference but it also means that participants in those arrangements lack uncontroversial ways to negotiate their differences.

Consequently, instead of a common language or discourse that unites, APEC especially is characterized by two distinct, interactive discourses, each of which identifies the other as problematic and consequently reinforces the other. In short, within ARF and APEC, as within ASEAN, sustained talking and interactions have performed social reinforcement functions; however, instead of unity or a sense of common cause, interactions have tended instead to reinforce ideas about the differences between ASEAN and APEC's "Western" membership. These exchanges, interactions, and resulting sense of difference, in turn, have contributed to a normative context more conducive to East Asian than to Asian Pacific regionalism.

A Return to the Big Picture:
Incremental Change, Cumulative Processes,
and the Evolution of Regional Systems

The complex interactions highlighted above and in these chapters give support to constructivist characterizations of social and ideational change as a multistage process that generally involves, first, ideational collapse and then consolidation around new strategies and new ideas, before the cycle begins anew.[12] At the same time, while affirming some of the conclusions of past constructivist studies, these chapters also add to our existing understandings of system change by highlighting three related dynamics that get less attention: (1) the roles played by lesser events and less dramatic shocks; (2) the evolutionary and incremental processes of change; and (3) the cumulative effects of ideas and processes on thinking and practice. Each of these dynamics is better revealed when we consider cooperation in more process-driven, less outcomes-driven or even events-driven terms.

With respect to the first, emphases on dramatic events and dramatic change may obscure other processes and interactions that move change. On the one hand, the conclusions here offer similar conclusions about the ways that events of great material consequence interact with existing expectations and ideas to produce the collapse of one orthodoxy and the emergence of another.[13] In this study on ASEAN, the period 1963 through 1967, which involved the collapse of "old-style nationalism" and confrontation and the emergence of a new, tentative regional ideology, provides such a juncture. These chapters also highlight a similar logic of change described in extant constructivist discussions that focus on dramatic events—that is, actors need reason or incentive to change their ways. In fact, anticipated material consequences (most often associated with extraregional developments) appear to be necessary stimuli before actors are ready and willing to change thinking and practice. This study also similarly concludes, however, that such shocks and events, in and of themselves, are insufficient explanations for change *and the kind of change* that follows.

These chapters thus affirm constructivist conclusions about the constrained and contingent nature of change. In fact, precisely because systems tend toward the status quo—be it due to ingrained habits and thinking or vested interests—the dramatic changes characteristic of critical junctures may be said to be quite rare. In these chapters, for example, few would dispute that events of 1963 through 1967 opened the door to a new era in the international relations of Southeast Asia, but it can be debated whether other events highlighted in these chapters constituted similar such critical junctures. Yet, as these chapters make clear, this is not to say that change was not taking place. Moved by both lesser and greater events, arguments for change still have effect, even in cases of less dramatic "shocks" and changes of course. Little changes affect subsequent arguments, shift the focus of debates, and ultimately lay the groundwork for different outcomes.

Our focus on dramatic challenges and changes, however, often leads us to overlook such smaller changes, as well as the ways that less dramatic challenges may still introduce critical instabilities and/or changes to existing thinking, which, in turn, may lead to and/or make possible larger changes down the line. For example, lesser changes can create new normative baselines from which subsequent challenges (large or small) will begin. The EAEG and Manglapus Initiative—both "failed initiatives"—offer illustrations of how lesser challenges served to destabilize status quo thinking, introduce new ideas, and offer new starting points for future discussion.

Lesser changes can also condition the direction of more dramatic change when crisis actually strikes. Here, the Asian financial crisis offers a particular illustration of some of the ways we might rethink "lesser" and "major" events. The 1997–1998 Asian financial crisis—unquestionably a "dramatic" event by most criteria—has been given great credit for facilitating the emergence of East Asian regionalism. However, "East Asia's" emergence as a possible regional response to challenges did not come from nowhere. It came from the ideas, politics, and momentum produced by prior EAEG, APEC, and ARF debates. Within ASEAN and as illustrated in Chapters 5 through 7, "lesser" events—notably the annual confrontations and tensions between ASEAN and Western counterparts, especially the United States, over trade, security, and regional frameworks, as well as human rights—had by 1997 already set in train normative changes and questions about the permanence and purpose of U.S. trade and security commitments, questions that factored large in the emergence of East Asian processes like the 6+3 and 7+3 processes, which preceded the advent of the 1997–1998 financial crisis.

In this sense, within ASEAN at least, these chapters provide some evidence to argue that the 1997–1998 Asian financial crisis may be better characterized in terms of the consolidation of—as opposed to the inspiration for—new thinking and new directions where East Asian regionalism was concerned. In short, while dramatic shocks can certainly catalyze the creation of new politics, such moments are not the only moments of change. As Pierson argues, "small" events can sometimes be normatively more consequential than "large" events at later stages.[14] These chapters thus offer reason to give more attention to the roles played by more "ordinary"—or, at least, less dramatic—events and changes in contributing to system change. Dramatic events and large-scale disappointments certainly can have transformative effects on a system, but as highlighted above and in these chapters, lesser events and lesser disappointments can at minimum play equally consequential roles.

The above dynamics give reason to expand our focus beyond dramatic events and junctures and the resulting characterizations of system change as defined by moments of discontinuity, involving sharp breaks with the past. In contrast, the above suggests that significant—indeed, dramatic—change can also result from more gradual and evolutionary processes. Such a conception of change may not challenge the standard multistage conception of system change described above so much as it supplements by describing the process of change under less dramatic conditions.

The above thus suggests that more attention might be paid to the ways that lesser changes interact with one another and cumulate to produce more significant social and material change. Again, lesser changes provide new baselines and agenda items that inform subsequent discussions; smaller changes and negotiations can also cumulate, expand realms of possibility, and create momentum. In that a focus on dramatic events can obscure these kinds of changes, what we may need instead are more process-driven, rather than event-driven or outcomes-driven, accounts of regionalism. Here, a conception of regionalism as an ongoing and cumulative dialogue on regional order can better reveal incremental and evolutionary changes and processes at work in consolidating support for new ideas and practices. As first argued at the beginning of this volume, a conception of cooperation and regionalism as an ongoing dialogue and cumulative process is more revealing of the variety of exchanges and changes that take place—social changes and exchanges that are not always visible in extant (material or constructivist) discussions of regionalism and regional change.

Conceiving cooperation as a cumulative dialogue and process thus captures not only the incremental nature of change but also the variety of exchanges and changes taking place. Indeed, it is able to capture smaller normative changes and interactive social renegotiations that are regular parts of politics; it is also revealing of larger, as well as evolutionary, patterns in the life of political systems. In addition, it can also provide insight into less tangible dynamics—for example, the ways that arguments and interactions cumulate to create certain perceptions, moods, and tensions; to affect changes in attitudes or receptiveness as regards particular issues and actions; to build expectations and momentum for conflict or cooperation; and to consolidate new thinking. Traced over time, these interactive and interdependent dialogues not only reveal how we got the politics we have today, but they may also offer us insight as to future trajectories. In this vein, I conclude with some reflections on what this ongoing dialogue and process tells us about the future of the United States in East Asia, East Asian regionalism, and ASEAN-Southeast Asia in the twenty-first century.

The United States in Twenty-First-Century East and Southeast Asia

The rhythms of ASEAN regionalism highlight interdependent dialogues on intra-ASEAN and extra-ASEAN relations. ASEAN regionalism's sensitivity to uncertainties in its great power relations underscores the point that while intramural reassurance was an important priority, members also viewed ASEAN, even during its earliest years, as providing an important framework with which to deal with the outside world.

Taken together, these chapters highlight not just the catalyzing role of extraregional uncertainties but also a patterned relationship that speaks to the dependencies that define ASEAN's relations with the outside world and major powers, especially the United States as a primary holder of important security, economic, and legitimacy goods.

These long-standing preoccupations with greater powers and states' particular sensitivity to U.S. policy changes and actions now inform in important ways recent East Asian trends. The emergence of East Asian regionalism—even if in its nascent stages—is most often viewed as the product of relatively new circumstances and conditions associated with the 1997–1998 Asian financial crisis. However, in conceiving regionalism as a cumulative series of negotiations and exchanges, I have highlighted some of the ways that the emergence of "East Asia" is also very much a continuation of a rethinking process that began well before 1997, even the culmination of a rethinking process that first began in the mid-1960s. Such rethinking has been about the requirements of regional security, self-determination, the nation–region relationship, and the roles that can and should be played by larger extraregional powers and lesser regional powers. In some important ways, ASEAN's arrival at "East Asia" is also an accumulation of forty years of rethinking U.S.–Southeast Asia relations.

Certainly, the United States factors large in ASEAN and in considerations of "East Asia." As highlighted above and in the last chapter, the acceleration of East Asian processes since the 1997–1998 Asian financial crisis has been very much a reflection of heightened questions about U.S. power and purpose in East Asia and thus the need for non–U.S.-based alternatives and supplements. Within ASEAN, such questions are far from new—as illustrated by the particular role played by U.S. uncertainties in triggering ASEAN's earliest regional renegotiations—but they have cumulated and intensified over time. Again, to think about recent East Asian trends or U.S.–ASEAN relations only in terms of the 1997–1998 crisis is to oversimplify the larger social, political, and contextual changes that helped make the crisis as significant as it was and in the ways that it was. As the previous chapters make clear, Southeast Asian interest in alternative regional arrangements did not emerge overnight but instead was built up over time, partly in response to recurring questions about U.S. power, purpose, and commitments in Southeast Asia. In this sense, the evolution of ASEAN regionalism—and now its spin-off regionalisms—also very much reflects one region's ongoing efforts to rethink and renegotiate its changing relations with the United States, as much one another.

The United States, of course, also factors large in East Asian processes as East Asia's most activist opponent. Its particular capacity to provide and deny goods has given it particular influence and leverage throughout Southeast and East Asia and, in turn, great ability to stymie East Asian processes—be it through overt coercion (as in the pressure brought to bear on Japan and Korea in EAEG and AMF debates) or through diversion (as in its promotion of bilateral trade agreements and security ties, thus diverting attention and resources away from regional processes whose gains are often less immediate and certain). Here, it is worth underscoring that the United States has not played a leading role in the development of regional cooperative arrangements in East or Southeast Asia. Even during the period 1990 to 2000—a period when global multilateralism seemed to take center stage in U.S. foreign policy—the United States was often described as being, at most, "lukewarm" toward new regional arrangements. While the United States did turn to a more multilaterally supportive rhetoric, its support for regional arrangements extended only so far as it did not challenge the primacy or U.S.–centrism of existing bilateral security arrangements.[15] U.S. objections to the AMF also took place during this period. Indeed, these chapters highlight a theme across administrations of Washington's active opposition to a variety of regional initiatives—ZOPFAN, SEANWFZ, APEC, the ARF, and most of all, exclusive East Asian arrangements like the EAEG and AMF. John Gershman is especially sharp in his conclusion: "Successive U.S. administrations have offered little support for regional initiatives under the auspices of the Association of Southeast Asian Nations; indeed, the United States has not acted as a partner with countries in the region since the end of the Cold War."[16]

This track record, itself, now factors into current assessments of U.S. power and purpose in East and Southeast Asia. Not only have the patterns, especially of the last two decades, fed the growing perception that U.S. and ASEAN interests and worldviews diverge in fundamental and critical ways, but Washington's efforts to stymie East Asian regional processes (which ultimately helps keep East Asia divided) now also feed a suspicion that Washington may not be interested in good intraregional relations, which is the basis for regional security. U.S. policies and arrangements, as Muthiah Alagappa has put it, may in fact be "retarding understanding and accommodation among the indigenous Asian powers."[17]

Recent developments have done little to alter the general trend. While U.S. efforts to reassert its presence post–September 11 have renewed some bilateral ties and links, they have also affirmed and underscored fundamental differences about both the sources of regional insecurity and how best to respond to them. Similarly, U.S. efforts to assist victims of the 2004 tsunami produced an uptick in Indonesian perceptions of the United States, only to be counteracted by U.S. Secretary of State Condoleezza Rice's no-shows at meetings of the ARF. Especially the 2005 decision—widely reported to be an expression of U.S. objections to Myanmar—served to confirm, rather than disconfirm, the view that (1) Washington did not think ASEAN that important; and (2) Washington was more concerned with criticizing Asian governments than having dialogue with them or supporting regional security processes.[18] In a related vein, U.S. Undersecretary of State for Public Diplomacy and Public Affairs Karen Hughes's "listening tour" of the Muslim world—a tour specifically aimed at improving the U.S. image abroad—not only failed to deliver but was mocked in some circles for being what one Indonesian analyst described as "a listening tour of one."[19]

In sum, while the United States continues to have great capacity to leverage and block developments, its "high-powered" efforts to stymie and undermine regional processes may ultimately do more to hurt its image in

East and Southeast Asia and thus consolidate conclusions as to the need for non–U.S.-based arrangements.[20] Indeed, previous U.S. actions and interactions with Southeast Asia (and East Asia) have created a social context that makes it more difficult for the United States to oppose East Asian efforts without negative backlash. This is not to say that ASEAN states do not continue to support a future U.S. role in East or Southeast Asia (they do very much); however, the terms of that role will now have to be renegotiated and rethought in light of changed and changing ideas and expectations about both the United States and their own roles. In other words, the future of the U.S.–ASEAN relationship will require Washington's understanding of the context that has been created. Some see signs of new U.S. engagement and expansion of bilateral (though not necessarily regional) ties that may reverse some of the trends of the last decade. But it will take more than a single fix or one or two public relations initiatives. Rather, it will take sustained attention of a particular sort and, most of all, mutual respect if current thinking is to be changed.

The Future of "East Asia"

As a later episode in an ongoing, cumulative dialogue on regional order, East Asia and especially the APT processes are an important product of interactive, interdependent, and cumulative debates about Southeast Asia's relations with one another, with the United States, with the Asia-Pacific, and now East Asia. In both APEC and the ARF, interactions produced a heightened sense of difference among Asian participants toward Western counterparts that formed part of the prism through which many later viewed and experienced the 1997–1999 financial crisis and the international response. The strengthening of the APT process is reflective of this heightened sense of difference, as well as diminished hope that institutions like the ARF and APEC might "bridge" Asian and Western institutional practices.[21] In this sense, the *content*—as much the emergence—of current East Asian processes has been very much shaped by the fact these processes emerged *after* the experiences of APEC and the ARF, rather than before.

At the same time, while East Asian trends have generated both optimism and concern about the rise of East Asia as a regional entity, "East Asia" remains a contingent and, most of all, contested process. Indeed, the debate on "East Asia"—what it is, what it is about, who it includes—is far from over. Developments since the 1997–1998 Asian financial crisis have both solidified and introduced new questions about East Asian regional trends.

Of particular note are the contradictory effects of China's growing capacities and influence. On the one hand, China's growth—like Japan's in the 1980s—is generating important economic integrating dynamics, dynamics that in this case were sped up by the Asian financial crisis. ASEAN's efforts to engage China in regional processes have also supported integrative trends, as have its efforts to nest collective ASEAN's bilateral relations with China within a wider regional framework. As an example of the latter, ASEAN states have sought to put bilateral initiatives from China, as well as from Japan—most notably the ASEAN-China Free Trade Area and Japan's Initiative for Development of East Asia—under the multilateral APT framework.[22] While such ASEAN efforts aim to dilute the leverage China and Japan have over ASEAN in bilateral relationships, they also continue to support the general East Asian trend.

On the other hand, as China grows, it also has the potential to challenge ASEAN's current centrality and its conceptions of region and regionalism. Meanwhile, concerns of other states about Chinese influence have helped to spur a flurry of bilateral activity, especially in trade. In that much of the activity has made ASEAN the hub of regional activity and has provided new networks and connections between Northeast and Southeast Asia, ASEAN states have tended to argue that recent bilateralism serves larger integrative goals. But, in that current bilateralism mostly involves different rules, scope, and conditions, it is also fragmenting and at least complicates efforts to create something like a larger East Asian free trade area or economic community.

Concerns about Chinese influence, especially from Japan but also from some ASEAN states, have also complicated the East Asian question with the emergence of the East Asian Summit (EAS) in December 2005 as a potential rival to the APT. When originally proposed and adopted, the EAS was supposed to develop incrementally as the logical extension of the APT process. However, Japanese insecurities led to a push for its early (and arguably premature) realization.[23] That move now muddies the East Asian process in significant ways.

Nowhere are questions about "East Asia" more clear than in EAS's membership and the requirements for membership. In the EAS, the APT states are joined by India, Australia, and New Zealand. In addition, the EAS holds out the possibility for even greater membership on the conditions that (1) states accede to ASEAN's TAC and (2) there is consensus among current members. Such expanded membership reflects important concerns about the recent East Asian trend, especially as regards the rise of China and the possible loss of ASEAN influence. The expanded membership is clearly aimed at diluting Chinese influence, while the decision to make TAC a critical condition of membership clearly reflects an effort to maintain ASEAN centrality in expanded regional processes.

Consequently, while original efforts and momentum behind the EAS reflected a desire, especially on the part of Malaysia, to give even greater, explicit, and institutional expression to the East Asian idea and APT processes, the EAS has emerged instead as a potential rival entity. (As Mahathir declared, "This so-called East Asia Summit" should instead be called the "East Asia Australasian Summit."[24] Indeed, in both its actual and potential membership, there are already parallels being drawn to the broader APEC process. Yet, in two critical ways the EAS is *not* like APEC: It does not include the United States, and it is not called the Asia-Pacific summit. In other words, while the EAS may rival the APT process, and though most would dispute whether all its members are in fact "East Asian," the fact that it is still called the *East Asian* Summit is also indicative of the increased normative legitimacy that "East Asia" now enjoys relative to some other rival regional concepts. East Asia is still a contentious idea, but developments like the EAS still illustrate some of the ways the debate has turned since the APEC/EAEG debates of the early 1990s.

Here, the APEC experience offers some cautionary notes for both our practice and our analysis of East Asian regionalism. In particular, the APEC experience underscores the importance of there being shared agreement about regionalism's fundamental purposes. Functional cooperation can help expand areas of agreement; but without agreement about fundamental purposes and processes, "cooperation" can also have more negative effects. In the final analysis, APEC's difficulties since its creation—and not just its post-1997 marginalization—reflect a lack of agreement among its members about APEC's fundamental purposes. Too much emphasis has been placed on APEC's diversity and informal regionalism in explanations of its marginalization. After all, ASEAN and the APT process are also informal and diverse in their membership, yet have been sites of greater regional activity and attention. Rather, the "strength" and durability of a regional institution may be less a function of binding rules than of the underlying foundational agreement on which all else is built.

Compared to APEC, East Asian and especially APT processes have arguably been built on greater consensus as to the need for East Asian cooperation and the value of regional processes for both economic and security reasons. In other words, there is greater agreement about the validity of processes in form and in content. That consensus has moreover now been solidified by the lessons drawn from crisis. It is also worth underscoring that APT areas of interest are also more wide-ranging, suggesting a more comprehensive kind of regional arrangement that is more like ASEAN than APEC. Nevertheless, in that there do remain fundamental *disagreements,* the process remains on uncertain ground. ASEAN's own success in transforming regional relations through dialogue offers hope for East Asia more broadly; but, again, as the APEC experience makes clear, greater dialogue and interaction do not always lead to improved relations. APEC, the ARF, APT, and now the EAS may all *look like* ASEAN in their adoption of ASEAN's informal regionalism, but they are nevertheless critically *not* ASEAN. Again, founding ideas and founding arguments have given ASEAN processes their meaning and made ASEAN what it is. By the same token, APEC, ARF, and the APT are products of different founding conditions and arguments. Consequently, while they may share ASEAN's consensual format, they may not in fact behave in the same ways, and informal regionalism may not have the same effects.

Such conclusions have implications for those who may look to ASEAN as a model for other more conflict-prone regions—be they Africa, South Asia, the Middle East, or Northeast Asia. The ASEAN model cannot simply be picked up and transplanted elsewhere. Again ASEAN's consensus-driven regionalism works because members' shared interpretations of their history of conflict and shared agreement about regional resilience have given that process a larger significance. Without that context of meaning, informal regionalism may not work the same ways elsewhere. Thus, just as it has now been proven that the "ASEAN way" is not the "Asian Pacific Way," it also may not be the South Asian way, African way, or the South American way. What remains to be seen is if it will become the "East Asian" way.

Ultimately, if a consensus-driven regionalism is to have similar ameliorating effects on East Asia as it did Southeast Asia, it will depend on there being fundamental agreement about what the process is all about. Only then, to quote Kim, "will it be safe to say in retrospect that the conception of East Asia as a region was 'an idea that would not go away.' "[25] In short, the future of East Asian regionalism—indeed, East Asian security—hinges on states' ability to strengthen the ideational glue, foundational agreement, and processes that can maintain relations in the face of adversity and division.

Whither ASEAN?

The last forty years have seen ASEAN evolve and expand in ways unforeseen by its founders. Indeed, developments have pushed the physical and ideological boundaries of region as originally understood in the late 1960s. Not only have treaties and norms originally forged for Southeast Asia alone now been made open to non–Southeast Asian actors, but ASEAN's coalition of lesser Southeast Asian states has also been playing an exceptional role in developing and anchoring unprecedented new Asian Pacific and East Asian frameworks. Its expansion into new regionalisms may also be considered an important institutional adaptation that has arguably helped sustain ASEAN's institutional relevance despite significantly changed circumstances from its founding.

Nevertheless, challenges remain great—and recent East Asian trends pose a particular challenge. Certainly, ASEAN states remain conflicted about East Asian trends. On the one hand, "East Asia" mitigates a particularly intense dependency on outside, especially U.S., markets as drivers of ASEAN growth, increases ASEAN leverage vis-à-vis Western trade partners, and offers ways to manage intensifying interdependencies among Northeast and Southeast Asian economies. In the political-security sphere, East Asian regionalism also offers the opportunity to build, if not community, then at least improved relationships through dialogue and functional cooperation. On the other hand, "East Asia," where China and Japan have historically dominated, comes with its own great power problems. The growing influence of China will be especially challenging—not only because China may have ideas that diverge from ASEAN's, along with influence that could be brought to bear, but also because of how others—notably Japan and the United States—may react to that growing influence. Most of all, as illustrated by intra-ASEAN debates over the creation of the APT secretariat, as well as the emergence of the EAS, ASEAN states also remain very much concerned about what "East Asia" means for the regional idea and regional ideal of Southeast Asia—resilient, self-determined, and unified.

In this sense, ASEAN's dilemmas and debates as regards "East Asia" remain very much the same in its themes and preoccupations. Again, East Asia is simply the latest chapter in a series of dialogues and exchanges on intra- and extraregional relations that were originally begun in the 1960s. Thus, even as the bounds of region continue to stretch, "Southeast Asia" remains an important organizing principle with great meaning in ASEAN.

This belief now informs and shapes the form, content, and parameters of an evolving East Asian regionalism. Certainly within ASEAN, affirmations of ASEAN remain a key component of a persuasive argument for new regional arrangements. Thus, it is worth underscoring that within ASEAN, its regionalist discourse on regional resilience remains the established, dominant, and thus legitimating regional ideology—and as such, it remains an important boundary on new regional ventures. In other words, just as nationalism once enabled and constrained ASEAN regionalism in the mid-to-late 1960s, the ASEAN ideology today makes possible, even as it constrains in important ways, how ASEAN states approach East Asia.

As for outside, non–Southeast Asian actors, ASEAN is also legitimating but in different ways. As in initial efforts to establish APEC and the ARF, others have sought ASEAN's support and accorded it centrality in large part because they recognize that ASEAN possesses legitimating properties that few other entities or actors have. Partly, one can say this is due to ASEAN's numbers; but it is also due to ASEAN's acknowledged status as the region's longest-running and most successful regional organization. Moreover, not only can ASEAN help legitimate and make more acceptable new regional arrangements, but it can also do the same for more questionable actors. China, Japan, and Australia, for example, all look to ASEAN at very least because they understand that they themselves lack the legitimacy and authority to lead regional processes. This dynamic widens the opportunity for ASEAN to shape new arrangements.

The result of these intra–Southeast Asian and extra–Southeast Asian dynamics is that East Asia is "ASEAN-ized"[26] in content and in form. In content, ideas about the value of inclusive engagement, a dialogue-driven regionalism, and their ameliorating effects on uncertain relations can all be counted among ASEAN's ideational and normative contributions. In form, ASEAN links new processes to its own, holds East Asian meetings in association with ASEAN meetings, and makes an ASEAN treaty the foundational basis of new regional arrangements. Indeed, TAC is now the most widely acceded to indigenously produced treaty in the region. Today, six non–Southeast Asian powers have acceded to TAC: China (2003), India (2003) Japan (2004), Russia (2004), Korea (2004), and Pakistan (2004). In 2006, the EU also indicated its intent to join TAC (now scheduled to be signed in 2009). Again, it is remarkable that it is a coalition of lesser powers that is at the center of this activity.

Nevertheless, the continued expansion of East Asian regional processes will continue to challenge ASEAN in profound ways, challenging states to reconsider long-held regional ideas and to think more clearly about what ASEAN is and represents. Nor will the challenges come only from outside. Challenges from within ASEAN and within member states will also test ASEAN, its existing consensuses, and its ability to adapt. Ongoing democratization in core states like Indonesia, the Philippines, and Thailand (whose 2007 constitution requires regional agreements to be ratified by the Thai parliament)[27] and political instability and legitimacy challenges faced by old and new members, as well as new understandings of security today, contribute to growing calls to rethink the nature and scope of regional organization.[28]

It is in this context of pressures from above, below, and sideways that ASEAN elites have pursued an ASEAN Charter. Adopted in November 2007 at ASEAN's thirteenth summit and entered into force in December 2008, the Charter aims to create an "ASEAN Community" by 2015 based on security, economic, and sociocultural pillars. Behind the Charter is a concern about ASEAN and ASEAN–Southeast Asia's future relevance not only vis-à-vis outside states but more importantly within Southeast Asia itself. Pushed especially by ASEAN's track 2 elites, the charter reflects a notable effort to rethink old practices and to recalibrate their forty-year-old organization in response to challenges of democratization and globalization, as well as "East Asia." Of particular note, the Charter's recognition of societal groups and transnational networks is reflective of a growing awareness that ASEAN's longevity will ultimately depend not just on elites, but also the "people."[29]

More generally, it also speaks to the fact that the "diversity" that has characterized the ASEAN process is becoming more so not just because new ASEAN members bring new perspectives and old ones are liberalizing but also because of new societal and transnational actors. Bringing home the point that ASEAN elite regionalism is in transition were the passing of Suharto and visits by Lee Kuan Yew and Mahathir, before his death in January 2008, just two months after the Charter was signed. Indeed, Suharto's death, which brought together the two remaining old men of ASEAN, was a reminder that ASEAN and the relative strength of its foundational consensuses have benefited in key ways from the fact that the process was dominated by a handful of leaders and ministers who moreover enjoyed a rare longevity in their positions. These include not just Suharto (thirty-one years), Lee Kuan Yew (thirty-one years), and Mahathir (twenty-two years), but also S. Rajaratnam (fifteen years), Adam Malik (eleven years), Mochtar KusumaAtmadja (ten years), Ali Alatas (eleven years), Tun Razak (six years as prime minister, three as deputy), and Abdullah Badawi (eight years as foreign minister, four years as deputy prime minister, and now five as prime minister). That longevity has helped insulate ASEAN processes, which in turn have helped incubate and grow ideas, relationships, and core consensuses that were key to ASEAN's survival during its formative decades. Neither ASEAN's new members, nor current founding members, nor the civil society groups clamoring for attention will have that same luxury or benefit of long-term relationship building or, for that matter, the direct and uniting experience of founding ASEAN at a time when nothing was taken for granted.

Perhaps most of all, the ASEAN Charter continues to reflect the driving normative dynamics and constraints described in preceding chapters. The particular preoccupation with ASEAN's relevance reflects a continued attachment to ASEAN, a strong belief that the future of all still depends on the unity of Southeast Asia, but also persistent concerns about the fragility of relations. As highlighted in these chapters, none of the other regional arrangements has the ability to inspire the same degree of concern and angst at the prospect of their disintegration and irrelevance. And to the extent that they do, it has more to do with ASEAN's relevance than, say, APEC's, ARF's, or the APT's. Again, the Charter's attempt to build "ASEAN community" is part of a necessary effort to build "Southeast Asia" so that it can hold its own not just in larger East Asian and other forums but also vis-à-vis its own members.

The Charter is thus also a response to perceived disintegrative threats from within the region. As historically, ASEAN's pursuit of unity remains premised on important assumptions and fears about Southeast Asia's inherent *disunity*. Similarly illustrative were states' last three leaders' summits, where officials felt that referencing "community" was not enough. Rather, lest anyone miss the point, they felt compelled to underscore their "oneness" with an adjective: "*One* Vision, *One* Identity, *One* Community" (eleventh Summit), "*One* Caring and Sharing Community," (twelfth Summit), "*One* ASEAN at the Heart of Dynamic Asia" (thirteenth summit). Thus, this tension between the normative objective of Southeast Asian unity and the assumed fragility of relations, which is at the center of regional resilience arguments, remain persistent and defining features of ASEAN.

Indeed, as evidenced by the ASEAN Charter, that assumption of Southeast Asian disunity may prove to be one of the larger constraints in efforts to reform and adapt the forty-year-old organization. Make no mistake, the ASEAN Charter, relative to the past, is a significant move toward a new ASEAN. At the same time, as a watered-down version of original pro-

posals, it is also a good illustration of the ways that regional resilience arguments continue to exert competing normative pressures on ASEAN states.
Unity must be pursued in the interest of regional resilience, but regional
resilience also demands that states not jeopardize the unity that exists. Thus,
states pursue an ASEAN Charter, but the assumed fragility of relations also
continues to constrain both process and outcome. Moreover, the current
process is additionally complicated by the addition of new members. Even
more than founding states, new members are reluctant to go beyond existing practices given their significant material constraints and disadvantages
as well as their newness to the ASEAN process. Indeed, in the process
of formulating the Charter, new members demonstrated that their numbers gave them significant influence.[30] Meanwhile, precisely because newer
members are less committed to and less trusting of the ASEAN process,
older members are reluctant to push them too much lest they bolt. In other
words, as long as regional resilience begins with the premise of national and
regional fragility, ASEAN's development on this question and others will
remain fundamentally and institutionally constrained.

The latest in a series of challenges from Myanmar offers another illustration. Despite unprecedented calls for revoking Myanmar's membership,
states have nevertheless remained reluctant to take stronger measures against
that regime. This reluctance partly reflects a concern about setting a precedent of intra-ASEAN interference; but it is also a reflection of a strong
belief that inclusion trumps exclusion. For ASEAN states, if the goal is to
move a target state in ways that are supportive of ASEAN as a whole, it
makes no sense to shut that target state out of the process. But most of all,
ASEAN is constrained by the fact that Myanmar *is* a part of Southeast Asia.
Especially given Myanmar's close relations with China, excluding Myanmar
would thus be contrary to ASEAN's regional resilience foundations.

In sum, both the less ambitious ASEAN Charter and ASEAN's limited
response to Myanmar illustrate the ways that ASEAN's founding arguments continue to have profound and lasting effects on an organization
and its evolution. In both cases, normative constraints come as much from
the moral imperative of maintaining unity as from resilience's premises of
national and regional fragility. In both cases, such competing normative
pressures produce *both* a more limited response than some would like *and
also* movement. Both, for example, still reflect an expansion of the regional
agenda and what regional actors talk about. As with past ASEAN initiatives, the ASEAN Charter is one step in a larger process—a point also made

by Surin Pitsuwan, ASEAN's newest Secretary General: "We must make the best of what we have and try to improve it for tomorrow."[31]

Thus, regionalism will continue to be constrained very much by founding ideas, but states' willingness—albeit gradual and often reluctant—to discuss contentious and formerly taboo issues also points to an organization that is more mature since its creation forty years ago. Indeed, it is worth underscoring that this is an organization that has adapted more than once to significant changes in its regional and global context.

Meanwhile, in the evolving process that is East and Southeast Asian regionalism, new challenges from within and without will continue to interact with competing ideas and discourses on region and regionalisms. Moreover, complex interactions will not necessary produce development in one linear direction. At times, such interactions and intersections will force important clarification of more established ideas and frameworks, while at other times, they will compel their modification and even replacement. All this serves to illustrate that ideas of region, regional organization, and regionalism are not static but dynamic, though there may be more enduring features. In ASEAN's case, debates about noninterference and East Asian regionalism may ultimately transform how the organization looks and works, but ideas about self-determination and regional resilience (though perhaps redefined) seem likely to remain more enduring features of regionalism in Southeast Asia and East Asia. Put another way, ASEAN is unlikely to disappear any time soon, but neither is it likely to remain completely the same. East and Southeast Asian regionalism will continue to be contested processes and cumulative dialogues in which old and new ideas about political organization in East Asia compete. ASEAN and its related regionalisms in this sense will remain evolving works in process. Indeed, it is through such dynamic interactions and contestations that we get East and Southeast Asia's unique regional expressions and outcomes.

Abbreviations Used in Notes and Bibliography

ADS   ASEAN Document Series
AFP   Agence France Press
AP   Associated Press
ASC   ASEAN Standing Committee
BP   Bangkok Post
CSEA   Contemporary Southeast Asia
CSIS   Centre for Strategic and International Studies (Jakarta)
CSM   Christian Science Monitor
EYC   Eighth Year Cycle
FEER   Far Eastern Economic Review
FPDA   Five Power Defence Arrangement
FRJ   Foreign Relations Journal (Philippines)
IHT   International Herald Tribune
IO   International Organization
IPS   Inter-Press Service
IQ   Indonesian Quarterly
IRAP   International Relations of the Asia Pacific
IS   International Security
ISEAS   Institute of Southeast Asian Studies
ISQ   International Studies Quarterly
JEN   Japan Economic Newswire
JMS   Joint Ministerial Statement

JP	Jakarta Post
NST	New Straits Times
NYT	New York Times
RSIS	Rajaratnam School of International Studies
SMH	Sydney Morning Herald
ST	Straits Times
WNC	World News Connection

Notes

1. Durian is a fruit common in much of Southeast Asia. It is as pungent as it is popular.

2. The argument about ASEAN's role in the construction of a Southeast Asian security community is most associated with Acharya, but most students of ASEAN have at one time or another weighed in. Acharya 1991, 1995, 1998, 2001. See also Alagappa 1991; Busse 1999; Buzan and Segal 1994; Dupont 1996; Emmerson 1996; Jones and Smith 2001; Narine 2002b; Simon 1982, 1998; Sopiee 1980; Tilman 1987.

3. Haacke 1998; Haas 1989: 282. Also, Wurfel 1996.

4. My conceptualization of regionalism as a "cumulative dialogue" or "series of negotiations" on regional organization draws on Kaye's study on Middle East multi-laterals, in which she argues that "multilateral cooperation must be appreciated as a process of interaction rather than solely as a set of outcomes" and on Barnett's study, which characterizes pan-Arabism as "a series of dialogues between Arab states regarding the desired regional order." See Kaye 2001; Barnett 1998: viii.

5. Antolik 1990; Soesastro 2003.

6. Leifer's work, which has been defining in the study of ASEAN, may be especially illustrative, even if his work is better described as implicitly, not explicitly, realist. See, e.g., Leifer 1986b, 1989, and 1996.

7. In cases like Indonesia, there is the belief that ethnic division had been one important reason for their conquest by the Dutch. See, for example, Elson 2006: 267–68.

8. This list can be compared to Alagappa's (2003) "pathways" to regional order.

9. Caballero-Anthony 2005; Emmers 2003.

10. Ravenhill 2001.

11. In particular, see Goldstein and Keohane 1993: 5–8.

12. As Johnston notes, focal points have a prominent place in neoliberal, contractual approaches toward institutions, but such approaches have oddly expressed little "curiosity about the social and historical origins of focal points." Johnston 2001: 490.

13. While there are historical examples of "Southeast Asian" regions, the particular Southeast Asian region that we know today as being the ten states of Indonesia, Malaysia, Singapore, Thailand, Philippines, Brunei, Cambodia, Laos, Vietnam, and Myanmar is unique.

14. Dirlik 1992.

Chapter 1

1. ASEAN website: www.ASEANsecorg/92.htm.

2. Peffer 1954: 311–312.

3. Those identifying ASEAN as a model or potential model for regional cooperation include: South Asian Association for Regional Cooperation (SAARC) (See, e.g., Jetly 2003); Economic Community of West African States (ECOWAS) (See, for example, Centre for Democracy and Development 2002); the Middle East (see Leifer 1998; Abdul Rahman Al-Rashid, The Arab View: The ASEAN Experiment, *Money Clips* (9 August)); the Shanghai Cooperation Council (see, for example, Tang 2002). See also United Nations Economic and Social Commission for Asia and the Pacific (2004).

4. Tan with Cossa 2001: 18.

5. Consider, for example, ASEAN's absence from earlier "neo-neo" theoretical debates. ASEAN received only one passing reference in Baldwin (1993) and none in Keohane's (1986) compilation of debates. ASEAN was better represented in political economy discussions, though as a subset of larger East Asian and Asian Pacific processes, which were similarly viewed critically. See, for example, Grieco's and Haggard's chapters in Mansfield and Milner 1997. Fawcett and Hurrell's (1996) volume on regionalism may best include ASEAN as part of the discussion; but here, too, ASEAN is mostly dismissed and not discussed at great length. Recent years have seen new interest due largely to Acharya's work (e.g., Acharya 2001, 2003/4, 2004), which by virtue of argument and prominence has become a particular focal point for theoretical discussion on ASEAN, for example, Jones and Smith 2001, Khoo 2004, special issue of *IRAP* 2005.

6. Leifer 1986b and Acharya 1992.

7. See Bates 1988, 387. See also Keohane 1988, 383–387, 384; Milner 1992, 468.

8. Luhilima 1987, 175.

9. Jorgensen-Dahl 1982, 45.

10. Kahler 2000, 549–571.

11. Katzenstein 1996a, 125.

12. Indonesia and Malaysia submitted their territorial dispute over Sipadan and Ligitan to the ICJ, which ruled in favor of Malaysia in 2002. Malaysia and Singapore similarly submitted their territorial dispute over Pulau Batu Puteh/Pedra Branca to the ICJ. While states' decision not to resolve disputes under TAC raise questions about the trust placed in ASEAN processes, the development as an indication of how far some intra-ASEAN relations have come is no less significant. See "M'sia, S'pore Exchange Documents on Pulau Batu Puteh," *Bernama* (May 9, 2003).

13. See, for example, Konjiing 1987; Lau 1990; Ojendal 2000; Rau 1981.

14. Katzenstein 1996a: 125. See also Crone, quoted in Friedberg 1993.

15. See also Acharya 2001; Adler and Barnett 1998: 3.

16. Kaye 2001.

17. Johnston 2001. See also Harris 2000.

18. See Barnett 1995.

19. At least five such "informal" meetings have taken place as of August 2007.

20. While realists may offer the China threat thesis, these meetings are consultative, and ASEAN states remain resistant to ASEAN's militarization. Also, the concept paper on which these meetings are based was adopted only in 2003 and the first meeting took place only in 2006, a time when China–ASEAN relations were doing well.

21. Kaye 2001: 13.

22. See chapter 1 in Acharya 2001. See also chapter 2 in Adler and Barnett. Even Acharya's excellent discussion (by his own self-admission) tends to make "testing" ASEAN norms a priority over the incremental processes of socialization he is also interested in. For a more general discussion of constructivism's insufficient attention to socialization's intervening processes, see Checkel 2001.

23. Acharya has in fact referenced all of the above. Acharya, 2002: 28. See also Wolters 1981; McCloud (1995), as well as Reid's (1999) rich discussion of Southeast Asia's commercial exchanges and trading networks during the fifteenth to seventeenth centuries.

24. For a different view, see Buzan 1998: 219. Writing on the Third World in general, Buzan mostly sees little utility in "dig[ging] in the arcadian mine of the social and political constructions that existed before the European imposition."

25. One can also add that none of Southeast Asia's historical mandala systems encompassed all of what we consider today to be Southeast Asia. As discussed by Wolters, early networks tended to be localized and even isolated, while later precolonial networks and kingdoms tended to be bound by geography or limited humanpower (Wolters 1981).

26. Acharya 2002: 32; Young 1966.

27. Modern states were foreign in that many, especially in insular Southeast Asia, adopted much of the old colonial boundaries, which had been put in place without regard for the various populations that lived there. See, for example, Bentley, 1986, especially 275–277; Steinberg 1987: 5; Vandenbosch 1946: 428–429.

28. For example, while ASEAN's style of regionalism may bear resemblance to Wolters' *mandala* system, it is also noteworthy that both Srivijaya and Majapahit empires, despite impressive maritime achievements, were still limited by physical barriers that prevented greater consolidation of the mainland, as well as a lack of human resources that hindered the complete consolidation of insular Southeast Asia. In other words, the Southeast Asia we know today has no historical precedent. See Fisher 1966: 102, 116–117; Fisher 1974: 5; and Gordon 1966: 6 (fn. 13).

29. O'Brien 2005. See also Hopf 1998.

30. For this reason, it may be more accurate to think of many of these states as "third world states,"not just lesser powers. See Buzan 1998; also Ayoob 1989, 1995.

31. Leifer 1974.

32. For a good overview of this literature, see Calder and Ye 2004.

33. Legro 2000.

34. Haas 1990.

35. Hopf 2002: 5.

36. Ba 2006.

37. See Johnston 2003b.

38. Wendt 1992: 415. In a different but also similar vein, some feminist theorists similarly argue the "innovative power" of the weak or powerless to come up with different solutions to their problems. See, for example, Carroll 1972.

39. See Hasenclever et al. 1997: 14–21, 136–224; Onuf 1998.

40. See Yee 1996: 97, 95.

41. See Emmerson 1996.

42. See Emmerson 1996: 37–39. See also Dewitt 1994.

43. Romulo 1969.

44. Payne 2001. See also discussion in Checkel 1999; Klotz 1995.

45. Cruz 2000. See also Finnemore and Sikkink 1998; Nadelman 1990.

46. Crawford 2002: 112–117.

47. Crawford 2002: 6–7, 57–78.

48. See, for example, discussion by Soloman 1970.

49. Anderson 1991.

50. Alagappa 1995a.

51. Ayoob 1995; Job 1992; see also Buzan 1991.

52. Alagappa 1998. See also Ayoob 1989; Buzan 1998, 1991; Collins 2003.

53. See, for example, Barker 2004. In practice, it often became a policy of rewarding supporters. Clapham (1970), discussing developmental nationalism in Southeast Asia and other postcolonial regions, characterizes the practice of developmental nationalism explicitly in terms of regime security.

54. For book-length treatment, see Narine (2002b), which makes sovereignty a central argument on ASEAN.

55. See Keohane 1988: 383–387, 384 (fn. 2).

56. The first ASEAN summit of ASEAN heads of government took place in 1976; however, such summitry did not become a regular and annual event until 1995.

57. For this reason, Laffey and Weldes also argue that ideas are better defined as "representations," not beliefs. Laffey and Weldes 1997: 216.

58. For excellent discussions on the domestic politics of ASEAN regionalism, see Nesadurai (2003a, b) and Solingen (1998).

59. See, for example, Kowert and Legro 1996; Chapter 1 in Goldstein and Keohane 1993.

60. See Kowert and Legro 1996: 493.

61. Adler 1997: 348.

62. Kaye 2001.

63. Wendt 1998: 105.

64. Antolik 1990; Soesastro 2003.

65. For a a recent and representative criticism of ASEAN's "imitation community," see Jones and Smith 2001.

66. Finnemore and Sikkink 2001: 402.

67. Onuf 1998: 59.

68. Crawford 2002: 15.

69. Higgott 1994: 370.

70. Laffey and Weldes 1997: 203.

71. See Mertus 2000; Risse-Kappen 1995; Sikkink 1998; Young 1991.

72. David 1991; Tetreault 1991.

73. Ghazali Shafie 1985; Rajaratnam 1969, quoted in Siagian n.d.: 141.

74. Listen to the ASEAN "song of unity" at www.ASEANsec.org/12346.htm.

75. Marshall 2002: 361.

76. Marshall 2002. See also Al-Ali 2002: 249–253.

77. Wendt 1992. For discussions on the role of (re)iteration in the strengthening of norms, see also Finnemore 1996b; Price and Tannenwald 1996; Schimmelfennig 2000.

78. Hopf 1998.

79. Hall, quoted in Yee 1996: 95.

CHAPTER 2

1. According to the ASEAN website: "The new ASEAN emblem represents a stable, peaceful, united and dynamic ASEAN. The colours of the emblem—blue, red, white and yellow—represent the main colours of the crests of all the ASEAN countries. The blue represents peace and stability. Red depicts courage and dynamism. White shows purity and yellow symbolises prosperity. The ten stalks of padi represent the dream of ASEAN's Founding Fathers for an ASEAN comprising all the ten countries in Southeast Asia bound together in friendship and solidarity. The circle represents the unity of ASEAN." <www.aseansec.org>

2. Meyer 1949: 72.

3. See, for example, Fisher 1953, 1966; Peffer 1954; Vandenbosch 1946. See also Emmerson 1984; Solheim 1985.

4. See, for example, Solheim 1985, 142–143; Steinberg 1987: 3.

5. Fisher 1974, 8. It also seems telling that for reasons of thematic coherence, scholarly discussions have often treated Southeast Asia in its two parts (mainland and insular), a practice likely encouraged and legitimated by the Eleventh Pacific Science Congress's 1966 Resolution 2.2, which specified the outlines of "Mainland Southeast Asia" and "Insular/Island Southeast Asia." See Emmerson 1984; Solheim 1985, 142–144.

6. Fisher 1974, 3. See also discussion in Mack and Ravenhill 1994, 6–7.

7. Compare, for example, Southeast Asia to Latin America, where Spanish imperialism offered a common point of reference, not to mention a common language.

8. Butwell 1964, 946.

9. Butwell goes so far to argue that the 1961 announcement about the formation of the federation marked a turning point in Southeast Asia's international relations in that it signaled a new (even if conflict-prone) focus on intraregional relations and international participation by Southeast Asian governments (as opposed to major powers relations or their relations with Southeast Asian client states). See Butwell 1964, 940–946.

10. Though ASA technically lasted until 1967, it was stalled half the time.

11. See Jorgensen-Dahl 1982, 14–23.

12. Ghazali Shafie 1998, 339, 345.

13. Ghazali Shafie 1998, 22.

14. That these ideas were clearly perceived as being in competition is illustrated by Tunku Abdul Rahman's decision not to send a representative to the Philippine conference.

15. See, for example, some of the local Philippine reporting during one of Tunku Abdul Rahman's visits to Manila to discuss ASA (Butwell 1964).

16. See Sukarno's comments in February 1963 (quoted in Gordon 1966, 69). See also, "Jakarta Worried about Growing Afro-Asian Support for Malaysia," *Malaysian Bulletin* (June 1965); Weinstein 1976, 168. Indonesia also had concerns that the new federation would try to annex Sumatra. See Shafie 1998, 364.

17. There is also evidence that suggests some in Indonesia were motivated by ideas of a "greater Indonesia" that would include Malaysia. See Gordon 1963/1964, 378–393; Weatherbee 1963, 342–343.

18. A number of articles in the *Far Eastern Economic Review* in summer 1966 put forward the argument that Confrontation was ultimately about Malaysia's failure or unwillingness to go through the rituals of deference to Indonesia. According to Gordon, the Indonesian leadership's dislike of the Tunku was personal and due to its "pent-up jealousies of Malaysia" and Tunku Abdul Rahman's attempt to speak for Malays and the region (Gordon 1964, 244–246).

19. Various questions have complicated the North Borneo question, including legal questions as to whether the Sultan of Sulu had originally leased or ceded the territory. Also unclear was the exact area in question and even who the real Sultan of Sulu was. See Gordon 1966, 14, 225, 227, including fn. 24. For a Philippine view of its claim, see Macapagal 1989 and Ramos 1977. For other interpretations of the Philippine claim, see also Butwell 1965, 43–48; Meadows 1965, 305–318; Wurfel 1967, 46–52. For the Tunku's views, see Tunku Abdul Rahman 1978, 136–141.

20. See excerpts of the unpublished and confidential report commissioned by Macapagal and written by Alejandro Fernandez outlining Philippine options with respect to North Borneo. Gordon 1966, 22–23.

21. Macapagal's term in office (1961–1966) was marked by a variety of tensions in Philippine-US relations: Anti-American protests, differences over military basing arrangements and criminal jurisdiction issues, war damages, parity rights, as well as specific events like a recently impounded shipment of tobacco (Gordon 1966).

22. That report detailed a confederation of Malaya, the Philippines, Indonesia and "possibly Thailand" and "envisaged the placing of Brunei, Sarawak, and North Borneo under the United Nations Trusteeship with the Philippines, Malaya, and Indonesia as joint administrators" (Butwell 1964, 943; Gordon 1966, 22–23; Ghazali Shafie 1998, 370). While some in the Philippines viewed the idea of pan-Malay brotherhood quite seriously, others, including the president and vice president, did not. Many also believe that regardless of Philippine intent, British "ineptness" and especially its refusal to acknowledge the Philippine claim were important reasons for the escalation of the conflict. See Jacobini 1964, 1144–1151; Starner 1963, 519–534; Wurfel 1963, 710.

23. See Ghazali Shafie 1998, 328, 363.

24. Gordon 1966: 68. Failing to block Malaysia from assuming its scheduled seat on the UNSC in 1965, Indonesia withdrew from the United Nations, becoming perhaps the only state to voluntarily withdraw from the United Nations for reasons other than political dissolution or unification.

25. Ghazali Shafie 1998, 336.

26. For a detailed discussion on the internal debate in the Philippines, see Gordon 1966, 25–30.

27. Jorgensen-Dahl 1982, 195.

28. This event is known by its acronym, GESTAPU-*Gerakan September Tiga Puluh* or Thirtieth of September Movement.

29. Final responsibility for events has been the subject of discussion among scholars, though official sources continue to pin the blame on the PKI. For discussions, see Anwar 1994, 28–31; Crouch 1988; van der Kroef 1970–1971, 557–577.

30. See Sukma 1999, 31.

31. See the government report cited by Gordon 1966, 28–30, 35, 40.

32. Butwell 1966, 48; Jacobini 1964, 1150; Wurfel 1963, 704.

33. Gordon 1966, 21.

34. See David Bonavia, "Marcos' One Hundred Days," *FEER* 52:6 (12 May 1966): 288.

35. See Gordon 1966: 28–30, 35, 40. See also Butwell 1966, 48.

36. Wilson 1964. See also, Starner 1963b, 41–47.

37. Thanat 1992: xix. See also Singh 1963, 535–543.

38. During an April 1967 visit to Singapore, British Defense Secretary Denis Healy "made clear that Britain would be out of mainland Asia by the late 1970s." See Lee 2000, 35.

39. Shafie paraphrasing the Tunku's views. Shafie 1998, 376.

40. See, for example, Lee Kuan Yew's 1966 comments quoted in Meow 1979, 8.

41. Tunku Abdul Rahman had originally not wanted to include Singapore into the proposed federation, but Lee Kuan Yew convinced the Tunku that including Singapore was necessary if both were to escape communism. See, for example, "Tunku Re-elected National President of UMNO for Fourteenth Year" (excerpts from Tunku Abdul Rahman's speech to the Eighteenth UMNO General Assembly, 15 May 1965), *Malaysian Bulletin* (June 1965). For the Tunku's views on Lee Kuan Yew and the circumstances leading up to separation, see Ghazali Shafie 1998 and Sheppard 1995: 146–151; for Lee Kuan Yew's views on union and separation, see Lee 1998: 410–453; 470–524; Han et al., 1998, 55–70.

42. See, for example, Harvey Stockwin, "Thrashing it Out," *FEER* (11 August 1966): 258.

43. Quoted in Josey 1968, 327–328.

44. Lee 2000, 43.

45. See Meow 1979, 9.

46. Harvey Stockwin, "Confrontation: After the Accord," *FEER* (16 June 1966): 510.

47. See Stockwin, "Uplift for ASA?" *FEER* (13 January 1966c, 42; Emmerson 1996, 63–65.

48. See Jorgensen-Dahl 1982, 32.

49. Bonavia (12 May 1966): 288; Far Eastern round-up 1966: 49; "Ganjang Konfrontasi?" *FEER* (26 May 1966): 351.

50. See Stockwin, "Tricky Negotiations," *FEER* (20–26 August 1967): 378; Weinstein 1976: 196–200.

51. See, for example, comments of Tun Razak quoted in Harvey Stockwin, "Interview with Tun Razak," *FEER* 52:10 (9 June 1966): 471. See also Jorgensen-Dahl 1982, 33.

52. Apparently, Malik's efforts put his job on the line more than once. For his efforts to end confrontation with Malaysia, he was also berated for cowardice by Sukarno (Derek Davies. The Java men. *FEER* [May 26, 1966], 353.)

53. Solidum 1974: 72.

54. As Gordon characterized sentiments in 1966, "any suspicion that [regional cooperation] is generated from outside of Asia can be the kiss of death" (Gordon 1966: 161).

55. Malaysia's now former Prime Minister Mahathir, commenting on ASEAN's founding. Mahathir nd: 2.

56. Malik 1980: xii.

57. Rajaratnam quoted in Stockwin, "Tricky Negotiations": 378.

58. Tunku Abdul Rahman 1978.

59. Quoted by Weinstein 1976: 175. See also comments of Suharto's powerful assistant for political affairs Lieutenant General Ali Moertopo (who also represented Indonesia in talks to end *konfrontasi*). Moertopo 1978, 30–32.

60. Declassified materials now detail just how much the United States intervened into Indonesia's politics. See *Foreign Relations of the U.S., 1955–1957*. See also Kahin and Kahin 1995.

61. Tunku Abdul Rahman 1966.

62. Among Western scholars, Fisher may draw the most explicit comparisons between Southeast Asia and the Balkans, seeing similarities in their "topographical fragmentation," "geographical position[s]," and minority problems as well as repeated invasions and attempts by external powers to dominate the region. Just as the Balkans are the "powder keg" of Europe, Southeast Asia is the "powder keg" of Asia. He also equates Southeast Asia's struggles for independence to the First Balkan War, and Southeast Asia's experience with konfrontasi to the Second Balkan War. See, for example, Fisher 1966, 9–10, 774. See also Brecher 1963, 213–235.

63. This idea of togetherness and resilience also informed Malaysian ideas about ASA. Explains Shafie, "The Tunku's proposal was instinctively a concept of togetherness (*berkampung*) to obviate communist subversive plots and to bring about its own version of internationalism or regionalism" (Shafie 1998: 345).

64. See Malik 1980: 271; Thanat 1964; and Thanat 1998, 83–86.

65. Thanat Khoman quoted by Young 1966: 67. See also Suharto quoted in Malik 1980.

66. Thayer 1990, 140.

67. ASEAN, "Verbatim Record of the Inaugural Meeting of ASEAN," 8 August 1967. Emphasis added.

68. Rajaratnam quoted in Chin 1997, 7.

69. South Vietnam did attend as an observer at ASEAN's 1969 and 1971 annual meetings as a guest of the host country (Malaysia in 1969 and Philippines in 1971) though significantly not as the guest of collective ASEAN.

70. Ghazalie Shafie 1998, 345. One might also note that Tunku Abdul Rahman's original ASA idea emerged at February 1958 meeting in Colombo.

71. Quoted in Chin 1997, 5.

72. See Chin 1997: 5 and fn 15.

73. Not until 1982, when "ASEAN Standing Committee definitively rejected Sri Lanka's application on grounds that it was outside the geographic confines of Southeast Asia" was the matter of Southeast Asia's western boundary finally settled.

While ASEAN's desire to remain distant from South Asian politics likely colored the ASEAN Standing Committee's rejection of Sri Lanka's 1981 application, its rejection on the basis of regional geography nevertheless contrasts with the less definitive stance taken in 1967. See Chin 1997: 5 and fn 15.

74. ASEAN, "Verbatim Record of the Inaugural Meeting of ASEAN," 8 August 1967, reprinted in *15th Anniversary* nd.

75. See, for example, Anwar 1998: 483–484. According to the *FEER* there was, until the end, still some uncertainty whether the compromise clause would be sufficient to appease Indonesian nationalists at home.

76. For a discussion of Indonesian concerns, see Weinstein 1976: 71–72, 168–9.

77. See Antolik 1990: 77.

78. ASEAN, "The ASEAN Declaration (Bangkok Declaration)," 8 August 1967.

79. Jorgensen-Dahl 1982, 37.

80. Quoted by Frances L. Starner, "Once Bitten, Twice Shy," *FEER* 57:3 (July 16–22, 1967): 151.

81. Rajaratnam quoted by Starner 1967: 151.

82. Tun Ismail bin Dato Abdul Rahman, Minister for Home Affairs and Acting Minister for Foreign Affairs, Address to the Foreign Correspondents Association, at Johore Bahru, 23 June 1966, in Boyce 1968: 237.

83. Cruz 2000, 276–277.

84. See Swidler 1986: 279. See also discussion in Cruz 2000: 281–282. For a more critical view about the significance of ambiguous situations, see Goldstein 1993: 12–18 and Kowert and Legro 1996.

85. Philpott 1995, 353.

86. Leifer 1989.

87. Rajaratnam quoted by Jorgensen-Dahl 1982: 73–74. See also comments of Thanat Khoman made in 1966, cited in Young 1966: 67; and Thanat's reflections on the creation of ASEAN in Thanat 1992: xviii.

88. Thanat 1992.

89. Leifer 1989: 20–21.

90. See, for example, Tunku Rahman's comments made to the Commonwealth Prime Minister's Conference in London, 14 September 1966, in "Commonwealth Prime Ministers' Conference . . . "; Djiwandono 1996; Suharto, "Address by the President of the Republic of Indonesia" in *Regionalism in Southeast Asia* 1975: 8.

91. Risse et al. 1999, 156.

92. ASEAN founding declaration, 1967. Available online at www.aseansec.org/1212.htm.

93. Writing on the Bretton Woods negotiations, Ruggie 1998, 870.

CHAPTER 3

1. Swidler 1986.

2. Malaysia discovered twenty-six armed Filipinos on an island near Sabah. See Bernardino Ronquillo, "Corregidor Questions," *FEER* (14/20 April 1968): 168. Antolik suggests that the situation might not have deteriorated quite so much had Malaysia offered the Philippines a face-saving way out (Antolik 1990: 71–72).

3. See Turnbull 1992: 617.

4. See Ganesan 1998: 21–36; Leifer 1989: 39; Wilairat 1975: 75.

5. Tunku Abdul Rahman's 1969 comments quoted by Pathmanathan 1977: 28, fn. 22.

6. See Mohamed bin Haron n.d. Antolik (1990) adds that U.S. domestic politics-racial riots, anti-Vietnamese protests, and the assassinations of Robert F. Kennedy and Martin Luther King-also contributed to the loss of confidence in the United States by members. See also "The Thai Foreign Minister in the U.S.," 1970: 15.

7. Romulo quoted by Terrill 1969: 25.

8. Terrill 1969.

9. See ministerial statements made to Third AMM in Siagian nd.

10. Nathan 1998: 537. See also Leifer 1996.

11. Tun Razak, Opening Statement to Third AMM in Siagian n.d.: 127. Opening statements by others echoed the same themes. See also Rajaratnam 1970; Thanat 1992: xvii–xviii.

12. Tunku Abdul Rahman Putra, Opening Statement to 1969 AMM, in Siagian n.d., 97.

13. Rajaratnam, Statement to 1974 AMM in Siagian n.d. See also comments of Philippine foreign minister in Siagian n.d.: 38.

14. Rajaratnam, Opening Statement to 1969 AMM in Siagian n.d., 112–113.

15. Thanat Khoman in Siagian n.d.:118.

16. It varied according to issue who "those" were. At the 1969 meeting, Thailand and the Philippines appear to advocate a more coordinated response to political-security developments. Later, Singapore would argue for more coordinated economic cooperation.

17. Suharto, Message to the Third AMM, in Siagian n.d., 103.

18. Razak to 1969 AMM in Siagian n.d.: 126. See also Tunku Abdul Rahman, Opening Statement 1969 AMM.

19. Tunku Abdul Rahman, Opening Statement 1969 AMM; also Rajaratnam, Opening Address to 1968 AMM in Siagian n.d.: 83–87.

20. Girling 1971: 56–65.

21. Acharya 1992: 7–21.

22. Pathmanathan 1977: 6. See also Malik 1980: 274. Malik directly links ZOPFAN to the "shifts in world politics" just described. Saravanamuttu 1984: 186–187.

23. See Pathmanathan 1977: 6.

24. For example, Prince Sihanouk's proposal that Laos and Cambodia be neutralized in 1960. Pathemanathan also discusses nonindigenously sourced proposals. See Pathmanathan 1977; Wilson 1975: 6–7.

25. Tun Razak to the 1970 NAM meeting, in what is considered to be his first major policy statement. Quoted by Wilson 1975: 3. See also, Mohamed bin Haron 1991; Pathmanathan 1977: 6; Hanggi 1991: 13–14.

26. Emmerson 1996.

27. Pathmanathan 1977: 22–23.

28. Wilson 1975: 3.

29. Mohamed bin Haron 1991.

30. See Hanggi 1991: 15.

31. Emmerson 1996: 67. See also Tilman 1987: 150.

32. Antolik 1990: 112.

33. See Malik 1980: 274.

34. At the U.N. vote, Malaysia and Singapore voted in favor, the Philippines against, and Indonesia and Thailand opted to abstain.

35. See Hanggi 1991: 17; and especially, Wilson 1975: 25–28.

36. Emmerson 1996; Wilson 1975: 29.

37. Kuala Lumpur Declaration, 1971 reprinted in ASEAN 1988: 34.

38. Antolik 1990: 114. Antolik discusses various compromises and concessions made to achieve agreement. See also, Hanggi 1991: 16–17, 19.

39. Romulo cited by Abisheganaden, "Southeast Asia Gets Nervous About Peace," *Nation* (Thailand) (12 March 1973).

40. Wilson 1975.

41. See Wilson 1975: 31–32.

42. Ghazali Shafie cited by Wilson 1975: 4–5. Tun Ismail also similarly expressed these same components in 1970. See Pathmanathan 1977: 19.

43. Mohamed bin Haron 1991.

44. Jusuf Wanandi, "Seeking Peace Amid Cambodia's Conflict," *FEER* (8 March 1994): 34.

45. See Joint Communiqué of the Eighth AMM reprinted in ASEAN 1988: 76–78.

46. Press Statement, "The ASEAN Foreign Ministers Meeting to Assess the Agreement on Ending the War and Restoring Peace in Vietnam and to Consider Its Implications for Southeast Asia, 15 Feb. 1973," reprinted in ASEAN 1988: 152–153.

47. Rajaratnam, Opening Statement to 8th AMM, in Siagian n.d.: 301.

48. See their opening statements to the 1975 AMM, in Siagian n.d.: 286–317.

49. Razak, Address by the Prime Minister of Malaysia at the opening ceremony of the 8th AMM, in Siagian n.d.: 292.

50. Quoted by Hanggi 1991: 39.

51. See Malik, Opening Statement to 8th AMM, Kuala Lumpur, 13 May 1975, Siagian n.d.: 313.

52. This is not to say that there were no objections to Vietnam, only that those most involved in ASEAN processes believed that Vietnam was theoretically eligible for ASEAN membership.

53. See *Joint Press Communiqué*, Meeting of the ASEAN Heads of Government, 23–24 Feb. 1976 in ASEAN 1988: 52. A similar clause was included in ASEAN's 1997 joint press communiqué, in which each of the Indochinese states, including Vietnam, was also identified by name.

54. A. Rahim bin Ishak 1974: 142–143.

55. See Leifer 1996: 11; Leifer 1986b: 124.

56. See Press Statement, "The ASEAN Foreign Ministers Meeting to Assess the Agreement on Ending the War . . . ," and "Joint Communiqué of the Ninth AMM" in ASEAN 1988: 152–3: 78–79.

57. See reference in Evans and Rowley 1984: 40.

58. The Thai request that U.S. troops leave may also have been partly a response to its being the only ASEAN country not included in Vice President Rockefeller's upcoming trip to Southeast Asia.

59. The "Five Regional Needs" were: "(1) the need to depend on one another; (2) the need to strengthen friendship among us and renew long dormant ties; (3) the need to live together in peace, in security, and in harmony; (4) the need to be collectively self reliant; and above all, (5) the need to have what is known in Buddhist

teachings as 'Knati-Dharma,' or Tolerance of one another's ways." See Chatichai, Opening Statement to Eighth AMM, in Siagian n.d.: 304–309.

60. Chia 1980: 121.

61. Specifically: "Mutual respect for the independence, sovereignty, equality, territorial integrity and national identity of all nations"; "The right of every State to lead its national existence free from external interference, subversion or coercion"; "Non-interference in the internal affairs of one another"; "Settlement of differences or disputes by peaceful means"; "Renunciation of the threat or use of force"; and "Effective cooperation among themselves." See *Treaty of Amity and Cooperation in Southeast Asia*, 1976, ASEAN website.

62. A year later, at ASEAN's second summit, leaders reaffirmed the direction set at Bali by elaborating the Secretariat's role as a channel for intra-ASEAN communications and receptacle of official reports of meetings, which it would then transmit to the ASC at the top of the ASEAN committee hierarchy. See Luhilima 1987: 175.

63. See Leifer 1986a: 123.

64. Rajaratnam, Opening Statement to 8th AMM in Siagian n.d.: 298–303.

65. Indonesia relations with Vietnam had remained intact throughout the Vietnam War.

66. Said Ghazali Shafie in 1996, "By bringing ASEAN to life via a Treaty of Amity and Cooperation, we [ASEAN members] expected that one day Vietnam would be able to join [ASEAN] by acceding to this treaty. When the Americans withdrew from Vietnam we asked Hanoi to do so and again in 1978–79 in the aftermath of their intervention into Cambodia. It was our policy of constructive engagement." Shafie quoted by Goodman 1996: 592–593.

67. "Uneasy Relations Near Home." *Times* (London) (2 Aug. 1977): 1.

68. Carlos P. Romulo, Opening Statement to Third AMM, in Siagian n.d.: 102.

69. Chanda, "Hanoi Tries a Friendly Line," *FEER* (16 July 1976): 13.

70. Chanda, "Foreign Relations," *FEER* (10 Sept. 1976); Das, "Hanoi's New War of Words," *FEER* (4 Feb. 1977): 10.

71. See Thanat Khoman, "Why Are We Chasing Mirages?" *Bangkok Post* (14 March 1976): 5

72. See Nayan Chanda, "Indochina Shot ASEAN Onto the World Stage," *FEER* (13 August 1982): 43–46; van der Kroef 1982: 1010–1012; Thayer 1990.

73. During this tour, only Singapore was omitted from the itinerary due to Singapore's refusal to return four Vietnamese responsible for the hijacking of an Air Vietnam plane bound for Singapore.

74. Thayer 1990: 145.

75. Antolik 1990.

76. Snitwongse 1997.

77. Antolik 1990: 122. See especially Chapters 7 and 8. See also, Crone 1996: 42.

78. See Antolik 1990: 119–131.

79. For example, ASEAN experienced success in confronting Australia over its International Civil Aviation Policy (1979–1981) and in securing GSP preferences for all ASEAN states, including Singapore, after New Zealand changed its policy in 1984. ASEAN is also frequently cited for its unity on issues regarding the New International Economic Order and early negotiations over the trade of synthetic rubber. See, for example, Esmara 1988: 3; Lau 1990: 119.

80. See Esmara 1988: 2.

81. See Alburo 1988: 39, en. 10.

82. See discussion in Chiew 1987.

83. Rajaratnam suggested in 1968 that "regionalism on the basis of bilateral or trilateral regional projects" might be more "practical" given their differences. See Rajaratnam, Opening Address to Second AMM, in Siagian n.d.: 85. See also Chia 1980; Esmara 1988; Lau 1990; Rau 1981.

84. See Weinstein 1976: 198–200. Strains of this view persist to the present day, though some think Indonesia may have an inflated view of its market size and potential. See, for example, Michael Vatikiotis, "A Mirage Market," *FEER* (17 May 1990); Carl Goldstein. "Steering Committee." *FEER* (15 Feb. 1990): 67.

85. According to that 1974 agreement, the two agreed that Singapore would provide Indonesia with bilateral trade statistics, leaving it to Indonesia to decide whether to publish them. In 2003, however, a misunderstanding arose when Jakarta (now a democracy without memory of the earlier agreement) took offense at Singapore's not publishing their bilateral trade numbers and accused Singapore of being unwilling to recognize Indonesia as a major trade partner. That misunderstanding has since been cleared, and there appears to be agreement to put aside the 1974 agreement. See Shoeb Kagda. "S'pore, Jakarta Bury the Hatchet on Trade Data Spat," *Business Times* (Singapore) (14 July 2003).

86. Examples include the division of the once jointly operated Malaysian Singapore Airline into Malaysian Airlines and Singapore Airlines; of their rubber and stock exchanges into two separate exchanges; and of their once common currency into two national currencies. See Doug Tsuruoka, "Saved by the Bull," *FEER* (18 Feb. 1990): 50–51.

87. See, for example, comments of Singapore Defense Minister Goh Keng Swee made in 1970. Chia 1980: 128.

88. See opening statements at 1974 AMM in Siagian n.d..

89. Rajaratnam, Opening Statement to 1974 AMM, in Siagian n.d.

90. See Raratnam's comments in Tasker, "All Hands on Deck," *FEER* (11 March 1977): 14.

91. Derek Davies, "The Message to Carter," *FEER* (17 June 1977): 8.

92. See Chia 1980.

93. *Joint Communiqué of the Seventh ASEAN Ministerial Meeting,* in ASEAN 1988: 74–76.

94. See *Declaration of ASEAN Concord,* Bali, 24 Feb. 1976, in ASEAN 1988: 36–38.

95. See Par. 11 of *Joint Press Statement of the Second Economic Ministers Meeting,* March 8–9 1976, in ASEAN 1988: 178.

96. Ravenhill 1995, 853.

97. See Tan 1987.

98. Ooi 1987.

99. As Stubbs explains, this relationship was a "metamorphosis" of the "triangular relationship" originally envisaged by U.S. policy makers after World War II. Originally, the triangle was to involve the United States providing capital and technology, Japan providing intermediate goods, and Southeast Asia providing raw materials. See Stubbs 1989: 531, 534; Siazon 1995: 25.

100. See Stubbs 1989: 520; Akrasanee, 1984. See also discussions of the flying geese model and its problems. Bernard and Ravenhill 1995: 171–210; Hatch 1996.

101. A UNDP study and an ISEAS study conducted in the 1980s identified these practices as the most common NTBs in intra-ASEAN trade. See Ooi 1987, 59.

102. See Tan 1996: 141.

103. Sudarsono 1986; Ooi 1987: 57; Ravenhill 1995.

104. See summary of these findings in Hill 1987; Meyanathan and Haron 1987: 25; Pangestu 1988, 149; Tan 1987: 65–66; also Alburo 1988, Parrenas 1998: 235.

105. See Hill 1987: 84–85.

106. See *Agreement on ASEAN Preferential Trading Arrangements*, Manila, 24 Feb. 1977, in ASEAN 1988, 293.

107. See *Declaration of ASEAN Concord* (24 Feb. 1976), and Preambles of both the *Agreement on ASEAN Preferential Trading Arrangements* (24 Feb. 1977) and *Basic Agreement on ASEAN Industrial Projects*, Kuala Lumpur, (6 March 1980), in ASEAN 1988: 36–38, 293–309, and 259–264.

108. Ferdinand Marcos, Opening address to Fourth AMM, Manila, in Siagian n.d.: 134.

109. See Rajaratnam's opening statements to ASEAN's 1969 and 1971 AMMs, in Siagian n.d.: 138–142, 111–112.

110. Rajaratnam, Opening Statement to 1974 AMM, in Siagian n.d.: 258–262.

111. Luhulima 1987: 172.

112. Rajaratnam (1970) argued that national consolidation and economic development were a "necessary precondition" of regionalism and that until that they completed that "nationalist phase of [their] history," regionalism had to be supportive of the national project. See Rajaratnam 1970: 25. See also his 1971 comments cited by Wilairat 1975: 46; Rajaratnam's Opening Statements to ASEAN's 1968, 1971, and 1973 AMMs, in Siagian: 85, 138–139, 216.

113. See Rajaratnam 1970: 25.

114. Malik 1980: 277.

115. See A. Rahim Ishak, Opening Statement to Fifth AMM, in Siagian n.d.: 206; see also, Soeharto's Opening Address to the 1974 AMM, in Siagian n.d.: 240–242.

116. For the economic nationalists that dominated Indonesia's policymaking process in the 1970s, trade liberalization was to be the last of ASEAN's immediate objectives and, at very least, subordinated to industrial cooperation.

117. Manila had originally proposed an ASEAN common market but then supported Singapore's free trade scheme instead.

118. Meyanathan and Haron 1987.

119. Wanandi 1984: 305.

120. See also Ba 1997.

121. See Alagappa 1987a: 187.

122. Jose Ingles, Message to the Fifth AMM, Siagian 197. See also, Rajaratnam's Opening statement to 1969 AMM, in Siagian n.d.: 141.

123. Ghazali Shafie 1982; "Malaysian Prime Minister's Closing Speech," *Radyo ng Bayan, Quezon City* (English) (15 December 1987)/ BBC (16 December 1987).

124. Soeharto, Address to the Second AMM, Jakarta, 6 Aug. 1968, in Siagian n.d.: 73.

CHAPTER 4

1. Alatas, Opening Address to Seminar on "ASEAN Strategies and Actions." 6 Aug. 1996. Available online at www3.itu.int/MISSIONS/Indonesia/arf.htm (Site of the Permanent Mission to the United Nations, Geneva."

2. Koh quoted by Terada 2003, fn 9.

3. See, for example, Acharya 2001; Ruland 2000: 434–438; Stubbs 2002.

4. See Thomas Friedman, "Indonesian Balancing Act," *NYT* (21 July 1997): A25.

5. Ba 2003; Whiting 1997.

6. These views were expressed in a briefing prepared by Siti Azizah Abod and Col. Jamil Rais Abdullah of the Malaysian Defense Ministry. See "Defense Analysts on Spratlys War Scenario," *Manila Business World* (21 April 1995), in *FBIS-EAS 95-079* (21 April 1995).

7. There is some uncertainty about when the Chinese actually built the structures. According to Segal 1996, the structures were built sometime in the three months before Jan. 1995, while Leifer 1996 suggests that they could have been built as much as six months earlier. As for when the Philippines discovered the structures, most reports pin it to Feb. 1995.

8. Wassana Nanuam. "China Offers installment Plan." *Bangkok Post* (26 May 1997); Tai Ming Cheung. "Air Arms Race Builds Tensions." *FEER* (15 Feb 1990): 54–55.

9. The idea of the "West" or to lump states into a "Western" category is, of course, as problematic as thinking of "Asia" as a coherent place. Here, I use it as a shorthand to refer mostly to the advanced, industrialized states of North America and Europe, as well as Australia. As Chapters 5, 6, and 7 further illustrate, using "the West" as shorthand is not completely unjustified in that emergent divisions are viewed by many participants in "Asia" versus the "West" terms.

10. See Wanandi 1985: 209.

11. See Evans and Rowley 1984: 54.

12. In 1988, Malaysia's permanent representative to the U.N. referred to the problem as one that "tax[ed] . . . the compassion of countries." See "Statement by UN Permanent Representative" 1988.

13. See Rodney Tasker, "ASEAN Toughens Up," *FEER* (26 July 1984): 32.

14. See Siddhi Savetsila, Opening Statement, 20th AMM, Singapore, June 15–20, 1987, in ASEAN 1988.

15. Consider, for example, that just six months earlier, Savetsila had been saying that Vietnam's occupation of Cambodia was "the greatest threat to [Thai] national security." See Savetsila 1988: 6–11.

16. Excerpts can be found in Innes-Brown and Valencia 1993 and Um 1991.

17. Richard Gourlay, "Meet the Neighbors," *Financial Times (London)* (December 5, 1988).

18. The election of Chatichai has been described as the "crucial turning-point in Thai policy towards Vietnam." For discussion of Thailand's internal, bureaucratic tensions, see, Maisrikrod 1994; Buszynski 1994: 721–738; Christopher Lockwood, "Thailand's Rulers Face Crisis Over Leadership Style," *Daily Telegraph* (24 March 1989).

19. See Jonathan Thatcher, "Southeast Asia Tries to Coordinate Cambodian Peace Moves," *Reuters* (20 Jan. 1989).

20. See Mochtar 1990: 166. See also Lee Kwok Kin, "Singapore Says Thailand Overtures to Phnom Penh Causing Concern," *Reuter Library Report* (2 July 1989).

21. See Innes-Brown and Valencia 1993: 335.

22. As Lee Kuan Yew acknowledged in 1965, "[T]his is not like a map . . . [that] you can take a pair of scissors and cut off Singapore and then . . . paste it in the South Pacific and forget about it. This is part of the mainland of the continent of Asia. And that Causeway . . . is part of history; and you are part of history. You are a part of this place as much as I am. . . ." (Han et al. 1998: 312).

23. See Antolik 1990, in which he refers to overlapping vulnerabilities as "security interdependencies." According to Antolik, the Philippines has the fewest. See also Emmerson 1996: 34–88. Consider also Indonesia's strategic doctrine of *ASEAN Kecil* (Inner ASEAN) whereby Indonesia considers Singapore and Kuala Lumpur more strategically important than Indonesian cities in the far eastern reaches of Indonesia. See Dupont 1996: 282–284 and fn. 29.

24. Confidential interview, Chulalongkorn University, Bangkok, Thailand, March 1998.

25. See Reginald Chua. "Will Cambodian Solution Weaken ASEAN Unity?" *Reuters* (22 June 1989). See also comments by Sukhumband Paribatra in Michael Vatikiotis, "Care to Join Us?" *FEER* (7 Dec. 1995): 23.

26. See Mochtar 1990: 167.

27. See "Prime Minister Proposes Inclusion of Indochina in ASEAN," *BP* (12 Jan. 1990): 9.

28. Buszynski 1998.

29. Nusara Thaithawat and Prinya Muang-akat, "Mekong Subregion Economic Conference Held - Hexagon Meeting Concludes," *BP* (17 Sept. 1994) in *FBIS-EAS-94-181*.

30. See Vatikiotis, "Care to Join Us?" *FEER* (7 Dec. 1995): 23.

31. In 1988 and 1989 the Philippines and Malaysia each sent representatives to talk trade with Vietnam, though it had yet to withdraw its forces from Cambodia. Suharto, accompanied by his foreign and economic ministers, followed in 1990. See Sukma 1999 and Keith Richburg, "Manila's Foreign Minister Ends Upbeat Hanoi Visit; Trade Expansion Vowed; Air Accord Reached," *Washington Post* (1 Dec. 1988): A45.

32. Paisai Sricharatchnaya, "Lee Sees Little Hope of Khmer Breakthrough," *Bangkok Post* (19 Sept. 1989). Rajaratnam, newly retired from public life, was harsher: "Playing the good Samaritan to a man-eating tiger is not clever politics, nor is it shrewd economics." See Rajaratnam 1989.

33. Despite the ban on investment, however, Singapore still ranked second among ASEAN states in terms of its investment in Vietnam as the ban did not apply to multinationals based in Singapore. See Vatikiotis 1995; and Harish Meta, "Singapore is Second Biggest ASEAN Investor in Vietnam," *Business Times* (16 Sept. 1991).

34. Rajaratnam 1989.

35. Ibid.

36. Rajaratnam 1989. See also Lee Kuan Yew's 1989 comments to Singapore's National Defense College in "Singapore's Lee Says Vietnam Must Be Taught a Lesson," *Reuter Library Report* (19 Sept. 1989). Views of Vietnam's "credibility gap" and "recurring pattern" of false promises were also expressed by Jusuf Wanandi in 1985. See Wanandi 1985: 209.

37. Rajaratnam 1989.

38. Quoted in Surya Gangadharan, "South-East Asia: ASEAN Scrambles to Do Business with Vietnam," *IPS* (15 Dec. 1990).

39. Gangadharan "South-East Asia . . ."

40. Richard Gourlay, "Meet the Neighbors," *Financial Times (London)* (5 Dec. 1988).

41. Gangadharan 1990.

42. In defending Thai policy in 1988, for example, Thai officials explicitly referred to the outside interest Vietnam was attracting. See Gourlay 1988.

43. Gourlay 1988.

44. Mahathir 1991.

45. See Innes-Brown and Valencia 1993: 345. See also, comments of Lao Deputy Minister of Foreign Affairs Soulivong Phrasithidethm in 1991, quoted in Jean-Claude Chapon, "Laos Ready to Consider ASEAN Offer of Cooperation," *AFP* (11 Aug. 1991).

46. This was one of three recommendations, the other two being to strengthen ZOPFAN and to strengthen links with dialogue partners. See, for example, Ian Stewart, "ASEAN Rethinks Indochina Policy," *SCMP* (23 Jan. 1992).

47. See "ASEAN Puts off Membership for Vietnam, Laos," *JEN* (25 Jan. 1992).

48. See confidential report cited by the Kyodo News Service. See "ASEAN Puts Off . . ." (25 Jan. 1992).

49. "KL Pushes Ahead with Proposal on Asian Grouping," *JP* (17 Jan. 1992): 1.

50. See, for example, Soesastro 1997a, 86–87.

51. Quoted in "Further on ASEAN Economic Ministers' Meeting: SRV's Membership Viewed," *Bangkok Post* (24 Sept. 1994), in *FBIS-EAS-94-187* (12 Nov. 1995).

52. That number is now closer to 700 meetings (at various levels) a year. See "Hamid Wants ASEAN to Remain Driving Force." Bernama (24 July 2006), WNC, 12 Sept. 2006.

53. For discussion on EU expansion, see Schimmelfennig 2000.

54. See Sopiee 1992. Some also considered the idea as a possible way to resolve the Cambodian problem. See P. Prashanth, "Could See New Regional Grouping Over Cambodia," *IPS* (23 June 1989). A proposal to create a new organization was also considered in 1973 by Bangkok and Manila, though it was not picked up.

55. Rajaratnam 1989: 360.

56. Mochtar 1992: 102.

57. Quoted by Antolik 1992: 151.

58. See Reuters, "US Serves Notice on Tyrants Threatening Security in Asia," *JP* (25 July 992): 12.

59. See Ramcharan 2000 and Haacke 2005. As Ramcharan and Haacke highlight, concerns about collective ASEAN became an important factor in debates to reform the "ASEAN Way."

60. Teresa Albor, "ASEAN Rejects West's Human Rights Tactics," *CSM* (29 July 1992): 6.

61. See, for example, Moller 1998.

62. Singapore was in favor of the 1997 timetable until 1996.

63. Author's discussions with track-two participants, Bangkok, Thailand, March 1998.

64. Dewi Fortuna Anwar, "Compelling Reasons for ASEAN to Delay Myanmar's Membership," *ST* (26 Oct. 1996).

65. As Buszynski notes, Thailand's espoused democratic goals of "constructive engagement" notwithstanding, its close association with SLORC put it in a difficult bind "should there actually be a democratic transition in Myanmar" as Thailand faces the real possibility that "a future democratic and populist regime . . . [w]ould punish [it] for cooperating for SLORC." See Buszynski 1998; Hamish McDonald, "Selling Out Old Friends," *FEER* (22 Feb. 1990): 16–17; 20–21.

66. The State Law and Order Restoration Council (SLORC)—renamed State Peace and Development Council (SPDC) in 1997—moved the capital from Yangon to Naypyidaw in 2006.

67. See also Corazon Aquino's comments in "Burmese Discontent 'May Poison All Asia,'" *Hong Kong Standard* (4 Nov. 1996).

68. Quoted by Singh 1997: x.

69. "SEA Leaders Gather . . . " (30 Nov. 1996); Agnes Wee, "Myanmar Will Join ASEAN When It is Ready" *Business Times (Singapore)* (2 Nov. 1996).

70. "ASEAN Ministers Prove Their Mettle," *BP* (2 Oct. 1996); "SEA Leaders Gather for Annual Summit," *Hong Kong Standard* (30 Nov. 1996).

71. Confidential interview with author, Department of Foreign Affairs, Manila, Philippines, Oct. 1997.

72. Confidential interview with author, Department of Foreign Affairs, Manila, Philippines, Oct. 1997.

73. Confidential interview with author, Ministry of Foreign Affairs, Bangkok, March 1998.

74. According to Romero (1998), Manila's willingness to compromise also stemmed from a sense of indebtedness to Jakarta for helping broker a peace agreement with the Moro National Liberation Front.

75. See Singh 1997: vii.

76. Paribatra 1994.

77. Nassara Sawatsawang, "Put Democracy Before ASEAN Role; SLORC Would Be More Welcome," *BP* (30 Oct. 1996); "Human Rights Can't be Taken Off Euro-Asia Agenda: EU," *JP* (11 Feb. 1997): 11; "Burma Unwelcome," *BP - Week in Review* (23 Feb. 1997).

78. Singh (1997). See also comments of Philippine Foreign Minister Domingo Siazon in "US and Europe Accused over Sanctions," *SMH* (2 May 1997): 11.

79. See "Soeharto Given Royal Welcome in Cambodia," *JP* (18 Feb. 1997): 1; "Laos, Indonesia Promise to Boost Economic Ties," *JP* (22 Feb. 1997).

80. "Between a Rock and a Hard Place," *The Nation* (25 April 1997).

81. Meidyatama Suryodiningrat, "ASEAN Considers Yangon's Entry," *JP* (31 May 1997).

82. "US to Keep Myanmar out of ASEAN," *JP* (27 April 1997): 2.

83. See "US and Europe Accused Over Sanctions," 11.

84. Anwar, "Compelling Reasons . . ."

85. Thanat 1998.

86. See 1995 op-ed by Ruslan Abdulgani, Indonesia's former minister of foreign affairs and permanent representative to the UN, "A Perceived Threat from the North: Japan or China," *Merdeka* (in Indonesian) (9 June 1995): 6 in *FBIS-EAS 95-*

112 (9 June 1995). For a discussion of the various perspectives in ASEAN, see Parrenas 1990.

87. Confidential interview with author, Bangkok, Thailand (April 1998).

88. For a discussion of some entrenched Indonesian elite views of Thailand, see also Weinstein 1976.

89. Emphasis added. Mochtar 1992: 102–103.

90. Chin 1997: 9.

91. On the necessity of constructive engagement toward China, see, for example, comments made by Jakarta-based CSIS's Wanandi. Wanandi, "Reining in China: It's US vs. East Asia on How to Do It," *IHT* (3 March 1993).

92. Mochtar 1992: 102.

93. "'ASEAN 10' Would Counter Chinese Might," *JP* (6 July 1995).

94. Goh quoted in "Australia in ASEAN "Just a Thinkable Idea," *ST* (18 Jan. 1996): 1.

95. Datuk Abdullah Bin Haji Ahmad Badawi, Keynote Address to Seventh SEA Forum (unpublished), 4 March 1996.

96. Datuk Abdullah Bin Haji Ahmad Badawi, Keynote Address to Seventh SEA Forum (unpublished), 4 March 1996.

97. Barnett 1996: 401.

98. The initiative emerged from 1995 summit of ASEAN heads (Hay 1996).

99. These measures were formalized at ASEAN's 1995 Summit in Bangkok, where they agreed to (1) increase CLM participation in future ASEAN activities; (2) share knowledge, experience in areas of interest; (3) assist in their transition to market economies; (4) assist in their preparation for AFTA participation. See Soesastro 1997a: 88–89.

100. See Chapter 14 in Australia, Department of Foreign Affairs and Trade (1997).

101. See "Gentle but Firm Way ASEAN Works," *NST* (30 July 1997). See also Mochtar 1992: 103.

102. Geoff Spencer. "ASEAN Defends Growing Links with Burma." *Associated Press* 18 July 1996.

103. Paribatra 1994.

104. Hurrell 1995: 334.

CHAPTER 5

1. See Vincent Lingga. "ASEAN Set for New Era of Cooperation." *JP* (27 Jan. 1992): 1; See also comments by Goh Chok Tong quoted by Yang Razali Kassim, "The Dawn of a New Epoch for ASEAN," *Business Times* (15 Jan. 1992): 2; Comments by Singapore Foreign Minister Wong Kan Seng in "Fourth ASEAN Summit" (17 Jan. 1992): 2; and Mari Pangestu, "Intra-ASEAN Economic Cooperation Becomes Imperative," *JP* (op-ed) (27 Jan. 1992): 4.

2. See Lestano 1995; Ravenhill 1995: 850–851; Stubbs 2000: 300.

3. Stubbs 1989.

4. Ravenhill 1995: 866.

5. See various ASEAN press releases and joint communiqués issued at AMMs between 1979 and 1983, in ASEAN 1988.

6. Akrasanee 1984.

7. See Mochtar, "Opening Statement to 18th AMM, Kuala Lumpur, 7 July 1985." See also various ASEAN press releases and joint communiqués for the period of 1979 to 1988 in ASEAN 1988–.

8. Soesastro 1989: 859.

9. See S. Dhanabalan's and Arun Panupong's Opening Statements to the 19th AMM, in ASEAN 1988.

10. Tommy T. B. Koh, "How Asia Should Respond to US Protectionist Threat," *FEER* 135:7 (12 February 1987): 61.

11. Siddhi Savetsila, quoted in Buszynski 1987: 778.

12. Antolik 1992.

13. Siddhi Savetsila, "Speech at the Luncheon Hosted in Honour of Gaston Sigur, US Assistant of State for East Asian and Pacific Affairs," Bangkok, Thailand, 18 Jan. 1988, in Siddhi Savetsila 1988. See also Munir Majid. "Asia's Regional Hopes." *World Press Review* (May 1996: 28–30.

14. Ghazali Shafie, 1986.

15. See Rodney Tasker. "Facing Up to Security." *FEER* (6 August 1992): 8.

16. Nathan 1998; see also Anwar 1992: 376–394.

17. See Leifer 1995; see also Nesadurai 1996: 31–57; Juwono Sudarsono. "The Diplomatic Scam Called Human Rights." *Jakarta Post* (11 April 1997): 1. See also comments of Indonesian foreign minister Ali Alatas in "Beware of New Regionalism." Kenneth Whiting, "Malaysia, the Reluctant Dragon Prospers," *AP* (3 May 1990).

18. See Stubbs 2000. For discussions focusing on the role of domestic coalitions and politics in the politics of AFTA and economic regionalism in Asia, see also Nesadurai 2003b; Solingen 1999; Jayasuriya 2003.

19. See Siddhi Savetsila, "Statement at the Opening Session of the 7th ASEAN-EC Ministerial Meeting, Dusseldorf, May 2, 1988, in ASEAN 1988.

20. Pangestu 1995a: 41.

21. Mochtar Kusumaatmadja (1986). Mochtar expressed a similar preference for a global approach in his opening statement to the 1985 AMM.

22. Mochtar Kusumaatmadja, "Opening Statement to 19th AMM, Manila, Philippines, 23–28 June 1986," reprinted in ASEAN n.d. *19th AMM*. See also Singapore's foreign minister S. Dhanabalan, "Opening Statement to 18th AMM, Kuala Lumpur, 7 July 1985," reprinted in ASEAN n.d. *18th AMM*.

23. See Pacifico A. Castro, "Opening Statement to 18th AMM, Kuala Lumpur, 7 July 1985." In ASEAN 1988.

24. See Tengku Ahmad Rithauddeen, "Opening Statement to the 19th AMM" in ASEAN n.d. *19th AMM*.

25. Siddhi Savetsila, "Opening Statement to 18th AMM, Kuala Lumpur, 7 July 1985" in ASEAN n.d. *18th AMM*.

26. Dhanabalan, Opening Statement to 18th AMM, Kuala Lumpur, 7 July 1985.

27. Singapore proposed to modify ASEAN's consensual decision-making practices in 1980 as well. At that time, it was the "five minus one" principle. Explained Lee Kuan Yew, "When four agree and one does not object, this can still be considered a consensus; and the four should proceed with the regional scheme." When Brunei joined in 1984, that principle became "six minus X." Lee quoted by Chia 1980: 113.

28. See S. Dhanabalan's and Arun Panupong's Opening Statements to the 19th AMM in ASEAN n.d. *19th AMM*.

29. Emphasis added. S. Dhanabalan, "Opening Statement to the 20th AMM, Singapore, 15 June 1987," reprinted in *20th AMM* in ASEAN n.d. *20th AMM*.

30. Ruth Youngblood, "ASEAN nations attack Western trade tactics," UPI (4 July 1989).

31. See, for example, the second Joint Statement of the Special AEMM in ASEAN 1989. See also comments of then-Thai Deputy Finance Minister Amnuay Viraban, "Let's Rewrite the Rules." *FEER* (March 9, 1989): 80, and Philippine Trade Secretary Jose Conception in Vatikiotis, "Little to Show at APEC's First Meeting," *FEER* 149:32 (August 9, 1990): 9.

32. See, for example, "ASEAN Fears Secret US–EC Farm Subsidy Deal" *Xinhua News* (3 May 1990).

33. "Joint ASEAN Statement on Uruguay Round" (30 July 1990). See also comments cited in Surya Gangadharan "GATT: Disappointed Asean Still Hopes for Successful Outcome," *Inter Press Service* (December 10, 1990).

34. While most prominent in the 1980s, discussions about the "Asia Pacific" can be traced as far back as 80 years ago (Woods 1994).

35. See discussion in Crone 1993.

36. Robin Pauley, "The Pacific Rim Initiative: An Idea Whose Time Has Come?" *Financial Times* (11 Aug. 1989): 4.

37. For a discussion of Australia's and especially Bob Hawke's motivations in proposing APEC, see especially Ravenhill 2001: 79–83.

38. Ravenhill 2001: 83.

39. Paul Handley, "What's In It For Us?" *FEER* 146 (30 Nov. 1989): 79.

40. Daniel Sneider, "Pacific Rim Nations Strengthen Economic Ties," *CSM* (6 Nov. 1989): 10.

41. Ravenhill 2001: 54–58; Yong Deng 1997: 101–107.

42. Ravenhill 2001. See also Crone 1993; Wanandi 1983.

43. See, for example, comments of Indonesian, Thai, Malaysian, and Singapore foreign ministers Ali Alatas, Siddhi Savetsila, Abu Hassan Omar, and Wang Kan Seng cited in Mark Baker, "ASEAN Cautious on Hawke Plan," *The Advertiser* (4 July 1989); Satoshi Isaka, "ASEAN Reasserts Its Regional Influence at Meeting of New Economic Organization," *Japan Economic Journal* (18 Nov. 1989): 5; Daniel Sneider, "Pacific Rim Nations Strengthen Economic Ties," *CSM* (6 Nov. 1989): 10; Misuk Woo, "Toward an 'Era of Pacific' in 21st Century," *JEN* (26 Oct. 1989).

44. See statements made by various ASEAN representatives. Paul Grigson, "Split over Proposal by ASEAN Anticipated," *SMH* (8 Nov. 1989): 7; Satoshi Isaka, "ASEAN Reasserts Its Regional Influence at Meeting of New Economic Organization," *Japan Economic Journal* (18 Nov. 1989): 5; Daniel Sneider, "Pacific Rim Nations Strengthen Economic Ties," *CSM* (6 Nov. 1989): 10; Siti Rahil Dolah, "ASEAN Sensitivities Expected to Play Crucial Role in APEC," *JEN* (25 July 1990).

45. See comments of various representatives and officials from ASEAN states: Satoshi Isaka, "ASEAN Reasserts Its Regional Influence at Meeting of New Economic Organization," *Japan Economic Journal* (18 Nov. 1989): 5; "Pacific Nations to Prepare for Economic Cooperation," *JEN* (14 Sept. 1989); "Canberra's Asia-Pacific Proposal Gets Cautions Nod," *FEER* 144:19 (11 May 1989): 20.

46. "Asia, Pacific Nations Discuss Cooperation without Accord," *JEN* (7 July 1989).

47. Daniel Sneider, "Pacific Rim Nations Strengthen Economic Ties," *CSM* (6 Nov. 1989): 10.

48. "ASEAN to Be Core of Asia Pacific Grouping," *JEN* (11 Sept. 1989).

49. Louise Williams, "Indonesia Sensitive about Hawke Plan," *SMH* (23 Oct. 1989): 5.

50. Ibid.

51. "ASEAN to Be Core of Asia Pacific Grouping," *JEN* (11 Sept. 1989); "Thailand against New Economic Grouping in Asia-Pacific Region," *Xinhua* (1 Nov. 1989).

52. See, for example, Misuk Woo, "Toward an 'Era of Pacific' in 21st Century," *JEN* (26 Oct. 1989).

53. This may have been due to ASEAN's negative reaction to a similar Japanese proposal for Asia Pacific cooperation earlier.

54. Paul Grigson, "Split over Proposal by ASEAN Anticipated," *SMH* (7 Nov. 1989): 7.

55. Satoshi Isaka, "ASEAN Reasserts Its Regional Influence at Meeting of New Economic Organization," *Japan Economic Journal* (18 Nov. 1989): 5. See also comments of one Thai official at the meeting, cited in Daniel Sneider, "Pacific Rim Nations Strengthen Economic Ties," *CSM* (6 Nov. 1989): 10.

56. See comments of U.S. Assistant Secretary of State for East Asian Affairs Richard Soloman and of a Tokyo foreign ministry official. Siti Rahil Dolah, "ASEAN Sensitivities Expected to Play Crucial Role in APEC," *JEN* (25 July 1990). See also Susumu Awanohara, "US Seeks Role in Widening Regional Economic Links," *FEER* 40 (5 Oct. 1989): 28.

57. See also Beeson 1999.

58. Bodde 1994: 37; Siti Rahil Dollah, "Asean Sensitivities Expected to Play Crucial Role in APEC," *JEN* (25 July 1990).

59. See Kahler 1994: 19–21.

60. Joint Statement, First APEC Ministerial Meeting, 6–7 Nov. 1989 on APEC website.

61. Chairman's Summary Statement, First APEC Ministerial Meeting, 6–7 Nov. 1989 (on APEC website, www.apec.org/). Also mentioned was the PECC, which also felt some rivalry with APEC.

62. WTO website, www.wto.org/.

63. As one illustration of how the MITI idea became very much Mahathir's, MITI officials in a 1998 interview session were loath to answer any questions on the EAEG, repeatedly answering that it was best to "ask Dr. Mahathir!" Confidential interview with author, MITI, Kuala Lumpur, February 1998.

64. Mahathir, "EAEC Idea Born of Frustration with West." *Nikkei Weekly* (5 February 1996): 19.

65. Nesadurai, 2000: 88.

66. Camroux 1994.

67. Quoted in George White and Teressa Watanabe. "Asian Economic Unity?" *Los Angeles Times* (4 March 1991): D1.

68. Dirlik 1992: 70–73.

69. See, for example, the opening statement of Lee Kuan Yew at 1987 AMM in ASEAN n.d. *20th AMM*.

70. Siddhi Savetsila 1988: 6–11.

71. Lim 1990: 21, 24–26.

72. "Malaysia Pressing for Asia 'common market,'" *Tin International* 2:64 (February 1991): 4.

73. Lim 1990: 24–26.

74. Chia (1998): 229. See also Lim 1996: 21, 24–26; Lim Chong Yah. Ahirudin Attan, "ISIS: Proposed Grouping Is to Counter Trading Blocs," *Business Times* (January 16, 1991) and B. K. Hoo, "More Positive Response to Economic Grouping Concept," (Malaysia) *Star* (January 16, 1991).

75. Lim 1990: 21, 24–26.

76. See, for example, Kahler 1994: 20; Dirlik 1992, 66–67; 70–93.

77. Baker 1995, 609. See also comments of U.S. Vice President Dan Quayle. "Asia Pacific Trade Blocs: Fortress or Fantasy," *FEER* (25 July 1991): 54.

78. In Baker's account, he also reveals that South Korea had, in fact, been sympathetic to the EAEG and the cause of "Asian solidarity" but was persuaded by the United States not to support it (Baker 1995, 609–611). For a discussion on Japan's views and the effect of U.S. pressure, see Terada 2003.

79. Baker quoted in Kaur, "U.S. All Out to 'Kill' the EAEC," *Business Times* (Malaysia) (6 Oct. 1995): 1.

80. "KL Pushes Ahead with Proposal on Asian Grouping," *JP* (17 Jan. 1992): 1; Vincent Lingga, "Indonesia Submits Items for CEPT," *JP* (24 Jan. 1992): 1.

81. See also comments of Malaysian FM Datuk Abu Hassan Omar. Michael Vatikiotis. "Little to Show at APEC's First Major Meeting." *FEER* (9 Aug. 1990): 9.

82. "ASEAN Adopts Common Tariffs on Imports," *Journal of Commerce* (1 Nov. 1990): 3A.

83. "Indonesia Urges New Approach for ASEAN Cooperation," *Xinhua* (30 Oct. 1990); "Ministers Alarmed over Stalled Uruguay Round," *UPI* (30 Oct. 1990). See also comments of Noordin Sopiee in Joyce Quek and Bernard Simon, "Asean Tries to Avoid Relegation to the Periphery," *Financial Times* (11 Sept. 1990): 7.

84. See comments of Singapore Trade Minister Mah Bow Tan quoted in "Singapore Reluctant to Join Trade Bloc," *Central News Agency* (3 Jan. 1991).

85. "Singapore Prime Minister in Malaysia to Hold Talks with Mahathir," *Bernama* (12 Jan. 1991).

86. "Singapore Supports Formation of Asian Economic Group," *JEN* (13 Jan. 1991).

87. "Thai Foreign Minister on Malaysian Proposal for East Asian Economic Grouping," *Xinhua* (16 Jan. 1991).

88. "Thai, Singapore Foreign Ministers Hold Talks," *Xinhua* (26 Jan. 1991); David Sanger, "Malaysia Trading Plan Seeks a Unified Voice," *New York Times* (12 Feburary 1991).

89. Lim Siong Hoon, "Malaysia's Brainchild Proves Problem for Partners," *Financial Times* (6 February 1991): 8.

90. See comments of Malaysian foreign minister Abu Hassan Omar. "Malaysia's Proposed Economic Bloc No Alternative to Multilateralism," *Bernama* (23 Jan. 1991)/BBC Summary of World Broadcasts (24 Jan. 1991).

91. "Malaysia's Proposed Economic Bloc No Alternative to Multilateralism," *Bernama* (23 Jan. 1991)/BBC Summary of World Broadcasts (24 Jan. 1991); "Malaysia Pressing for Asia 'Common market,'" *Tin International* 2:64 (February 1991): 4; David Sanger, "Malaysia Trading Plan Seeks a Unified Voice," *New York Times* (12 Feburary 1991).

92. Per an informal Malaysian government paper on the EAEG. Gwen Robinson, "Voice of East Asia Needs Choral Backing," *JEN* (2 March 1991); "Malaysia Urges Japan to Join East Asia Trade Bloc," *Bernama* (25 February 1991).

93. "Plan for ASEAN Summit Discussed by Singaporean, Indonesian Leaders," *Xinhua* (4 March 1991).

94. "Reactions Mixed to Call for Economic Grouping," *Japan Economic Journal* (16 March 1991).

95. See, for example, sentiments of Goh Chok Tong in "Goh Sees Benefits from Trade Bloc," *Business Times* (14 Jan. 1991); Philippines' Secretary of Foreign Affairs Domingo Siazon in Siazon 1995: 24–25; and former Philippine finance minister Cesar Virata quoted in Ahirudin Attan, "ISIS: Proposed Grouping Is to Counter Trading Blocs," *Business Times* (16 January 1991).

96. As stated by one observer describing the views of ASEAN delegates at the 1991 APEC meeting in Seoul. Gwen Robinson, "Asia Forum Cutting Political Teeth," *Nikkei Weekly* (23 Nov. 1991).

97. Koh quoted by Terada 2003: 260.

98. See Vatikiotis 1993: 360–361.

99. The first was a private gathering of senior officials at APEC March 4–5 in Cheju, South Korea; the second was a SEOM on March 17. "Trade Bloc Not Endorsed," *Courier Mail* (18 March 1991).

100. "Malaysian Trade Minister Defends Trade Zone Idea," *JEN* (6 April 1991).

101. There were reports that it was Singapore's idea to characterize the EAEG as a consultative forum. Both the PECC and Goh's arguments to Japan took place in May 1991.

102. See Michael Vatikiotis, "ASEAN: Initiatives Test," *FEER* (11 July 1991):13.

103. Joint Statement of 23rd ASEAN Economic Ministers Meeting, Malaysia (7–8 Oct. 1991) at www.aseansec.org.

104. See comments of Dhanabalan above, also comments made by Abdul Jabar, Malaysia's spokesman for the Malaysian Embassy in Washington, DC. See "ASEAN Called on to Step up Common Trade Arrangements," *JP* (13 Jan. 1992).

105. See "ASEAN Called on to Step up Common Trade Arrangements," *JP* (13 Jan. 1992); "KL Says RI Undercuts its Palm Oil Market," *JP/AFP* (5 June 1992); George White and Teressa Watanabe, "Asian Economic Unity ?": D1; Tyabji 1990: 33.

106. ASEAN Secretariat (1992).

107. See, for example, various comments by ministers. "Philippines Urges EC-type Economic Pact for ASEAN," *Central News Agency* (31 July 1991); Peter Kandiah, "ASEAN Hammers out Brass-Tack Plans," *Nikkei Weekly* (3 Aug. 1991): 20.

108. Mark Magnier, "SEA Trade Zone Backed by Leaders," *Journal of Commerce* (22 June 1991): 1A.

109. See Singapore Declaration of 1992, ASEAN website.

110. Quoted by Antolik 1992: 145.

111. The CEPT scheme also included a fast-track scheme under which tariffs for fifteen product groups (vegetables, oils, fertilizer, rubber products, pulp and paper, wooden and rattan furniture, gems and jewelry products, cement, pharmaceuticals, plastics, leather products, textiles, ceramics and glass products, copper cathodes, and electronics) would be lowered to 0 to 5 percent by 2003.

112. This would become the "10 minus X" principle with the addition of new membership.

113. See Article I, Paragraph 3 in "Framework Agreement on Enhancing ASEAN Economic Cooperation, 28 Jan. 1992," reprinted in ASEAN 1992–, 7.

114. See Section 8 in "Singapore Declaration of 1992," in ASEAN 1992–: 19–20.

115. See Singapore Declaration, in ASEAN 1992.

116. For example, how to determine ASEAN content, rules of fair competition, and the harmonization of standards. The 1992 CEPT scheme was also criticized for its lack of a dispute settlement mechanism.

117. As one ASEAN official put it, for example, "In principle, we don't want to lose our identity. ASEAN will be the basis of unity for us." Misuk Woo, "Toward an 'Era of Pacific' in 21st Century," *JEN* (26 Oct. 1989).

118. Joyce Quek and Bernard Simon, "ASEAN Tries to Avoid Relegation to the Periphery," *Financial Times* (11 Sept. 1990): 7; Sopiee 1996.

119. See, for example, Goh Chok Tong, "Regionalism and Multilateral Trade: Discovering Ways Forward," Speech to Tenth International General Meeting of the Pacific Economic Cooperation Council Conference, March 1994.

120. See comments of Tommy Koh. "Business Affairs" *FEER* (31 Jan. 1991), 32.

121. Corazon Aquino in "Philippines Urges EC-type Economic Pact for ASEAN," *Central News Agency* (31 July 1991).

122. Anand quoted in "Thai Prime Minister at ASEAN Summit Foresees a New Era for Southeast Asia," *Bernama* (27 Jan. 1992)/BBC Summary of World Broadcasts (30 Jan. 1992).

123. Siazon 1995.

CHAPTER 6

1. "Economic, Security Issues Dominate ASEAN Summit," *Indonesia Times* (15 Dec. 1987).

2. See "Pragmatic Politics" (Interview with Lee Kuan Yew (31 May 1990); Siti Rahul Dollah, "ASEAN Hopes Bush Trip Will Ease US-Japan Trade Friction," *JEN* (31 Dec. 1991). See also Leifer 1996.

3. Daniel Williams, "Rebuilding Military Ties to Tokyo," *Washington Post* (19 Feb. 1995), A48.

4. Indonesia was also concerned about the inclusion of the Natuna Island area in Chinese maps.

5. Leifer 1996: 17, 35.

6. Lee 1997; Wanandi 1996a.

7. Whiting 1997; Ba 2003.

8. See, for example, *Bernama*, "Aquino's comments in "Philippine President Interviewed on ASEAN Relations," BBC Summary of World Broadcasts (25 Aug. 1986).

9. See Fernando del Mundo, "Aquino Claims Power over Nuke Ban Issue," *UPI* (June 21, 1988).

10. Yasmin Arquiza, "Senate Gives Final Approval to Anti-Nuclear Bill," *AP* (6 June 1988)

11. This legislation basically reinserted (though not explicitly) a clause on the Philippines' support for an SEANWFZ that had been taken out of the draft constitution.

12. See Manglapus' comments cited in Cameron Forbes, "Manila Bets Both Ways," *SMH* (14 Dec. 1987): 11.

13. Antolik 1990: 162, 82. See also Ramon Isberto, "Philippines: Insists Asia Must Share Burden of US Bases." *Inter Press Service* (May 4, 1990); "Security in Southeast Asia," *JP* (16 Nov. 1987). Philippine officials have also expressed the view that U.S. bases may actually detract from Philippine security by making the Philippines more of a military target. See Aquino's comments in Robert Reid, "Aquino: Bases to Be Determined Primarily By Filipino Not Regional Interests," *AP* (September 14, 1989).

14. As discussed in Chapter 3, that predicament reflected the tension between the perceived need for some degree of security commitment from greater powers and ASEAN states' interest and desire to be architects of their own destiny.

15. For discussion, see Wurfel 1990: 170–171.

16. Apparently, nearly half the Senate had gone on record saying exactly that.

17. See Keith Richburg, "Filipinos Irritated by What They Describe as U.S. Interference," *Washington Post* (1 Nov. 1986): A20.

18. "Staying on in the Pacific," (London) *Times* (31 March 1988). See also Manglapus's comments in same article.

19. Humphrey Hawksley, "Takeshita Puts 2 Billion Dollars Seal on ASEAN Summit: Japan Aid Package Underlines Key Role in South-East Asia," (London) *Times* (16 Dec. 1987).

20. Raul S. Manglapus (op ed), "Blaming the Philippines," *Washington Post* (21 Sept. 1988): A19.

21. Keith Richburg, "Japan Pledges to Aid Southeast Asia," *Washington Post* (16 Dec. 1987): A38; Manglapus 1987.

22. Humphrey Hawksley, "Aquino Ruffles ASEAN Calm on US Bases Issue," (London) *Times* (15 Dec. 1987). See also, "Staying on in the Pacific," (London) *Times* (31 March 1988).

23. See, for example, "Decision on US Bases Affected by Singapore's Offer," *JEN* (10 Aug. 1989). See also comments of Thai Prime Minister Kukrit Pramoj in Siti Rahul, "S'Pore's Offer to Host US Bases Stirs ASEAN Controversy," *JEN* (30 Aug. 1989).

24. See comments of U.S. Ambassador Paul Wolfowitz in Michael Vatikiotis, "Nuclear-Free Plan Upsets US," *Guardian* (6 Jan. 1988).

25. Those officials included Secretary of State George Shultz, NSC Director for Asian Affairs Richard Childress, State Department Regional Affairs Director Charles Schmitz, Ambassador to Indonesia Paul Wolfowitz, Assistant Secretary of State Gaston Sigur, and President Ronald Reagan.

26. Quoted by Luhilima 1992.

27. V. Tenorio, "Offer by Singapore Affects US Bases," *SMH* (8 Aug. 1989): 11.

28. Peter Hastings, "ASEAN's Uncertainty over Glasnost," *SMH* (21 Aug. 1989): 16.

29. See "Unease over Bases," *JP* (13 Jan. 1992).

30. N. Balakrishnan and Michael Vatikiotis, "Blood and Money," *FEER* (1 March 1990); Paul Jacobs, "Move Should Not Cause Concern," *ST* (10 Jan. 1992).

31. Lim Siong Hoon, "Kuala Lumpur, Singapore Clash over US Bases," *Financial Times* (11 Aug. 1989): 3; Keith Richberg, "Southeast Asia Debates U.S. Security Umbrella," *Washington Post* (21 Aug. 1989): A18; "Malaysia Ticks off Singapore over US Bases," *JEN* (10 Aug. 1989).

32. UMNO's youth wing is also sometimes used to express more strongly senti-ments of more diplomatically constrained officials. "Mahathir's Party Opposes U.S. Bases in Singapore," *JEN* (16 Aug. 1989).

33. "US Bases Issues High on Suharto-Lee Summit Agenda," *JEN* (5 Oct. 1989).

34. [No Title] Reuter / *SMH* (15 Aug. 1989): 9.

35. Quoted in Siti Rahil, "S'Pore's Offer to Host US Bases Stirs ASEAN Con-troversy," *JEN* (August 30, 1989).

36. Sayidiman Suryohadiprojo, "Opinions Vary over US-S'pore Agreement," *JP* (July 9, 1992).

37. "Decision on US Bases Affected by Singapore's Offer," *JEN* (10 Aug. 1989). See also Ortiz 1991.

38. "Malaysian Prime Minister Opposes Permanent US Bases in Singapore," BBC Summary of Worldbroadcasts (16 Aug. 1989). See also Siti Rahul, "S'Pore's Of-fer to Host US Bases Stirs ASEAN Controversy," *JEN* (30 Aug. 1989).

39. "No US Base in Singapore," *SMH* (9 Oct. 1989): 12.

40. The announcement was made January 5. Mahathir went on record January 6 and Indonesia January 7 stating that they had no objections to the additional arrange-ments. See "Mahathir Allays Fears over US Naval Shift to Singapore," *JEN* (6 Jan. 1992); "Southeast Asia Open to More U.S. Military," UPI (7 Jan. 1992).

41. Malaysian Foreign Minister Abu Hassan Omar quoted in "Malaysia Reiter-ates Stance," *JEN* (November 13, 1990).

42. In the case of Indonesia, which had been most publicly opposed to the bases, there were reports that Suharto sent his Defense Minister General Benny Murdani to lobby Manila privately to keep the bases. See Tom Fawthrop, "Following Destiny and Sukarno's Ghost," *SMH* (10 Sept. 1988): 24; Wanandi 1991.

43. See Peter Osbourne, "ASEAN Sets Directions," *Australian Financial Times* (23 April 1992); Reuter, "US Pondering . . . " *JP* (4 January 1992): 3.

44. "Decision on US Bases Affected by Singapore's Offer," *JEN* (10 Aug. 1989). See also comments of Thai Prime Minister Kukrit Pramoj in Siti Rahul, "S'Pore's Offer to Host US Bases Stirs ASEAN Controversy," *JEN* (30 Aug. 1989).

45. The study was published in Telstra, published by Indonesia's government-run National Institute of Defense. "Study Calls for US Bases to Remain in Philippines," *SMH* (14 Oct. 1989): 20.

46. See, for example, AFP, "News Leak Delays . . ." *JP* (6 Jan. 1992); Wanandi 1996a, 128; AFP, "Malaysia Supports US, Britain Presence in Asia" *JP* (16 April 1997): 6; Leifer 1996: 7.

47. Siti Rahil Dollah, "US Negotiating Access to ASEAN Nations," *JEN* (9 Nov. 1990).

48. Siti Rahul Dollah, "Singapore-US Military Facilities Pact Sets Regional Trend," *JEN* (13 Nov. 1990).

49. See also Wanandi's comments in Keith Richburg, "Many Asians Fear Poten-tial Military Threat From Japan," *Washington Post* (4 Aug. 1990): A18; Shiro Yone-nama, "Manglapus Seeks 'Equitable' Philippine-US Relations," *JEN* (11 Nov. 1989).

50. Don Oberdorfer, "US-Japan Relations Seen Suffering Worst Downturn in Decades," *Washington Post* (1 March 1992): A1, 26.

51. William Dobson, "Now Vietnam Needs America to Ward off China," *CSM* (17 April 1997).

52. Every opening statement at the 1992 AMM made mention of the South China Sea.

53. "Worries about China," *Asia Week* (7 Aug. 1992): 20–24; and Tasker, "Facing up to Security," *FEER* (6 Aug. 1992): 8–9.

54. "Share Info on Regional Security, Minister Says," *ST* (12 March 1990). This view was also publicly expressed by ASEAN foreign ministers collectively and individually at a press conference at the 1995 AMM. See "ASEAN Says US Military Presence . . . ," (3 August 1995).

55. See, for example, the views of Alan T. Ortiz, the Philippines' National Security Adviser in 1991. Ortiz 1991.

56. Raul Manglapus, Foreign Secretary of the Philippines to the National Press Club, *Federal News Service* (1 March 1991).

57. "Philippine Minister Calls for ASEAN Defense Cooperation," *Xinhua* (25 Nov. 1989). This view would in fact grow in strength between 1989 and 1992. See comments of Anand Panyarachun in Antolik 1992.

58. See comments of Manglapus in Tim Johnson, "ASEAN Meeting to Seek Consensus on Cambodia," *JEN* (22 July 1990).

59. See Joint Communiqué of 23rd AMM (24–25 July 1990), in ASEAN 1990.

60. Djalal (2000).

61. See Joint Communiqué of the 23rd AMM (24–25 July 1990) in ASEAN 1990.

62. Sanjiv Prakash, "ASEAN Acquires New Teeth, New Words," *Defence and Foreign Affairs Strategic Policy* (November 1990): 13.

63. As one ASEAN representative concluded from the U.S. action: "There is less reason for the superpowers to court us. We have to work harder to make ourselves relevant." Sheila Tefft, "ASEAN Nations Seek to Strengthen Ties," *CSM* (1 Aug. 1990): 4.

64. See, for example, discussion in Nesadurai (1996).

65. Quoted in Mack and Kerr 1995, 126. See also comments of Singapore's foreign minister in Oh Kwee Ngor, "Wanted: Peace, Freedom and Neutrality," *JEN* (1 Dec. 1990).

66. For a more extended discussion, see Caballero-Anthony 2005: 124.

67. Philippine sources cited in "Philippines to Seek Foreign Advice on US Military Bases," *Xinhua* (9 March 1991).

68. See Manglapus' comments to 1991 AMM. "Masanori Kikuta, "ASEAN Consensus Emerging on Need for Security Talks," *JEN* (19 July 1991).

69. Manglapus 1991.

70. Manglapus 1991.

71. ASEAN diplomat cited in Ruth Youngblood, "Security Issue Likely to Dominate Talks between Asians, Allies," *UPI* (21 July 1991).

72. See, especially, discussion in Chapter 5 in Caballero-Anthony 2005.

73. Masanori Kikuta, "ASEAN Consensus Emerging on Need for Security Talks," *JEN* (19 July 1991).

74. 1991 Joint Communiqué of 24th AMM, in ASEAN 1991.

75. Mervin Nambiar, "Japan Calls for Security Talks between ASEAN and Trading Partners," *AFP* (22 July 1991). See also comments of Ali Alatas from the *Jakarta Post,* cited in "Indonesian Foreign Minister on Japan's Security Proposal," *Xinhua* (25 July 1991).

76. Caballero-Anthony 2005: 125.

77. Vatikiotis, "Crux of the Matter," *FEER* (16 Jan. 1992): 24–25.

78. Quoted in Vatikiotis, "ASEAN: United, for What?" *FEER* (20 June 1991): 28.

79. Peter Mackler, "ASEAN States Differ on Security Outlook," *JP* (24 Jan. 1992), 4.

80. While the South China Sea workshops were not officially authorized by an ASEAN decision (the way the Manila and Bangkok Seminars were), it was clearly approved by "ASEAN" in the sense that Hasjim Djalal, the workshop's initiator, solicited the support from all the ASEAN capitals in 1989. Its "ASEAN" character was then affirmed by the fact that its first meeting in 1990 limited participation to ASEAN states before extending it to all claimants in 1991.

81. The Manila and Bangkok Seminars were also cited in the 1991 communiqué as "useful and constructive building blocks" for the enhancement of regional security. In addition, the listed fora here are just the ones with formal approval from ASEAN. As part of the dialogue preceding the 1992 summit, one can also include the activities of ASEAN-ISIS and the various gatherings organized by member institutes, including the Asia Pacific Roundtables, begun in 1987. While ASEAN-ISIS was not explicitly mentioned in the 1992 Declaration, ASEAN-ISIS efforts would be explicitly commended by ministers in their 1993 communiqué. See Caballero-Anthony 2005: 162–168; and Joint Communiqué of 26th AMM in ASEAN 1994.

82. See, for example, comments of Philippine military Chief of Staff Gen. Lisandro Abadia's summary of the Manila Seminar's conclusions. Ramon Isberto, "Increased Defense Cooperation Seen," *IPS* (5 Nov. 1991).

83. "Internal Problems Remain Biggest Threat to ASEAN Security: ASEAN Experts," *Xinhua* (7 June 1991).

84. Mervin Nambiar, "Japan Calls for Security Talks between ASEAN and Trading Partners," *AFP* (22 July 1991). See also comments of Ali Alatas from the Jakarta Post, cited in "Indonesian Foreign Minister on Japan's Security Proposal," *Xinhua* (25 July 1991).

85. See, for example, comments of various ASEAN experts and Malaysian armed forces chief Gen. Hashim Mohd Ali at Manila Seminar. "Internal Problems Remain Biggest Threat to ASEAN Security: ASEAN Experts," *Xinhua* (7 June 1991); Ramon Isberto, "ASEAN to Speed up Search for New Security Order," *IPS* (1 Oct. 1991).

86. Surya Gangadharan, "ASEAN Defense Pact Looks Like Non-Starter," *IPS* (4 April 1991). Ramos and others also recognized the challenge to ASEAN core principles. See "Philippine Minister Calls for ASEAN Defense Cooperation," *Xinhua* (25 Nov. 1989).

87. "Japanese Proposal of Regional Security Dialogue Receives Mixed Response," BBC Summary of World Broadcasts (23 July 1991). See also Peter Mackler, "ASEAN States Differ on Security Outlook"; Mack and Kerr 1995: 123–124; and Kerr 1994: 397–409.

88. As Alatas described them, the JIMs were not necessarily negotiations but would provide "an informal framework for preliminary contact and hopefully an exchange of views among the contending parties." David Jenkins, "ASEAN Renews Call for Hanoi Withdrawal," *SMH* (6 July 1988): 11.

89. See 1991 AMM on Manila Seminar.

90. For Wanandi's comments, see Ramon Isberto, "ASEAN No Longer Coy about Defence Cooperation," *IPS* (10 June 1991). See also "Asia-Pacific Security Forum Based on PECC Planned," *JEN* (18 Nov. 1992).

91. Quoted in Nicholas Cumming-Bruce, "Pacific Rim States Launch Security Forum," *Guardian* (27 July 1993): 9.

92. Reginald Chua and Mary Kwang, "Signing of Pact by Vietnam, Laos Will Boost Peace, Stability," *ST* (23 July 1992).

93. Manglapus 1991.

94. On this latter point, see the 1993 Joint Communiqué of the 26th AMM, in ASEAN 1994.

95. For discussions of Indonesia's and Singapore's early reservations about engagement, see the chapters by Leifer and Khong in Johnston and Ross 1999. See also chapter by Acharya on Malaysia.

96. See, for example, Lee Siew Hua, "Light Touches for Spontaneous ARF Conversation," *ST* (25 July 1994). See also comments of Singapore's Foreign Minister Wong Kan Seng in Alex Dacanay, "ASEAN Settles Tift over Trade Forum," *Nikkei Weekly* (2 Aug. 1993): 23.

97. Ramon Isberto, "ASEAN No Longer Coy about Defence Cooperation," *IPS* (10 June 1991); "Aquino Pushes for ASEAN Security Grouping," *JEN* (6 June 1991). See also comments of Malaysian Defense Minister Najib Razak in Peter Goodspeed, "Asian Nations Tackle New Challenges: Economic, Security Concerns Top ASEAN Meeting Agenda," *Toronto Star* (21 July 1991).

98. See Ramon Isberto, "ASEAN No Longer Coy about Defence Cooperation," *IPS* (10 June 1991).

99. See comments of Secretary of State Baker. Hari Maniam, "Baker Urges Against Replacing Proven Security Arrangements That Include U.S.," *AP* (25 July 1991).

100. See, for example, Jusuf Wanandi, "Securing Asia's Future" *FEER* (July 15, 1993): 23.

101. Simon 1998.

102. See Victor Mallet . "Survey of Malaysia." *Financial Times* (28 August 1992): iv.

103. Vatikiotis, "Assessing the Threat," *FEER* (June 1991): 29; Jacob, "ASEAN Officials to Propose Roping in India and Myanmar in ARF," *ST* (10 April 1996).

104. Said Thai Deputy Foreign Minister Surin Pitsuwan, "ASEAN Will Always Have the Driver's Seat [in ARF]." Kassim, "ASEAN Will Always Have Driver's Seat," *Business Times* (25 July 1994).

105. Leifer 1996: 41.

106. Exerpts from Mahathir's Opening Statement to Fifth ASEAN Summit, in *Business Times* (15 Dec. 1995): 1.

107. "Thai Foreign Minister Backs Burma's Admission into ARF," *BP* (3 May 1996).

108. Almonte also added that as the only established regional institution in East Asia that moreover was "already in place, ASEAN offered a convenient forum for major-power dialogue at the end of the Cold War." See Almonte 1997/1998: 81. See also Wanandi, "Seeking Peace in Cambodia's Conflict," *FEER* 34; "Regional Security Depends on Big Powers," *JP* (30 May 1995).

109. See especially Leifer 1999.

110. See Concept Paper for the Establishment of an ASEAN Defense Ministers Meeting on ASEAN website. According to that paper, ASEAN defense officials have regularly participated in ARF meetings, ARF Senior Officials' Meeting

(ARF-SOM), ARF Inter-Sessional Group on Confidence Building Measures (ARF-ISG-CBM), the ARF Security Policy Conference (ASPC), and the ARF Defence Officials' Dialogue (ARF-DOD).

111. See Mazen Nagi, "ASEAN Should Declare Itself Boldly as Nuclear Free Zone," *ST* (2 Oct. 1995).

112. Bertha Henson, "EAEC and Amity Two Hottest Issues," *ST* (23 Jan. 1992); see also Manibhandu and Chetchotiros, "Govt Pushes for Wider Backing," *BP* (23 Jan. 1992); AFP, "Anand Wants Big Five to Sign ASEAN Treaty" *JP* (Jan. 1992) 1.

113. Alatas in "Personalities and Policies," *Business Times* (24 July 1993).

114. Full text available at www.ASEANsec.org.

115. Emphasis added. See Protocol Amending the Treaty of Amity and Cooperation in Southeast Asia, Manila, 15 Dec. 1987 on ASEAN website.

116. One immediate reason for the protocol was to allow Papua New Guinea (a state "outside Southeast Asia") to participate in what had been an exclusively Southeast Asian treaty. The desire to include but not include PNG in ASEAN processes also speaks to the fuzziness of the Southeast Asian concept at the margins.

117. "Anand Wants Big Five to Sign ASEAN Treaty," *JP/AFP* (20 January 1992): 1.

118. See "ASEAN Officials Feel Need to Review ZOPFAN," (23 Feb. 1993). See also, Alatas' comments in "Personalities and Policies," *Business Times Weekend Edition* (24 July 1993): 2.

119. See also "ASEAN Scraps Plans . . ." *AFP* (24 Jan. 1992).

120. "ASEAN Finalizing Nuclear Free Zone Treaty" *JP* (13 Oct. 1995); Yang Razali Kassim, "Don't See ARF as Problem Solving Tool," *Business Times* (27 July 1994); Kavi Chongkittavorn, "ASEAN Summit in Bankok," *Nation* (26 July 1993): 6.

121. See "ASEAN Has Plan of Action to Create Zone of Peace, Neutrality" *ST* (26 July 1993): 22.

122. See ASEAN Joint Communiqué, 25 July 1998 on ASEAN website; see also, "India Agrees to Sign TAC Protocol," (Bangkok) *Nation* (24 Aug. 1998).

123. Christine T. Tjandraningsih, "Questions Still Spread over Meaning of Pact," *JEN* (10 Dec. 1995).

124. Lee Siew Hua, "Arms-Free Zone Pact 'Must Have N-Powers' Backing to be Effective,' " *ST* (12 Dec. 1995).

125. Leifer 1996.

126. "Nuclear Freedom in ASEAN" *NST* (11 Dec. 1995).

127. All but the Philippines have since ratified.

128. Leifer 1996: 53.

129. See Wanandi 1997: 192. See also, Hernandez 1995b: 31.

130. See comments of Alatas in Kassim, "ASEAN Member States Agree on US Presence," *BT* (29 Oct. 1992); "ASEAN Says US Military Presence Welcome, but Not Bases," *JEN* (3 August 1995).

131. Leifer 1996. See also Emmers (2003), who describes an unconventional "balance of power" approach reflective of ASEAN states' material constraints, whereby power is constrained not by military power but through political channels.

132. Reuters, "Japan PM Talks on ASEAN in KL," *JP* (9 Jan. 1997), 11.

133. Michael Leifer has been a strong proponent of this view. See Leifer, "ASEAN Bigger Does Not Mean More Clout," *ST* (3 July 1997); and Leifer 1996.

CHAPTER 7

1. "East Asian Shipwreck," *Financial Times* (16 February. 1998).

2. See, for example, Godement 1999; Haggard 2000; Jomo 1998; Noble and Ravenhill: 2000; Sachs 1998a; Wade 2000; Wang 2000; See also, McLeod and Garnaut 1998.

3. See especially Ravenhill 2001: 106–108. As Ravenhill puts it, Canberra (and Washington) won over Suharto with a successful appeal to his vanity.

4. See Ravenhill 2001: 107–108.

5. Elek 2003: 262–5.

6. Bodde 1994: 37. Bodde was U.S. ambassador and first executive director of the APEC Secretariat.

7. See, for example, discussion of U.S. pressure on Japan and Korea in Kwon 2002: 190–193.

8. Bodde 1994: 37.

9. Just as Indonesia became known as "Mr. No" in early intra-ASEAN trade liberalization debates, Malaysia acquired the same moniker among many in APEC. Informal conversation with Korean foreign ministry officer.

10. Kamachy Sappani, "ASEAN Slams US, Canada over Trade Talks," *JEN* (30 July 1990); Michael Vatikiotis, "Little to Show at APEC's First Major Meeting," *FEER* (9 Aug. 1990): 9.

11. See Cossa 2003. See also Crone 1993 for discussion of ASEAN's earlier concerns.

12. Gallant and Stubbs 1997.

13. "PM Mahathir Satisfied with Action Agenda." *BBC Summary of World Broadcasts* (19 November 1995).

14. This is according to Philippines' former foreign minister Domingo Siazon. See Terada 2003.

15. Yang Razali Kassim, "Prospective EAEC Members Hold Talks, Agree to Meet More Often," *Business Times* (26 July 1994).

16. See Terada 2003: 254, 261–262.

17. Mahbubani 1995.

18. Lee Kuan Yew and Mahathir especially associated with Asian values arguments. See, for example, Mahathir and Ishihara 1995; Zakaria 1994. These arguments started to gain prominence in 1992.

19. Anwar 1996.

20. In addition to foreign and finance ministers, economic ministers have also met on a regular basis. There have also been ministerial-level meetings (though less regular and less frequent) on the environment, migration, science and technology, and labor and employment.

21. See "The Asia Europe Meeting," available online at http://ec.europa.eu/external_relations/ASEM/intro/index.htm.

22. See Yeo 2000.

23. See Anthony Blass, "Bad Omen for America?" *Nation* (March 2, 1996): A5. See also ASEM website: http://ASEM.inter.net.th/ASEMinfo/background.html.

24. See also Narramore 1998.

25. "Singapore Prime Minister in Malaysia to Hold Talks with Mahathir," *Bernama* (12 Jan. 1991). Many in ASEAN were already noting the contradiction and

"paradox" of U.S. policies as early as 1991, but the issues in APEC and the actual emergence of NAFTA made those concerns more real. See Edith Terry, "Asia's Rising Star," *Globe and Mail* (24 Dec. 1991).

26. See Stubbs 2002.

27. Writes Yeo, "For the Asians, the political symbolism of having sixteen European leaders journey to Bangkok was in and of itself important. It was to be a symbol of Asia's new status on the world stage, and Europe'a recognition of that status" (Yeo 2000: 117).

28. Yang Razali Kassim, "Asia-Europe Summit to Debut in March in Bangkok," *Business Times* (4 May 1995).

29. Gilson 2002.

30. Jaqueline Lee, "Burma Issue Highlights Conflicting Cultures," *IPS* (17 Feb. 1997).

31. See comments of Tommy Koh in "ASEM Gives ASEAN Clout," AsiaWeek (14 Feb. 1997); and Philippine Foreign Minister Siazon in Lee, "Burma Issue Highlights Conflicting Cultures."

32. Stubbs 2002.

33. Milner 2003: 285–6.

34. Higgott and Phillips 2000: 360.

35. Berger 1999.

36. Solingen 2001: 518.

37. Higgott and Phillips, 2000: 363. See also "Asian Shipwreck"; "Asian Safety Net," *JP* (29 Sept. 1997): 4.

38. Tay, Estanislao, and Soeastro 2001: 208.

39. See, for example, opening statements of ASEAN ministers and leaders at July 1997 AMM (on ASEAN website).

40. "Asian Safety Net," *JP* (29 Sept. 1997): 4.

41. The passage was initiated by Thailand's foreign minister Prachuab Chaiyasarn. See Susanne Ganz, "ASEAN Urges Cooperation to Stop Currency Speculation," *JEN* (25 July 1997).

42. Anil Penna, "ASEAN to Push IMF for Rules to Rein in Financial Speculators," *AFP* (19 Sept. 1997).

43. Cited in Anil Penna, "ASEAN Puts Regional Monetary Fund Proposal on Ice," *AP* (19 Sept. 1997).

44. "ASEAN to Use Collective Strategy to Counter 'Economic War': Malaysia's Anwar," *AFX* (4 Sept. 1997).

45. "ASEAN to Mount Collective Action to Beat Speculation," *AFP* (4 Sept. 1997).

46. The original agreement was described as "an ASEAN reciprocal currency or 'swap' arrangement which would provide immediate short term credit facilities for emergency foreign exchange financing to an ASEAN country with temporary international liquidity problems." See Joint Communiqué of Second Heads of Government Meeting, 4–5 Aug. 1977, ASEAN website. The agreement was then extended in five-year increments.

47. "ASEAN Inks Customs Pact, to Promote Finance Cooperation," *JEN* (1 March 1997).

48. Ted Berdacke, "SE Asia to Explore Currency Fund Plan," *Financial Times* (3 March 1997): 4.

49. Elaine Lim, "Buffer Fund to Weather Disruptions," *NST* (2 March 1997): 3.

50. "Asian Safety Net," *JP* (29 Sept. 1997): 4.

51. See, for example, P. Parameswaran, "Rupiah Crashes as SE Asia's Currency Turmoil in Fourth Month," *AFP* (3 Oct. 1997).

52. Jirapreey Keawkumnurdpong, "Currency Crisis Hits ASEAN Fund," *Nation* (27 Aug. 1997).

53. Ravi Velloor and Edward Tang, "Regional Support Fund on the Cards at ASEAN Meet," *ST* (19 Sept. 1997).

54. Thomas Crampton, "ASEAN States Seek Regional Fund," *IHT* (20 Sept. 1997): 13.

55. Patrick McDowell, "Southeast Asian Regional Currency Decision Mooted," *AP* (September 18, 1997).

56. For a discussion of Japan's motivations behind the AMF proposal, see Altbach 1997.

57. Direct contributors to Thailand's rescue package were International Monetary Fund (IMF), Japan, Thailand, China, Hong Kong, Indonesia, South Korea, Malaysia, and Singapore. Sakakikara Eisuke had been interested in an AMF type fund as early as 1995. See Calder and Ye 2004.

58. See "IMF Opposed," *AFX* (23 Sept. 1997).

59. Chang and Rajan, 1999: 273; Rapkin, 2001: 375.

60. See comments of Stanley Fischer, IMF First Deputy Managing Director in "IMF, Southeast Asian Finance Ministers at Odds over Rescue Fund," *AFP* (23 Sept. 1997).

61. Comments of IMF's Deputy Managing Director Stanley Fischer. "IMF, Southeast Asian Finance Ministers at Odds over Rescue Fund," *AFP* (23 Sept. 1997).

62. P. Parameswaran, "Rupiah Crashes as SE Asia's Currency Turmoil in Fourth Month," *AFP* (3 Oct. 1997).

63. See statement of ASEAN secretary general Ajit Singh and Fidel Ramos (who was that year's ASEAN chair) cited in Kieron Flynn, "Southeast Asian Leaders Seek United Defense for Embattled Currencies," *AFP* (October 1, 1997).

64. "IMF, Southeast Asian Finance Ministers at Odds over Rescue Fund," *AFP* (23 Sept. 1997).

65. These conditions are according to a three-page communiqué issued following the meeting. See Al Labita, "Asian Fund Will Be Tied to IMF and not Japan, Officials Agree," *Business Times* (20 November 1997).

66. Lee Kim Chew, "Clinton Seeks to Restore Asia's Financial Stability," *ST* (25 November 1997).

67. Irene Ngoo, "Mahathir Reiterates Call to Register Currency Traders," *ST* (27 Nov. 1997).

68. Malaysian Finance Minister Clifford Herbert in "Southeast Asian Senior Officials Dismiss ASEAN Fund," *AFP* (30 Nov. 1997).

69. "Battle of Wills," *Asia Week* (20 March 1998).

70. IMF policies prolonged the period before recovery. Not only did they result in a liquidity crisis and exacerbate deflationary pressures, but they also grew the Southeast Asian population (especially in Thailand and Indonesia) that was below the poverty line. See Sachs 1998b.

71. See Terada 2003: 264–265.

72. There were also important intra-East Asian differences that stood in the way of the AMF's creation in 1998; however, my point here is to highlight how U.S. actions influenced and shifted ASEAN perceptions.

73. Chang and Rajan 1999: p. 273; Wesley 1999.

74. Higgott 1998; Webber 2001: 355. See also Beeson 2002: 11; "Opportunity Knocks," *Financial Times* (October 21, 1997); Michael Vatikiotis, "Pacific Divide," *FEER* (November 6, 1997): 14.

75. These views are most associated with Malaysia, but they were prominent even in those countries most known for their support of the United States and its policies, such as South Korea, Japan, and Thailand, as well as Malaysia and Indonesia (Milner 2003).

76. See also the conclusions of Beeson on APEC vis-à-vis the IMF (Beeson 1999).

77. "APEC Mulls Fund to Buffer Currency Attacks," *JEN* (11 Sept. 1997).

78. Nesadurai 2006.

79. Indonesian official Kobsak Chutikul quoted by Romulo T. Luib, "Begging for a More Relevant Asia-Pacific Economic Group," *Business World* (1 October 1999): 6.

80. See "APEC and the Decline of Leadership," *Business Daily* (26 November 1998).

81. Nesadurai 2006.

82. See "APEC and the Decline of Leadership," *Business Daily* (26 November 1998).

83. The Manila Framework, whose membership overlaps APEC but was created outside of APEC, can similarly be seen as "a telling commentary" on APEC's perceived problems (Ravenhill 2002: 240).

84. Rowley, "Go-Ahead Seen for Asian Bond Market Plan," *Business Times-Singapore* (28 July 2003). See also discussion in Beeson 2002b: 198.

85. See, for example, Ramcharan 2000 and Haacke 2005.

86. In 2002 Severino reflected that the extreme post-crisis assessments of ASEAN may have been the product of overly high expectations. To quote Severino, "Before the financial crisis people had an exaggerated set of expectations of ASEAN . . . When the financial crisis struck . . . the pendulum swung to the other extreme." Jake Lloyd Smith, "Five Years on the ASEAN Tiger," *SCMP* (28 October 2002): 1.

87. See discussion in Acharya 2001.

88. Kassim 2008.

89. See discussion in Beeson 2002: 197.

90. Quoted in Smith, "Five Years . . ." (28 October 2002).

91. This dynamic where ASEAN's institutional reform is driven by how outside actors view the coherence of the organization is also found in the case of ASEAN's intramural noninterference norm. For example, concerns about how Myanmar is affecting ASEAN's credibility vis-à-vis external actors appear to be a stronger force than a concern for human rights behind ASEAN's reassessment of non-interference. See, for example, Haacke 2005; Katsumata 2007; Ramcharan 2000.

92. "Relegated to the Sidelines," *Asia Week* (4 Aug. 2000).

93. See Alejandro Reyes, "Southeast Asia Adrift," *Asia Week* (September 1, 2000).

94. Berger 1999: 1024.

95. Nesadurai 2003b: 62–63.

96. Soesastro 2003.

97. See especially Ravenhill 2007.

98. Senior Thai official cited in Achara Pongvutitham, "Indonesia, Malaysia May Bow out of AFTA Tarriff Plan," *Nation (Bangkok)* (September 15, 1998).

99. "ASEAN Needs East Asian Regionalism," *JP* (30 Aug. 2000). "Coming Together," *Asia Week* (4 Aug. 2000): 73.

100. Chua Lee Hoong, "China 'Open' to FTA with ASEAN," *ST* (November 26, 2000): 10.

101. East Asian Vision Group 2001; East Asian Study Group 2002.

102. Bracken 2003.

103. Severino 2007.

104. See JMS of APT Finance Ministers, 6 May 2000. Available online at www .mofa.go.jp/region/asiapaci/asean/conference/asean3/index.html.

105. See JMS of APT Finance Ministers Meeting 2002. Available online at www .aseansec.org/4918.htm.

106. Brunei, Indonesia, Japan, Korea, Philippines, Thailand, Vietnam.

107. Quoted in the "Joint Statement of East Asia Cooperation," Nov. 28, 1999; accessed at www.mofa.go.jp/region/asia-paci/ASEAN/pmv9911/joint.html. See also JMS of APT Finance Ministers, 6 May 2000.

108. Stubbs 2002.

109. Hew 2006.

110. Asian Development Bank 2008, Chapter 5.

111. Japan Ministry of Finance at www.mof.go.jp/english/if/as3_070505.htm.

112. See comments by various ASEAN-ISIS representatives in "We Must Stick Together," *Asia Week* (1 Sept. 2000).

113. Hernandez quoted in Reyes, "Southeast Asia Adrift."

114. Wanandi 2000. See also Eric (Chu Cheow) Teow. "Challenges to East Asia." *Asiaweek.* (15 September 2000): 129.

115. Hew and Anthony 2000.

116. "'ASEAN Plus 3' Should be Called E. Asia Economic Group." *JEN* (4 August 2003).

117. Confidential Interview with author, Ministry of Industry and Trade, Kuala Lumpur, Aug. 2002.

118. P. Parameswaran, "Malaysian Proposal for 'ASEAN Plus Three' Secretariat Evokes Fears," *AFP* (26 July 2002).

119. Kavi Chongkittavorn, "The Future of ASEAN: ASEAN+3 or 3+ASEAN." *Korea Herald* (10 October 2002).

120. Saiful Azhar Abdullah, "Plus 3 'home' dogs Asean" *NST* (29 July 2002).

121. "ASEAN Considers Strengthening 'ASEAN plus 3' Cooperation," *JEN* (27 July 2002). See also comments of Philippine foreign minister Siazon. Saiful Azhar Abdulla, "Plus 3 'Home' Dogs ASEAN," *NST* (29 July 2002).

122. See especially comments of Siazon in Keith Richberg, "Asians, West Clash over Human Rights; Few at ASEAN See U.S. Concerns as Valid," *Washington Post* (30 July 1997).

123. See Jayakumar's "Summing Up Notes" from Joint Press Conference of first meeting of ASEM foreign ministers, 15 Feb. 1997, at Japan Ministry of Foreign Affairs website at www.mofa.go.jp/policy/economy/asem/index.html.

124. See Roberto Coloma, "Asia-Europe Meeting Highlights Clash of Political Cultures," *AFP* (16 Feb. 1997).

125. Low. 2005.

126. See Kahler 2000. Kahler's economic/functional redundancy applies more to the U.S. views of APEC.

127. See Hew and Anthony 2000: 22; Narine 2002a. Noting ASEAN's weak central banking system and general lack of resources, both conclude that it is "entirely unreasonable" (to quote Narine) to expect that ASEAN could have done more.

128. See, for example, Hew and Soesastro 2003.

129. "We Must Stick . . ."

CONCLUSION

1. Thanat 1992.

2. As Hay observes, "Structural factors are certainly crucial [and] . . . While contexts present opportunities to actors, it is the conduct of these actors which determines the extent to which such opportunities are realized" (Hay 2002: 165–166).

3. Checkel 2004: 238.

4. Legro 2005.

5. As Legro argues, if change is to follow collapse, there must be some clear alternative ("replacement idea") to the old orthodoxy. See Legro 2005: 35.

6. Khong 1997, 296.

7. As Legro argues, for example, "What is key [to the consolidation of ideas] . . . is not whether the new ideas actually caused the success but whether success seems to follow the adoption of new policies, which are perceived to be the source of the desirable outcomes." See Legro 2005: 38.

8. See Hay 2002: 166.

9. See Johnston 2003b: 126 and fn 85.

10. See, for example, Beyers 2005; Brecher 1963.

11. Checkel 2005, 807.

12. Finnemore and Sikkink 1998; Haas 1990; Legro 2000; and Sikkink 1998. See also Barnett 1996 and Berger 1996.

13. See Legro 2005.

14. Pierson 2004.

15. See, for example, Blair and Hanley 2001, in which Admiral Dennis C. Blair, Commander in Chief of the U.S. Pacific Command during Clinton's second administration, adopts the language of security communities but still defines it mostly in terms of a bilateralism centered on the U.S. role (albeit an "enriched bilateralism").

16. Gershman 2002: 60.

17. Alagappa 2003: xi–xii.

18. See also Ba 2007.

19. Informal statement made in November 2005 by an Indonesian analyst just after Hughes's visit to Indonesia in October.

20. Ralph A. Cossa, "President Bush's Press Conference: Missing the Point," *Policy Forum Online*, 05-38A, Nautilus Institute, San Francisco, May 5, 2005; "Highlights: Malaysian, Singapore Press 18 Nov 05," *FBIS/WNC* (18 November 2005). Elizabeth Economy, "Losing Our Lead," *Newsday*, November 20, 2005.

21. See Hill and Tow 2002: 176–177 for a discussion of ARF as a "bridging model."

22. On the IDEA being subsumed under the APT process, see Albar 2002.

23. Terada 2006.

24. Seth Mydans, "As an Asian Century Is Planned, U.S. Power Stays in the Shadows," *NYT* ((December 13, 2005): A11; "Malaysia Defends Australia, NZ Inclusion in East Asia Summit," *Kyodo News Service* (December 12, 2005).

25. Kim 2004.

26. Borrowing from Haacke (2003) and Haas (1989)'s discussions, mostly on the Asia Pacific.

27. Nirmal Ghosh, "No Delay on ASEAN Charter," *ST* (18 Oct. 2007).

28. Tay et al. 2001.

29. See, for example, Katsumata and Tan 2007.

30. Sukma 2008.

31. Quoted in Stanley Weiss, "Sifting Schizoid ASEAN's Reality from Rhetoric," *Asia Times* (21 November 2007).

Bibliography

Abisheganaden, Felix. 1973. Southeast Asia gets nervous about peace. *Nation* (12 March).

Acharya, Amitav. 1991. The Association of Southeast Asian Nations: "Security community" or "defence community." *Pacific Affairs* 64: 159–78.

———. 1992. Regional military-security cooperation in the Third World: A conceptual analysis of the relevance and limitations of ASEAN. *Journal of Peace Research* 29: 7–21.

———. 1995. A regional security community in Southeast Asia? *Journal of Strategic Studies* 18(3): 175–200.

———. 1997. Ideas, identity, and institution-building: From the "ASEAN way" to the "Asia-Pacific way?" *Pacific Review* 10(1): 319–46.

———. 1998. Collective identity and conflict management in Southeast Asia. In *Security communities,* ed. Emanuel Adler and Michael Barnett, 198–227. Cambridge, U.K.: Cambridge University Press.

———. 2001. *Constructing a security community in Southeast Asia: The problem of regional order.* London: Routledge.

———. 2002. *Quest for identity.* Oxford, U.K.: Oxford University Press.

———. 2003/2004. Will Asia's past be its future? *IS* 28(3): 149–64.

———. 2004. Norm localization and institutional change in Asian regionalism. *IO* 58: 239–75.

Asian Development Bank. 2008. Emerging Asian regionalism. Manila: Asian Development Bank.

Adler, Emanuel. 1997. Seizing the middle ground: Constructivism in world politics. *European Journal of International Relations* 3(3): 319–63.

———. 1998. Conditions of peace. *Review of International Studies* 24(5): 165–91.

Adler, Emanuel, and Michael Barnett, eds. 1998. *Security communities.* Cambridge, U.K.: Cambridge University Press.

Aggarwal, Vinod, and Charles E. Morrison, eds. 1998. *Asia-Pacific crossroads: Regime creation and the future of APEC.* New York: St. Martin's Press.

Akrasanee, Narongchai. 1984. *ASEAN economies and ASEAN economic cooperation.* Philippines: Asian Development Bank.

Al-Ali, Nadje. 2002. Gender relations, transnational ties and rituals among Bosnian refugees. *Global Networks* 2(3): 249–53.

Alagappa, Muthiah. 1987a. ASEAN institutional framework and modus operandi: Recommendations for change. In *ASEAN at the crossroads: Obstacles, options & opportunities in economic co-operation,* ed. Noordin Sopiee, Chew Lay See, and Lim Siang Jin, 183–230. Kuala Lumpur: ISIS Malaysia.

———. 1987b. *Towards a Nuclear-Weapons-Free Zone in Southeast Asia.* Kuala Lumpur: ISIS Malaysia.

———. 1991. Regional arrangements and international security in Southeast Asia. *CSEA* 12(4): 269–301.

———. 1995a. *Political legitimacy in Southeast Asia: Quest for moral authority.* Stanford, CA: Stanford University Press.

———. 1995b. Regionalism and conflict management: A framework for analysis. *Review of International Studies* 21: 359–87.

———, ed. 1998. *Asian security practices: Material and ideational influences.* Stanford, CA: Stanford University Press.

———. 2003. *Asian security order.* Stanford, CA: Stanford University Press.

Albar, H. E. Dato Seri Syed Hamid. 2002. Statement to IDEA Meeting, August 12, in Tokyo, Japan.

Alburo, Florian. 1988. ASEAN initiatives for economic integration or cooperation: What's in a name? In *ASEAN economic cooperation: A new perspective,* ed. Hendra Esmara. Singapore: Chopmen Publishers.

Almonte, Jose T. 1997/1998. Ensuring the "ASEAN Way." *Survival* 39(4): 80–92.

Altbach, Eric. 1997. The Asian Monetary Fund proposal: A case study of Japanese regional leadership. *Japanese Economic Institute Report* 47: 1–14.

———. 1998. Growing pains: ASEAN at 30. *Japanese Economic Institute Report* 23.

Anderson, Benedict. 1991. *Imagined communities: Reflections on the origin and spread of nationalism.* Revised edition. London: Verso.

Antolik, Michael. 1990. *ASEAN and the diplomacy of accommodation.* Armonk, NY: M. E. Sharpe.

———. 1992. ASEAN's Singapore rendezvous: Just another summit? *CSEA* 14(2): 142–53.

Anwar, Dewi Fortuna. 1992. Indonesia in a changing regional and international environment. *IQ* 20(4): 376–94.

———. 1994. *Indonesia in ASEAN.* Singapore: ISEAS.

———. 1996. Regionalism versus globalism: A Southeast Asian perspective. *Korean Journal of Defense Analysis* 18(2): 29–52.

———. 1998. Indonesia: Domestic priorities define national security. In *Asian security practices: Material and ideational influences,* ed. Muthiah Alagappa, 477–512. Stanford, CA: Stanford University Press.

Anwar, Ibrahim. 1996. *The Asian renaissance.* Singapore: Times Books International.

Ariff, Mohamed. 1996. *AFTA in the changing international economy.* Singapore: ISEAS.

ASC. 1992. *ASEAN economic cooperation for the 1990s (A report of the ASC).* Philippines: ASEAN Secretariat and Philippine Institute for Development Studies (PIDS).

ASEAN website: www.aseansec.org/.

ASEAN. n.d. *18th AMM and PMC with the dialogue partners, Kuala Lumpur, 7–13 July 1985.* Jakarta: ASEAN Secretariat.

———. n.d. *19th AMM and PMC with the dialogue partners, Manila, 23–28 June 1986.* Jakarta: ASEAN Secretariat.

———. n.d. *20th AMM and PMC with the dialogue partners, Singapore, 15–20 June 1987.* Jakarta: ASEAN Secretariat.

———. n.d. Verbatim record of the inaugural meeting of ASEAN. In *15th Anniversary of the ASEAN, 8 August 1982.* Jakarta: ASEAN Secretariat.

———. 1986. *Statements by the ASEAN heads of government at AMMs 1968–1985.* Jakarta: ASEAN Secretariat.

———. 1988. *ADS 1967–1988.* 3rd ed. Jakarta: ASEAN Secretariat.

———. 1989. *ADS 1989.* Jakarta: ASEAN Secretariat.

———. 1991. *ADS 1989–1991.* Jakarta: ASEAN Secretariat.

———. 1992. *ADS 1991–1992.* Jakarta: ASEAN Secretariat.

———. 1994. *ADS 1992–1994.* Jakarta: ASEAN Secretariat.

———. 1995. *ASC Annual Report: 1994–5.* Jakarta: ASEAN Secretariat.

———. 1996a. *29th AMM and PMC with dialogue partners (PMC), and third ARF (ARF).* Jakarta: ASEAN Secretariat.

———. 1996b. *ASC Annual report: 1995–6.* Jakarta: ASEAN Secretariat.

———. 1996c. *ASC report 1995–6.* Jakarta: ASEAN Secretariat.

The Asia Europe Meeting. Available online at: http://ec.europa.eu/external_relations/ASEM/intro/index.htm.

ASEAN-ISIS. 1991. *A time for initiative: Proposals for the consideration of the fourth ASEAN summit.* Jakarta: ASEAN-ISIS. Asia-Pacific Economic Cooperation. Available online at: www.apec.org/.

Australia, Department of Foreign Affairs and Trade. 1997. *The new ASEAN: Vietnam, Burma, Cambodia, and Laos.* Canberra: Department of Foreign Affairs and Trade.

Ayoob, Mohammed. 1989. The Third World in the system of states: Acute schizophrenia or growing pains? *ISQ* 33(1): 67–79.

———. 1995. *The Third World security predicament: State making, regional conflict, and the international system.* Boulder: Lynne Rienner Publishers.

Ba, Alice D. 1997. The ASEAN regional forum: Maintaining the regional idea in Southeast Asia. *International Journal* (Autumn): 635–56.

———. 2003. China and ASEAN: Renavigating relations for a 21st century Asia. *Asian Survey* 43 (4): 622–47.

———. 2006. Who's socializing whom? Complex engagement and Sino-ASEAN relations. *Pacific Review* 19(2): 157–79.

———. 2007. Between China and America: ASEAN's great power dilemmas. In *China, the United States, and Southeast Asia: Contending perspectives on politics, security, and economics,* ed. Evelyn Goh and Sheldon W. Simon. New York: Routledge.

Baker, James A. III. 1995. *The politics of diplomacy.* New York: G. P. Putnam's Sons.

Baldwin, David, ed. 1993. *Neorealism and neoliberalism: The contemporary debate.* New York: Columbia University Press.

Barker, Joshua. 2004. Satellite nation: The anatomy and afterlife of developmental nationalism in Indonesia. Paper presented at Asian Nationalisms Project (Workshop II), Sept. 27.

Barnett, Michael N. 1995. The United Nations and global security: The norm is mightier than the sword. *Ethics and International Affairs* 9: 37–54.

———. 1996. Identity and alliances in the Middle East. In *The culture of national security,* ed. Peter Katzenstein, 400–50. New York: Columbia University Press.

———. 1998. *Dialogues in Arab politics.* New York: Columbia University Press.

Bates, Robert H. 1988. Contra contractarianism: Some reflections on the new insitutionalism. *Politics and Society* 16(2–3): 387–401.

Bautista, Lilia R. 1992. Developing Philippine competitiveness in global markets: Part II. *CRC staff memos, no. 28.*

Beeson, Mark. 1999. Reshaping regional institutions: APEC and the IMF in East Asia. *Pacific Review* 12(1): 1–24.

———. 2002a. East Asia and the international financial institutions: The politics of regional regulatory reform. *Southeast Asia Research Centre Working Papers No. 32.* Hong Kong: City University of Hong Kong.

———. 2002b. *Reconfiguring East Asia.* London: RoutledgeCurzon.

Bentley, G. Carter. 1986. Indigenous states of Southeast Asia. *Annual Review of Anthropology* 15: 275–305.

Berger, Mark. 1999. APEC and its enemies: The failure of the new regionalism in the Asia Pacific. *Third World Quarterly* 20(5): 1013–30.

Berger, Thomas U. 1996. Norms, identity, and national security in Germany and Japan. In *Culture of national security: Norms and identity in world politics,* ed. Peter J. Katzenstein, 317–56. New York: Columbia University Press.

Beyers, Jan. 2005. Multiple embeddedness and socialization in Europe. *International Organization* 59(4): 899–936.

Bhakti, Ikrar Nusa. 1992. Facing the 21st century: Trends in Australia's relations with Indonesia. *IQ* 20(2): 142–55.

Blair, Dennis, and John Hanley. 2001. "From wheels to webs." *Washington Quarterly* (Winter 2001): 7–17.

Bodde, William Jr. 1994. *View from the 19th floor: Reflections of the first APEC.* Singapore: ISEAS.

Boyce, Peter. 1968. *Malaysia and Singapore in international diplomacy: Documents and commentaries.* Sydney, Australia: Sydney University Press.

Bracken, Lyall. 2003. China-Southeast Asia relations: On the inside track. *Comparative Connections.* 5(3). Available online at: www.csis.org/media/csis/pubs/0303qchina_seasia.pdf.

Brecher, Mark. 1963. The subordinate state system of Southern Asia. *World Politics* 15(2): 213–35.

Busse, Nikolas. 1999. Constructivism and Southeast Asian security. *Pacific Review* 12(1): 39–60.

Buszynski, Leszek. 1987. ASEAN: A changing role. *Asian Survey* 27(7): 764–86.

———. 1994. Thailand's foreign policy: Management of a regional vision. *Asian Survey* 34(8): 721–38.

———. 1998. Thailand and Myanmar: The perils of "constructive engagement." *Pacific Review* 11(2): 290–305.

Butwell, Richard. 1964. Malaysia and its impact on the international relations of Southeast Asia. *Asian Survey* 4(7): 940–46.

———. 1965. The Philippines: Prelude to elections. *Asian Survey* 5(1): 43–48.

———. 1966. The Philippines: Changing of the guard. *Asian Survey* 6(1): 43–48.

Buzan, Barry. 1988. Southeast Asian Security Complex. *CSEA* 10(1): 1–16.

———. 1991. *People, states, and fear.* Boulder, CO: Lynne Rienner Publishers.

———. 1998. System versus units in theorizing. In *International theory and the Third World,* ed. Stephanie Neuman, 213–34. New York: St. Martin's Press.

Buzan, Barry, and Gerald Segal. 1994. Rethinking East Asian security. *Survival* 36(2): 3–21.

Caballero-Anthony, Mely. 2005. *Regional security in Southeast Asia.* Singapore: ISEAS.

Calder, Kent, and Min Ye. 2004. Regionalism and critical junctures: Explaining the "organizational gap" in Northeast Asia. *Journal of East Asian Studies* 4(2): 191–227.

Camroux, David. 1994. *"Looking east"* . . . *and inwards: Internal factors in Malaysian Foreign Relations During the Mahathir Era, 1981–1994.* Australia-Asia paper, no. 72 (October). Brisbane: Centre for the Study of Australian Asian Relations.

Carroll, Bernice. 1972. Peace research: The cult of power. *Journal of Conflict Resolution* 16(4): 585–61.

Casimiro-Ortuoste, Maria Consuelo. 1995. ASEAN regional forum: Multilateralizing security in the Asia Pacific. *Kasarinlan* 10(4): 37–46.

Centre for Democracy and Development. 2002. From regional security to regional integration in West Africa: Lessons from the ASEAN experience. Working Paper #5 (June). Available online at: www.cdd.org.uk/pdf/ECOWASworkingpaper.pdf.

Chang Li Lin and Ramkishen S. Rajan. 1999. Regional responses to the Southeast Asian financial crisis. *Australian Journal of International Affairs* 53(3): 261–81.

Checkel, Jeffrey. 1999. Norms, institutions, and national identity in contemporary Europe. *ISQ* 43: 83–114.

———. 2001. Why comply? Social learning and European identity change. *IO* 55(3): 553–88.

———. 2003. Social construction and European integration. In *European Union: Readings on the theory and practice of European integration,* 3rd edition, ed. Brent F. Nelson and Alexander Stubb. Boulder, CO: Lynne Rienner Publishers.

———. 2004. Social constructivisms in global and European politics: A review essay. *Review of International Studies* 30: 229–44.

———. 2005. International institutions and socialization in Europe. *International Organization* 59(4): 801–26.

Chia Siow Yue. 1980. ASEAN economic cooperation: Singapore's dilemma. *CSEA* 2(2).

———. 1998. The ASEAN free trade area. *Pacific Review* 11(2): 213–32.

Chiew, Eddie. 1987. ASEAN co-operation in food and agriculture: Looking back and looking forward. In *ASEAN at the Crossroads: Obstacles, options & opportunities in economic co-operation,* ed. Noordin Sopiee, Chew Lay See, and Lim Siang Jin. Kuala Lumpur: ISIS Malaysia.

Chin Kin Wah. 1995. ASEAN: Consolidation and change. *Pacific Review* 8(3): 424–39.

———. 1997. ASEAN: The long road to "one Southeast Asia." *Asian Journal of Political Science* 5(1): 1–19.

Clapham, Christopher. 1970. The context of African thought. *The Journal of African Studies* 8(1): 1–13.

Collins, Alan. 2003. *Security and Southeast Asia: Domestic, regional, and global issues.* Boulder, CO: Lynne Rienner.

Commonwealth prime ministers' conference: Prime minister's views on world situation—Southeast Asia. 1966. *Malaysian Bulletin* (October).

Cossa, Ralph A. 2003. U.S. approaches to multilateral security and economic organizations in the Asia-Pacific. In *US hegemony and international organizations,* ed. Rosemary Foot, S. Neil MacFarlane, and Michael Mastanduno, 193–215. Oxford, U.K.: Oxford University Press.

Crawford, Neta C. 2002. *Argument and change in world politics.* Cambridge, U.K.: Cambridge University Press.

Crone, Donald. 1993. Does hegemony matter? The reorganization of the Pacific political economy. *World Politics* 45: 501–25.

———. 1996. New political roles for ASEAN. In *Southeast Asia in the new world order: The political economy of a dynamic region,* ed. David Wurfel and Bruce Burton, 36–51. New York: St. Martin's Press.

Crouch, Harold. 1988. *The army and politics in Indonesia.* Revised edition. Ithaca, NY: Cornell University Press.

Cruz, Conseulo. 2000. Identity and persuasion: How nations remember their pasts and make their futures. *World Politics* 52: 275–312.

Darwanto, Herry. 1997. Trade liberalisation in Indonesia: Impacts and issues. *IQ* 25(2): 110–27.

David, Steven R. 1991. Explaining Third World alignment. *World Politics* 43(2): 233–56.

De Cunha, Derek, ed. 1996. *The evolving Pacific power structure.* Singapore: ISEAS.

Dewitt, David. 1994. Common, comprehensive, and cooperative security. *Pacific Review* 7(1): 1–15.

Dhanabalan, S. 1987a. Economically dynamic ASEAN and regional stability. *FRJ* 2(2): 154–60.

———. 1987b. Taking stock of ASEAN before looking to the future. *FRJ* 2(2): 120–22.

Diez, Thomas. 2001. Europe as a discursive battleground: Discourse analysis and European integration studies. *Cooperation and Conflict* 36(1): 5–38.

Dirlik, Arif. 1992. The Asia-Pacific idea: Reality and representation in the invention of regional structure. *Journal of World History* 3(1): 55–79.

Djalal, Hasjim. 2000. South China Sea island disputes. *The Raffles Bulletin of Zoology,* Supplement No. 8 (The Biodiversity of the South China Sea): 9–21.

Djiwandono, J. Soedjati. 1986. *Southeast Asia as a nuclear-weapons-free zone.* ASEAN series. Kuala Lumpur: ISIS Malaysia.

———. 1991. *ZOPFAN: Is it still relevant?* Jakarta: CSIS.

———. 1996. Defence cooperation between member-states of ASEAN. *IQ* 24(4): 339–51.

Dupont, Alan. 1996. Indonesian defense strategy and security: Time for a rethink? *CSEA* 18(3): 275–97.

East Asian Study Group 2002. Final report. Submitted to ASEAN Plus Three, Phnom Penh. Available online at: www.aseansec.org/4918.htm.

East Asian Vision Group 2001. Towards an East Asian community: region of peace, prosperity, and progress. Available online at: www.aseansec.org/4918.htm.

Eikenberry, Karl. 1996. China's challenge to Asia-Pacific stability. In *Southeast Asia in the new millennium,* ed. Richard Ellings and Sheldon Simon, 89–122. Armonk, NY: M. E. Sharpe.

Elek, Andrew. 2003. APEC and the construction of Pacific Rim regionalism (reviews). *Economic Record* 79(245): 262–5.

Elson, R. E. 2006. Indonesia and the West: An ambivalent, misunderstood engagement. *Australian Journal of Politics and History* 52(2): 261–71.

Emmers, Ralf. 2001. The influence of the balance of power factor within the ASEAN Regional Forum. *CSEA* 23(2): 275–91.

———. 2003. *Cooperative security and the balance of power in ASEAN and the ARF.* London: RoutledgeCurzon.

Emmerson, Donald K. 1984. "Southeast Asia": What's in a name? *Journal of Southeast Asian Studies* 15: 1–21.

———. 1994. From confrontation to cooperation in Southeast Asia: Lessons and prospects. In *The future of the Pacific Rim: Scenarios for regional cooperation,* ed. Barbara K. Bundy, Stephen D. Burns, and Kimberly V. Weichel, 156–71. Westport, CT: Praeger Publishers.

———. 1996. Indonesia, Malaysia, and Singapore: A regional security core? In *Southeast Asia in the new millennium,* ed. Richard Ellings and Sheldon Simon. Armonk, NY: M. E. Sharpe.

Esmara, Hendra. 1988. ASEAN economic cooperation: An overview of the issues. In *ASEAN economic cooperation: A new perspective,* ed. Hendra Esmara. Singapore: Chopmen Publishers.

Estanislao, Jesus. 1997. Internal dynamics of one Southeast Asia: Economic and social aspects. In *One Southeast Asia in a new regional and international setting,* ed. Hadi Soesastro, 79–82. Jakarta: CSIS.

Evans, Grant, and Kelvin Rowley. 1984. *Red brotherhood at war: Vietnam, Cambodia, and Laos since 1975.* London: Verso.

Fawcett, L., and Andrew Hurrell. 1995. *Regionalism in world politics.* Oxford, UK: Oxford University Press.

Fifield, Russell H. 1958. *The diplomacy of Southeast Asia: 1945–1958.* New York: Harper and Brothers.

Finnemore, Martha. 1996a. Institutional environments and organizations: Structural complexity and individualism. *IO* 50(2): 325–47.

———. 1996b. *National interests in international society.* Ithaca, NY: Cornell University Press.

Finnemore, Martha, and Kathryn Sikkink. 1998. International norm dynamics and political change. *IO* 52(4): 887–89.

Finnemore, Martha, and Sikkink, Kathryn. 2001. Taking stock: the constructivist research program in international relations and comparative politics. *Annual Review of Political Science* 4: 391–416.

Fisher, Charles A. 1953. The concept of South-East Asia. *Eastern World* 7(3): 12–4.

———. 1966. *South-East Asia: A social, economic, and political geography.* 2nd edition. London: Methuen & Co.

———. 1974. Geographical continuity and political change in Southeast Asia. In *Conflict and stability in Southeast Asia,* ed. Mark Zacher and R. Stephen Milne, 3–44. Garden City, NY: Anchor Books.

Friedberg, Aaron. 1993. Ripe for rivalry: Prospects for peace in multipolar Asia. *International Security* 18(3): 5–33.

Funston, John. 1999. Challenges facing ASEAN in a more complex age. *CSEA* 21(2): 205.

Gallant, Nicole, and Richard Stubbs. 1997. APEC's dilemmas: Institution-building around the Pacific Rim. *Pacific Affairs* 70(2): 203–19.

Ganesan, N. 1998. Malaysia-Singapore relations: Some recent developments. *Asian Affairs: An American Review* 25:1 (Spring 1998): 21–37.

Gershman, John. 2002. Is Southeast Asia the second front? *Foreign Affairs* 81(4): 60–74.

Ghazali Shafie, M. 1966. Permanent Secretary for Foreign Affairs, interview reprinted in *Malaysia Bulletin* (August).

———. 1975. ASEAN's response to security issues in Southeast Asia. In *Regionalism in Southeast Asia*, 23. Jakarta: CSIS.

———. 1982. *ASEAN: Contributor to stability and development.* Kuala Lumpur: Ministry of Foreign Affairs.

———. 1985. ASEAN and security. Speech to Pine Tree Club, October 27, in Singapore.

———. 1986. Security concerns in the Asia-Pacific region and prospects for regional cooperation. Paper presented at the International Seminar on Peace and Security in the Pacific. Institute of International Area Studies, Tokyo. Sept. 10–12 1986.

———. 1998. *Ghazali Shafie's memoir on the formation on Malaysia.* Bangi, Selangor: Universiti Kebangsaan Malaysia.

Gilson, 2002. *Asia meets Europe: Interregionalism and the Asia-Europe Meeting.* Cheltenham, England: Edward Elgar.

Girling, J. L. S. 1971. Regional security in Southeast Asia. *Journal of Southeast Asian studies.* 2: 56–65.

Godement, Francois. 1999. *The downsizing of Asia.* London and New York: Routledge.

Goldstein, Judith. 1993. *Ideas, interests, and American trade policy.* Cornell studies in political economy. Ithaca, NY: Cornell University Press.

Goldstein, Judith, and Robert O. Keohane, eds. 1993. *Ideas and foreign policy: Beliefs, institutions, and political change.* Cornell studies in political economy. Ithaca, NY: Cornell University Press.

Goodman, Allan. 1996. Vietnam and ASEAN: Who would have thought it possible? *Asian Survey* 36:6 (June 1996): 592–600.

Gordon, Bernard. 1963/1964. The potential for Indonesian expansion. *Pacific Affairs* 36(4): 378–93.

———. 1964. Problems of Regional Cooperation in Southeast Asia. *World Politics* 16(2): 222–53.

———. 1966. *The dimensions of conflict.* Englewood Cliffs, NJ: Prentice-Hall.

Gourevitch, Peter A. The Pacific Rim: Current debates. *Annals of the American Academy of Political and Social Science.* 505: 8–23.

Grieco, Joseph. 1997. Systemic sources of variation in regional institutionalization in Western Europe, East Asia, and the Americas. In *The political economy of regionalism*, ed., Edward Mansfield and Helen Milner. New York: Columbia University Press.

Haacke, Jurgen. 1998. The ASEANization of regional order in East Asia: A failed endeavor? *Asian Perspective* 22 (3): 7–47.

———. 2003. *ASEAN's diplomatic and security culture.* London: Routledge.

———. 2005. "Enhanced interaction" with Myanmar and the project of a security community: Is ASEAN refining or breaking with its diplomatic and security culture? *Contemporary Southeast Asia* 27(2): 188–216.

Haas, Ernst B. 1990. Reason and change in international life: Justifying an hypothesis. *Journal of International Affairs* 44(1): 209–40.

Haas, Michael. 1989. *The Asian way to peace: A story of regional cooperation.* New York: Praeger Publishers.

Haggard, Stephan. 1997. Regionalism in Asia and the Americas. In *The political economy of regionalism*, ed., Edward Mansfield and Helen Milner. New York: Columbia University Press.

———. 2000. *The political economy of the Asian financial crisis.* Washington, DC: Institute for International Economics.

Han Fook Kwang, Warren Fernandez, and Sumiko Tan. 1998. *Lee Kuan Yew: The man and his ideas.* Singapore: Straits Times Press.

Hanggi, Heiner. 1991. *ASEAN and the ZOPFAN concept.* Pacific strategic papers. Singapore: ISEAS.

Harris, Stuart. 2000. Asian multilateral institutions and their response to the Asian Economic Crisis: The regional and global implications. *Pacific Review* 13(3): 495–516.

Hasenclever, Andreas, Peter Mayer, and Volker Rittberger. 1997. *Theories of international regimes.* Melbourne, Australia: Cambridge University Press.

Hassan, Mohamed Jawhar, and Thangan Ramnath, eds. 1995. *Conceptualizing Asian-Pacific security—Papers presented at Second Meeting of CSCAP Working Group on Comprehensive Security and Cooperative Security.* Kuala Lumpur: ISIS Malaysia.

Hatch, Walter. 1996. *Asia in Japan's embrace: Building a regional production alliance.* New York: Cambridge University Press.

Hay, Colin. 2002. *Political analysis: A critical introduction.* New York: Palgrave.

Hay, Simon J. 1996. The 1995 ASEAN summit: Scaling a higher peak. *CSEA* 18(3): 254–74.

Hernandez, Carolina. 1995a. ASEAN post–Cold War security strategy for the Asia-Pacific. *Kasarinlan* 10(3): 53–74.

———. 1995b. View from the Philippines. In *Multilateral activities in South East Asia,* ed. Michael Everett and Mary A. Sommerville. Washington, DC: National Defense University.

Hettne, Björn. 1993. Neo-mercantalism: The pursuit of regionness. *Cooperation and Conflict* 28(3): 211–32.

Hew, Denis. 2006. Economic integration in East Asia: An ASEAN perspective. *UNISCI Discussion Papers.* May: 49–58.

Hew, Denis, and Mely C. Anthony. 2000. ASEAN and ASEAN + 3. *NIRA Review* Autumn: 21–6.

Hew, Dennis, and Hadi Soesastro. 2003. Realising the ASEAN economic community by 2020: ISEAS and ASEAN ISIS approaches. *ASEAN Economic Bulletin* 20(3): 292–296.

Higgott, Richard. 1994. Ideas, identity, and policy coordination in the Asia-Pacific. *Pacific Review* 7(4): 367–79.

———. 1998. The international politics of resentment: Some longer term implications of the economic crisis in East Asia. *New Political Economy* 3(3): 333–56.

Higgott, Richard, Richard Leaver, and John Ravenhill, eds. 1993. *Pacific economic relations in the 1990s: Cooperation or conflict?* Boulder CO: Lynne Reinner.

Higgott, Richard, and N. Phillips. 2000. Challenging triumphalism and convergence: The limits of global liberalization in Asia and Latin America. *Review of International Studies* 26: 359–79.

Higgott, Richard, and Richard Stubbs. 1995. Competing conceptions of economic regionalism: APEC versus EAEC in the Asia Pacific. *Review of International Political Economy* 2(3): 516–35.

Hill, Cameron J., and William T. Tow. 2002. The ASEAN regional forum: Material and ideational dynamics. In *Reconfiguring East Asia,* ed. Mark Beeson, 161–84. London: RouteldgeCurzon.

Hill, Hal. 1987. Challenges in ASEAN economic cooperation: An outsider's perspective. In *ASEAN at the crossroads: Obstacles, options & opportunities in economic co-operation*, ed. Noordin Sopiee, Chew Lay See, and Lim Siang Jin. Kuala Lumpur: ISIS Malaysia.

Hopf, Ted. 1998. The promise of constructivism in international relations theory. *IS* 23(1): 171–200.

———. 2002. *Social construction of international politics.* Ithaca, NY: Cornell University Press.

Hurrell, Andrew. 1995. Explaining the resurgence of regionalism in world politics. *Review of International Studies* 21: 332–58.

Ibrahim, Anwar. 1992. Address to Asia Society, Washington DC 21 Sept. 1992. *Foreign Affairs-Malaysia* 25 (3).

Ikenberry, John G., and Charles Kupchan. 1990. Socialization and hegemonic power. *IO* 44(3): 283–315.

Indonesia, Department of Information. 1976. *ASEAN: Towards peace, progress, and prosperity.* Jakarta: Department of Information, Indonesia.

Indonesia, Indonesian Embassy in Thailand. 1968. *The Second ASEAN Ministerial Meeting, Djakarta August 7–8.* Jakarta: Indonesian Embassy.

Indonesia, Ministry of Defence. 1995. *The policy of the state defence and security of the Republic of Indonesia.* Jakarta: Indonesia Ministry of Defence.

Innes-Brown, Marc, and Mark J. Valencia. 1993. Thailand's resource diplomacy in Indochina and Myanmar. *CSEA* 14(4).

International Relations of the Asia Pacific 5:2 (August 2005). Special Issue on Constructing Security Communities.

Jacobini, H. B. 1964. Fundamentals of Philippine policy toward Malaysia. *Asian Survey* 4(11): 1144–51.

Jakarta worried about growing Afro-Asian support for Malaysia. 1965. *Malaysian Bulletin,* June.

Japan Ministry of Finance website: www.mof.go.jp/english/if/as3_070505.htm.

Jayakumar, S. 2003. "Summing up notes" from Joint Press Conference of first meeting of ASEM foreign ministers, 15 Feb. 1997. Japan Ministry of Foreign Affairs; available online at: www.mofa.go.jp/policy/economy/asem/index.html.

Jayasuriya, Kanishka. 2003. Introduction: Governing the Asia Pacific—Beyond the "New Regionalism." *Third World Quarterly* 24(2): 199–215.

Jetly, Rajshree. 2003. Conflict management strategies in ASEAN: Perspectives for SAARC. *Pacific Review* 16(1): 53–76.

Job, Brian. 1992. *The (in)security dilemma: The national security of third world states.* Boulder, CO: Lynne Rienner Publishers.

Johnston, Alastair Iain. 2001. Treating international institutions as social environments. *ISQ* 45(4): 487–516.

———. 2003. Socialization in international institutions. In *International relations theory and the Asia-Pacific,* ed. G. John Ikenberry and Michael Mastanduno, 107–62. New York: Columbia University Press.

Johnston, Alastair Iain, and Robert S. Ross. 1999. *Engaging China: The management of an emerging power.* London and New York: Routledge.

Jomo, K. S. 1998. *Tigers in trouble.* London: Zed Books.

Jones, David Martin, and Michael L.R. Smith. 2001. ASEAN's imitation community. *Orbis* 46 (1): 93–109.

Jorgensen-Dahl, Arnfinn. 1982. *Regional organization and order in South-East Asia.* Hong Kong: MacMillan Press.

Josey, Alex. 1968. *Lee Kuan Yew,* vol. 1. Singapore: Times Books International.

Kahin, Audrey R., and George Kahin. 1995. *Subversion as foreign policy.* Seattle: University of Washington Press.

Kahler, Miles. 1994. Institution-building in the Pacific. In *Pacific cooperation: Building economic and security regimes in the Asia-Pacific region,* ed. Andrew Mack and John Ravenhill, 16–39. St. Leonards, Australia: Allen and Unwin.

———. 2000. Legalization as strategy: The Asia-Pacific case. *IO* 54(3): 549–71.

Kassim, Yang Razali. 2008. Suharto: The end of an ASEAN era. *RSIS Commentary* (27 January).

Katsumata, Hiro. 2007. Human rights and democracy: from big talk to concrete action? In Katsumata and Tan, *People's ASEAN, government's ASEAN. RSIS Monograph* #11.

Katsumata, Hiro, and Tan See Seng. 2007. *People's ASEAN and government's ASEAN.* RSIS Monograph #11.

Katzenstein, Peter J. 1996a. Regionalism in comparative perspective. *Cooperation and Conflict* 31(2): 123–59.

———, ed. 1996b. *Culture of national security: Norms and identity in world politics.* New York: Columbia University Press.

Kaye, Dalia Dassa. 2001. *Beyond the handshake.* New York: Columbia University Press.

Keck, Margaret, and Kathryn Sikkink. 1998. *Activists beyond borders: Advocacy networks in international politics.* Ithaca, NY: Cornell University Press.

Keohane, Robert O., ed. 1986 *Neorealism and its critics: New directions in world politics.* New York: Columbia University Press.

———. 1988. International institutions: Two approaches. *ISQ* 32: 379–96.

Kerr, Pauline. 1994. The security dialogue in the Asia-Pacific. *Pacific Review* 7(4): 397–409.

Khong, Yuen Foong. 1997. Making bricks without straw in the Asia Pacific. *Pacific Review* 10(2): 289–300.

Khoo, N. 2004. Deconstructing the ASEAN security community: A review essay. *International Relations of the Asia-Pacific* 4: 35–46.

Kim, Samuel. 2004. Regionalization and regionalism in East Asia. *Journal of East Asian Studies* (2004): 39–67.

Klotz, Audie 1995. *Norms in international relations: The struggle against apartheid.* Ithaca, NY: Cornell University Press.

Konjing, Khaisri. 1987. ASEAN economic cooperation on commodities: Looking back and looking forward. In *ASEAN at the crossroads: Obstacles, options & opportunities in economic co-operation,* ed. Noordin Sopiee, Chew Lay See, and Lim Siang Jin. Kuala Lumpur: ISIS Malaysia.

Kowert, Paul, and Jeffrey Legro. 1996. Norms, identity, and their limits: A theoretical reprise. In *Culture of national security: Norms and identity in world politics,* ed. Peter J. Katzenstein, 451–97. New York: Columbia University Press.

Kroef, Justus M. van der. 1970–1971. Interpretations of the 1965 Indonesian coup: A review of the literature. *Pacific Affairs* 43(4): 557–77.

———. 1982. Kampuchea: Diplomatic labyrinth. *Asian Survey* 22(10): 1009–33.

Kwon, Youngmin. 2002. *Regional community-building in East Asia.* Seoul: Yonsei University Press.

Laffey, Mark, and Jutta Weldes. 1997. Beyond belief: Ideas and symbolic technologies in the study of international relations. *European Journal of International Relations* 3(2): 193–237.

Lau Teik Soon. 1990. ASEAN diplomacy: National interest and regionalism. *Journal of Asian and African Studies* 25(1–2): 114–27.

Lee Kuan Yew. 1998. *The Singapore story.* Singapore: Simon and Schuster Asia.

———. 2000. *From Third World to First: The Singapore story: 1965–2000.* New York: Harper Collins.

Lee Lai To. 1997. East Asian assessments of China's security policy. *International Affairs* 73(2): 251–62.

Legro, Jeffrey. 2000. The transformation of policy ideas. *American Journal of Political Science* 44(3): 419–32.

———. 2005. *Rethinking the world: Great power strategies and international order.* Ithaca, NY: Cornell University Press.

Leifer, Michael. 1974. Great power intervention and regional order. In *Conflict and stability in Southeast Asia,* ed. Mark W. Zacher and R. Stephen Milne, 181–201. Garden City, NJ: Doubleday.

———, ed. 1986a. *The balance of power in East Asia.* Basingstoke, U.K.: Macmillan.

———. 1986b. The role and paradox of ASEAN. In *The balance of power in East Asia,* ed. Michael Leifer, 119–31. Basingstoke, U.K.: Macmillan.

———. 1989. *ASEAN and the security of South-East Asia.* London: Routledge.

———. 1995. Civil society In the Indonesian context (excerpt from a paper presented at a seminar titled *Indonesia and the World*). *JP* (October 23).

———. 1996. *The ASEAN Regional Forum,* Adelphi Paper 302. New York: Oxford University Press for the International Institute for Strategic Studies.

———. 1998. The ASEAN Regional Forum: A model for cooperative security in the Middle East. Working Paper 1998/1, Department of International Relations, Australian National University.

———. 1999. The ASEAN peace process: A category mistake. *Pacific Review* 12(1): 25–38.

Leong, Stephen. 2000. The East Asian Economic Caucus: "Formalized" regionalism being denied. In *National perspectives on the new regionalism in the south,* ed. Björn Hettne, András Inotai, and Osvaldo Sunkel. Houndsmill, U.K.: Macmillan.

Lestano, 1995. ASEAN economic performance. Discussion Paper 3. Centre for International Management and Development Antwerp. August.

Lim, Linda Y. C. 1990. ASEAN: New modes of economic cooperation. In *Southeast Asia in the new world order: The political economy of a dynamic region,* ed. Bruce Burton and Daniel Wurfel, 19–35. New York: St. Martin's Press.

Low, Low. 2005. Asia-Pacific Economic Cooperation (APEC): The first decade. (Book Review). *ASEAN Economic Bulletin* 22(2): 245–48.

Luhilima, C. P. F. 1987. ASEAN institutions and modus operandi: Looking back and looking forward. In *ASEAN at the crossroads: Obstacles, options & opportunities in economic co-operation,* ed. Noordin Sopiee, Chew Lay See, and Lim Siang Jin, 161–82. Kuala Lumpur: ISIS Malaysia.

———. 1992. ASEAN, the South Pacific Forum and the changing strategic environment. *IQ* 20(2): 207–18.

Macapagal, Diosdado. 1989. The Philippine claim to Sabah. *FRJ* 4(4): 160–73.

MacIntyre, Andrew. 1995. Ideas and experts: Indonesian approaches to economic and security cooperation in the Asia-Pacific region. *Pacific Review* 8(1): 159–72.

Mack, Andrew, and Pauline Kerr, eds. 1995. The evolving security discourse in the Asia-Pacific. *Washington Quarterly* 18: 123–24.

Mack, Andrew, and John Ravenhill, eds. 1994. *Pacific cooperation: Building economic and security regimes in the Asia-Pacific region*. Sydney, Australia: Allen & Unwin.

Mahathir bin Mohamad. n.d. "Keynote address to the first ASEAN economic congress." In *ASEAN at the crossroads: Obstacles, options & opportunities in economic co-operation,* ed. Noordin Sopiee, Chew Lay See, and Lim Siang Jin. Kuala Lumpur: ISIS Malaysia.

———. 1991. From confrontation to cooperation: ASEAN's agenda for a cooperative peace. Keynote speech to Bali International Conference on the ASEAN countries and the world economy: Challenge of change, March 3–5, in Bali, Indonesia.

Mahathir bin Mohamad and Ishihara, Shintaro. 1995. *The voice of Asia: Two leaders discuss the coming century.* Tokyo: Kodansha International.

Mahbubani, Kishore. 1995. The Pacific way. *Foreign Affairs* (January/February): 100–12.

Maisrikrod, Surin. 1994. "The peace dividend" in Southeast Asia: The political economy of new Thai–Vietnamese relations. *CSEA* 16(1): 46–66.

Malaya, Federation of. 1961. *ASA: Report of the first meeting of foreign ministers on economic and cultural cooperation among Southeast Asian countries and statement of policy.* Malaya: Federation of Malaya.

———. 1962. *ASA: Report of the special meeting of foreign ministers.* Malaya: Federation of Malaya.

———. 1963. *ASA: Report of the second meeting of foreign ministers.* Malaya: Federation of Malaya.

Malik, Adam. 1980. *In the service of the republic.* Singapore: Gungung Agung (S) PTE.

Manglapus, Raul S. 1987. ASEAN neutrality and the U.S. bases. *FRJ* 2(1): 147–51.

———. 1991. ASEAN security dialogue: Modality for peace. Keynote address at ASEAN and the Asia-Pacific region: Prospects for security cooperation in the 1990s conference, June 5–7, in Manila. Sponsored by Department of Foreign Affairs of the Philippines and Department of Foreign Affairs of Thailand.

Mansfield, Edward, and Helen V. Milner. 1997. *The political economy of regionalism.* New York: Columbia University Press.

Marshall, Douglas A. 2002. Behavior, belonging, and belief: A theory of ritual practice. *Sociological Theory* 20(3): 360–80.

Mauzy, Diane K. 2000. ASEAN: Challenges of regional political and economic cooperation. In *The Asia-Pacific in the new millennium,* ed. Shalendra Sharma, 257–84. Berkeley: Institute of East Asian Studies, University of California.

McCloud, Donald G. 1995. *Southeast Asia: Tradition and modernity in the contemporary world.* Boulder, CO: Westview Press.

McLeod, Ross H., and Ross Garnaut, eds. 1998. *East Asia in crisis: From being a miracle to needing one?* London: Routledge.

Meadows, Martin. 1965. Recent developments in Philippine-American relations. *Asian Survey* 5(6): 305–18.

Meow, Seah Chee. 1979. *Singapore's position in ASEAN co-operation.* Occasional Paper No. 38. Singapore: Chopmen Enterprises.

Mertus, Julie. 2000. Considering nonstate actors in the new millennium: Toward expanded participation in norm generation and norm application. *Journal of International Law and Politics* 32: 537–66.

Meyanathan, Sahathavan, and Ismail Haron. 1987. ASEAN trade cooperation: A survey of the issues. In *ASEAN at the crossroads: Obstacles, options & opportunities in economic co-operation,* ed. Noordin Sopiee, Chew Lay See, and Lim Siang Jin. Kuala Lumpur: ISIS Malaysia.

Meyer, Milton W. 1949. Regional cooperation in Southeast Asia. *Columbia Journal of International Affairs* (Spring): 68–77.

Milner, Anthony. 2003. Asia-Pacific perceptions of the financial crisis: Lessons and affirmations. *CSEA* 25(2): 284–305.

Milner, Helen. 1992. International theories of cooperation among nations: Strengths and weaknesses. *World Politics* (April): 466–96.

Mochtar, Kusuma-Atmadja. 1986. Prospects for peace in Southeast Asia. *FRJ* 1(2): 139–55.

———. 1990. ASEAN security cooperation: An Indonesian perspective. *CSEA* 12(3): 161–71.

———. 1992. The promise of the ASEAN summit. In *Southeast Asia: The way forward.* Kuala Lumpur: ISIS-Malaysia.

Moertopo, Ali. 1978. Political and economic development in Indonesia in the context of regionalism in Southeast Asia. *IQ* 6(2).

Mohamed bin Haron (Embassy of Malaysia Moscow). 1991. ZOPFAN—From conception to confusion: A personal commentary. Paper presented at ASEAN Experts Group Meeting on ZOPFAN, January 5–6. Kuala Lumpur: ISIS Malaysia.

Moller, Kay. 1998. Cambodia and Burma: The ASEAN way ends here. *Asian Survey* 38(12): 1087–104.

Nadelman, Ethan A. 1990. Global prohibition regimes. *IO* (Autumn): 479–526.

Narine, Shaun. 1997. ASEAN and the ARF: The limits of the "ASEAN Way." *Asian Survey* 37(10): 961–78.

———. 1998. Institutional theory and Southeast Asia. *World Affairs* 161(1): 33–47.

———. 2002a. ASEAN in the aftermath: The consequences of the East Asian Economic Crisis. *Global Governance* 8(2): 179–94.

———. 2002b. *Explaining ASEAN.* Boulder, CO: Lynne Rienner.

Narramore, Terry. 1998. Communities and citizens: Identity and difference. *Citizenship Studies* 2(1): 69–88.

Nathan, K. S. 1988. The role and significance of ASEAN in world politics. *Foreign Relations Journal* 3(4): 76–88.

———. 1998. Malaysia: Reinventing the nation. In *Asian security practice: Material and ideational influences,* ed. Muthiah Alagappa, 513–48. Stanford, CA: Stanford University Press.

Nesadurai, Helen. 1996. APEC: A tool for US domination? *Pacific Review* 9(1): 31–57.

———. 2000. "In defense of national economic economy." *Pacific Review* 13(1): 73–113.

———. 2003a. Attempting developmental regionalism through AFTA: The domestic sources of regional governance. *Third World Quarterly* 24(2): 235–53.

———. 2003b. Globalisation, domestic politics and regionalism: The ASEAN Free Trade Area. London: Routledge.

———. 2006. APEC and East Asia: the challenge of remaining relevant. In *APEC and the search for relevance: 2007 and beyond.* Canberra: National Library of Australia.

Neuman, Stephanie, ed. 1998. *International theory and the Third World*. New York: St. Martin's Press.

Noble, Gregory, and John Ravenhill, eds. 2000. *The Asian financial crisis and the architecture of global finance*. Cambridge, U.K.: Cambridge University Press.

O'Brien, Robert 2005. Global civil society and global governance. In *Contending perspectives in global governance*, eds., Alice D. Ba and Matthew J. Hoffmann. New York: Routledge.

Ojendal, Joakim. 2000. Regionalization in East and Southeast Asia. In *National perspectives on the new regionalism in the south*, ed. Björn Hettne, András Inotai, and Osvaldo Sunkel. Houndsmill, U.K.: MacMillan Press.

Onuf, Nicholas. 1998. Constructivism: A user's manual. In *International Relations in a Constructed World*, ed. Vendulka Kubalkova, Nicholas Onuf, and Paul Kowert, 58–79. Armonk, NY: M. E. Sharpe.

Ooi Guat Tin. 1987. ASEAN preferential trading arrangements: An assessment. In *ASEAN at the crossroads: Obstacles, options & opportunities in economic co-operation*, ed. Noordin Sopiee, Chew Lay See, and Lim Siang Jin, 55–62. Kuala Lumpur: ISIS Malaysia.

Ortiz, Alan T. 1991. Towards Asia Pacific regional security. ASEAN Experts Group meeting on ZOPFAN, January 5–6, in Kuala Lumpur, ISIS Malaysia.

Palmer, Ronald, and Thomas Reckford. 1987. *Building ASEAN: 20 years of Southeast Asian cooperation*. New York: CSIS and Praeger Publishers.

Pangestu, Mari. 1988. Comments. In *ASEAN economic cooperation: A new perspective*, ed. Hendra Esmara. Singapore: Chopmen Publishers.

———. 1995a. ASEAN free trade area: An Indonesian perspective. *IQ* 23(1): 39–49.

Paribatra, Sukhumbhand. 1994. From ASEAN six to ASEAN ten: Issues and prospects. *CSEA* 16(3): 243–58.

Parrenas, Julius Caesar. 1990. China and Japan in ASEAN's strategic perceptions. *CSEA* 12(3): 198–224.

———. 1998. ASEAN and Asia-Pacific economic cooperation. *Pacific Review* 11(2): 233–48.

Pathmanathan, Murugesu. 1977. *Conflict management in Southeast Asia: A neutralized Malaysia?* Kuala Lumpur: University of Malaya.

Pattugalan, Gina Rivas. 1995. ASEAN approaches to managing regional security. *Kasarinlan* 10(4): 6–19.

Payne, Rodger A. 2001. Persuasion, frames and norm construction. *European Journal of International Relations* 7(1): 37–61.

Peffer, Nathaniel. 1954. Regional security in Southeast Asia. *IO* 8(3): 311–15.

Philpott, Daniel. 1995. Sovereignty: An introduction and brief history. *Journal of International Affairs* 48(2): 353–68.

Pierson, Paul. 2000. Not just what, but when: Timing and sequence in political processes. *Studies in American Political Development* 14 (Spring): 72–92.

Price, Richard, and Nina Tannnenwald. 1996. Norms and deterrence. In *Culture of national security*, ed. Peter Katzenstein, 114–52. New York: Columbia University Press.

A. Rahim bin Ishak. 1974. Regionalism in Southeast Asia: Commitment or integration? In *Regionalism in Southeast Asia: Papers presented at the first conference of ASEAN students of regional affairs*, Jakarta, October 22–25. Jakarta: CSIS.

Rahman, Tun Ismail bin Dato Abdul. 1966. Minister for Home Affairs and Acting Minister for Foreign Affairs, Address to the Foreign Correspondents Association, June 23, in Johore Bahru. Reprinted in Peter Boyce (1968) *Malaysia and Singapore in international diplomacy: Documents and commentaries*. Sydney, Australia: Sydney University Press.

Rahman, Tunku Abdul. 1978. *Viewpoints.* Kuala Lumpur: Heinemann Educational Books (Asia).

Rajaratnam, S. 1989. Riding the Vietnamese tiger. *CSEA* 10(4): 347–51.

Ramcharan, Robin. 2000. ASEAN and non-interference: A principle maintained. *CSEA* 22(1): 60–88.

Ramos, Narciso. 1977. *Philippines brings the Sabah dispute to the UN.* Manila: Republic of the Philippines.

Rapkin, D. 2001. The United States, Japan, and the power to block: The APEC and AMF cases. *Pacific Review* 14(3): 373–410.

Rau, Robert L. 1981. The role of Singapore in ASEAN. *CSEA* 3(2): 99–112.

Ravenhill, John. 1995. Economic cooperation in ASEAN. *Asian Survey* 35(9): 851–66.

———. 2001. *APEC and the construction of Pacific Rim regionalism.* Cambridge, U.K.: Cambridge University Press.

———. 2007. Fighting irrelevance: An economic community with "ASEAN characteristics." Working Paper 2007/3. Canberra: Department of International Relations at Australian National University.

Regionalism in Southeast Asia: Papers presented at the First Conference of ASEAN Students of Regional Affairs, Jakarta, October 22–25. Jakarta: CSIS.

Reid, Anthony. 1999. *Charting the shape of early modern Southeast Asia.* Chiang Mai, Thailand: Silkworm Press.

Reyes, Narciso G. 1986. The ASEAN summit syndrome. *FRJ* 1(2): 49–78.

Reynolds, Craig J. 1995. A new look at the old Southeast Asia. *Journal of Asian Studies* 54(2): 419–46.

Risse, Thomas, Daniela Engelmann-Martin, Hans-Joachim Knopf, and Klaus Roscher. 1999. "To Euro or not to Euro? The EMU and identity politics in the European Union. *EJIR* 5(2): 147–87.

Risse-Kappen, Thomas. 1995. Ideas do not float freely: Transnational coalitions, domestic structures, and the end of the Cold War. In *International relations theory and the end of the Cold War,* ed. Richard Ned Lebow and Thomas Risse-Kappen, 187–222. New York: Columbia University Press.

Romero, Segundo E. 1989. Philippine foreign relations in a period of transition. *FRJ* 4(4): 73–98.

———. 1998. The Philippines in 1997: Weathering political and economic turmoil (A survey of Asia in 1997, part II). *Asian Survey* 38(2): 196–202.

Romulo, Carlos. 1969. *Rejoining our Asian family.* Manila: Republic of the Philippines.

Ruggie, John. 1998. What makes the world hang together? Neo-utilitarianism and the social constructivist challenge. *IO* 4(52): 855–85.

Ruland, Jurgen. 2000. ASEAN and the Asian crisis: Theoretical implications and practical consequences for Southeast Asian regionalism. *Pacific Review* 13(3): 421–41.

Sachs, Jeffrey. 1998a. The East Asian financial crisis. *Brookings Papers on Economic Activity* (Spring).

———. 1998b. The IMF and the Asian flu. *American Prospect* (March-April).

Said, Edward. 1993. *Culture and imperialism.* New York: Knopf.

Saravanamuttu, Johan. 1984. ASEAN security in the 1980s: The case for a revitalized ZOPFAN. *CSEA* 2(6): 186–96.

Siddhi Savetsila. 1988. *Collection of speeches 1988.* Bangkok: Ministry of Foreign Affairs.

Schelling, Thomas. 1960. *Strategy of conflict.* London: Oxford University Press.

Schimmelfennig, Frank. 2000. International socialization in the new Europe: Rational action in an institutional environment. *European Journal of International Relations* 6(1): 109–39.

Segal, Gerald. 1996. East Asia and the constrainment of China, *IS* 20(4): 107–35.

Severino, Rodolfo. 2007. ASEAN beyond forty. *CSEA* 29(3): 406–24.

Sharp, Paul. 1999. For diplomacy: Representation and the study of international relations. *International Studies Review* 1(1): 33–57.

Sheppard, Mubin. 1995. *Tunku: His life and times, the authorized biography of Tunku Abdul Rahman Putra al-Haj*. Kuala Lumpur: Pelanduk Publications.

Siagian, Boni Ray, ed. n.d. *Eighth year cycle, eighth year cycle*. Jakarta: ASEAN National Mass Media Department of Information and ASEAN National Secretariat.

Siazon, Domingo L. Jr. 1995. Emergence of geoeconomics and its impact on regional security. *Kasarinlan* 10(3): 23–52.

Sikkink, Kathryn. 1998. Transnational politics, international relations theory, and human rights: A new model of international politics is needed to explain the politics of human rights. *PS: Political Science and Politics* 31: 517–21.

Simon, Sheldon. 1982. *The ASEAN states and regional security*. Stanford, CA: Stanford University Press.

———. 1995. Realism and neoliberalism: International relations theory and Southeast Asian security. *Pacific Review* 8(1): 5–24.

———. 1998. Security prospects in Southeast Asia. *Pacific Review* 11(2): 195–212.

Singapore, Ministry of Foreign Affairs. 1995. *Joint communiqués, ministerial statements, and international conventions that Singapore is a party to, 1995*. Singapore: Ministry of Foreign Affairs, Public Affairs Directorate.

Singh, Ajit. 1997. Introduction. In *One Southeast Asia in a new regional and international setting*, ed. Hadi Soesastro. Jakarta: CSIS.

Singh, Bilveer. 1991. American military facilities in Singapore: Enhancing the creation of a zone of peace, freedom, and regional zecurity. *Asian Defense Journal* (January): 16–9.

———. 1992. *ZOPFAN and the new security order in the Asia-Pacific region*. Kuala Lumpur: Pelanduk Publications.

Singh, L. P. 1963. Thai foreign policy: The current phase. *Asian Survey* 3(11): 535–43.

Snitwongse, Kusuma. 1997. Thailand and ASEAN: Thirty years on. *Asian Journal of Political Science* 5(1): 87–101.

Soesastro, Hadi. 1989. The political economy of deregulation in Indonesia. *Asian Survey* 29(9): 853–69.

———. 1997a. Challenges to AFTA in the 21st century. In *One Southeast Asia in a new regional and international setting*, ed. Hadi Soesastro, 83–92. Jakarta: CSIS.

———. 2003. ASEAN: Regional economic cooperation and its institutionalization. Economic Working Papers Series, no. 071. Jakarta: Centre for Strategic and International Studies.

Sopiee, Noordin. 1989. The Cambodian conflict, 1978–1989. In *Peace in the making*. Ed. Rohana Mahmood. Kuala Lumpur: ISIS.

Solheim, Wilhelm. 1985. "Southeast Asia": What's in a name? Another point of view. *Journal of Southeast Asian Studies* 16: 142–43.

Solidum, Estrella. 1974. *Towards a Southeast Asian community*. Quezon City, Philippines: University of the Philippines Press.

Solingen, Etel. 1998. *Regional orders at century's dawn*. Princeton, NJ: Princeton University Press.

————. 1999. ASEAN, quo vadis? Domestic coalitions and regional co-operation. *CSEA* 21(1): 30–53.

Soloman, Richard. 1970. Boundary concepts and practices in Southeast Asia. *World Politics* 23(1): 1–23.

Sopiee, Noordin. 1980. Contemporary sources of conflict. In *Regional security developments and stability in Southeast Asia*. Singapore: ISEAS.

————. 1992. The Cambodian conflict, 1978–1989. In *Peace in the making: Proceedings of the third Asia-Pacific roundtable: Kuala Lumpur, June 16–19, 1989*, ed. Rohanna Mahmood. Kuala Lumpur: Institute for Strategic and International Studies.

————. 1996. *EAEC: Fact and fiction*. Malaysia: ISIS.

Starner, Frances L. 1963a. Malaysia and the north Borneo territories. *Asian Survey* 3(11): 519–34.

————. 1963b. Philippines: Politics of the "new era." *Asian Survey* 3(1): 41–47.

Steinberg, David Joel, ed. 1987. *In search of Southeast Asia*. Honolulu: University of Hawaii.

Stubbs, Richard. 1989. Geopolitics and the political economy of Southeast Asia. *International Journal* 44 (Summer): 517–40.

————. 2000. Signing on to liberalization: AFTA and the politics of regional economic cooperation. *Pacific Review* 13(2): 297–318.

————. 2002. ASEAN Plus Three: Emerging East Asian regionalism? *Asian Survey* 42(3): 440–56.

Sudarsono, Juwono. 1986. Religious, ethnic, and ideological dissension in the ASEAN states. In *Internal and external security issues in Asia*, ed. Robert Scalapino, Seizaburo Sato, and Jusuf Wanandi. Berkeley: Institute of East Asian Studies, University of California, Berkeley.

Sukma, Rizal. 1992. Security arrangements in Southeast Asia: A challenge for ASEAN in the post Cold War era. *IQ* 20(3): 273–86.

————. 1999. *Indonesia and China*. London: Routledge.

————. 2008. Building the ASEAN community: How useful is the ASEAN charter? Paper prepared for the Sentosa roundtable on Asian security 2008. January 17–18, 2008, Sentosa Island, Singapore.

Suriyamongkol, Marjorie. 1988. *Politics of ASEAN economic cooperation*. Singapore: Oxford University Press.

Swidler, Ann. 1986. Culture in action: Symbols and strategies. *American Sociological Review* 51(2): 273–86.

Tan, Gerald. 1987. ASEAN preferential trading arrangements: An overview. In *ASEAN At the crossroads: Obstacles, options, and opportunities in economic cooperation*, ed. Noordin Sopiee, Chew Lay See, and Lim Siang Jin. Kuala Lumpur: ISIS Malaysia.

————. 1996. *ASEAN economic development and co-operation*. Singapore: Times Academic Press.

Tan See Seng and Ralph A. Cossa. 2001. Rescuing realism from the realists: A theoretical note on East Asian security. In *Many faces of Asian security*, ed. Sheldon Simon, 15–47. Lanham, MD: Rowman and Littlefield.

Tang Shiping. 2002. The future of the Shanghai Cooperation Organization. *IDSS Perspectives*. Available online at: www.ntu.edu.sg/idss/Perspective/research_050223.htm.

Tay, Simon S. C, Jesus P. Estanislao, and Hadi Soesastro. 2001. *Reinventing ASEAN*. Singapore: ISEAS.

Terada, Takashi. 2003. Constructing an "East Asian" concept and growing regional identity: From EAEC to ASEAN + 3. *Pacific Review* 16(2): 251–77.

———. 2006. Forming an East Asian community: A site for Japan–China power struggles. *Japanese Studies* 26(1): 5–17.

Terrill, Ross. 1969. Bangkok, Manila. *Atlantic Monthly:* 22–27.

Tetreault, Mary Ann. 1991. Autonomy, necessity, and the small state: Ruling Kuwait in the twentieth century. *IO* 45(4): 565–91.

The Thai Foreign Minister in the U.S., Interview of Thanat Khoman on 8 Oct. 1970. *Asia Pacific Record* 1:8 (Nov. 1970), 15.

Thambipillai, Pushpa, and J. Saravanamuttu. 1985. *ASEAN negotiations: Two insights.* Singapore: ASEAN Economic Research Unit, ISEAS.

Thanat Khoman. n.d. *Collected statements of Foreign Minister Thanat Khoman, October 1965–October 1966 (Vol, 2).* Bangkok: Department of Information, Ministry of Foreign Affairs.

———. 1992. ASEAN conception and evolution. In *ASEAN reader,* ed. K. S. Sandhu et al. Singapore: ISEAS.

———. 1998. [No title]. In *ASEAN towards 2020: Strategic goals and future directions,* 83–86. Kuala Lumpur: ISIS Malaysia.

———. 1998. Reflections on ASEAN: What we did right, where we went wrong—Lessons for the future. In *ASEAN towards 2020: Strategic goals and future directions.* Kuala Lumpur: ISIS Malaysia.

Thayer, Carlyle A. 1990. ASEAN and Indochina: The dialogue. In *ASEAN into the 1990s,* ed. Alison Broinowski. London: Pallgrave Macmillan.

Thomas, Nick. 2001. Building an East Asian community. *Asian Perspective* 26(4).

Tilman, Robert O. 1987. *Southeast Asia and the enemy beyond: ASEAN perceptions of external threats.* Boulder, CO: Westview.

Turley, William. 1985. *Confrontation or coexistence.* Bangkok: Chulalongkorn University.

Turnbull, C. M. 1992. Regionalism and nationalism. In *Cambridge history of Southeast Asia,* Vol. 2, ed. Nicholas Tarling. Cambridge, U.K.: Cambridge University Press.

Tyabji, Amina. 1990. The six Asian economies: 1980–1988. In *ASEAN into the 1990's,* ed. Alison Broinowski. London: Pallgrave Macmillan.

Um, Khatharya. 1991. Thailand and the dynamics of economic and security complex in mainland Southeast Asia. *CSEA* 13(3): 245–70.

U.S. State Department. n.d. *Foreign relations of the United States, 1955–1957,* vol. XXII, Southeast Asia. Washington, DC: U.S. Government Printing Office.

Valencia, Mark. 1996. The Spratly imbroglio in the post–Cold War era. In *Southeast Asia in the new world order: The political economy of a dynamic region,* ed. David Wurfel and Bruce Burton, 244–69. New York: St. Martin's Press.

Vandenbosch, Amry. 1946. Regionalism in Southeast Asia. *The Far Eastern Quarterly* 5(4): 427–38.

Vatikiotis, Michael. 1993. Indonesia's foreign policy in the 1990s. *CSEA* 14(4): 360–61.

———. 2003. Catching the dragon's tail: China and Southeast Asia in the 21st century. *CSEA* 25(1): 65-78.

Viraphol, Sarasin. 1987. The Philippine bases in context. *FRJ* 2(1): 152–55.

Wade, Robert. 2000. Wheels within wheels: Rethinking the Asian crisis and the Asian model. *Annual Review of Political Science:* 3(1): 85–115.

Waltz, Kenneth W. 1979. *Theory of international politics.* Reading, MA: Addison-Wesley.

Wanandi, Jusuf. 1983. Pacific economic cooperation: An Indonesian view. *Asian Survey* 23(12): 1271–80.

———. 1984. Security issues in the ASEAN region. In *ASEAN security and economic development*, ed. Karl Jackson and M. Hadi Soesastro, 19–26. Berkeley: University of California Press.

———. 1985. ZOPFAN and the Kampuchean conflict. *IQ* 13(2): 206–13.

———. 1991. Peace and security in Southeast Asia. *IQ* 19(4): 313–25.

———. 1992. Australia-Indonesia security relationship. *IQ* 20(2): 156–67.

———. 1996. ASEAN's China strategy: Towards deeper engagement. *Survival* 38: 117–28.

———. 1997. Old and new strategic developments in the Asia-Pacific. *IQ* 25(2): 185–96.

———. 2000. East Asian regionalism: The way ahead. *ST.* December 4.

Wang, Yunjong. 2000. The Asian financial crisis and its aftermath: Do we need a regional financial arrangement? *ASEAN Economic Bulletin* (August).

Weatherbee, Donald E. 1963. Indonesia and Malaysia: Confrontation in Southeast Asia, *Orbis* 7(Summer): 336–51.

Webber, D. 2001. Two funerals and a wedding? The ups and downs of regionalism in East Asia and the Asia-Pacific after the Asian crisis. *Pacific Review* 14(3): 339–72.

Weinstein, Franklin B. 1976. *Indonesian foreign policy and the dilemma of dependence.* Ithaca, NY: Cornell University Press.

Wendt, Alexander. 1987. The agent-structure problem in international relations theory. *IO* 41(3): 335–70.

———. 1992. Anarchy is what states make of it: The social construction of power politics. *IO* 46(2): 391–425.

———. 1998. On constitution and causation in international relations. *Review of International Studies* 24: 101–18.

Wesley, Michael. 1999. The Asian crisis and the adequacy of regional institutions. *CSEA* 21(1): 54–73.

Whiting, Allen. 1997. ASEAN eyes China. *Asian Survey* 37(4): 299–322.

Wilairat, Kawin. 1975. *Singapore's foreign policy: The first decade,* field report series no. 10. Singapore: ISEAS.

Wilson, David. 1964. Thailand: A new leader. *Asian Survey* 4(2): 711–15.

Wilson, Dick. 1975. *The neutralization of Southeast Asia.* New York: Praeger.

Wolters, O. 1981. Culture, history, and region in Southeast Asian perspective. In *ASEAN: Identity, development and culture,* ed. R. P. Anand and P. V. Quisumbing, 1–40. Quezon City: University of the Philippines Law Center.

Woo Sik Kee, In-Taek Hyun, and Kisoo Kim, eds. 1995. *APEC and the new Pacific community: Issues and prospects.* Seoul: The Sejong Institute.

Woods, L. 1994. *Asia Pacific diplomacy: Nongovernmental organisations and international relations.* Vancouver, BC: UBC Press.

World Trade Organization website: www.wto.org/.

Wurfel, David. 1963. A changing Philippines. *Asian Survey* 4(2): 702–10.

———. 1967. The Philippines: Intensified dialogue. *Asian Survey* 7(1): 46–52.

———. 1990. Philippine foreign policy. In *The political economy of Southeast Asia,* ed. David Wurfel and Bruce Burton. London: MacMillan Press.

———. 1996. The "new world order" in Southeast Asia: Some analytical explorations. In *Southeast Asia in the new world order: The political economy of a dynamic region,* ed. David Wurfel and Bruce Burton. New York: St. Martin's Press.

Wurfel, David, and Bruce Burton, eds. 1996. *Southeast Asia in the new world order: The political economy of a dynamic region.* New York: St. Martin's Press.

Yee, Albert. 1996. The causal effects of ideas on policies. *IO* 50(1): 69–108.

Yeo, Lay Hwee. 2000. ASEM: Looking back, looking forward. *CSEA* 22(1): 113–44.

Yong Deng. 1997. *Promoting Asia Pacific economic cooperation.* New York: St. Martin's Press.

Young, Kenneth T. Jr. 1966. *The Southeast Asia crisis.* Dobbs Ferry, NY: Oceana Publications.

Young, Oran. 1991. Political leadership and regime formation: On the development of institutions in international society. *IO* 45(3): 281–308.

Zakaria, Fareed. 1994. A conversation with Lee Kuan Yew. *Foreign Affairs* 73(2): 189–94.

Zakaria Haji Ahmad. n.d. Images of American power: Perspectives from Southeast Asia. Occasional Paper. Malaysia: Universiti Kebangsaan Malaysia.

———. 1986. The world of ASEAN decision-makers: A study of bureaucratic elite perceptions in Malaysia, the Philippines, and Singapore. *CSEA* 8(3): 192–211.

Index

Studies in Asian Security

A SERIES SPONSORED BY THE EAST-WEST CENTER

Muthiah Alagappa, Chief Editor
Distinguished Senior Fellow, East-West Center

Minimum Deterrence and India's Nuclear Security
By Rajesh M. Basrur
2006

Rising to the Challenge: China's Grand Strategy and International Security
By Avery Goldstein
2005

*Unifying China, Integrating with the World:
Securing Chinese Sovereignty in the Reform Era*
By Allen Carlson
2005

Rethinking Security in East Asia: Identity, Power, and Efficiency
Edited by J. J. Suh, Peter J. Katzenstein, and Allen Carlson
2004